MAN, EARTH AND SPACE

MAN, EARTH AND SPACE

VOLUME NINETEEN

The Caxton Publishing Company Limited

LONDON

CONTENTS

FOREWORD

By Sir Bernard Lovell, O.B.E., F.R.S., Professor of Radio Astronomy at the University of Manchester and Director of the Jodrell Bank Experimental Station.

Throughout the recorded history of man there has always been a firm belief that the universe could be described in terms of the knowledge actually available at that epoch of history. Prior to the age of Galileo it was unthinkable that the Earth was not the centre of the universe. Then for another two and a half centuries the solar system was believed to be at the centre of the universe. This concept persisted into the 20th century. Furthermore there was a persistent belief that the system of stars known as the Milky Way comprised the totality of the universe. Indeed, it is only 30 to 40 years ago that these egocentric concepts gave way before the increased resolving power and penetration of the large optical telescopes which came into operation on the American continent. These telescopes revealed that the solar system is in a remote part of a spiral galaxy (the Milky Way) containing 100,000 million stars, which is itself only one amongst trillions of similar galaxies distributed throughout vast regions of time and space.

The acquisition of this great knowledge of the universe inspired man with the conviction that his eyes, assisted by modern optical instruments, were the only effective means for making observations which would help to refine his knowledge of the universe and of its extent and development in time and space. In our contemporary life this belief has also been shown to be erroneous. The discovery in 1932 of long wave radiation from space (radio waves) was disregarded by astronomers. Now the sight of large radio telescopes in various parts of the world testifies to the further extension of man's view of the universe.

During the last two decades radio telescopes have revealed features of the universe which have been entirely unsuspected; for example, the quasars – a type of object in the universe believed to be at distances of thousands of millions of light years, generating enormous amounts of energy by processes which appear to be without parallel in our terrestrial environment. Today we believe that at least one quarter of all extragalactic objects are quasars, and yet until 1962 their existence was quite unsuspected. Again, until 1968 no one would have maintained that some star-like objects in the Milky Way would be generating radio signals in precisely timed bursts of about one second. The discovery of pulsars has revealed the existence of these strange processes and in 1969 one of these was shown to be associated with a star (in the Crab Nebula) whose apparently steady light was the result of the emission of pulsed light with a period of thirty milliseconds.

Today we must still attempt to describe the universe in terms of the phenomena which we can study now, but the belief that our description will remain valid for long is becoming hard to sustain. The ability to study the universe from scientific instruments orbiting in space opens the entire electromagnetic spectrum to our observation. The few observations already made in the ultra-violet and X-ray region serve to illustrate that the universe is far more complex than we can envisage from looking at it with our earth-bound optical and radio telescopes. The despatch of men to the moon and instruments to the planets are in the grasp of modern technology. So it is with an almost breathless excitement that we await the next discovery.

NEW VIEWS
OF THE UNIVERSE

From the beginning of recorded history, at least, man has studied the heavenly bodies. He quickly distinguished between the fixed stars, which shine by their own light, and the planets moving among them that were eventually recognised as cold objects, made visible only by the light they reflected. Much of this study was inspired by the vain hope of being able to predict the future from the movements of the stars and the planets, but the accurate measurements that were made led to the formulation of the laws of planetary movement and to the realisation that the nature and behaviour of the stars, planets and other bodies could be understood in scientific and mathematical terms.

His aim then became to find out about the planets – were they like the Earth, how distant were they, could there be life on them; about the stars – how did they produce their light, how did they come into being, what were they made of; and about the universe itself – did it have boundaries, was it formed at a particular time, or had it always been much as it is now, changing only imperceptibly and locally? All these questions are the province of astronomy and are raised in the next section, but astronomy, until approximately the end of the Second World War, suffered from crippling limitations. The skies had to be studied from the Earth, and the study was limited to the objects that could be seen by the eye, assisted by telescope and camera.

The Sun and the other stars emit electromagnetic radiation over a very wide range of wavelengths, of which heat, light, and radio waves represent particular selections, and some of this is reflected or otherwise affected by the planets. However, most of this emission, much of which would be harmful to life, is absorbed by the Earth's atmosphere. All that can penetrate is visible light, with a small amount of ultra-violet and infra-red radiation, and radio waves covering a small range of frequencies. Of this, the visible light with its accompanying radiation is all that can be used by the astronomer's telescope and camera. Until relatively recently, he has had to formulate his theories without any knowledge of the nature of the other emissions from the stars. Two developments from wartime technology, radio astronomy and the use of artificial satellites in space, have freed him from this limitation, and the latter had made possible, for the first time, direct investigation of our nearest neighbours.

Radio astronomy is a science to which an exact birthdate, December 1932, can be assigned, for this was the date on which an American, Karl Jansky, published an account of receiving radio waves from space. He had been investigating short-wave radio interference, caused by thunderstorms in particular, for the Bell Telephone Company, and he had discovered that, apart from the characteristic crackle of a storm, a relatively steady hiss could be detected by his receiver, and that this hiss reached its maximum intensity when his aerial was pointed towards the centre of our galaxy, the direction of the greatest concentration of stars. The only pre-war successor to Karl Jansky was another American, Grote Reber, who built the prototype of the reflecting radio-telescopes that are so widely used nowadays and who published the first radio map of the skies in the early 1940s. Since then, radiotelescopes,

starting with Sir Bernard Lovell's at Jodrell Bank, have multiplied and radio astronomy has developed enormously, in the early days largely through the use of wartime radar techniques. The study has yielded a great revelation of the nature of the universe, together with some new mysteries.

One discovery was the shape of our galaxy. The Sun, together with its planets, including the Earth, is part of a galaxy containing about 100,000 million stars. It has been surmised that these are in the form of a disc that swells in the centre, and that when we look at the Milky Way, we are looking through the thick part of the disc, towards the edge; but the exact shape could not be seen, partly because our view of the centre is obscured by clouds of interstellar dust. Radio waves pass through this dust. Hydrogen, the gas, is invisible, but it emits radio waves in space, and a map of the radio emission from hydrogen reaching us reveals the shape of our galaxy, which is permeated by the gas. Radio astronomy can do more than discover the direction of sources; it can also show the speed and direction of their movements. The radio waves from hydrogen have a definite frequency, but this frequency will appear to be increased if the source is moving towards us and decreased if it is moving away, in the same way as the pitch of a train whistle appears to be altered if the train is moving relative to the listener. A careful mapping of our galaxy has shown that it consists of a dense central core surrounded by spiral arms, looking something like the pattern left by a burning Catherine-wheel, and that the arms are rotating much faster than the centre. We, and the Sun, are near the edge of one of the arms.

Hydrogen gas is diffuse and invisible, but other sources of radio waves are visible single objects in the sky. One of the most interesting of these is in the constellation Taurus and is a star which, like radio astronomy itself, has a recorded birthday. During the year 1054 A.D., Chinese astronomers noticed a new and brilliant star, and this has now been photographed and shown to be a vast cloud

A view from the control room of the 250-foot diameter radio telescope at the Jodrell Bank Experimental Station, Cheshire.

The Earth photographed from over the Moon, a picture taken during the flight of the Apollo 8 manned spacecraft, December 1968. The craters of the Moon are clearly visible in the foreground. The Moon's colour is probably caused by a shift in the colour response of the film; the surface is in fact grey.

of gas, expanding at the rate of 70 million miles a day. What the Chinese astronomers had recorded was the explosion of a dim star, near the end of its life, in an enormous thermo-nuclear explosion. The process is known as the formation of a supernova, and the 'star' is within our galaxy, about 4,000 light years away.

This radio source is known as the Crab Nebula and is within our galaxy, but other galaxies also emit radio waves, and these have given radio astronomers an opportunity of attacking the question of whether or not the universe had a beginning and will have an end. The optical astronomers had evidence that the universe we see is expanding and that the most distant of the galaxies are receding the most rapidly. This would seem to suggest that the universe had a beginning in some form of explosion whose date can be calculated from the rate of explosion, by working out when

it must have started. This theory—the 'Big Bang Theory'—is opposed by the 'Steady State Theory', which holds that the matter that the galaxies take with them as they travel outwards is replaced by the slow creation of matter throughout space, so that the universe has always much the same appearance. Optical telescopes have not been able to produce enough evidence to decide between the two theories; radiotelescopes, however, are so much more sensitive—all the energy detected on all the radiotelescopes since radio astronomy started is less than is needed to lift a playing card a couple of centimetres—that they can see nearly to what must be the edge of the expanding universe. There is a higher density of radio sources there than nearer the centre, and hence presumably a higher density of galaxies, which seems to support the idea that they are the farthest thrown products of a big bang. There should be no unduly high concentration there if the steady state theory is correct. The radio astronomers also think they have discovered some background heat in the universe, left over from the fireball of the big bang. Most astronomers now believe the evidence points towards the origin of the universe in a big bang.

Radio astronomy is helping to answer some of the problems that optical astronomy cannot deal with, but it has also raised new problems of its own. Most of the powerful radio sources have turned out to be either supernovae, like the Crab Nebula, or galaxies, and these are relatively large. However, a few intense, small sources, true radio stars, have been detected. As radio astronomy became more refined, these radio stars could be given exact positions in the sky, and some of them were found to be visible stars. At first these were thought to be relatively normal, rather dim, stars in our galaxy. If the universe is expanding so that the furthest stars recede most quickly, one can find out how far away a star is by measuring how quickly it is receding, and the result for one of these dim stars showed that it was about 1,500 million light years away, well outside our galaxy. This was a sensational discovery—Martin Schmidt, the Dutchman who made it in 1963 is reported to have told his wife, 'Something terrible happened today, if what I think is true'—because it meant that the star was dim only because it was so far from us. Really it must be the size of a star but at least several hundred times as bright as a normal galaxy. It was named a quasar, a word derived from 'quasistellar object' and the name does nothing to conceal the mystery. There is no known process by which a celestial body could give off this much energy for more than a hundred years or so, but enough quasars have now been discovered to show that the average life must be much more.

One attempt to find out more about quasars led instead to the discovery of another group of mysterious objects. The space around us—'empty space'—is filled with clouds of charged particles, and irregularities in these clouds affect radio waves in the same way as irregularities in our atmosphere affect the light from the stars. The radio stars appear, to the radiotelescope, to twinkle. The smaller the apparent size of a radio star, the more pronounced this radio twinkling will be, so measuring it can eventually lead to an estimate of the star's size. A group of radioastronomers under Dr Antony Hewish therefore set out in 1967 to sweep the skies with a special kind of radiotelescope, looking for good examples of radio twinkling from quasars. Radiotelescopes record the intensity of the waves they receive on long strips of paper, and this one poured out four hundred feet of paper a week. One can tell computers to go through results like these, looking for scintillation, but the Cambridge astronomers fortunately decided to look through the records themselves. The girl who had this task noticed that they seemed to show a regular beat occasionally, coming from a particular position in space. This was so unlikely that even when later results confirmed the discovery, the group was reluctant to announce it, in case all they had recorded was some radio interference. They were even more reluctant to publish one of their early suggestions for a source in space. There was no known astronomical mechanism that could produce a series of radio pulses, and the astronomers were forced to recognise that they might be getting a signal from an intelligent creature on some other world in space. Eventually they ruled this out, and since then, so many pulsating radio stars—pulsars, as they are called—have been discovered that a natural, physical explanation has to be found. Unfortunately, the behaviour of the pulsars, like that of the quasars, defies explanation by any normal process. The most plausible theory is that the pulses

come from a collapsed, 'dead' star—a neutron star—rotating so that a radio source on its surface sweeps a beam through space like a celestial lighthouse.

Radiotelescopes, using the radio waves that can penetrate the Earth's atmosphere, have solved many astronomical problems and suggested some new ones. The use of artificial satellites and rocket-borne instruments has enabled astronomers to study radiation that cannot penetrate the Earth's atmosphere, and has at the same time removed an unenviable peculiarity of astronomy as a science. Previously, it could hardly be called a genuine experimental science, as it could reach none of its objects of study. Instead, it had to be content with radiation emitted or reflected by the heavenly bodies and able to penetrate the atmosphere, and the few samples of celestial matter that dropped to the Earth as meteorites. Now the Moon and the nearer planets can be visited and experimented on, using experiments similar to those used directly on Earth.

The use of artificial satellites is another technique that has a definite birthdate—4 October 1957. This was the date on which the Soviet Union astonished the world by announcing that it had put what then seemed an incredibly heavy (184 lb) satellite, Sputnik 1, into orbit around the Earth. Almost a month later, Sputnik 2, a much heavier satellite, carrying a living dog, was launched, and it became clear that travelling observatories, manned and unmanned, and free from the restrictions of the Earth's atmosphere, were soon to be available. Glimpses of the sky as seen from above our atmosphere had been seized by rocket-borne instruments as they peered briefly into space before falling back to Earth; space travel brought with it the possibility of continuous observation.

Sputnik 1 carried no instruments, but even so, from the effect of

Below: Launch of the Saturn V rocket carrying Apollo 8 from Cape Kennedy.

Photograph of the Moon's surface taken by the spacecraft Lunar Orbiter II.

ignorance of how the planets have come into being is so profound that these estimates are really barely disguised guesswork. We need the knowledge that can come from satellite investigations. Already, unmanned explorations have shown that Venus is a hot, inhospitable planet—its surface temperature is about 475°C. They have tested its atmosphere and measured its magnetic field, to find, surprisingly, that it has none. The trips by men to the Moon have been preceded by a succession of hard and soft landings that showed that the Moon is not covered by a deep layer of dust, as had been believed, and that the density and chemistry of the rocks approximated to those of basalt. These landings measured the Moon's gravitational force with accuracy unimaginable in earlier times, and the orbiting satellites with their cameras have charted the Moon more completely than the Earth is mapped. The dense bodies that lie beneath some of the Moon's seas, and which probably caused them by crashing into the Moon from space, were discovered by their disturbing effects on the path of an orbiting satellite.

The ultimate adventures in space exploration, though, are the manned flights. Man is a more inventive investigator than the instruments he devises, and the chance of discovering the completely unexpected makes the hazard and expense of these trips worthwhile. Manned explorations of the Moon and planets are the most expensive scientific experiments ever devised, but they are also the most stimulating. The first sight of the Moon as the satellites approach, and the views of the Earth from the Moon were exhilarating as well as informative, and space flights to further and further planets will draw man on as the exploration of unknown terrestrial areas drew him on in earlier times. The history of exploration lists many hazardous voyages, but none have gone so far, nor with so little hope of surviving an unpredicted hazard.

Space exploration can be justified by scientific interest and adventure, but the techniques have paid commercial and social dividends as well. Rather surprisingly, the early twentieth century, scientific age though it was, relied for high speed, long distance communications on submarine cables which were easily overloaded, and on radio which electrical storms could make erratic. The later part of the century has seen many of the dreams of science-fiction come true, and it was a science-fiction writer, Arthur C. Clarke, who first suggested using satellites for communication. He pointed out that a satellite 22,300 miles up would rotate at the same speed as the Earth and thus appear to be stationary above it; that three such satellites could cover the Earth, as one would be visible from any point on it; and that satellites could be used as relay stations for radio and television. Their transmissions would be relatively unaffected by radio disturbances, and they could carry a multitude of messages infinitely more cheaply than the comparable number of cables. These 'stationary' satellites have shown their value commercially and it has since become clear that communication by satellite is an important and economic way of spreading information and education through the world.

Weather forecasting is another valuable application of satellite tecnnology. Meteorology has always been handicapped by the difficulty of getting enough observations to make reliable forecasts, but the Earth is now ringed by weather satellites that report on cloud formations and on the movements of storms far more comprehensively than was formerly possible. Reliable weather forecasting has saved thousands of people from death in storms, and millions of pounds by avoiding crop disasters. The rockets used to launch the satellites were developed for military purposes, but the benefits of the space age can literally cover the world.

gravity it gave more accurate information about the shape of the Earth than had been obtainable before, and it showed that the air was unexpectedly dense 150 miles up. The first American satellite, Explorer 1, launched on 31 January 1958, was tiny— it weighed only 31 lbs—but it made a totally unexpected discovery about the space that surrounds the Earth. The satellite travelled in an orbit that went from 200 miles above the Earth at its nearest to nearly 1,600 miles away at its furthest, and it carried equipment to measure the intensity of the cosmic rays, the charged atomic particles that strike the Earth from outer space. They are largely absorbed by the atmosphere, and the cosmic ray counters in the satellite predictably showed that the intensity of the radiation increased as the satellite got further from the Earth. Then, unpredictably, they stated that there was no cosmic radiation at all 600 miles up. This seemed impossible, and the scientist in charge, James Van Allen, at first thought that the counters had failed. Then he realised that they might have been overloaded by an excess of radiation. Later experiments showed this to be true. The Earth has been found to be surrounded by patchy belts of charged particles named the Van Allen belts. Even a simple satellite is clearly a powerful research tool.

Gradually the instruments in the artificial satellites have told us more and more, particularly about the Moon and the planets. It is symptomatic of the difficulty of obtaining knowledge in astronomy that the question of the nature and origin of the Moon and planets should be so open. It is commonly held that the universe is so large that there must be, somewhere, another Sun like our own, surrounded by planets, with intelligent life on one of them. Astronomers have even boldly stated how far one would have to travel in space to be statistically sure of reaching such a planet. But our

THE EARTH IN THE UNIVERSE

Ancient ideas of the universe

Science is the classification of facts and the recognition of their significance in the order of nature. That there is an order of nature has been believed from the earliest times, but whereas the ancients conceived it as a set pattern or blue-print to which nature conformed, modern scientists conceive it as a statistical effect resulting from the random motions of myriads of charged particles through vast aeons of time. The ancients recorded the movements of the stars and observed the common phenomena of the Earth, but considered that the order which these facts express could be discovered by reason alone. They performed experiments and thus acquired new facts, but these were treated as fresh evidence for old theories, rather than as a basis on which new theories might be erected.

Astronomy is the one physical science that can advance on a basis of plain observation without experiment and, in its early stages, without instruments of precision; hence its early development by the Greeks. It is difficult now to realize the tremendous intellectual leap needed in these early stages. The primitive astronomical observer considered himself at the centre of a circular plane extending to the horizon with a hollow hemisphere overhead. On this he followed the diurnal rotation of the heavens; superimposed on that, the slower seasonal motions of Sun and Moon relative to fixed stars, and the apparently erratic motions of the planets. Observations at first were confined to noting the order of rising and setting and the position on the horizon.

By combining observation with reasoning of a kind that can only be called metaphysical, as it demanded logical consistency and intelligibility, the Greeks passed beyond the primitive view to state the fundamentals of astronomical theory. They argued that the Earth must float freely in space, because a support is unthinkable; that it must be spherical because there is no reason for asserting any asymmetry. Several thinkers had suggested that the Earth might be moving and Aristarchus actually put forward the heliocentric theory of the solar system, but in the absence of decisive evidence his hypothesis was rejected.

During the Middle Ages there came a revival of interest in science, and for the first time for a thousand years the classic 'authorities' began to be questioned. Particularly outspoken was Roger Bacon (c. 1214–1294), who advocated the experimental method of appealing to nature rather than to Aristotle, and of basing theories on discovered facts rather than adapting new facts to fit old theories. In the 16th and 17th centuries Nicolaus Copernicus (1473–1543) and Galileo Galilei (1564–1642) broke clear away from tradition in spite of determined religious opposition.

Instruments

As soon as Galileo learnt of the first telescopes being made in Holland he constructed his own more powerful instruments, c. 1610. He was the first to use the telescope scientifically.

The space missile enables man to break away from the limits formerly set him by nature. With it he may make observations from outside the atmosphere, a viewpoint which extends his knowledge of the Earth, the solar system, and the universe.

The revival of scientific method caused all previous religious and philosophical theories about the universe to be examined and amended so as to conform with observed phenomena. This process is a continuing one, since new observations often make current theories invalid so that they have to be adapted or replaced by new hypotheses. Thus today the Earth is known not to be the centre of either the solar system or the universe. This conclusion is the result of the analysis of measurements and observations made possible by the use of instruments. Through them man is obtaining a more complete view of the universe and a better understanding of its phenomena.

Powerful instruments have revealed that the Sun is a member of a family of stars numbering approximately 100,000 million, known as the Galaxy; and that innumerable other galaxies exist all at immense distances from each other. From these facts we begin to appreciate the enormous size of the universe. Our own galaxy is not in any way a special member of the cosmos; it is just one of the countless galaxies that our instruments have located in their search of the heavens.

Many types of astronomical instrument are in use today, of which the most fundamental is the telescope. First used to aid the human eye, optical telescopes are now used in conjunction with photographic plates, spectrographs, photoelectric cells linked to recording mechanisms, and other devices. The radio telescope is used to detect radio waves emanating from the cosmos. Basically a radio antenna fitted with an amplifier and recorder, it has greatly extended the range of the astronomer's observation.

Outstanding among the 'eyes' introduced in recent years are the artificial satellites carrying instruments beyond the Earth's dust-laden atmosphere. They can obtain pictures giving a much clearer view of the distant galaxies and of the members of our own solar system, the images being transmitted back to Earth by radio.

Ptolemy's concept of the universe placed the Earth at the centre, as shown in this 17th century print. Round the Earth revolve the Sun, the Moon, and the planets.

Spectroscopes are used to record the spectrum of a star from which its composition may be deduced, while the study of nuclear physics advances the understanding of the origins and conditions of cosmic energy. All major observatories have access to electronic computers which can carry out prodigious high-speed calculations formerly impossible. By the analysis of advancing

Far left: Galileo's telescopes in the Museum of the History of Science, Florence. Galileo used these instruments scientifically; a man of an essentially experimental nature, the great Italian scientist was the first to make regular observations of heavenly bodies. He thereby laid the foundations of modern studies of the universe. *Left:* The Schmidt telescope at the Palomar observatory, California, has a clear aperture of 48 in. and a main mirror 72 in. in diameter. This instrument is designed to photograph large areas of the sky with relatively short exposures; its photographs are used for the compilation of statistics from which the composition of the vast numbers of distant stars and galaxies may be analyzed.

researches into nature, obtained with ever-improving instruments such as these, we are moving slowly towards a fuller understanding of the universe.

The outer galaxies

The distances from the Earth to galaxies outside our own are so enormous that it is almost impossible for us to visualize them. The faintest observable galaxies are thought to be thousands of million light-years away. Light travels at 186,000 miles per second, so *one* light-year (the distance travelled by light in a year) is about 5,866 thousand million miles. This gives an idea of the enormous area of space that comes within the scope of man's instruments, and of the vast time scales involved in the study of the most distant objects known.

The speed of light is so great that it can be considered infinite at the level of day-to-day experience; the time light takes to travel on Earth is infinitesimal, and results in virtually instantaneous perception of the light emitted. But this is not the case in terms of astronomy. The light from the Sun takes about $8\frac{1}{2}$ minutes to reach the Earth, that from the nearest star $4\frac{1}{3}$ years, and that from the most distant star in our galaxy 50,000 years. The great galaxy of Andromeda, one of the nearest, is 2,000,000 light-years away. Thus when we look at the sky we do not see something there as it is now; in the case of the Sun we see what happened $8\frac{1}{2}$ minutes before and in the case of the galaxies up to several thousand million years ago.

Another extremely important discovery, made with spectroscopes linked to the most powerful telescopes focused on various galaxies, is that they are retreating from us at speeds which vary in proportion to their distances from us. The speed is relatively low in

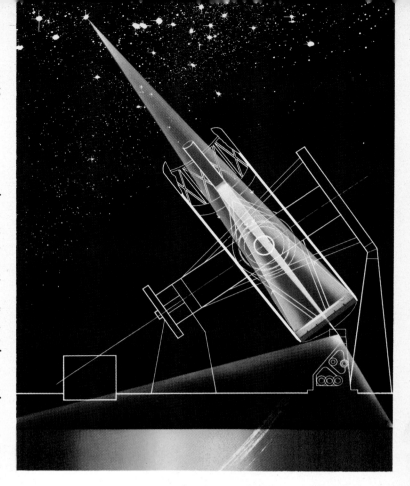

Above: An illustration showing how a reflecting telescope is used to investigate the radiation emitted by heavenly bodies. The light from a star is collected by the primary mirror and focused on a prism, which disperses the light into its component wavelengths. From the spectrum so produced, the density, temperature, and chemical composition of the heavenly body can be deduced by means of known physical laws. *Below:* A reflecting telescope at Mount Wilson, California, which has a primary mirror 100 inches in diameter.

The discovery of the galaxies considerably broadened the field of astronomical research and stimulated the formulation of theories of the structure and activity of the universe. Stellar systems have their own internal dynamics and fall into various groups: elliptical galaxies, spiral galaxies, and irregular galaxies. The great galaxy in Andromeda, one of the nearest to our own (almost 2 million light-years away), is shown on the left. It is a spiral galaxy with mainly bluish stars in the spiral arms. The colour indicates a process of evolution; the redder stars in the nucleus are probably older.

Evidence is now mounting that strange and violent events occur at the centres of galaxies. This object, the galaxy NGC 5128, is also known as the radio source Centaurus A. Dark clouds of dust seem to encircle the galaxy's bright centre, and this originally suggested to astronomers that two galaxies were here seen in collision. But detailed mapping has shown that the areas of radio emission are on either side of the galaxy. At the galaxy's edges, at right angles to the dark lane, are two strong radio sources. Farther away from the galaxy are two larger but fainter sources of radio emission, one on each side of the galaxy. Astronomers think that these symmetrically placed radio-bright areas were caused by two explosions in Centaurus A, one more recent than the other.

million years ago caused by a very high concentration of matter in a very restricted space. It might seem that because this recession can be observed from our own galaxy our position in the universe is a privileged one; but this belief is disproved by the arguments of relativity which state that an observer from another galaxy would witness the same process.

The relativity argument is that the cosmos does not change in appearance regardless of the point from which it is observed. Though the analogy is necessarily inadequate, the situation may be compared to a group of observers standing on different points of the surface of a sphere that is swelling steadily like a balloon. Each of these observers would see the others recede at speeds in proportion to their distance from him.

Others reject this idea of an expanding universe. They maintain that the concept of relativity should apply not only to observers at different points in space but also those placed at different points in time. The effect of this argument is to postulate the same description of the phenomena of the universe for all observers regardless of space or time. Therefore, if an observer 20,000 million years ago had taken the same set of measurements with the instruments used today he would have reached the same conclusions regarding the behaviour of the universe as a whole.

To explain this, the concept of continuous creation has been put forward. This states that, although the stars and galaxies are ageing and 'dying', the energy they emit in doing so remains within the universe; it is suggested that this energy then becomes the new material from which new stars, and hence galaxies, are formed. Thus the spaces opened up by the recession of the galaxies are filled and the *status quo* is maintained.

Both theories are, however, working hypotheses that act as guides for research, and neither is a definitive description of the universe.

The Galaxy

Our own galaxy consists of about 100,000 million stars, most of them located in the spiral arms. The Sun with its solar system is situated about two-thirds of the distance from the nucleus to the periphery. The Galaxy (as it is usually termed) has a flattened

nearby galaxies and increases enormously the farther away the galaxies are situated. The most distant are retreating at approximately 90,000 miles per second.

The immense tracts of space that exist and the speed with which the galaxies retreat across them have resurrected the problem of the finite and the infinite. This has given birth to the science of cosmogony, the propounding of physical and mathematical theories of the nature of the universe. The most important of these theories are those of Einstein and others developed from them.

Some theories maintain that the speeds of the retreating galaxies are the result of an original 'explosion' dating from about 10,000

Right: Galaxy M 51 in the constellation Canes Venatici, seen from the Earth in plan, with its magnificent spiral arms and a small irregular satellite galaxy to the left. *Far right:* The spiral galaxy NGC 4594 in the constellation Virgo, seen from the Earth in profile.

shape, with a diameter of about 90,000 light-years and a depth of about 2,500 light-years. In this mass are contained about 99% of the stars, the remainder being distributed throughout a spherical area about 90,000 light-years in diameter.

The sphere also contains numerous globular clusters, about a hundred of these consisting of groups of about 100,000 stars, located in a space several hundred light-years in diameter. The American astronomer Harlow Shapley noted that the distribution of these clusters in space formed a spherical structure with its centre located near the Milky Way, towards Sagittarius. He thought this centre was about 50,000 light-years from the Earth, a figure later modified to 30,000 light-years. Shapley's observation made it possible to locate the centre of the Galaxy accurately. This does not mean that we can distinguish the nucleus of our galaxy through an optical telescope. The stars there are so numerous that they form an almost impenetrable barrier, and there are also dense clouds of cosmic matter which conceal whatever lies beyond them. Recently, however, using radio-telescopes, astronomers have been able to pick up radiation which appears to emanate directly from the galactic centre. These waves have a length outside the optical range, so can be detected only by radio-telescopes.

Masses of gas about 10,000 light-years away from the nucleus have also been detected. These are receding from the galactic centre at a speed of 30 miles per second. This is an important discovery since it suggests that gases have been expelled from the galactic nucleus. This would support the theory that considerable dynamic activity is taking place at the nucleus and would link it with similar activity in many other galactic nuclei.

The stars of the Galaxy

The spectrograph is probably the most important of the various instruments which have contributed to the formulation of modern concepts of the universe. It separates the light from a luminous source into its component colours and photographs the resulting spectrum. Distinct types of spectral band are produced by the atoms of different elements present in the star in particular states of temperature and pressure, so that the chemical and physical make-up of the star may be deduced. By this method it has been established that hydrogen is by far the most abundant element in the universe. Next comes helium, followed by the other elements in lesser quantities. Apart from certain exceptions, the greater the element's atomic weight, the less it occurs.

The surface temperatures of stars can be discovered by examining the distribution of light intensity through the entire spectrum, one of several types of information which may be deduced from

A globular cluster (M13) in the constellation Hercules. Clusters of this type form a 'halo' around the Galaxy and contain large numbers of stars (about 100,000). These are formed during the first phase of the process of galactic evolution.

these intensity profiles. Distance and photometric measurements are also of fundamental importance, since they enable the true intensity, or absolute magnitude, of the star to be calculated. This is done by correcting the apparent (observed) brightness for the diminishing effect of the star's distance. Stellar temperatures range from about 2,000° C. to a maximum of 30,000° C. Absolute magnitudes range from about 1/100 of our own Sun's luminosity to about 10,000 times this value.

In the early 1900s, the German Hertzsprung and the American Russell independently drew up charts for the stars whose spectra and luminosities were known, plotting absolute magnitude against spectral type. The result was that the points plotted on the chart were not evenly distributed, but were confined to clearly defined zones. They showed, for example, that a given temperature can exist on two totally different types of star, the larger of the two being many times greater in volume than the smaller. Thus the former are termed *giants* and the latter *dwarfs*.

Spectral analysis also showed that the matter making up the stars is in a gaseous state. This posed several problems regarding the structure of stars between their surfaces and their cores.

A star's luminosity is energy radiated from it. Where did this energy come from? Theorists have long been studying the problem. In their research they used known physical laws relating to the equilibrium of fluids, adapting and improving in cases where they could not be applied to astronomy as they stood. They then produced the first stellar models based upon these laws. On this basis

Part of the Milky Way seen on a clear night. It demonstrates the characteristic lens-shape of our galaxy, which is in fact spiral, seen here from within. The dark areas are clouds of cool, obscuring dusts and gases.

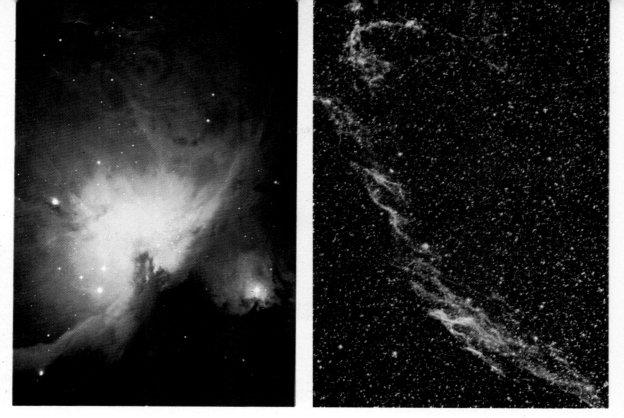

Right: The Orion nebula is a huge gas cloud seen illuminated by stars contained within it, notably a mutiple star, the 'Trapezium', so called from the shape formed by its four principal stars. *Far right:* Part of the filamentary nebula in the constellation Cygnus. This nebula is probably formed from the remnants of the explosion of an unstable star which took place about 50,000 years ago. The explosion threw off a shell of gas that has expanded at extremely high speed and now has a diameter of approximately 180 million million miles. The filaments are part of this shell seen edgewise on.

The Hertzsprung-Russell diagram showing, on the vertical scale, the luminosity or absolute magnitude of the stars, calculated with reference to a standard distance of 33 light-years from the Earth; for example, the Sun is shown to be a star of magnitude 5, and its size is indicated by the factor 5. The horizontal scale shows the spectral types classified in a sequence of decreasing temperature. The diagram shows that stars fall into groups: supergiants, giants, medium-sized stars, and dwarfs. These are shown with their relative dimensions approximately illustrated. The chart also shows the evolution of the stars; on this scale, our own Sun is a young-to-middle-age star in the main sequence.

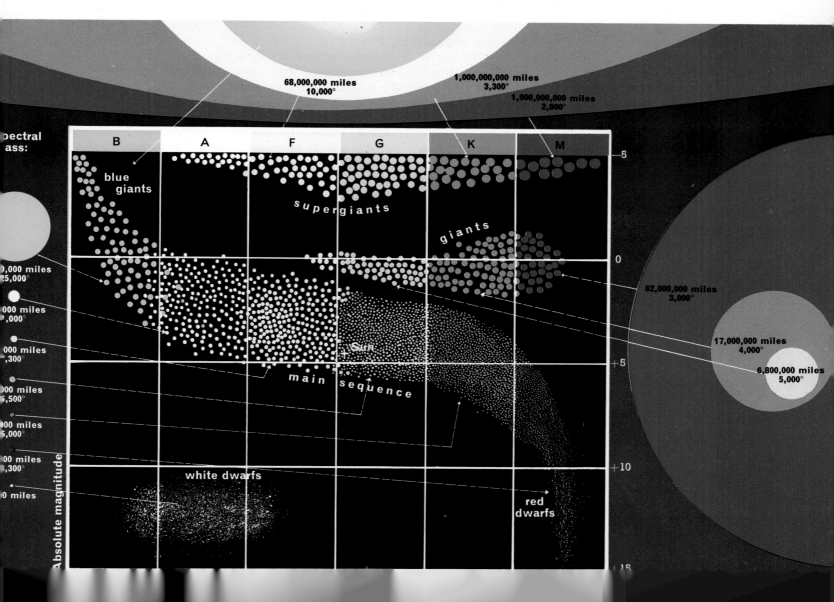

The Trifid nebula in the constellation Sagittarius consists of superheated gases. The small dark spots may be stars in the process of being formed.

the Sun was shown to have the following characteristics:

    Surface: radius 432,475 miles; temperature 5,710° C.
                density 0.00002 g/cc.
    Centre: temperature 13,600,000° C.; density 98 g/cc.

The calculation of the enormous temperatures and core densities of the stars together with what was already known about the behaviour of atomic nuclei has enabled the source of their energy to be established. At such high temperatures and pressures, it is known that atomic nuclei would fuse together. First two hydrogen nuclei would combine, followed by a third and fourth. The resultant particle of four hydrogen nuclei would produce the nucleus of helium gas. The helium nucleus weighs less than four hydrogen nuclei, indicating a loss of matter as a result of the fusion. This loss represents energy produced during the fusion process, in accordance with Einstein's famous equation stating that energy is proportional to mass: $E = mc^2$. This is the source of the stars' energy.

But as energy is produced by the conversion of hydrogen nuclei into helium, a star will continue to radiate only so long as there is a supply of hydrogen. When this supply is exhausted, the star evidently undergoes changes in its internal structure. In fact, stars are in a constant process of evolution. The largest stars end their lives in an explosion (the phenomenon known as the *supernova*),

evidently forming pulsars, while smaller stars fade away more peacefully, becoming white dwarfs.

A star, which according to most astronomers is originally formed as a result of the gravitational contraction of a diffuse mass of interstellar matter, completes its evolutionary cycle in a variable period depending on its total constituent mass. The Sun's cycle spans several thousands of millions of years. Smaller stars have a longer evolution, while larger ones may have lifetimes as brief as 10,000 years.

The solar system

The concept of an essentially evolving and dynamic universe naturally applies also to our own planet. The Earth was born during an evolutionary process which also produced the other planets in the solar system; this may have been the same process that produced the Sun, or may have occurred subsequently.

The age of the Earth can be calculated in various ways. One method utilizes the presence of uranium in many rocks. The uranium atom has a nucleus of 238 particles (92 protons, 146 neutrons) forming an unstable group. Periodically one of these particles breaks away from its neighbours until the nucleus assumes a different character. This process of disintegration continues until the nucleus has achieved stability. By then, another element has been formed, lead, which has 206 particles (82 protons, 124 neutrons). The presence of uranium in rocks clearly shows that not enough time has elapsed for the element completely to have broken down into lead. By analysing the lead content of uranium found in rocks it can be established that the age of the Earth is about 5,000 million years.

Another method of estimating the Earth's age is to analyse the movement of the Moon round our planet. Many scientists believe that in the early stages of the formation of the Earth and the Moon, the two bodies were much closer to one another than they are now. The Earth rotated faster on its own axis, taking an estimated 4 hours 45 minutes for one revolution compared with the present 24 hours, and the Moon also rotated and revolved at a higher speed. The powerful gravitational attraction of the two bodies resulting from their greater proximity produced strong tidal effects which have resulted in the Moon being pushed away from the Earth. As the distance increased the tidal effect diminished, being replaced by the balanced rotational periods observed today. The fact that there

Saturn, the second largest of the planets, with its characteristic rings; these are formed by numerous very small particles, probably the fragments of a former satellite.

are still tides on the Earth indicates that an absolute balance has not yet been reached. Scientists estimate that the period of time it has taken to reach its present stage is between 4,000 and 5,000 million years and it has been calculated that eventually a state of equilibrium will be reached, when both the Earth and the Moon will have axial rotational periods equal to the period of the Moon's revolution around the Earth. This will result in an Earth day lasting 47 days. Throughout this period the Moon will continue to show the same face to the Earth, and ultimately the Earth will always present the same face to the Moon.

The knowledge of the universe that we have acquired by the use of instruments gives us a picture of intense dynamism in which time spans are measured in thousands of millions of years. The fact that the Earth, the Moon, and possibly the Sun are the same age seems to indicate that all three bodies were formed at the same time.

Some astronomers believe that the process was broadly as follows. A huge cloud of gas in space began to contract and rotate. The speed of rotation increased as it contracted, and most of the constituent material of the nebula was spread out in the plane of its rotation – the *equatorial plane*. This equatorial zone was subjected to very intense cooling and condensed into the planets. The Sun remained as the nucleus of the resulting solar system.

This theory explains many observed facts: that all the planets revolve in the Sun's equatorial plane, that the direction of their revolutions is the same as that of the Sun's rotation, and that the axes of rotation of the planets are all more or less perpendicular to their plane of revolution.

This interpretation has been modified as a result of certain criticisms. For example, some scientists suggest that the gas cloud came into contact with the already existing Sun at an early stage in its history, and the planets were formed from the cloud as it condensed while revolving about the Sun.

The Moon

In recent years the Moon has assumed a particular importance, as a result of the possibility of it being used as an extra-terrestrial base for space exploration. Until a short time ago the astronomer's interest in the Moon had to be concentrated mainly on its movement round the Earth and the delineation of its surface features. The question of its internal structure was not neglected, but progress was limited by the small amount of information about the Moon's interior which could be obtained by observers on Earth.

The orbits of the nine planets around the Sun. The red bands show the orbits of 1,500 small planets known as asteroids or minor planets (the largest of these, Ceres, is about 480 miles in diameter). The orbits of the four planets nearest to the Sun are shown in orange. The orbits of two of the major planets, Jupiter and Saturn, are shown in red. The outer orbits in blue are those of Uranus, Neptune, and Pluto. The elliptical orbits outside the equatorial plane of the Sun are the paths of two comets, also members of the solar system.

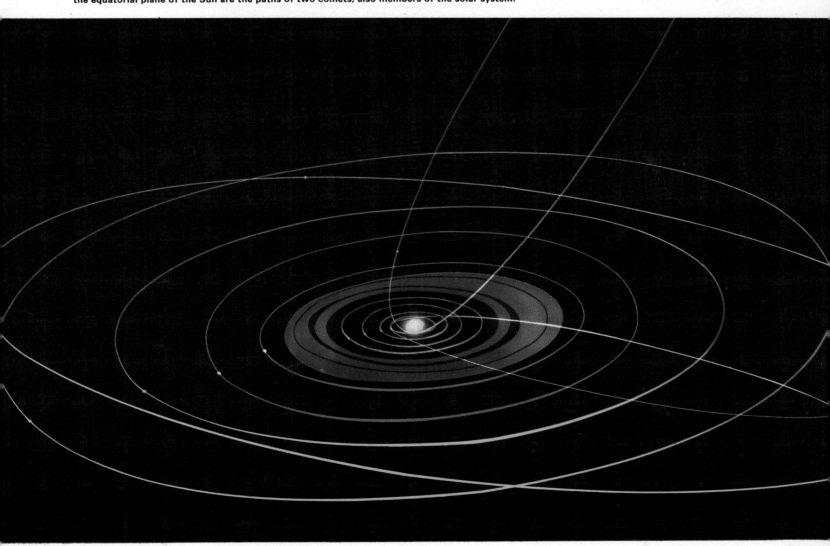

	Mean distance from Sun (millions of miles)	Equatorial diameter (miles)	Period (years)	Orbital inclination to plane of ecliptic	Density (water=1)	Mass (Earth=1)	Number of natural satellites
Mercury	35·98	3,010	0·24	7° 0'	5·50	0·05	0
Venus	67·24	7,650	0·62	3° 23'	5·25	0·82	0
Earth	92·96	7,926	1·00	0°	5·52	1·00	1
Mars	141·64	4,220	1·88	1° 51'	3·94	0·11	2
Jupiter	483·64	88,760	11·86	1° 18'	1·33	317·89	12
Saturn	886·70	74,160	29·46	2° 29'	0·71	95·14	10
Uranus	1,783·1	29,300	84·01	0° 46'	1·70	14·52	5
Neptune	2,794·1	30,100	164·79	1° 46'	1·77	17·25	2
Pluto	3,666·2	3,700	248·4	17° 10'	5·5?	0·10	0

An oblique view of the lunar farside photographed from the Apollo 11 spacecraft in lunar orbit, looking southwest. The large crater in the centre of the picture is International Astronomical Union crater No. 308, which is located at 179° east longitude and 5·5° south latitude. I.A.U. crater No. 308 has a diameter of about 50 miles. The rugged terrain seen here is typical of the farside of the Moon. *NASA.*

VIKING ON MARS

Mars has become almost as familiar a body as the Moon thanks to space-probe exploration that culminated in the landing on Mars of two *Viking* craft in 1976.

Through a telescope, Mars appears as a small orange disk with white polar caps and vague dark markings that seem to change in size and intensity during each Martian year. Earlier this century, astronomers were inclined to think that these dark areas might be vegetation, and some even claimed to see canals which they believed were built by intelligent beings to bring water from the melting polar caps to irrigate crops nearer the Martian equator.

But the red sands of Mars have turned out to be less hospitable than that. In 1971-1972, the American space probe *Mariner 9* photographed Mars in detail from orbit, but failed to reveal either signs of vegetation or the supposed network of artificial canals. Instead, it showed an arid, near-airless world of stark geological contrasts, including gigantic lunar-like craters formed by the impact of meteorites, a volcanic mountain named Nix Olympica that is larger than the volcanic Hawaiian islands on Earth, chaoctic terrain where subsurface ice has apparently melted, and a Martian Grand Canyon caused by a fault in the crust of the planet. *Mariner 9*'s photographs also showed what appeared to be dried-up river valleys, evidence that the climate of Mars may once have been warmer and wetter in the past.

From the *Mariner 9* results, scientists selected a

Above: Artist's impression of the *Viking* lander spacecraft on the surface of Mars. The American bicentennial *Viking* mission consisted of two unmanned spacecraft launched in August and September 1975. *Below:* Diagram of the lander showing the positioning of some of its scientific instruments.
NASA

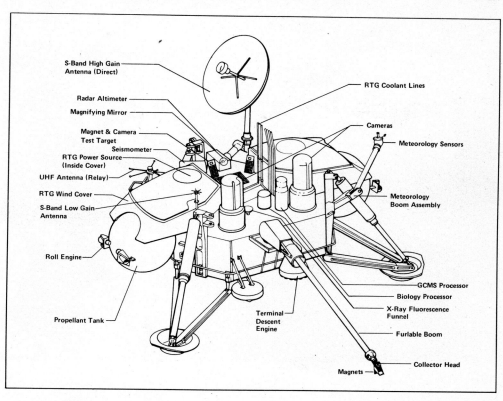

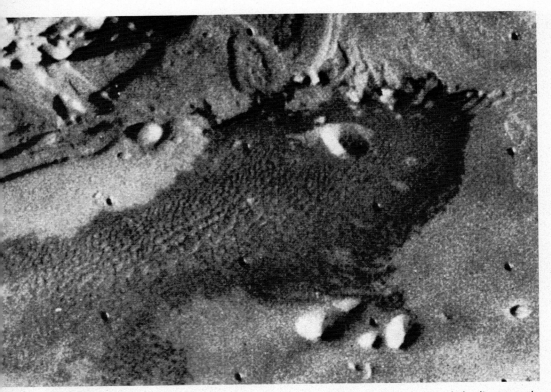

number of promising landing sites for the more ambitious *Viking* project, which was to land two automated probes on the surface of the red planet. Prime requisites were a smooth, flat surface, so that the landers would not tip over on touchdown, and a warm lowland area where traces of water might still exist, giving prospects for life.

In August and September 1975 the two *Viking* spacecraft set out on their 10-month flights to Mars. The first arrived at Mars on June 19th, 1976, and went into orbit to spy out potential landings sites in more detail. Eventually, a safe site was located in the north-western part of the lowland basin known as Chryse, where liquid water is believed to have flowed over the surface during the wet times on Mars. Then the lander separated from its mother craft, which remained in orbit to relay data back to Earth.

Under control of its on-board electronic brain, the lander descended to the surface of Mars, using parachutes and retro-rockets to brake its fall. On July 20th, 1976, seven years to the day after the first men landed on the Moon, the *Viking 1* lander touched down on Mars.

The photographs it sent back, in black and white and colour, showed a rock-strewn landscape like that in a stony desert on Earth. These pictures immediately squashed one of the more extreme theories about Mars—that large organisms, like cacti, might be visible sprouting from the surface. Mars in colour turned out to be very red indeed, apparently due to the presence in its rocks and soil of large amounts of iron oxide—in effect, rust. One surprising discovery was that the sky on Mars appears pink, as a result of fine sand and dust particles suspended in the atmosphere. The surface was firm enough to support the weight of *Viking*, and men could apparently walk around on Mars as safely as on the Moon.

What little air there is on Mars is mostly carbon dioxide (the polar caps are largely frozen carbon dioxide, not frozen water), with a pressure about equal to that at a height of 20 miles above Earth. However, *Viking*'s instruments found a trace of nitrogen, a vital substance for organisms on Earth, which suggested that conditions may once have been suitable for life to form. *Viking*'s meteorology sensors reported light winds and air temperatures ranging from $-86°C$. just after dawn to about $-30°C$. in early afternoon, the warmest part of the day.

But most eagerly awaited were the results from *Viking*'s automated biology laboratory. First, a long robot arm reached out to scoop a handful of Martian soil, which it carefully tipped into funnels leading to the experiment chambers. Three tests were run on the samples in an attempt to incubate possible Martian micro-life.

During these tests, gases were given off by the samples. This could indicate life, with the gases resulting from the 'breathing' of invisible organisms —or, more likely, the gases could be the result of chemical reactions caused by the large amounts of oxygen locked up in the Martian soil. The readings were frustratingly ambiguous—and in view of the importance of the result, scientists were cautious in their interpretation of the findings. Whatever the truth Mars is a sufficiently fascinating world to be worthy of further detailed study.

After this excitement, the landing of the second Viking craft on September 3rd was almost an anti-climax. Whereas scientists had been hoping to see sand dunes at its selected landing site nearer the pole, the lander photographs instead showed a rock-strewn landscape similiar to that at the first *Viking* site.

Above: Huge Martian sand dunes photographed by *Viking 1*, just south of the equator, during its reconnaissance for a possible landing site for *Viking 2*. *Below:* Part of the surface of Mars. The arrow points to the debris kicked up be the impact of a protective cover ejected from the spacecraft.
Popperfoto

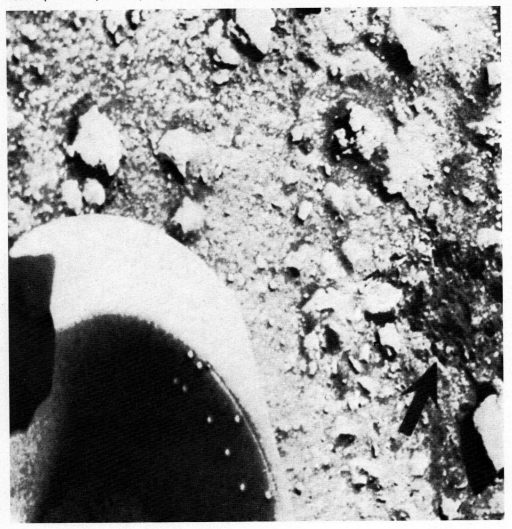

Apollo 12 astronauts, Charles Conrad Jr., Alan L. Bean, and Richard F. Gordon Jr., made their Moon landing in November 1969. *Left:* A television camera is inspected prior to detaching it from Surveyor 3 on the lunar surface. Surveyor 3 soft landed in the Ocean of Storms in April 1967. In the background is the lunar module Intrepid. *Right:* One of the astronauts holding a container of lunar soil collected during the *Apollo 12* extra-vehicular activity. The astronaut wears a check-list on his left wrist to facilitate the following of the pre-planned activity. *JAS/NASA.*

With the advent of the space age, it became possible to send a great variety of probes to the Moon. Most of these were concerned with photographing the Moon in greater detail than possible from Earth, both to learn more about the Moon's surface and also to spy out safe landing sites. For the first time, men saw what the reverse side of the Moon looked like. The photographic probes showed that the Moon's far side is much rougher and mountainous than the near side. Craters abound, but there are no great, flat plains of dark volcanic lava.

Other probes were sent to land on the Moon. They found that the Moon's surface was hard on top, and not covered in deep drifts of soft dust as some astronomers had feared. Craters were found to exist down to a few inches across, and the lunar topsoil behaved like wet beach sand. However, its composition was measured to be like that of earthly volcanic rock. The continual impact of small meteorites had churned it up to make a compacted but powdery top layer.

Following the automatic pathfinder probes came the *Apollo* series of manned landings. On these expeditions, men walked across the Moon and collected samples of its soil and rocks. Analysis back on Earth confirmed the general findings of the first analyses made by the robot probes, but showed that the Moon has definite differences in its detailed composition from the Earth. This may signify that the Moon formed near to the Earth, but from slightly different material.

The Moon has no atmosphere, and so its surface is open to erosion by the small cosmic hailstones called micrometeorites. These have a 'gardening' effect—they churn up the surface over millions of years. However, there is little other form of erosion on the surface. Although the astronauts found evidence that the Moon is slightly warm inside and may once have had a magnetic field, very little activity has taken place for thousands of millions of years. Even the youngest Moon rocks collected were formed about 3,000 million years ago; this is probably the age of the great lunar plains. The oldest rocks date back about 4,500 million years, showing that the Moon is of similar age to the Earth.

The investigation of the Moon allows us to understand our own planet better. The Moon's surface has been compared to a Rosetta Stone of the solar system, because it has remained relatively untouched for so long. The short series of *Apollo* landings, although they told us much about the Moon, are only the first efforts to study our nearest neighbour in space. Seismometers left on the surface have radioed back evidence of meteorite impacts, and the nature of other seismic signals suggests that small Moonquakes still shake the lunar interior.

Study of seismic signals has enabled astronomers to work out the internal structure of the Moon, but far more work remains to be done on this and other aspects before we can build up an accurate picture of the Moon's true nature. Hopefully multinational bases will be set up on the lunar surface in the coming years for study not only of the Moon but also to examine the sky without the blanketing effect of the Earth's atmosphere.

HOW THE EARTH IS MADE

The shape of the Earth

The first and most elementary consideration in studying our planet is its shape. The idea of a horizontal surface is an easy one to grasp. For many practical purposes, such as building roads and houses, we regard the Earth's surface as a flat plane from which perpendicular lines are parallel to each other. But of course the 'horizontal' surface on which we carry out our measurements is really curved. *Geodesy*, the measurement of the Earth on a large scale, shows that the vertical lines we draw from it are not in fact parallel but are inclined towards the poles.

All terrestrial measurements are based on an ideal model of the Earth known as an *ellipsoid of revolution*. This is a spheroid slightly flattened at the poles – the shape formed by a fluid mass rotating on its own axis. This model is a theoretical approximation, since the Earth is such a complex shape that it has avoided accurate mathematical definition. For convenience, therefore, it is conventionally expressed by the model of an ellipsoid of revolution, with a constant equatorial radius and a larger polar radius which is also constant.

Measuring the Earth in classical times

The Pythagorean philosophers were the first to suggest that the Earth was a sphere, in the 5th century B.C. In the following century the first proof of its spherical shape was advanced by philosophers such as Eudoxus of Cnidus and Aristotle. At the same time attempts were made to measure the circumference of the Earth, but the results obtained were extremely inaccurate. Then Eratosthenes of Cyrene (c. 276–c. 194 B.C.) used the meridian arc between Alexandria and what is now Aswan to calculate the Earth's size. He obtained a distance corresponding to about 24,500 miles in circumference, only a few hundred miles less than that obtained by modern measurements.

The accuracy of Eratosthenes' measurements was not recognised and more faith was placed in the most celebrated geographical work of the ancient world, the eight volumes written in the 2nd century A.D. by the astronomer and geographer Ptolemy of Alexandria. He gave the Earth's dimensions as much smaller than they actually are, his measurement of the meridian arc corresponding to a circumference of about 20,000 miles. Ptolemy's *Geography* was rediscovered and translated into Latin by Italian humanists in 1405. Though it contained serious errors, it inspired Columbus to undertake his momentous voyage of discovery; something he might never have done had he known the true distance between the coasts of Europe and Asia in the westward direction. The work was considered highly authoritative for many years; not till Cook's voyage of 1775 was the existence of Ptolemy's supposed Terra Australis Incognita disproved.

The origins and development of modern geodesy

The broad scientific development of the late Renascence inspired other methods of inquiring into the shape and behaviour of our planet, and modern geodesy has its origins in the second half of the 17th century.

Newton's discovery of the law of gravity enabled him (and also Huygens) to put forward the hypothesis of the flattening of the poles. The law of gravity states that bodies attract each other with a force in direct proportion to their masses and in inverse proportion to the square of their distance apart. It was proposed that the effect of gravity together with centrifugal force on a rotating fluid mass – such as the Earth at its formation – would cause the poles to be flattened, and this supposition was checked by the use of pendulums.

The oscillatory period of a pendulum depends on the force of gravity, which is inversely proportional to the distance from the Earth's centre. Thus it is apparent that a variation in the period of oscillation indicates a variation in the distance between the instrument and the centre of the Earth. This experiment was performed by two French scientific expeditions working in the equatorial regions of the Andes and in Lapland in 1736–37. Their measurements showed that Newton's hypothesis was correct.

At the same time, the French expedition in the Andes made an extremely important discovery. It was observed that the great mountain masses exerted a much smaller force of attraction than had been expected. Mount Chimborazo was particularly surprising,

Left: The Pacific Ocean photographed from a space capsule orbiting the Earth, clearly showing its spherical shape. Exploration of space has given man a more objective view of his own planet, permitting the observation of geographical phenomena that are impossible to see from the Earth itself.

Right: According to Anaximander (6th century B.C.) the Earth was flat and surrounded by the Oceanus river. The notion of a flat Earth was first discarded by the Pythagoreans. *Far right:* In the 6th century A.D. religious leaders required the denial of the spherical shape of the Earth. To some the existence of the Antipodes was in any case absurd, as is shown by this drawing by Cosmas Indicopleustes, a Byzantine friar.

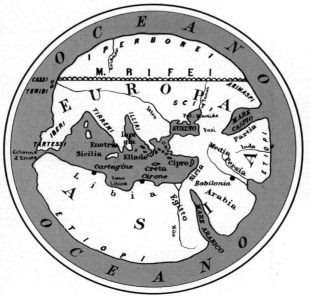

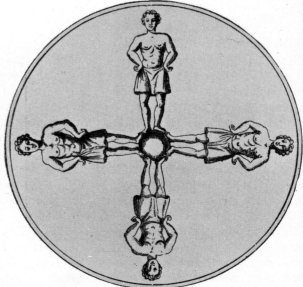

since the great mass of this mountain was expected to make its presence much more strongly felt to the extremely sensitive pendulum being used. This strange gravimetric behaviour was attributed to its volcanic nature. This reasoning, although mistaken, did contain a glimmer of truth which was to come to light more than a hundred years later.

In 1855, in fact, Pratt and Airy were measuring gravity in the Himalayan range and noticed an appreciable difference between the direction of the vertical indicated by the plumb line and that theoretically determined by reference to the surface of the ellipsoid of revolution. From this they deduced that the great mountain chains were composed of lighter material than that found in the lowlands.

This was checked on all the continents and also, recently, in the depths of the oceans. The instruments used are called *gravimeters*, which are very sensitive scales that register the slightest variations in weight of a constant mass caused by variations in the force of gravity acting upon it. By these tests the whole phenomenon was recorded. In the ocean depths there was an abnormal increase of weight, though the overlying water is far lighter than the material making up the land areas.

The shape of the Earth derived from this further knowledge is known as the *geoid*. This gives a far more accurate representation of the physical shape of the Earth than the mathematicians' ellipsoid. It cannot, however, be defined in mathematical terms, and for this reason the dimensions of the ellipsoid of revolution are still used generally, as agreed by international conventions in 1924.

At this point it is of interest to consider what other anomalies of gravity have been revealed by the study of geodesy. Using Newton's law of gravity, the mass of the Earth can be calculated. For this purpose the forces exerted on a sample body by the Earth and by another large body, of known mass, are compared. By this method the mass of the Earth is found to be 5,000 million million million tons, or 5×10^{21} tons.

Once the mass is known, the mean destiny of the Earth may be calculated. This works out at 5.52 g/cc, but the average density of the materials comprising the Earth's crust on which we stand is less than 3 g/cc. From this it must be concluded that underneath the outer crust there are other materials of higher density.

What are these materials and what is their physical state? In fact, what is contained in the Earth's core? The drilling of boreholes and the science of seismology are helping to answer these questions.

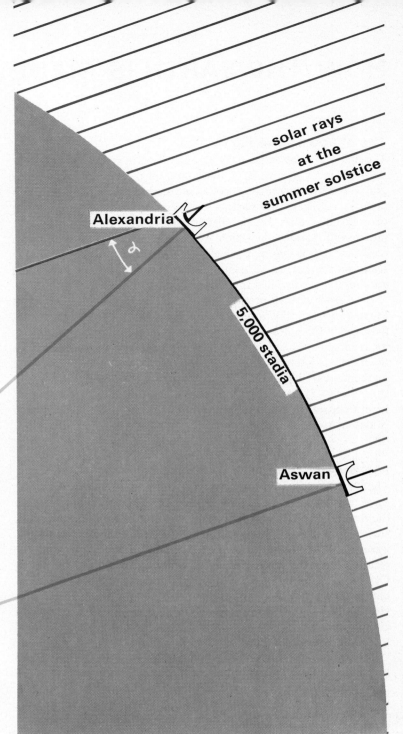

The Earth's heat

Boreholes drilled in mining operations have revealed that beneath a depth of about 60 to 150 feet – that is, the level penetrated by the atmosphere's thermal influx – the temperature rises by an average of 1° C approximately every 120 feet. This is called the *geothermic gradient*. The figures are average, because results vary from place to place, depending on the types of rock concerned, the proximity of volcanic activity or thermal springs, and chemical reactions that generate heat. The origin of this terrestrial heat is not clear. Nothing is known of any heat the Earth might have inherited during its formation, because little has been discovered for certain about this process.

On the other hand, the Earth possesses a significant source of heat of its own, arising from the disintegration of radioactive materials present in rocks: uranium, thorium and potassium-40. But these materials are present in relatively abundant quantities only in the outer shell of the planet. The deeper rocks contain much smaller amounts; it is not known whether there is any at all in the innermost core of the Earth, or whether possibly some form of nuclear reaction takes place there and generates heat.

If the geothermic gradient were constant right down to the centre of the Earth, the core would have a temperature of about 200,000° C. It is however agreed that the gradient becomes less steep at a depth still unknown. This belief is based on the observation that volcanic lavas from the deepest levels erupt at the surface at temperatures no higher than 1,300° C, whereas the Earth's temperature at a depth of even one-tenth of its radius would be of the order of 4,000° to 10,000° C if the gradient was constant. Nonetheless, the fact remains that temperature does increase with depth, reaching about 2,000° C at a depth of 40 miles.

Left: The measurement of an arc of the Earth's meridian as carried out by Eratosthenes in the 3rd century B.C. With an instrument that was virtually a sundial, he measured the angle of incidence of the Sun's rays at the summer solstice in Alexandria. Knowing that, on the same day, the Sun would be at its zenith over Syene (now Aswan), where he was born, he determined the angle formed by two radii from the Earth's centre passing through the two cities. It was equal to 1/50 of the full circle; that is, his measured arc between the two cities was 1/50 of the Earth's circumference. Knowing also the actual distance between the two cities, Eratosthenes was able to calculate the Earth's circumference as 250,000 stadia, a measurement close to the 24,900 miles recorded by modern instruments. (The angle in the diagram is deliberately exaggerated for clarity.)

Right: A representation of the Earth by an anonymous author in an 8th century A.D. atlas. It shows the inhabited face of the planet surrounded by the Oceanus river, which penetrates the Mediterranean through the Strait of Gibraltar (the Pillars of Hercules). The river divides the Earth into distinct regions, with Asia (the site of the terrestrial paradise and the cradle of mankind) shown at the top. Africa, with the River Nile, is at the bottom on the right, opposite Europe.

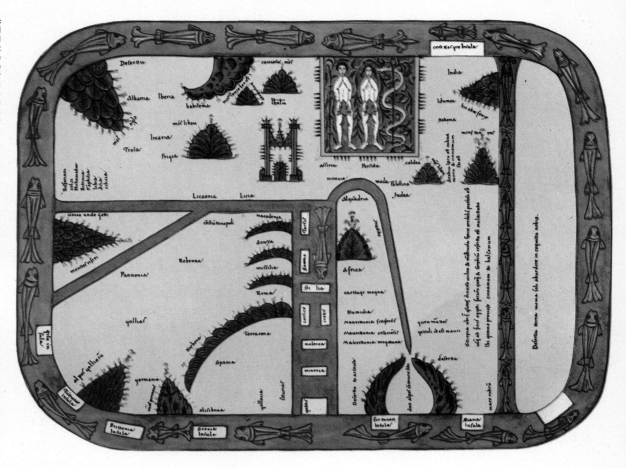

The observation of volcanic and seismic phenomena gave rise to the theory of a central fire in the Earth's core that fed fires, such as volcanoes, on the surface. This theory was put forward at the end of the 17th century by the Jesuit Athanasius Kircher, who illustrated it in his work *Mundus Subterraneus.*

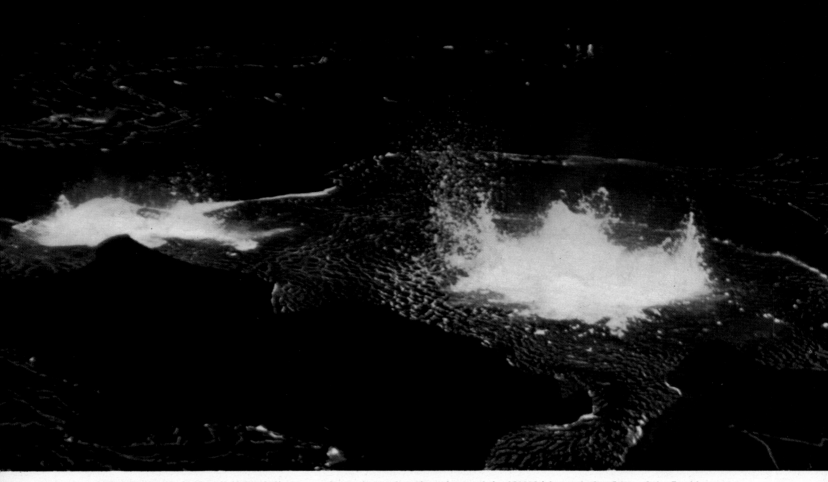

Volcanic eruption in Hawaii. Volcanic lava comes from a layer of partly molten rock (c. 1200°C.) beneath the plates of the Earth's crust.

Temperature and pressure effects

The material inside the Earth is not in a fluid state. If it were, the force of attraction between the Moon and the Earth would so affect the Earth's outer shell that we would all be wrenched away into space and then plunged downwards again several times a day, in the same way that the tides operate but with far greater dislocation. Pressure increases with depth, but although the effect of an increase in temperature is to transform solid bodies into liquids or even gases, increases of pressure have the opposite effect.

A body in the gaseous state has a critical temperature at which it remains in that state even if its pressure is increased. In such conditions it is the density of the body that increases. Scientists have calculated that the gaseous material in certain stars is so dense that if it were brought to the Earth it would weigh several tons per cubic inch.

Complex theoretical calculations have reached a fair approximation of the increase in pressure and density between the outer and inner parts of the globe. These calculations show that pressure

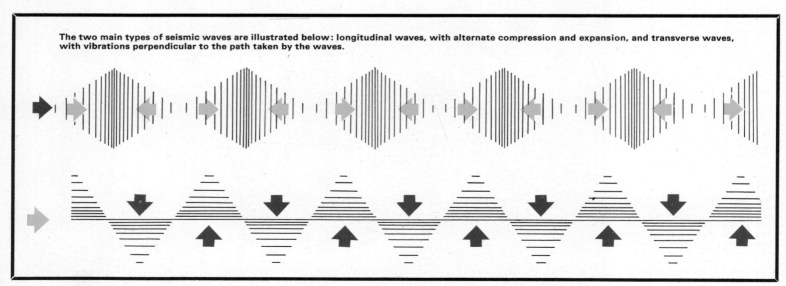

The two main types of seismic waves are illustrated below: longitudinal waves, with alternate compression and expansion, and transverse waves, with vibrations perpendicular to the path taken by the waves.

rises at a uniform rate until it reaches 3.9 million atmospheres at the Earth's centre. The density of the material seems to undergo a first increase from 3.2 to 4.5 g/cc at a depth of about 550 miles, and reaches 5.5 g/cc at a depth approaching 1,800 miles. At this point there appears to be a sharp increase up to 9.7 g/cc, followed by a more gradual increase to 12 g/cc near the Earth's centre. After this, there is a further big increase at the centre itself.

These calculations provide no more than a number of clues to help solve the mysteries of the Earth's interior. To obtain a clearer idea another phenomenon must be studied, that of seismic waves.

How seismic waves move

Scientists know that a sudden and swift disturbance taking place at a certain spot in the Earth's interior – known as the *focus* or *hypocentre* of an earthquake – causes vibrations that spread out in all directions as elastic waves. In practice, each particle affected by the earthquake tends to resume its former position by vibration in two ways: by alternate compression and expansion and by oscillations whose plane of vibration is respectively parallel and perpendicular to the direction of the seismic waves. The waves produced are of two types: *longitudinal* waves and *transverse* waves, the latter being the slower moving of the two.

These seismic waves have been observed to follow a curved trajectory, according to the density of the surroundings. The curve is fragmented into smaller curves, the resultant shape resembling that of a festoon. Each small curve is marked by sudden changes of velocity in response to sudden changes of the surrounding density.

It has been established that these sudden deviations all occur at identical depths. This has led to the identification of the so-called surfaces of discontinuity, which can be defined as surfaces separating layers of material of differing chemical and physical composition, as if the Earth was built of a series of concentric wrappings.

The Mohorovičić discontinuity (known as the *Moho*), named after the scientist who discovered it in 1909, is situated at a depth varying between 15 and 30 miles according to the thickness of the crustal plates. In mountainous areas it is found at greater depths. Between the Earth's surface and the Moho the velocity of the longitudinal waves varies according to the rock medium encountered, from about 3½ to 4½ miles/sec.

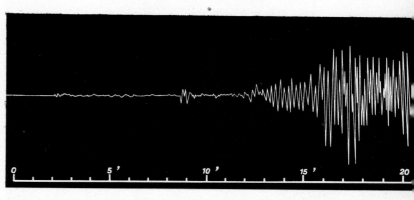

A seismogram recorded at a station situated 3,000 miles from the epicentre of an earthquake. It shows longitudinal waves until the 8th minute. They come from the focus together with the transverse waves, which occur here between the 8th and the 12th minutes. These are followed by a third type of wave, which is recorded as very broad strokes on the instrument. These come from the epicentre and travel along the Earth's surface. Representing the visible signs of an earthquake, they are known as long waves.

Below the Moho the seismic velocity is about 5 miles/sec. An important point is that the discontinuity is only about 3 miles beneath the ocean floor, or 6 or 7 miles below sea-level.

Between the Moho and a depth of about 1,800 miles, the behaviour of seismic waves is different again. At a depth of about 90 miles, their velocity is just under 5 miles/sec. At nearly 600 miles there is a sharp change to 6½ miles/sec – this level being known as the Repetti discontinuity, again named after the scientist who discovered it. Below this the velocity increases to 8 miles/sec.

However, at 1,800 miles down there is a sharp reduction of the velocity of longitudinal seismic waves to below 5 miles/sec, and beyond this point the movement of transverse waves can no longer be recorded. This is the Gutenburg discontinuity. It encloses the Earth's nucleus, which itself contains an even smaller nucleus, a kind of seed, whose presence is detected by another abrupt change in the velocity of longitudinal waves about 3,000 miles deep.

With these data in their possession, scientists immediately began to try to discover what sort of materials would make seismic waves behave in this manner. They established that down to the Gutenberg discontinuity the waves behaved as if they were

Seismic waves change their direction as they move according to the density of the material through which they are moving. Seismograms have in this way revealed an increase of density at a depth of between 15 and 30 miles below the land surface, and just below the seabed. This is known as the Mohorovicic discontinuity. From this it is concluded that the Earth's crust, consisting of blocks of sial, floats on a layer of higher density sima.

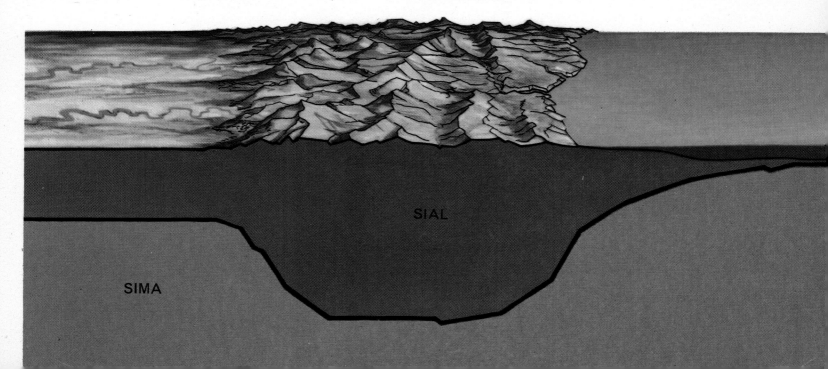

SIAL

SIMA

Wiechert's seismograph for recording seismic waves. It consists basically of an inverted pendulum, whose inertia prevents it being affected by earth tremors, and a frame anchored firmly to the ground. The relative movement of the two is recorded on a moving chart by a stylus. Particularly sensitive seismographs use a moving light beam focused on sensitive paper.

passing through solid bodies, albeit of varying densities. In the nucleus, however, they behaved as they do on the Earth's surface when passing through liquids or gases.

The Earth's internal structure

The study of seismic waves tells us more about the Earth's internal structure, but does not lead to any absolute conclusions. Scientists have tried other ways, but have always had to satisfy themselves eventually with hypotheses, such as the following:

The Earth is made up of a series of concentric layers, namely:

1) The solid crust, to a depth of between 20 and 35 miles, made up of plates of rocks with a density of just under 3 g/cc. These rest on material of a slightly higher density. This crust is relatively very thin. The surface separating it from the underlying material is indicated by the Mohorovičić discontinuity.

2) The upper mantle, a layer of material with a density of 3·3 to 4·3 g/cc with a temperature exceeding 1,000°C. and thus in a molten state. The pressure keeps the viscosity of this material at a standard level similar to that of molten glass. This layer goes down to about 900 miles.

3) The lower mantle with densities up to 7 g/cc and temperatures around 4,000°C, situated between 900 and 1,800 miles down. This layer, indicated by the Gutenberg discontinuity, is also viscous, but has a different composition.

4) The outer core, enclosing a smaller solid nucleus or inner core, has a density between 9 and 12 g/cc and a temperature of about 10,000°C. This section is in a fluid state and its nature is not entirely known.

The Earth reacts to brief shocks like a body having twice the rigidity of steel. To shocks of longer duration it behaves like a highly plastic body.

The rocks of the lithosphere

There is still the problem of the composition of the Earth's rocks. Rocks found recently in Cyprus and Greenland are thought to have come from the mantle. Before that we could only observe the shallow layer directly.

The study of rocks exposed to the surface reveals several layers. First, a blanket of *sedimentary rocks*, consisting mainly of layers (strata), and composed of fragments of pre-existing rocks that have been exposed to erosion and of rocks of chemical and organic origin. Sedimentary rocks are usually deposited in a gradual process on the sea floor, and on dry land. Their depth can often be measured on the Earth's surface and in zones near dry land. They scarcely exist on the ocean floors or at the bottom of the great ocean trenches.

We are witnessing the destruction and the formation of these rocks. The land we walk on consists of loose particles that in time will form layers of these rocks. Sedimentary rocks are a product of the erosion of dry land surfaces and the accumulation of plant or animal remains, and have been in formation since the Earth's atmosphere formed. Generally the sedimentary rocks situated at the Earth's surface are of comparatively recent origin. The oldest ones, because of the various upheavals and changes that have

Sedimentary rocks. *Far left:* encrustations of geyserite, a mineral of hydrothermal origin. The mineral's chief component is silica, which is dissolved in the very hot waters that rise from the subsoil and which precipitates into various shapes when cooling. In this picture of the Yellowstone National Park, the silica has formed a terraced structure. *Left:* A conglomerate of recent formation composed of detritus and large pebbles, which have been more or less cemented together.

A view of the Colorado plateau in the Dinosaur National Monument near Colorado's border with Utah. At this point (Harper's Corner) the Yampa River runs into the Green River, a tributary of the Colorado. The picture shows a section of rocks of sedimentary origin. Sedimentary rocks make up only some 5% of the lithosphere, although they are found to a great extent throughout the continents.

affected the Earth during the many millions of years of its existence, have changed often through being swallowed into the depths of the crust where the temperature and pressure are different from those at the surface.

In this way they have acquired different characteristics producing another type of rock *metamorphic rocks*. These rocks are those whose original structure has been changed—to a slight degree at the surface and more radically deep down. Because of the Earth's long existence, the proportion of these rocks is greater than that of the sedimentary rocks.

Where these metamorphic rocks are exposed they can often be seen to be closely associated with the *granitic rocks*. These are magmatic rocks, formed from the slow cooling, deep down and away from the atmosphere, of molten rock masses that, because of the conditions of temperature and pressure, have developed a crystalline structure.

These rocks are rich in silica, either pure in the form of quartz or combined with aluminium and other elements (potassium, sodium, calcium, etc.). They have a low mass, their density being about 2·7 g/cc, and seismic waves pass through them slowly.

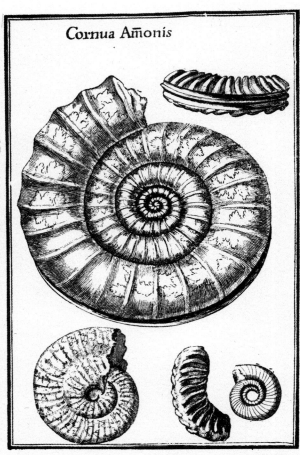

Cornua Amonis

Sedimentary rocks. *Left:* Calcareous stratifications dating from the lower Cretaceous (Mesozoic era) and containing fossil cephalopods like the ammonites *(right)* from *Lang's Fabulosa Historia Lapidum Faguratorum* (1708).

Two examples of metamorphic rock. *Left:* Crystalline calcareous rock (marble) of the Apuane Alps. *Below:* Schist from the Val d'Aosta, a schistose rock that splits easily into laminations and is used as roof tiles. These two rock types are different in origin and have been subjected to different metamorphic processes.

Mont Blanc is a gigantic mass of granite with its foundations deep in the Earth's crust. A magmatic, intrusive rock, granite appears to form the most important part of the continental masses. It is relatively light, composed mainly of silica and aluminium (sial) in varying proportions.

Photographs taken of thin sections of sedimentary, metamorphic, intrusive, and extrusive rocks. The rocks are prepared for microscopic inspection by being cut in slices 0.01 – 0.05 mm. thick, and mounted in slides. They are then examined under a polarizing microscope.

Fusulinus limestone (mag. × 35)
A sedimentary rock containing fossil fusulinids, an important genus of Formanifera that inhabited the seas during the Carboniferous period. The photograph shows the internal structure of the fossil.

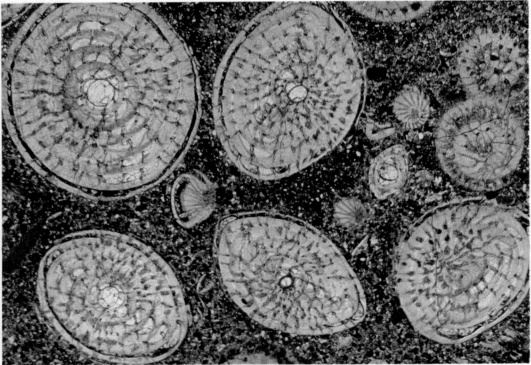

Nummulitic limestone (× 10)
Another sedimentary rock, containing Nummulites, fossils characteristic of the Eocene and Oligocene epochs. Accumulation of their shells on the sea-floor contributed to the formation of the calcareous rocks, layers of which are very common in the Italian pre-Alps.

Carrara marble (× 130)
A rock formed from the recrystallization of a calcareous rock when subjected to metamorphic activity. The slide shows the characteristic structure of calcite crystals (calcium carbonate) arranged in a mosaic, and in places penetrating each other.

Mica-schist (× 50)
A metamorphic rock composed basically of quartz and mica with a few other minerals. The quartz can be seen clearly (grey and white crystals). The mica (blue or yellow strips) is of the muscovite type. Mica-schist is one of the most common forms of rocks in the Alps.

Granite (× 50)
An intrusive and highly acid rock, characterized by the presence of quartz and felspars (silicates of aluminium with other alkaline metals such as sodium and potassium, or alkaline earths such as calcium or barium). The slide shows the felspars as greyish banded crystals. The greenish-red crystal in the centre is biotite, a form of mica.

Basalt (× 130)
An extremely basic extrusive igneous rock composed of olivine (or peridot, a mixture of silicates) and pyroxene.

23

The Devil's Tower, which stands near the Belle Fourche River in Wyoming, is a block of basalt, a columnar structure in the course of cooling. Basalt, is a basic rock with a low silica content and contains mainly magnesium. It is a volcanic rock common on the ocean floors.

Some scientists have suggested recently that the granitic rocks may have originated from the fusion of all the other rocks already mentioned. In fact, experiments have shown that by melting these rocks in the proportions in which they are found in the Earth's crust, a magma is obtained with a chemical composition very similar to that of granite.

Geophysicists have deduced that the continents are composed of largely basaltic and granitic rocks which they call *sial* because of the silicon and aluminium content. Recent observations also show that ocean floors contain materials from the mantle.

If we go back to what has been said above about the distribution deep down of different materials of varying density and the velocity of the seismic waves passing through them, we can deduce that the layer of granite varies between about 6 and 25 miles in thickness. It is thicker under mountainous areas.

The ocean floors are where new crust is being created. By observing the increase in the velocity of seismic waves and the density of the material responsible for this increase, geophysicists have deduced that the rocks there consist of basalt with a low silica content and with a preponderance of magnesium and sodium. This basaltic layer, because of the prevalence of silicon and magnesium, is known as the *sima*.

The thickness of this layer extends to the Mohorovičić discontinuity, which occurs at a depth of between 15 and 30 miles. Beneath this layer seismic waves and gravimetric readings have revealed the existence of rocks even more basic than the basaltic layer which are consequently known as ultrabasic. These rocks are only occasionally found on the surface of the Earth; they are known as dunites, and are composed almost exclusively of magnesium silicates and iron.

Analogic hypotheses

Measurements of seismic waves and gravimetric readings carried out deep down cannot be compared with those carried out in the rocks nearer the Earth's surface. Scientists believe that the sima layer of ultrabasic rocks reaches a depth of about 900 miles, but they do not know what forms of aggregation are present at that level.

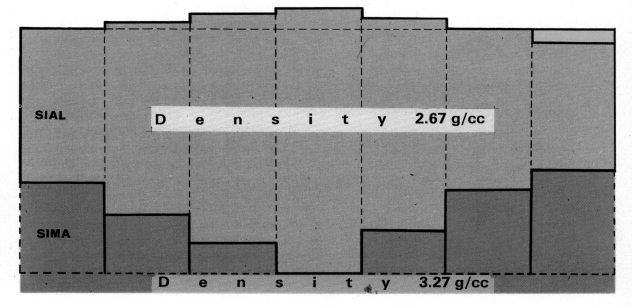

SIAL

D e n s i t y   2.67 g/cc

SIMA

D e n s i t y   3.27 g/cc

According to the theory of isostasy, the materials forming the continental masses (sial) all have comparable densities, since they float on the substratum of sima. Thus the higher the mountain range the deeper it penetrates into the Earth's crust. In the diagram, the upper horizontal broken line represents sea level: the lower one a depth of nearly 50 miles. Mount McKinley (below) has roots deep in the crust.

One of the vast tablelands of Western Australia, a characteristic example of the Earth's dry-land areas in both altitude and morphology.

Beneath this level and down to 1,800 miles (the depth of the Gutenberg discontinuity), it is believed that the rocks are made up mainly of olivine and silicotes.

The composition of the Earth's core has been partly deduced from the examination of meteorites. These are thought to be cosmic material that has not been formed into a planet, the theory that they are parts of an exploded planet now being generally rejected. There are two basic types: the *aerolites*, largely composed of heavy ultrabasic rocks, and the *siderites*, containing a high proportion of iron and nickel. An intermediate class, the *siderolites*, are made of both rock and metal. All classes also contain small amounts of other elements, but none has yet been found to contain any matter not found on Earth. This supports the theory that the bodies of the solar system are all composed of similar materials, and the average composition of all meteorites suggests that the proportion in which they contain the various elements is similar to that found in the Earth and the Sun.

From this it has been concluded that the Earth's core is made up mainly of an alloy of iron and nickel. This is known as *nife*, after the symbols for nickel and iron, which are Ni and Fe.

The isostatic theory

If all the above facts are now viewed in relation to each other, there emerges an extremely important phenomenon. First of all, that the crust is not a continuous mass but made up of separate parts, some of which form the continents. Beyond the depth at which the solid, crystalline sial is believed to end, namely that level where the change in the velocity of seismic waves indicates a density of 3 g/cc and temperatures of about 1,000° C., the materials present must be in a highly viscous state. The inference, therefore, is that the solid, light sial floats on the dense, plastic sima.

Next, it must be noted that the gravitational acceleration, when adjusted for latitude and altitude, is lower than it should be in theory for mountains and greater for oceans and deep depressions.

We then consider the greater thickness of the sial layer under mountain systems, and we are again able to deduce that the sial layer floats on the sima substratum. In mountainous areas the sial layer is immersed at greater depth in the sima than in low-lying areas.

This phenomenon takes the form of an equilibrium between the sial and sima layers. The equilibrium is known as *isostasy*, and is similar to that between water and floating bodies, which is known as hydrostatic equilibrium. In practice, the surface separating the sial from the sima should resemble the surface topography, creating the effect of mountains mirrored in a pool.

It is known that the variation between the average altitude of the dry-land area and the average depth of the sea is over 15,000 ft. This corresponds exactly to the height that a tabular-shaped block of sial would rise above the sima substratum when we consider that 20 miles is the average thickness of the sial and its density is only six-sevenths that of the sima.

Isostatic equilibrium is not found everywhere, however, because the Earth's surface is incessantly exposed to erosion. The eroded material falls away from its parent mass, which consequently becomes lighter. The areas receiving the eroded material become heavier in their turn. Then the lighter masses tend to rise and heavier ones sink, owing to the disturbance of the sima layer.

On the assumption that the sima layer has a density of 3.2 g/cc, it has been calculated that the removal through erosion of 3,000 feet of sial rock with a density of 2.7 g/cc would cause a rise of the sial amounting to 2,531 feet, so that the effective decrease through erosion would be reduced to 469 feet.

Parallel to this, the deposition of eroded material with a density of 2.2 g/cc to a depth of 3,000 feet would cause the part of the sial thus laden to sink 2,062 feet, so that its effective height increase would amount to only 938 feet.

It must be pointed out, however, that the laws of plasticity in time do not mean that the sial layer sinks into the sima with every variation of weight. Plastic deformation in time also depends on the amount of resistance put up by bodies submitted to pressure. If this does not reach a certain level, which varies with each body, then no deformation takes place. This is demonstrated in the case of the Grand Canyon in Colorado, where the diminution of weight through erosion has not disturbed the rock stratification, which has remained perfectly horizontal.

On the other hand, the diminution of weight resulting from the melting of the ice-cap that covered the interior of Scandinavia during the Ice Age (Gulf of Bothnia) caused that region to rise by 600–1,000 feet during the last 9,000 years. The region is still rising at an estimated 3 feet a century, and has another 150 feet to rise before reaching its isostatic equilibrium.

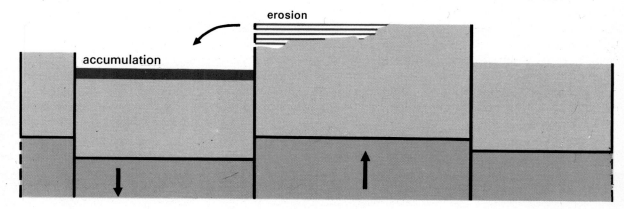

The continuous processes of erosion to which the surface of the Earth is exposed result in a reduction in the weight of the rock masses, while the material removed forms an additional load on the area where it is deposited. A good example of this process is provided by the Grand Canyon of the Colorado *(below)* where the eroded rock masses have been raised. The rock strata have remained perfectly horizontal throughout.

THE EARTH'S CRUST SHAPED FROM WITHIN

Mobility of the Earth's crust

The theory of isostasy, as described above, suggests that the Earth's crust moves on a large scale. This movement is evident from observations of phenomena which we can see around us.

Volcanoes and seismic disturbances are obvious signs of the intense dynamism that occurs within the Earth; the chemical and thermal activity of volcanoes being linked with the mechanical action of earthquakes. The movements in the Earth's crust trigger seismic activity. But the most widespread proof of the crustal movements can be seen (even at the surface) in the deformation of the materials making up the solid crust. The most spectacular examples of this deformation are to be found in mountain ranges and rift valleys.

In many of these the rock masses had their origins beneath the sea, formed by rock sediments or by vast accumulations of shells and coral. These still bear fossil traces left by creatures that once led a marine life. The strata of these rocks may no longer be horizontal, as they must have been when they were submerged, but instead may be tilted or folded.

The mountains that are formed by deformation of the Earth's crust are evidence of the ways in which it is subjected to extreme pressure and change.

There are two main types of tectonic structures: *fractures*, which are deformations of a rigid type, and *folds*, which are deformations of a plastic nature.

Generally, the type of deformation depends on the nature of the rocks affected, their degree of resistance, and the duration of the process. For example, sedimentary rocks, which are composed of alternating layers with varying degrees of resistance (some, like the clays, being plastic), have a different behaviour pattern from homogeneous layers of crystalline rock. Also, a rock mass that has been subjected to deformation acquires considerable

This photograph is a striking illustration of how the Earth's crust can be deformed by internal forces.

A wall of the Sass Pordoi in the Dolomites. These mountains are examples of the tremendous dislocations to which the Earth's crust is subjected. The rocks, once beneath the sea, now stand high above the plains.

resistance, so that subsequent pressure almost always produces a rigid type of deformation.

Rigid deformations: fractures

The mobility of the Earth's crust falls into two broad categories. First, there are dislocations that affect the entire thickness of the crust on a continental scale. These movements are marked by radical changes not only in the topography of land areas, but also in the relationship between land and sea; they give rise to the complex movements of *orogenesis* or mountain building. In the second category are those pressures that act only on rocks at the surface, causing dislocations on a much smaller scale.

Tectonic forces shape the Earth's surface warping and fracturing it. Rocks, especially sedimentary ones, are minutely fractured and break into blocks of regular shapes. These small-scale fractures are determined by planes of least resistance to pressure. These planes are formed during cooling in the case of volcanic rocks,

A fault in a bed of Cretaceous marble, shown up by the dark layer of silica. This was produced as a result of local activity. The small, scale-like fractures are characteristic of this type of sedimentary rock, although the curvature shows that it has a certain degree of plasticity.

A huge fault extending for hundreds of miles in Canada. It separates two Pre-Cambrian formations: on the left, granitic rocks; on the right, sedimentary rocks. A smaller fault can be seen in the centre, forming the coastline of a peninsula on Lake MacDonald, near the Great Slave Lake.

or by variations of pressure during the process of deformation, or by the different conditions affecting sedimentary rocks during their consolidation. They are to be distinguished from the actual fractures produced by the tectogenetic process which are due to tectonic forces greater than the plasticity of the rock masses they act on.

Often the fracture is not accompanied by a corresponding movement of the rock beds, and some strata slide along the crack so that the beds which were previously continuous become out of alignment. A break of this type is known as a *fault*. Faults are classified by the resulting relationship between the two rock sections affected. If the rock beds have merely become misaligned at the fault-plane, the fault is a *normal* one. If, however, the beds moved in such a way as to overlap, it is called a *thrust* fault.

The normal fault is produced by a force that pulls the rock beds apart. The thrust fault is the result of lateral pressure that breaks the beds and forces them to overlap. Both indicate the presence of a horizontal force acting on the beds. These horizontal forces play an important part in large-scale tectonic phenomena along the edges of the plates of which the crust is formed.

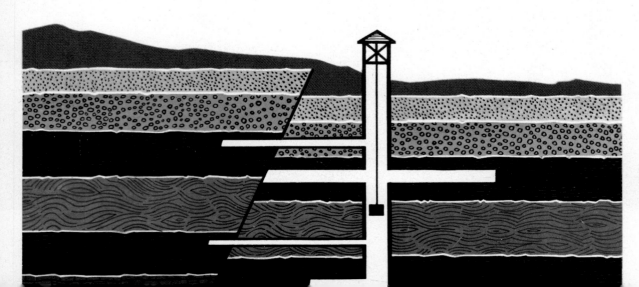

An illustration of the importance of identifying faults in mining. The continuity of the vein has to be located within the various layers of rock.

Plastic deformations: folding

Folding may be small-scale, or large-scale, arising from tectonic forces, and various other factors.

The crystal-line metamorphic rocks show folding on a small scale. The minute folding is caused through the settlement of the rock at great depth where rock masses of a very plastic nature undergo a process of recrystallization. Rocks with a high clay content may also show folding of a small order, possibly due to the effects of certain kinds of turbulence during the sedimentation of the rocks or to the effects of freezing and thawing of the water content which cause changes in the volume of the rock mass. In each of these cases the amount of folding involved is on a small scale, ranging from a few inches to several feet.

Deformation of the Earth's crust produces folding on a much larger scale, involving entire systems of stratification of a more or less homogeneous composition. This type of folding occurs in two forms, *anticlines* and *synclines*. These can be readily distinguished by the age-sequence of the strata relative to the *nucleus* of the fold. If we take a book as an example, the nucleus would be represented by the centre pages. If the nucleus of the fold contains the oldest rocks then it is an anticline, and has the overall shape of the letter A; if, however, the nucleus comprises the rocks of most recent formation then the fold is a syncline, with the shape of the letter V.

In some cases the rocks are not simply bent, but are turned back into flattened loops known as overfolds, which causes the order of the bedding to be reversed so that older rocks lie above younger ones.

The photograph below, taken in Zagros (Iran), clearly shows an example of an anticline. *Right:* Phases in the evolution of an inclined fold into an overfold, a faulted fold, and finally into a deformed mass where the beds have been fragmented

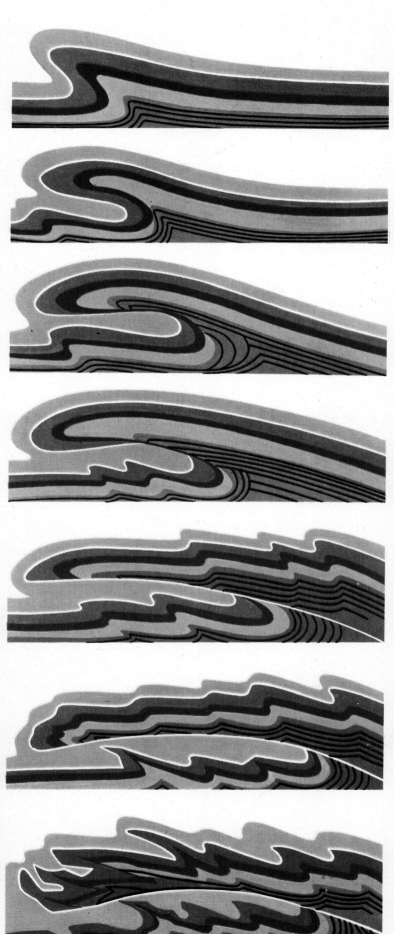

An anticline in the Elburz Mountains in Iran. The broken lines show the line of the anticline which has been attacked by erosion.

A gigantic fold in Iran, photographed from the air, is highlighted by the lack of vegetation. Its size is indicated by the village shown inside the black circle. The top layers of the anticline have been worn away to expose the layers of rock beneath.

The theory of continental drift

To explain compression on a gigantic scale, Alfred Wegener proposed the theory of *continental drift* in 1910. It was based on the observation that the sial floated in the sima, obeying the principles of isostatic equilibrium. Wegener found that the eastern coastline of the South American continent and the opposite west African coast corresponded, like pieces in a jigsaw puzzle, and that fossils found on the two coasts were similar. He found equivalent correspondences between the other continents, leading him to suggest that all the continental masses once formed a single unit which has since split and drifted apart.

Wegener called this original single continent Pangaea, and stated that it drifted slowly towards the west. About 100 million years ago, the mass began to break up into distinct sections which drifted apart until they reached the positions they are in today.

To understand Wegener's conception of Pangaea we have to think not just of the dry-land area of a continent, but also of any part of it that may now be submerged under what is known as an *epicontinental sea*, but is nonetheless still part of the sial mass.

Wegener's theory seemed to explain the formation of the Alps and other similar mountain systems such as the Andes and Rockies.

These mountain ranges usually occur along the edges of a continental mass. In a continent drifting to the west, its westward shore would push ahead like the prow of a ship into the underlying sima on which it floated. The sima's resistance would form corrugations or crumpling in the land mass; that is, mountain ranges. At the same time, the eastern shores of the dry-land areas would lag behind because of the braking action of the sima. This effect would create island chains along the eastern shores of the dry-land areas, such as the West Indies and Azores in the case of North and South America. Biological evidence, such as the occurrence of similar species of 'rain-worms' in South America, southern Africa, Australia, and India, strongly supports Wegener's theory of continental drift or a variation of it. Wegener's theory failed to provide a satisfactory explanation of certain phenomena. In particular, the validity of the correspondence between opposed continental coastlines, in the light of what is known of the morphology of the floor of the Atlantic, has only recently been confirmed.

The theory raised one major problem which puzzled Wegener himself, and this was the identification of the motive force which caused such massive displacement. The hypothesis stimulated much research culminating in the present theories of plate tectonics.

The forces that contort the sediments into mountains often form a succession of parallel mountain ranges. The parallel ranges of the Dolomites *(above)* are a formidable barrier in southern Europe. They are formed largely of limestone, that once lay beneath the seas.

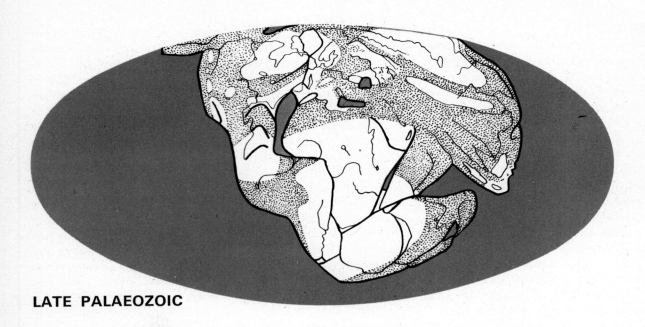

LATE PALAEOZOIC

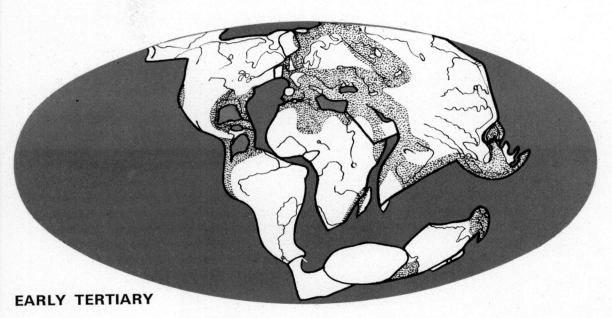

EARLY TERTIARY

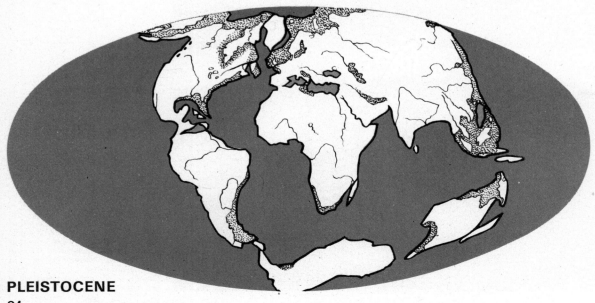

PLEISTOCENE

The Matterhorn (*right*) and Monte Rosa form part of two different folds of old rock (gneiss), the former course of which is shown in the diagram (*below*) by broken lines. These folds have encompassed the sedimentary formations in the syncline that existed prior to the folding. The sediments also show intrusions of volcanic rock (the lenticular shapes). Erosion has stripped the upper fold almost completely, leaving only isolated fragments such as the Matterhorn pyramid. The huge arching cannot be caused entirely by tangential pressure, since this would involve the deeper rocks whose plastic behaviour is quite different from that of the upper rocks above them.

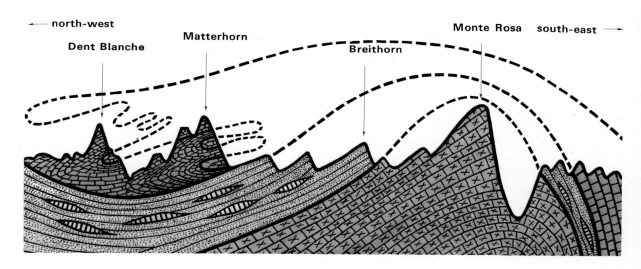

← north-west

south-east →

Dent Blanche   Matterhorn   Breithorn   Monte Rosa

The theory of the formation of the continents from a primordial continuous crust. Convection currents (indicated by arrows) deform the crust, which is subsequently attacked by erosion at B, with accumulation of detritus at the depressions (A) marked by the broken line. There is only limited erosion at C, where the currents move upwards. Once heat balance is reached and the convection currents cease, the zones of accumulation settle according to the principle of isostasy, and the nucleus areas (D) are formed. The areas worn down become depressions forming the oceans (E), containing traces of the sial crust (F). These currents were considered to be sufficient to explain Wegener's theory of continental drift.

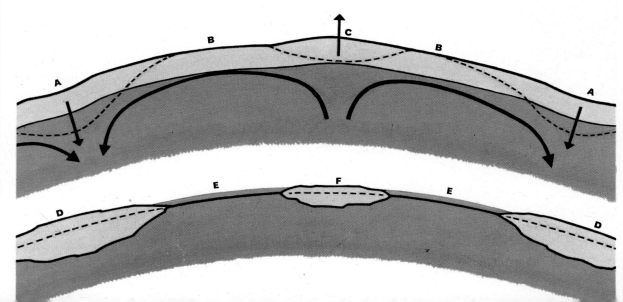

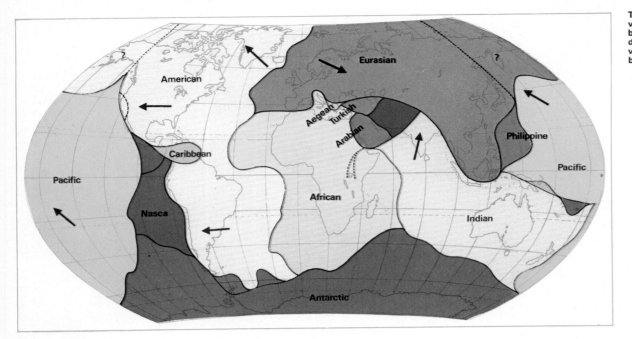

This map shows the plates into which the Earth is at present broken. They move in different directions causing earthquakes, volcanic activity, and mountain building.

This is a colour composite of three black and white photographs of Monterey Bay in California. The city of San Jose and the southeastern tip of San Francisco Bay is in the upper left corner. Agricultural fields in the San Joaquin Valley are shown in the upper right; the variations in the red tones indicated different crop types and different stages of maturity. The linear feature running from the lower right to the upper left is the famous San Andreas fault. The San Andreas fault in California is where two plates of the Earth's crust move alongside each other causing numerous earthquakes. These movements are a constant threat to the safety of San Francisco.

Modern hypotheses of tectonics

More than 40 years passed after Wegener formulated his theory of continental drift before the concept was widely accepted by earth scientists. Geomagnetic data, closer studies of the geology, and computer estimates to show the fit of the continents have all added support to the theory.

The theories of "*plate*" *tectonics* suggest that the crust of the planet is broken into plates. These plates move in different directions. Most geological activity occurs at the edges of these rigid plates where they run beneath each other, alongside each other, or where they are splitting apart.

It has been difficult to find the exact motive force causing the plates to move although it is known that radioactivity generates intense heat and currents in the mantle beneath. Geomagnetic studies of the materials on the ocean beds suggest that they are spreading out from the mid-ocean ridges. The mantle beneath is welling up and adding new crust to the edges of the plates thus gradually pushing them apart.

Where the plates move into each other the edge of one of the plates sinks into the mantle and the crust is thus gradually destroyed. In this way the plates are slowly re-cycled.

Of special interest is Iceland which stands on the mid-Atlantic ridge. An examination of recently formed rocks shows that Iceland is slowly getting wider.

Folded rock layers in the Alps show they have been crumpled by enormous forces. These mountains are formed by the collision of the rigid plates that form the Earth's crust. Rocks and fossils that formerly lay horizontally beneath the seas have risen thousands of feet above sea level.

Bottom: Careful study of rocks on the sea bed have shown differences in their magnetism. These studies have enabled scientists to trace their history and have suggested that rocks welling up in the centre of the oceans push the continents apart and make the oceans wider. *Right:* Experiments are carried out in laboratories to examine the mechanisms by which mountains may be built. This is Grigg's experiment to demonstrate orogenesis caused by currents of magma. The rotation of two drums in a sub-stratum made up of a concentrated solution of sodium silicate forms a symmetrical structure in the crust which is composed of a mixture of sand and soil. When only one of the drums rotates, the resulting structure is asymmetrical.

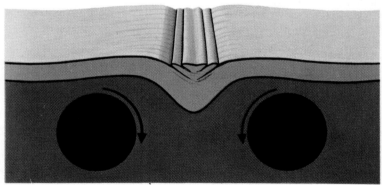

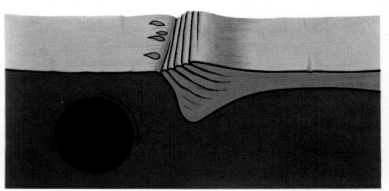

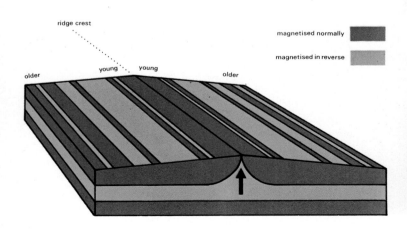

ridge crest

older   young   young   older

magnetised normally

magnetised in reverse

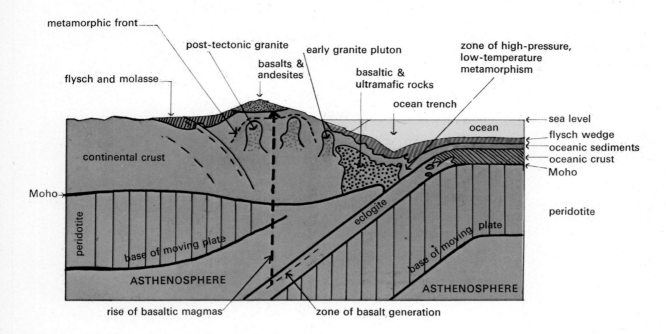

metamorphic front

post-tectonic granite   early granite pluton

basalts & andesites

basaltic & ultramafic rocks

zone of high-pressure, low-temperature metamorphism

flysch and molasse

ocean trench

sea level

ocean

flysch wedge

oceanic sediments

oceanic crust

Moho

continental crust

Moho

peridotite

eclogite

peridotite

base of moving plate

base of moving plate

ASTHENOSPHERE

ASTHENOSPHERE

rise of basaltic magmas

zone of basalt generation

Phases in the formation of topography

According to modern theories the formation of relief structures on the Earth's surface takes place as a result of the plates that form the Earth's crust meeting each other and buckling up. At the same time they scoop sediments into mountain ranges. This stage does not necessarily determine the ultimate form of the landscape. The cordillera systems, originating in such uplifts, are immediately subjected to erosion, the material removed by this process being transported eventually to the seas. Areas newly exposed to erosion are round the eastern coast of the Asian continent from the Indonesian archipelago to the Aleutian Islands.

The deformations that take place occur spasmodically rather than continuously, and extend through time as well as space. Thus, even in the systems that form the New Fold mountain ranges some sections can be seen that were deformed earlier than others. The American cordillera systems, for example, were formed over a considerable period of time. While the deformations in the Andes date back about 150 million years to the Jurassic period, those in the Californian mountain ranges belong to the Pliocene (about 7 million years ago) and the Quaternary (2 million years ago) and are presumed still to be taking place.

At the same time that the mountains are eroded sedimentation takes place. The new rocks formed are clays, sands, and limestones. These accumulate to depths of several miles. Through compacting due to pressure, a process of recrystallization and cementation then takes place, forming schistose rocks in compact layers known as *shales*. If these layers alternate with thin layers of other rocks, they form a very plastic rock mass known as *flysch*.

These rocks may be subsequently injected with intrusions of basic magma. A typical example of this is the greenish serpentine

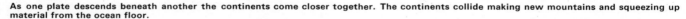

As one plate descends beneath another the continents come closer together. The continents collide making new mountains and squeezing up material from the ocean floor.

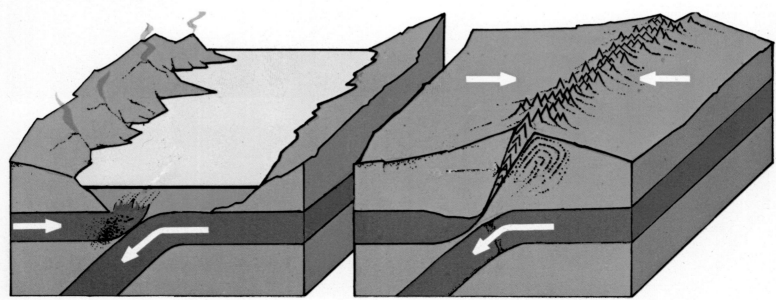

rock found in the European Alps. The sediments are also subjected to extreme metamorphic pressure as a result of the formation of intrusions known as *batholiths*.

The detritus worn away by erosion from the higher parts of the relief structure is deposited as *molasse*, a generally coarse-grained material, in elongated basin areas undergoing subsidence around the region where the mountain system is in formation. These sediments become involved in the orogeny and are deformed and dislocated, so that the developing system reabsorbs its own detritus. The Swiss plateau is an example of this.

The major uplift of the whole mass is immediately followed by renewed erosion, which carves out the relief. The following pattern emerges:

a) An inner zone plastically deformed during the preparatory phases, then flattened and subsequently rigidly deformed by the final displacements, resulting in a complex of large fractured masses.

b) An outer zone built on the lower slopes, marked by plastic deformations.

c) A region between the mountain system and the rest of the landscape unaffected by the orogenic process. This is usually in the form of a hollow, which receives sediments from erosion of the mountain system.

The basic elements of a mountain system, the central section of the Alps. The Adamello, *top*, represents the inner zone of the system. A plain (the Po valley), *below*, lies outside the system. The Verona pre-Alps (background) represent the outer zone of the system.

The form of the Massif Central in France suggests that it resulted from peripheral disturbances caused by the great Alpine upheaval. Its fractures were later injected with extensive magmatic intrusions and developed volcanic cones which are now inactive.

Other major types of orogenesis

We have seen how crustal warpings connected with orogenesis are less severe beyond the mountain ranges. These dislocations are less intense and more widespread, generally taking the form of uplift or subsidence, or fluctuations in the horizontal axis of large crustal sections. Extremely interesting examples of these peripheral changes include the large depressions known as *rift valleys*. Typical of these are the Rhine trench which runs northwards from Basle, and, on a very much larger scale, the Great Rift Valley in Africa.

The process of mountain building may be marked by a lull, or, at least, a significant decrease of crustal movements. Then the principal process is erosion, causing a progressive dismantling and flattening of the relief structure until it is reduced to platforms which are affected only by large-scale displacement.

These platforms are sometimes overlaid by horizontal beds of sediments of land or sea origin, in complete *unconformity* with the underlying strata, which, being part of an older mountain chain, are folded and fractured.

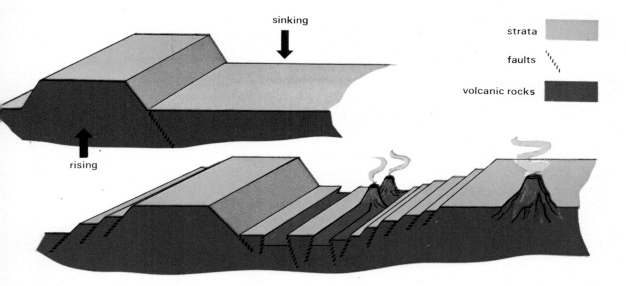

sinking

rising

strata

faults

volcanic rocks

Section of a trench caused by subsidence of a mass affected by two or more faults. The diagram is based on the Rhine trench, the bottom of which is covered with marine sediments (more recent in origin than the sediments on the river's banks) topped by alluvial deposits.

Volcanic rocks filling the floor of the Great Rift Valley in Kenya conceal the full depth of the tear. East Africa broke along old fault lines when the Red Sea and the Gulf of Aden opened. The East African rift is small compared to the one that made the Atlantic Ocean.

These areas are known as *tablelands*. They have a flat surface, and consist of a succession of horizontal strata, the different types of rock showing as distinct layers. Much of Africa is made up of such tablelands.

Parts of these platforms can be subjected to slow erosion over a wide area, accompanied by the accumulation of larger layers of sediments. These form in *sedimentary basins*, which are extremely important in that many of them contain oases.

The pattern of a continent in growth

Platforms can become involved in mountain-building to a more or less marked degree. For example, mountain systems of recent formation (Alpine Systems) contain large masses of rocks that were already corrugated and flattened in previous orogenic cycles known as the Hercynian phase, which took place about 250 million years ago during the upper Palaeozoic era.

The most ancient orogenics are found in the African land mass, and scientists have calculated that they took place about 3,000 million years ago. (The Earth is about 4,500 million years old.)

The old routes of the continents themselves are thought in one theory to be the result of a primordial orogenies which lacerated the surface film of the planet as it cooled and solidified; this concentrated masses of sial, which were divided by deep trenches, to form primitive oceans. It is also suggested that the continents were formed when island arcs were brought together.

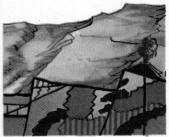

Great block mountains may be lifted along faults and tilted as can be seen in the Sierra Nevada (*left*) of California. The mountain in the front of the picture is the stump of the Alabama mountains, a high range that has been nearly worn away by the forces of erosion.
Below: Eroded tablelands in Mauritania. They consist of calcareous sediments and were formed during earlier periods of subsidence. They rest on the rigid African land mass.

Right: The topography of the island of Spitzbergen, like that of Scandinavia is the product of the erosion that has all but demolished the mountains of the Caledonian orogeny. Other earlier mountain-building phases have been identified dating back to the Palaeozoic era.

Below: This photograph, taken from space shows the north-west African coast. From this height, the continent appears quite visibly as a contorted and fractured part of the Earth's crust.

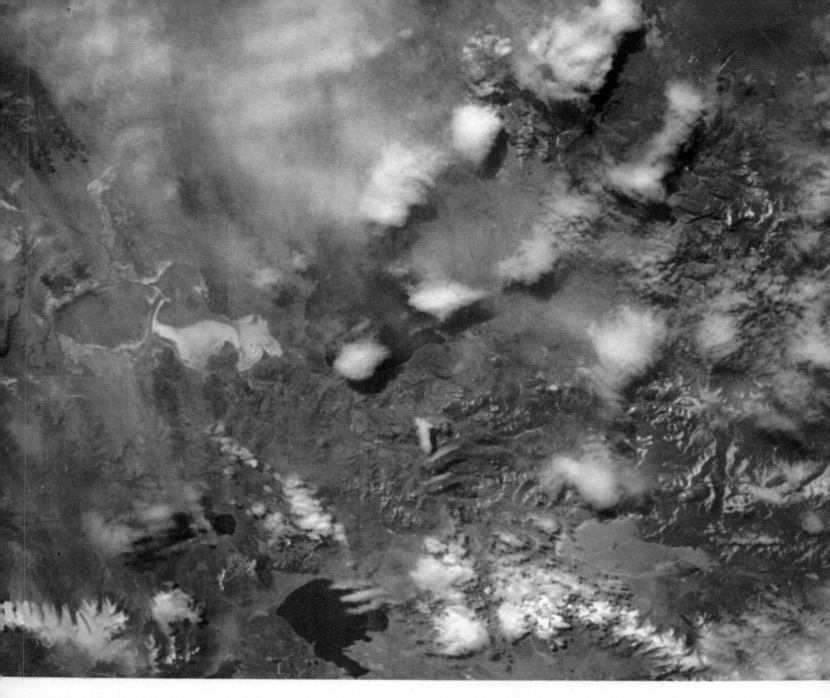

Structural interpretation of the world's regions

Each major region of the world seems to have as its nucleus a framework comprising a strong primordial structure consisting of old consolidated platforms. Deformed rock masses stand at the edge of this framework, as if they have been added later. Their position in relation to the inner zone and the periphery depends upon their age. The topographical relief of dry-land areas reflects this distribution of major structural types.

In Europe, the framework is located in the east and towards the north, where the continent is unbroken and level. Elsewhere, Europe is broken up into numerous islands and peninsulas situated in epicontinental seas. The land areas here show deformations of different kinds. In the far north there are the Caledonian mountain systems, which form the topography of Scotland, Norway, and Spitzbergen. In the centre and the south-west there is the Hercynian system, which begins with the strikingly fractured Iberian Plateau and passes through France, the Rhine, central Germany, and Bohemia to reappear in the Ukraine. Finally, in the south, there are the more recently formed systems including the Pyrenees,

the Alps, the Apennines, the Carpathians, and the Balkans.

Africa has a completely different structure. Its unbroken, massive shape indicates that it is almost entirely made up of a Pre-Cambrian shield, fractured in various places, and affected in its central and eastern regions by a colossal zone of faults. From the beginning of the Cretaceous period, these faults created the Great Rift Valley, a vast tectonic trench lined with lakes and bordered by imposing volcanoes. Deformed rock masses are present only at its outer edges – at the Cape of Good Hope (Caledonian), in Morocco and Kabylia (Hercynian), and at the Algerian coast (Alpine).

In Asia, however, the great Pre-Cambrian masses are located at the fringes of the continent: to the north on the Siberian plain, a subsidence area between the Urals and the River Lena. To the south, the two squat peninsulas of Arabia and Deccan suggest that at some time in the remote past they formed part of a single vast continent, together with Africa, Australia and Antarctica. Geologists have named this *Gondwana*. If Asia is studied closely it has the appearance of being made up of several blocks formed by the breaking up of a single land mass.

Left: The Tibetan plateau photographed from the United States space capsule *Aurora 7*. Below the clouds can be seen snow-capped mountain chains, valleys, and lakes. The plateau, the largest and highest on Earth, is situated next to the great folded mountains of the Himalaya and north of the Sinkiang depression.

The Blue Mountains are one of the highest parts of the mountains folded up along the entire eastern border of Australia. The Pre-Cambrian mass of the west of Australia has remained rigid.

Volcanic cones in the Aleutian archipelago. This enormous chain of partially submerged mountains is an example of mountain-building which is still in progress.

Mount Erebus, an active volcano situated on Ross Island in the Antarctic. The Antarctic continent is an old, rigid block with a mountain system of recent formation connected, through Graham Land, with the Andes.

The central and eastern belts of Asia, however, are dominated by corrugated rock masses. These are typified by the old massifs, which extend from the Caucasus to Tien Shan and southern Siberia, excluding the Kamchatka peninsula. They belong to the Hercynian phase in the outer regions, and to the Caledonian phase in the inner regions such as Siberia. There are also the folded mountain chains that form the very high and uniform systems of Anatolia and the Himalaya, as well as the great island arcs off the eastern Asian coast.

On the American continent the Pre-Cambrian masses are located adjacent to the Atlantic coast. The North American shield extends from the Great Lakes to the extremely intricate Arctic archipelago, and to Greenland, which, with Grant's Land, is bordered on the north and east by Caledonian mountains which are a continuation of similar structures in northern Europe and northern Asia. To the south of the Great Lakes the shield descends to the enormous sedimentary layer in the Mississippi River basin, an area of subsidence. The east and west are bordered by folded mountains: the Appalachians (Hercynian) and the western cordilleras.

The structure of South America is similar. Here, the shield has been split into two blocks, forming Guyana and Brazil, joined by the great subsidence basin of the Amazon and bordered towards the Pacific by the orogenic belt of the Andes, which began to undergo upheavals during the Mesozoic Era.

Oceania is another huge Pre-Cambrian shield, comprising central and western Australia. It is bordered on the east by three orographic systems: the Caledonian and Hercynian, which created the eastern mountain chains and Tasmania; the Papuasic, which built New Guinea, New Caledonia, and New Zealand; and, more recently, the Solomonic, which created the archipelagos of Melanesia.

Antarctica is also an old block, with a system of folded mountains of recent formation connected with the Andean system through the Southern Antilles and Tierra del Fuego. Its traces are visible in the Graham Land Peninsula.

Morphology of the sea bottom

To obtain a comprehensive picture of the great structural units of the Earth's surface, we must try to determine the shape of the submerged parts located under the oceans, which cover more than 70% of the Earth's surface. This is a difficult task, since only a small quantity of data is available. The human eye can see little

Direct knowledge of the ocean floor is still limited to depths that can be reached by divers (*far left*), bathyspheres, or information obtained with special instruments on oceanographic vessels. Indirect knowledge is gained from test borings of the ocean floor (*left*) or from data obtained by radio-sonde and other techniques.

An aerial view of the sea bottom off Bahrain in the Persian Gulf, made possible by the extreme clarity of the water.

The true oceanic area of the Pacific is where the greatest depths are recorded and where the ocean floor is composed mainly of sima. This area extends eastwards from the so-called andesitic line, to the west of which the prevalent rocks are sial (including andesite). The vast area of the ocean is subdivided by ridges that are not so marked or so regular as those of the Atlantic. These ridges support the Polynesian archipelagos, in particular the coral atolls such as those in the Society Islands (*above*). The ridge on which these islands stand is parallel to the Tuamotu archipelago, and, to the south-east, joins the more imposing ridge at Easter Island.

more than about 200 feet down, and relatively few observations have been made by bathyspheres, which can descend to greater depths.

Other observations have been made by a number of different techniques: the measurement of acceleration due to gravity, the behaviour of sonic and seismic waves, the measurement of the Earth's magnetic field, and the extraction of the material of the ocean floor by test borings. Ideas regarding the morphology of the ocean bed have been classified by these observations. Its convexity has been noted, as have various types of relief structure, arranged from the centre to the peripheries in a distinctive pattern.

The development and projection of the *continental shelf*, which forms the continuation of the dry-land area to a depth of about 600 feet, have been established. It has been calculated that its breadth is in inverse proportion to the overlying topography of the dry-land area, so that it is broader at the edge of level areas and narrower or absent near mountains. Its average breadth is estimated as just over 45 miles and its total surface area as 7.6% of the total marine area.

Both shelf and slope are marked by varied relief features. The platform has formations like those seen on dry land: valleys, rocky peaks (which may emerge as islands), humps, and hollows. These are all covered in sediments carried down to the sea by rivers and redistributed by tides and currents. The slope has deep furrows called *submarine canyons*, which may be connected with major river valleys on the dry land. The existence of these features is today explained by the change of sea-level that has taken place during the last 20,000 years, since the end of the great Pleistocene Ice Age. During the Ice Age the sea-level was about 260 feet lower than it is now, so that the areas now submerged would then have been affected by atmospheric erosion. It is, unusual to find cases where the relief appears to have a strictly structural origin, such as slow subsidence and displacement from the shore mass through faulting and folding.

Oceans with depths ranging from 6,500 to 20,000 feet extend over 83% of the total marine area of the Earth. The ocean floor consists mainly of large basins that are roughly as long as they are wide. The Atlantic basins are situated along the sides of an S-shaped ridge, which runs from north to south. In the Pacific, four vast basins are separated by ridges that in many places form the basic support for atolls.

The actual oceanic area of the Pacific is limited to a zone east of the so-called *andesitic line*, a belt that runs along the eastern coast of Japan and the Bonin and Mariana Islands. It cuts through between the Gilbert and Ellice Islands and Samoa on one side and the Solomon Islands, Fiji, the Kermadec Islands, the Chatham Islands, and Macquarie Island on the other. All the volcanoes to the west of the line are explosive and emit andesitic lavas, while those to the east are effusive with basaltic lavas.

The floor of the Atlantic Ocean at the coast of the United States (63° W, 31° N). The drawing is based on a physiographic diagram prepared by the Lamont Geological Observatory, and shows the chief morphological elements of this part of the Atlantic deeps. The heights have been exaggerated twentyfold. The most important features are the great canyon at the mouth of the Hudson River, the continental slope, and the submarine topography, part of which emerges to form Bermuda. Depths are given in metres.

In the Atlantic there is a mid-ocean ridge system that runs southwards from Iceland and is crossed by major fractures.

The Indian Ocean has a Y-shaped ridge, the two arms of which run from Socotra Island and off Karachi.

Besides ridges, two other unusual types of relief structures have been identified, particularly in the Pacific: *peaks* and *guyots* (or tablemounts). Both are like very high and isolated mountains, but while the peaks are conical in shape, the guyots (called after a 19th-century American geographer) are truncated, as if they had been eroded by atmospheric action. Peaks and guyots are thought to be volcanic phenomena.

The *abyssal trenches*, situated mainly along the edges of the continents, occupy 1.2% of the Earth's total marine area. The greatest depths are registered in the Mariana Trench (36,204 feet) and the Philippine Trench (34,580 feet). The trenches are narrow, long and festoon-shaped, and, except for the very long trench between Peru and Chile, are always associated with at least one ring of volcanic islands beyond which lies a basin more than 6,500 feet deep.

49

A view from about 20,000 feet of the island partly destroyed by the explosion in 1883 of Krakatoa, near Java. The volcanic phenomena of Indonesia, as in other great island arcs situated above deep ocean trenches, suggest that this is a meeting place of crustal plates.

Structural interpretations of the ocean bed

Seismic investigations have revealed that the crust of the ocean bed is only 6 or 7 km thick. They have also shown that there is a system of mid-oceanic ridges encircling the world. It is thought that these ridges are formed where the Earth's mantle rises to the surface to form a new crust. In so doing it adds rocks to the crustal plates and as it spreads it makes the oceans wider and causes the continents to drift. A spread of an inch or two a year would have been enough to form the ocean floor of the Atlantic during the past 200 million years.

The abyssal deeps are the only areas on the Earth that coincide with earthquakes having foci between about 1,000 and 2,000 feet deep (the only dry-land area affected by Earth movements of this type is the Hindu Kush). The foci are arranged at depth along a plane that runs obliquely to the continental masses, never towards the centre of the ocean, and with an angle of slope of about 45°.

We know that earthquakes are the result of abrupt dislocations of sections of the Earth's crust along fault planes. Thus the margins of these zones along the trenches experience intense crustal activity and are composed of fault planes, covered by a zone of intense fractures rendering them highly unstable.

Magmatic activity and metamorphism

Eruptive phenomena are the result of chemical and mechanical processes that take place deep in the Earth's crust. Rocks are produced and redistributed both by the reabsorption of surface rocks into the Earth and by the formation of new rocks deep down. Metamorphism is the change brought about by the effects of very high temperature and pressure on the rocks. The effect of this process is that the crystals of the rock tend to realign themselves in a common direction, thus changing the texture of the rock and determining its schistosity. At a greater depth a further process takes place which causes recrystallization of the rock. When rocks are carried into the deeper parts of the crust they become subject to greater transformation.

Metamorphism occurs at temperatures above about 600°C and involves the fusion of the rocks concerned. This fusion is gradual, and first of all forms *migmatites*, which are mixed rocks that have been partially fused but still contain noticeable traces of the original rock. The next stage produces *magma*, which is a completely re-fused and regenerated rock, but since it is not the primordial type it is known as *palingenetic magma*. These changes are known collectively as *ultrametamorphism*.

Metamorphism and ultrametamorphism clearly occur with greater intensity in crustal zones subject to dislocation and deformation where orogenesis and magmatic and granitic intrusions occur. The rise of magma to higher levels and to the surface of the Earth is a typical phenomenon of these zones.

Magmatic intrusions into solid rocks which contain the flow generate another series of metamorphic phenomena caused by the effects of the differing temperatures of the two types of material coming in contact and the highly fluid state of the magma intruding into the country-rock. This is known as *contact-metamorphism*.

Plutons

We must distinguish here between magma that intrudes into rocks beneath the surface of the Earth and remains there, so that the injected rocks take a long time to cool, and the surface extrusion

A zone of volcanoes and earth-quakes occurs where the down-going Pacific plate moves beneath the edge of the Philippines plate.

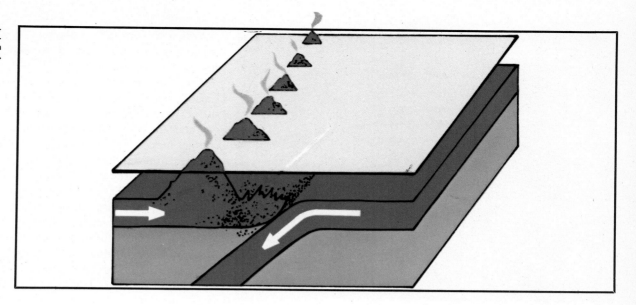

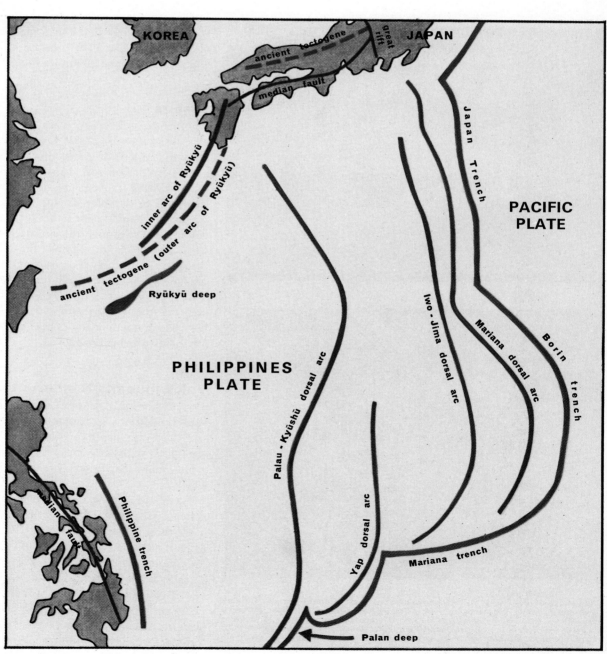

KOREA

ancient tectogene

great rift

JAPAN

median fault

inner arc of Ryūkyū

ancient tectogene (outer arc of Ryūkyū)

Ryūkyū deep

Japan Trench

PACIFIC
PLATE

PHILIPPINES
PLATE

Palau - Kyūshū dorsal arc

Iwo - Jima dorsal arc

Mariana dorsal arc

Bonin trench

median fault

Philippine trench

Yap dorsal arc

Mariana trench

Palan deep

The chart shows a series of ridges running from the abyssal deeps south of Japan. The arrangement of the complex suggests that a continuous process of destruction of the old crust is taking place where the Pacific Plate meets the Philippines plate.

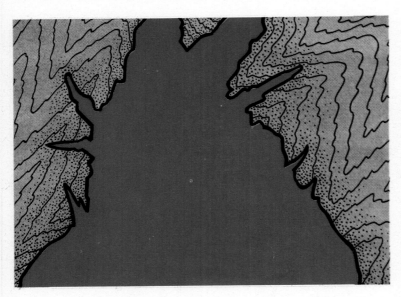

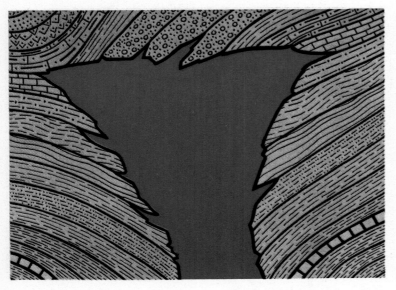

Three types of plutonic intrusion accompanied by structural contortion and contact-metamorphism in the encasing rocks. *Top:* A laccolith, a lenticular intrusive mass thrust into sedimentary beds causing the overlying strata to bulge. *Centre:* A batholith with lateral protrusions (the stippled areas indicate the parts of the encasing rocks affected by metamorphism). *Bottom:* An ethmolith, a funnel-shaped intrusion that has caused the encasing rocks to fold downwards.

in which the magma cools very rapidly. In the latter case the magma is known as *lava*. The magma that remains beneath the surface forms *plutonic* rocks.

These factors are of extreme importance in the shaping of the Earth's surface. Volcanic rocks build up new structures on the surface, while the plutonic rocks deform the crust by the mechanics of their injection and change its lithological structure through contact-metamorphism and the intrusion of new rocks.

When atmospheric erosion brings the plutonic rocks to light, they show a variation of structural forms intruded into beds of country-rock.

Batholiths are large-scale magmatic intrusions, but are also known by the other names according to the way in which they have intruded into rock beds. For example there are those that follow the stratification of the rock beds to form slabs, as in *sills*, or those that push the hither beds upwards to form *laccoliths*. These are especially common in tableland areas such as the high plateaux of the Piedmontese Alps and the Rocky Mountains.

Volcanic intrusions that cut straight across the rock beds so as to be discordant with them are called *dykes*. These are narrow, vertical intrusions that can sometimes run for hundreds of miles along the surface, as in the case of the Great Dyke in Rhodesia, which is more than 300 miles long.

Diapirs

Another form of rock mass that thrusts upwards through pre-existing strata is the *diapir*. Diapirs are not of magmatic origin; they are deposits of salt thrust upwards either by hydrostatic pressure arising from their low density compared with surrounding rocks, or by crustal movements of the surrounding strata setting up squeezing or pumping effects. Though the salt is of a much higher plasticity, diapirs pierce the rock beds as they rise. When the diapir breaks through the surface its salt content runs like molten wax. In tableland regions, the diapir usually fails to break through the surface, thus causing the formation of salt domes or pillars.

Diapirs play an extremely important part in the formation and preservation of petroleum deposits. By rising and cutting through the beds containing the deposits, they block all means of escape for these valuable products.

Volcanoes and their eruptive material

The effusion of magmas as lava at the surface of the Earth causes volcanic activity. Volcanoes represent a link between the surface and the lower depths of the Earth's crust, so that they provide geologists with a means of studying directly the genetic and evolutionary conditions of rock material of magmatic origin, which forms 80% of the Earth's crust.

The shape of a volcano is determined by the type of magmatic material it erupts. This material erupts at very high temperatures in the three physical states; solid, liquid, and gaseous. The material, including the gaseous matter, solidifies on cooling.

Gaseous eruptions almost always indicate volcanic activity of a highly explosive kind known as *Vesuvian*. Eruption of gaseous matter can reach very large proportions even in moderate cases.

The eruption of solid material, known as *pyroclastic rocks*, takes place in a violent manner. The material includes blocks of rock formed from lava solidified in the volcano's throat; rocks torn

A phase in the eruption of a volcano in which huge quantities of gaseous material are emitted. This eruption, which took place in 1963, created the island of Surtsey, off the coast of Iceland.

from surrounding formations; and *volcanic bombs*, which are shot out in a viscous state and which solidify into spherical or pear-shaped lumps of stone or *pumice*, which has a sponge-like structure. Small rock fragments made up of volcanic sand, ash, and dust are known as *lapilli*. These mingle with the gases produced during an eruption to form the smoke-cloud that occurs before and during the phenomenon.

Larger fragments usually come to rest in the immediate vicinity. The smaller material is sometimes transported for miles on air currents, as in the case of the Krakatoa eruption in 1883, when it rose to a height of about 50 miles and floated in the atmosphere for several years, circulating round the Earth several times.

Volcanic *breccias* and *tuffs* are derived from the cementation of volcanic materials. *Ignimbrites* represent loose material that has accumulated together without cementation taking place, and originate during the 'rain of fire' phase of an eruption.

Lastly, there are the *lavas*, which erupt in a molten state with a surface temperature ranging from 1,000° to 1,300° C. Prior to this stage the lava is considerably cooler with a temperature of about 600° C. The cooling is brought about through contact with the

volcanic throat as the lava rises. However, near the surface, processes of oxidation and other chemical reactions arising from the gases trapped in the magma cause a sharp temperature increase.

Volcanic magma at great depths is kept in a solid state by the combined effects of temperature and pressure. The chemical reactions that take place near the surface transform it into a fluid state, and increase its capacity to rise.

Surface topography caused by volcanic eruptions

The shape that solidified lava assumes depends mainly on the cooling processes involved, and these in turn are connected with the chemical and mineralogical composition of the material.

There are two main types. *Pahoehoe lavas* – a name given to them by the people of Hawaii – have a gnarled appearance and resemble coils of rope. These are the 'ropy' lavas, formed by the rapid cooling of the lava's thin outer skin while the material underneath remains in a fluid state and continues to flow. Lavas can remain at high temperatures and in a viscous state for several decades.

Aa lavas – another Hawaiian term – form irregular blocks and

The eruption of Kilauea in Hawaii in 1960, with the emission of fluid lava in the form of 'fire fountains'.

slag. This is because the fairly thick, half-congealed skin is carried along by the still molten lava underneath, but as the skin is insufficiently plastic to form ropy lava it cracks.

The most spectacular forms of lava eruption are those that form shields, platforms and tablelands. These are typical of eruptions that take place across vast areas split by fissures carrying a system of craters. In these areas lava eruptions can cover thousands of square miles to produce accumulations more than half a mile thick. A comparatively modest example of this is the Laki system in Iceland, which extends for 15 miles with 105 craters, and which covered an area of more than 200 square miles in a single eruption. This type of volcanic activity, mainly basaltic in content, was much more widespread in earlier geological times. The Parana region of Brazil has nearly 300,000 square miles affected by such eruptions, while the high plateau of lava in the Rocky Mountains extends over an area of about 150,000 square miles, the newest layer having been added only 150 years ago.

The greatest expanse of lava is that located at the bottom of the Pacific Ocean, where molten rocks well up to form new crust.

Right: One of the most extensive eruptions of lava is at Laki, in Iceland. The lava erupted through a line of craters and covered an area of several hundred square miles. This has resulted in a great platform which has subsequently been gouged by torrential streams. *Below:* Layers of volcanic ash which buried Herculaneum during the eruption of Vesuvius in 79 A.D. The ashes hardened into *tuffs,* which can be seen on the left of the photograph. *Below right:* 'Ropy' lava on Vesuvius. This is lava that solidified at the skin but remained in a fluid state underneath. The skin has been rippled into a rope-like pattern by the continuing flow.

Forms derived from central eruptions

The shapes of volcanoes are numerous and are determined by the type of lava erupted, land movements, and erosion. Forms constructed solely of lava can take the shape of shields, domes, or spines. A typical volcanic cone can consist either exclusively of solid detritus, or of alternate layers of lava and detritus in the form known as *strato-volcanoes*.

Violent eruptions can cause huge depressions of a roughly circular shape known as *calderas*. Calderas are large subsidence basins resulting probably from successive sinking of a crater wall. Some calderas measure up to 12 miles across.

Volcanic necks are spines that protrude from the landscape and represent columns of lava that solidified in the throat of the volcano before being exposed by erosion of the surrounding rocks.

Above: Mount Ngauruhoe in New Zealand, with its perfect conical shape and small eruptive cloud. This volcano belongs to the most common category, lava cones. *Below left:* The rim of the inner crater of Aso, a volcano in Kyushu, Japan. The cavity has layers of slag or scoria, indicating successive phases of activity. *Below right:* The small caldera of Tamadaba in Gran Canaria.

Four types of volcanic eruption. The Hawaiian type (*top left*) emits a continuous stream of liquid lava. The crater is a lake of lava which overflows. The Strombolian eruption is marked by lava in a continuously simmering state, but which erupts only at intervals: the gas and scoria either fall back into the crater or run down the volcano's slopes, as seen (*centre left*) in a photograph of a volcano in Samoa. The Vulcanian type emits viscous lava which soon solidifies and plugs the crater, ultimately causing an explosion which expels ashes, gas, and pulverized lava, as in the case of Parícutin in Mexico (*bottom left*). The photograph *top right* shows a terrifying example of a spine of lava rising from a volcano in Hawaii.

The processes that take place after volcanic activity has come to an end (secondary vulcanism) are numerous. They include solfataras (*right*), which send out jets of very hot water vapour containing hydrogen sulphate and carbon dioxide; bubbling mudlakes (*far right*), formed in the cavity of the fumarole; and geysers, such as those in the Yellowstone National Park (*below*), which are intermittent jets of water and high-temperature water vapour caused by constant renewals of temperature and pressure.

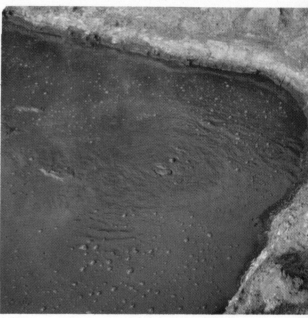

Types of eruption

Eruptions involving a large-scale flow of basalt belong to the *Hawaiian* type. The lava in this case is in a highly fluid state and contains gaseous compounds; such eruptions are very rarely explosive. The *Strombolian* type of eruption is explosive; the *Vulcanian* type is marked by viscous lava effusions, and the preliminary explosions send out a huge column of smoke and a mixture of solids and gases to a great height. In the *Peléan* type the smoke cloud is very hot and extremely destructive, and known as a *nuée ardente* (glowing cloud). It is named after Mont Pelée, in Martinique, which erupted in 1902 and destroyed the entire city of St. Pierre. *The Vesuvian* or *ultravulcanian* type of eruption is the most dangerous and destructive of all.

Eruptions are only a spasmodic form of volcanic activity. The slow cooling of magma or the presence of still active furnace beds deep down is shown at the surface by phenomena of various kinds, some of which are of great practical use to man. Typical of these are the *fumaroles*, which are ejections of gaseous products. Their chemical composition and temperature are determined by their distance from the furnace beds and the lapse of time since the

59

previous eruption. Fumaroles range from the anhydrous ones, which emit white clouds of chlorine, fluorine and chlorides at a temperature of about 500° C, to the cool ones, which emit sulphur compounds at temperatures between 40° and 100° C. Boric acid and sulphur are quite common deposits around such fumaroles. Cooler fumaroles, often only slightly warmer than the air temperature and rich in carbon dioxide, are called *mofettes*. They indicate the near-extinction of a volcanic cycle and are often connected with thermal springs. Typical examples are the *geysers* of Iceland and New Zealand, which are high temperature emissions that occur intermittently, functioning like the safety-valve of a steam boiler.

Distribution of volcanic activity

About 450 volcanoes have shown themselves to be active in historic times, and another 150 have become extinct comparatively recently. More than 80% of the active volcanoes are situated around the Pacific Ocean, forming the well-known 'fire belt'. In addition, there are the volcanic systems more or less in a state of emergence from the waters of the central Pacific and the islands of Hawaii.

About 50 active volcanoes are situated along the central axis of the Atlantic, between Jan Mayen Island, the Azores, Sao Paulo, Ascension Island, St Helena, and Tristan da Cunha. This volcanic chain continues off the southern coast of Africa into the islands of Bouvet, Prince Edward, Crozet, Kerguélen, and Heard. The Canary and Cape Verde Islands and a group aligned between Cameroun and the Guinea Islands comprise another ten active volcanoes.

Mount Ararat stands on the Armenian high plateau. It is one of the largest volcanic structures, nearly 17,000 feet high.

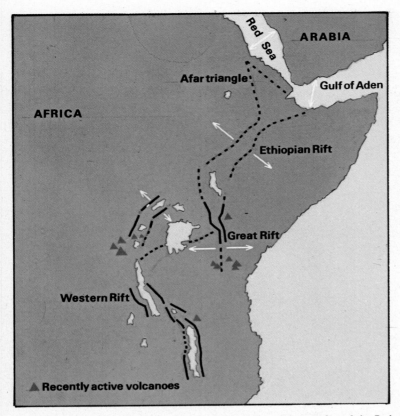

The diagram shows a slight divergence in the direction of the opening of the Red Sea and the Gulf of Aden. This is due to the remarkable rifting of the African continent. Another result of the rifting has been the incorporation of the Afar triangle, formerly part of the Red Sea basin, into the continent itself. The rifting in east Africa has also caused considerable volcanic activities (see diagram below).

In the Indian Ocean the volcanoes form an arc around Madagascar (where there are inactive volcanoes) between the Comoro Islands and Réunion together with the arc of the Southern Antilles and the two volcanoes Erebus and Terror discovered in Antarctica in 1841. There is also the great arc of the Sunda Islands, which vulcanologists associate with the Pacific 'fire-belt'.

A great alignment of volcanoes connected with the Earth's largest system of faults runs along the tectonic trenches from Syria through the Red Sea, Ethiopia, and beyond Lake Nyasa in Africa. This alignment has about a dozen active volcanoes, but it includes many more that are now extinct.

The Mediterranean area has some 20 volcanoes arranged in an arc running from southern Italy through Sicily, the Aegean Sea, Asia Minor, and the southern shores of the Caspian Sea.

The distribution of volcanoes has led geologists to believe that they are influenced by the movements of the plates that form the Earth's crust. The alignment along the inner cordilleras of vol-canoes situated in zones of orogenic activity, together with the absence of volcanic activity from the outer-arc zones, seems to give weight to the hypothesis that these volcanoes are linked with the descent of one plate beneath another along the deep ocean trenches. Magma wells up through what scientists refer to as 'hot spots'. Other geologists hold the theories that volcanoes occur above fault lines.

Volcanoes and earthquakes

It is of interest that the earthquake line seems to follow that of the volcanoes, and deep seismic foci coincide with the great ocean trenches. It is thought that the common origin of volcanoes and earthquakes both indicate movement along the edges of the crustal plates. Earthquakes are the violent symptoms of movements in the Earth's crust, and therefore, like volcanoes, they are most frequent in orogenic zones.

The San Francisco earthquake of 18th April 1906 was the catastrophe that led American geologists and structural engineers to make a systematic study of seismic phenomena. The earthquake was apparently caused by sudden movement along the fault structures affecting the coastal mountain system of California. A major element in the disaster was the San Andreas fault, between two crustal plates, which at various points was subjected to vertical dislocation separating the two sections of land by about 3 feet. Horizontal displacement of up to 20 feet split gas and water mains.

The power of an earthquake to change the shape of the surrounding topography depends on its *intensity*. This is measured on an international logarithmic scale, which provides for up to 12 levels of intensity. The intensity levels are calculated on the basis of the time taken by each particle affected by the seismic movement to return to its position of rest and the greatest distance the particle moves from this position in the course of the earthquake. Earthquakes of the first level of intensity can be detected only by the most sensitive instruments. Those with an intensity of the twelfth level cause total destruction of all man-made structures and transform the topography on a large scale by dislocating huge masses of the crust, diverting rivers, and contorting rock formations.

Scientists today obtain a more accurate idea of an earthquake's force by measuring its *magnitude*, which is the energy developed in the focus of the seismic movement. On this basis, earthquakes with a magnitude of 9 develop an energy of 10^{27} ergs. An example of an extremely intense earthquake was that which shook Assam in August 1950. Its magnitude of 8.6 was the highest recorded since seismographs were first used. It affected an area of more than a million square miles and radically changed the topography of the eastern Himalaya, where thousands of square miles of land and vegetation were swept away by landslides, subsidence, and flooding from rivers diverted from their courses.

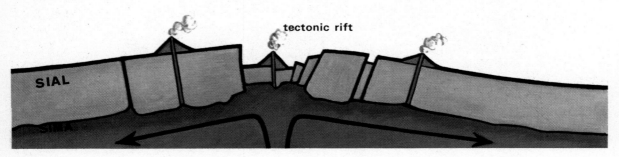

The theory of convective currents explains the formation of crato-genic volcanoes, which have no connection with orogenesis. The rise of magma causes fracturing and faults in the sial crust. In the subsidence zones and adjacent faults, eruptions take place at the crust, chiefly as emissions of basalt originating in the sima.

The destructive force of earthquakes has always terrified man, and is the result of changes in the Earth's crust. Sometimes, the movement is so slight as to be almost imperceptible. On a geological time-scale the action alters the appearance of the Earth's surface. The photographs show the effects of an earthquake in Alaska *(top)* and the ruins of an old church in Mexico *(bottom)* with the volcano Paricutin in the background; the birth of this volcano caused widespread devastation.

THE EARTH'S CRUST SHAPED FROM OUTSIDE

THE ATMOSPHERE

Characteristics

Deformations of the Earth's solid crust are caused by internal forces. The outer surface of the crust is also subject to changes and deformations as a result of a number of external agents, the most important of which is *atmospheric action*. A typical example of such action is water which acts to shape the topography of the Earth in the form of vapour in the air and as precipitation. These affect the Earth's surface both physically and chemically.

The atmosphere consists of several concentric layers round the Earth, each different from the others and separated by discontinuity zones known as *pauses*. Half of the atmosphere's weight is concentrated in the first $2\frac{1}{2}$ miles from the Earth's surface, and 90% of it in the first 12 miles. This lower portion constitutes the air we breathe. The density decreases by 75% of its initial value for every rise of 6 miles. At sea level it is 1.3 g/l and at 500 miles it is reduced to 10^{-14} g/l. In these upper regions, the atmosphere is so rarefied that it no longer behaves like a gas. At an altitude of 1,500 miles the density value of interstellar space is found, of one atom per cubic centimetre. The link between the Earth's atmosphere and that of the sun is thought to be composed of atoms of hydrogen which meet as they emanate from the two bodies.

The troposphere

The *troposphere* is that part of the atmosphere in direct contact with the Earth's surface. It contains the main mass of the atmosphere and 75% of its water-vapour content, and is the zone that carries our weather. As well as including gases and variable amounts of water vapour, the troposphere also carries a large variety of matter received from volcanic eruptions, combustion of all kinds, and the breathing of living organisms.

The troposphere has an average thickness of $7\frac{1}{2}$ miles. At the equator it is about 10 miles thick, and at the poles 5 miles. Temperatures in the troposphere decrease by 1° C for every rise of 600 feet. Because of the different thicknesses of the troposphere at the poles and the equator, the temperature of the troposphere

This photograph from space shows the lower layers of the Earth's atmosphere diffusing the last light of the Sun, which is sinking behind the horizon. The progressive decrease of the diffusion of the Sun's radiations in an upward direction is due to the absence of particles in suspension. In the troposphere these particles diffuse mainly the shorter wavelengths (blue in the spectrum). This causes the light gradation of light blue, dark blue, and finally black above a sunset. The redness of the Sun at the horizon is due to the longer waves (red in the spectrum), which can penetrate the thicker atmosphere more easily than the short blue rays.

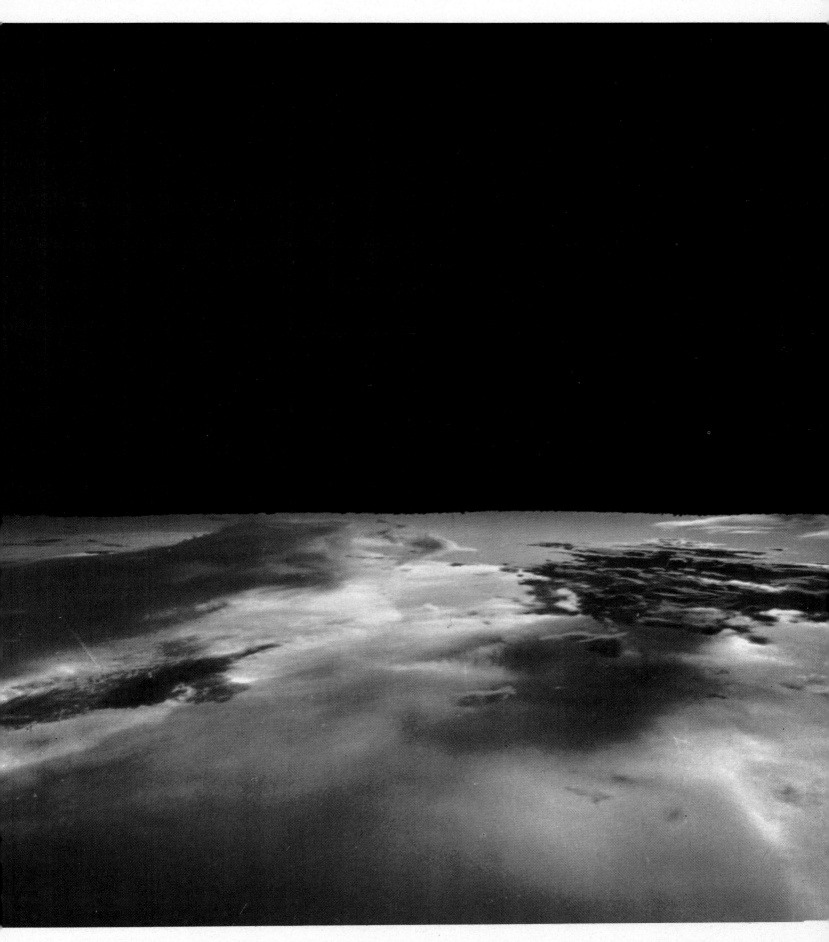

The troposphere is the thinnest but densest layer of the atmosphere surrounding the Earth. It is the zone that contains the weather.

ceiling is about −80° C above the equator, and −45° C above the poles. The progressive decrease of temperature ends at the *tropopause*, a thin layer that marks a reversal in temperature behaviour. This is the zone where two extremely violent air currents from the stratosphere, known as *jet streams*, run from west to east above the 40th parallels of the two hemispheres.

The stratosphere

The *stratosphere* lies above the troposphere and rises to an altitude of about 50 miles. Density values drop considerably, but the chemical composition of the air remains constant. Water content is reduced to 0.01%, and since there is a complete absence of the matter (other than man's space hardware) that pollutes and darkens the troposphere the stratosphere is clean and dry.

High-frequency radiation in the form of ultra-violet rays from the Sun transforms the oxygen (O_2) into ozone (O_3) so that a layer is formed known as the *ozonosphere* at levels between 10 and 30 miles, with a maximum concentration of 15 miles. This layer filters the Sun's ultra-violet rays, which would kill all forms of life if they reached the ground at their full intensity.

Low temperatures averaging −50° C are maintained both at the floor and at the ceiling of the stratosphere. But at levels between 30 and 40 miles energy arising from the absorption of ultra-violet rays by the ozonosphere creates the so-called *warm layer*, where temperatures range from 15° to as high as 170° C.

The ionosphere

The *stratopause* marks the ceiling of the stratosphere, which is followed by the *ionosphere*. Here there is a further rapid decline in density values so that at a level of 100 miles conditions of pressure are equivalent to an air vacuum. At 50 miles molecules of oxygen break apart, reverting to their atomic state, and molecules of nitric oxide are formed. This starts off a process of *ionization* in which an electron is removed from an atom or a molecule to form a positive ion, or an electron is added to an atom or molecule to form a negative ion. The ionized particles are located in the ionosphere in three layers known as the *D*-, *E*-, and *F*-layers. These layers reflect electromagnetic waves and thus make possible radio communication from opposite sides of the Earth.

The energy arising from solar radiation, which is effectively a massive bombardment of particles in space, causes a progressive increase in temperature. At an altitude of 100 miles the temperature is −21° C, at 150 miles it rises to 650° C, and beyond 300 miles (in the *exosphere*) it reaches 2,000° C. These temperatures reflect the degree to which the particles have been activated and have acquired energy, and are known as *kinetic temperatures*.

In the ionosphere, protons released from the Sun come into collision with atmospheric particles at a velocity of 6,000 miles/sec, causing a luminescence known as an *aurora*. This occurs most frequently at an altitude of 60 miles but the most spectacular example, the Aurora Borealis, which appears as a tremendous drapery of multi-coloured lights visible at night in latitudes north of the 50th parallel, takes place at altitudes of between 500 and 600 miles.

Another luminescent phenomenon, the so-called *noctilucent* clouds, can be seen at the stratopause, between the 45th and 60th parallels. These are probably caused by the formation of ice crystals in the low temperature part of the stratopause.

Air temperatures in the troposphere

About 35% of the Sun's radiation is sent out into space again by diffraction and reflection. This takes place in every planet, causing it to give out a light known as the *albedo*. Some 14% of the Sun's radiation is absorbed directly into the Earth's atmosphere and turned into heat. Only 51% actually reaches the surface of the Earth, raising its temperature to an average of 14.4° C. The

The Aurora Borealis seen from Alaska. Auroras are due to the collision of high-speed atomic particles, and the most spectacular displays take place at altitudes of 500 to 600 miles.

Earth's particles become activated to a certain degree so that the planet itself becomes a radiant body, sending out low-frequency infra-red rays which carry heat. The effect of air in the troposphere can be compared with that of the glass in a greenhouse. It lets through the luminous high-frequency rays of the Sun but is opaque to the Earth's infra-red rays, which are held back and reflected mainly by the water vapour and clouds.

The activation of the Earth's surface as a radiant body differs according to conditions. Snow and ice coverings reflect 70% to 90% of the Sun's ray, so that the heating process in such conditions is extremely slow and affects only a limited thickness. A covering of vegetation, grass and trees reflects from 10% to 37% of the solar energy received. Some of this is used up in the respiration process. Dark dry land reflects only 8% to 14% so that the heating process is relatively rapid and affects a greater thickness of the ground. Daily variations in irradiation affect thicknesses of up to 3 feet, but annual ones can affect the ground to a depth of as much as 45 feet or more.

Water is more transparent and conducts heat both through molecules and convection and through the motion of waves, currents and tides. Here the daily heating process extends to a depth of 21 feet, while the annual effect reaches down to 650 feet.

It is evident, therefore, that an equal quantity of solar energy received by the Earth is dispersed more in water than on land, and consequently water takes longer to heat and cool than land. In quantitative terms, the thermal capacity of land is 0.6 that of water,

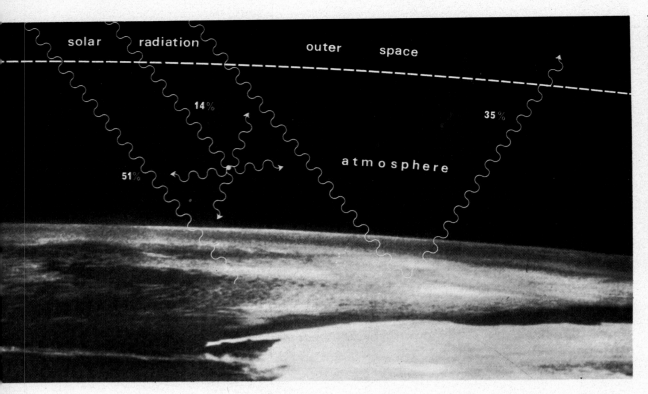

The energy the Earth receives from the Sun represents only a tiny fraction of the total energy given out by the Sun. The atmosphere surrounding our planet acts like the glass of a greenhouse. It lets through most of the Sun's rays but prevents heat dispersion into space. This heat is given out by the Earth as long waves, and is mostly contained by the water vapour in the air. The diagram (*left*) shows how the total energy from the Sun to the Earth is distributed: 51% is absorbed by the Earth, 35% is reflected back into space, producing the albedo, a luminosity that we can see in other planets, and 14% is directly absorbed into the atmosphere. These are global values; the heat received from the Sun and that lost through the atmosphere balance each other during the course of a day or a longer period in relation to all the Earth's surface, but the figures cannot be applied to individual places.

causing the distinction between maritime and continental climates.

The varying proportion and distribution of the variable components of the air in the troposphere, particularly H_2O, CO_2, and O_2, also affect the amount of radiation received. Dry, calm air, such as that in the tropics and the cold zones, absorbs little infra-red radiation. High mountains with their summits in a dry atmosphere are consequently transparent to both solar and terrestrial radiation, and are hence known as 'windows of the Earth'.

Clouds reflect radiations of all wavelengths, so that the cooling of the Earth's surface during a clear night is about seven times greater than during a cloudy night. The temperature variations in the air of the troposphere are also influenced by the movement of the air. The compression brought about by a column of air moving downwards, for example, produces heat energy. This is a common phenomenon when air masses pass over a high mountain chain and descend on the slopes of the other side. The converse is true of rising air masses, since the air uses heat energy and becomes cooler.

The Earth's shape and temperature distribution

The amount of solar energy that reaches the limit of the troposphere is almost constant, varying only by 1 or 2%. It averages 1.94 calories per minute per square centimetre, and is called the *solar constant*. This energy is not spread out evenly over the surface of the Earth, because of the planet's spherical shape and the fact that it rotates and revolves. For this reason, the angle of incidence between solar radiation and tangents to the Earth's surface is larger at the equator than at the poles. Therefore, at higher latitudes, the same

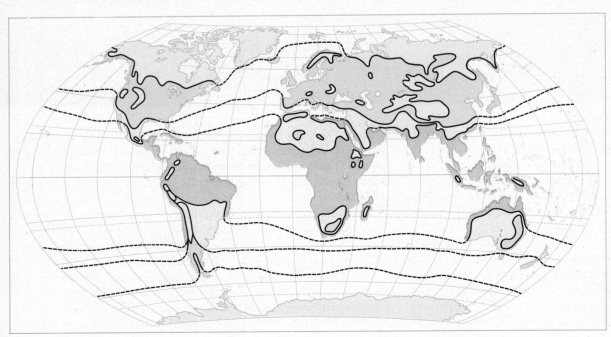

DURATION OF FROST

no frost

sporadic frost

less than 275 days per year

more than 275 days per year

amount of energy is dispersed over a greater area and is filtered through a thicker layer of air.

Between latitudes 37° North and 37° South the amount of energy received from the Sun is greater than that irradiated, while towards the poles the reverse is the case. For example, in the latitude band between 0° and 10°, the annual energy balance is positive and corresponds to 1.1×10^{12} kilojoules/sec; (1 joule/sec = 1 watt). Conversely, between latitudes 80° and 90°, taking into account the smaller area of the Earth's surface round the poles, the balance is a negative one of -2.2×10^{10} kilojoules/sec.

The continuous transfer of energy from the equator to the poles, accomplished by horizontal movements of the air in the troposphere and by ocean currents, modifies the theoretical conditions of temperature caused by solar radiation. Thus there is no progressive heating of zones with a positive energy balance nor cooling of areas of negative energy balance. The distribution of clouds also affects the amount of heat transferred to the equatorial zone, which consequently is not the hottest zone on the Earth. The Earth's highest temperatures are recorded in the tropics, where the air is clear, just as the lowest temperatures are recorded in the circumpolar regions and not at the poles.

The southern hemisphere is colder than the northern one for two reasons. As far as latitude 50° the southern hemisphere is more oceanic, so that the water's thermal capacity assumes a more important role; and the continental ice mass of Antarctica absorbs an enormous quantity of heat as it melts, drawing this heat from the waters of the ocean and from neighbouring land masses.

The movement of the Earth

Temperature distribution on the Earth, with its variations from pole to pole and over the year, is also affected by a number of other phenomena: the rotation of the Earth round its own axis, the tilting of the axis, and the parallelism of the axis as the Earth revolves round the Sun.

The Earth's rotation determines night and day. If the other factors were not present, night and day would have an equal duration of 12 hours at every point on the Earth's surface. The tilting of the Earth's axis at an angle of 66°33′ to the orbital plane varies the duration of night and day according to latitude. The ratio of night to day at any particular latitude would be invariable if the Earth did not also revolve round the Sun.

This revolution round the Sun takes place with the positions of the Earth's axis always parallel to themselves so that the planet does not appreciably change direction in space. Thus any imbalance of solar radiation to the various latitudes is eliminated. Because of this parallelism through the passage of the year, every part of the planet receives solar radiation for six months of the year; thus every part of the globe receives the same amount, the distribution being varied according to the season.

The duration of night and day at the equator is always the same, since the circle of illumination that constantly separates the night-side of the Earth from the day-side is at the globe's greatest circumference and divides the equator into two equal parts. As a result of the angle of tilt of the Earth's axis, the Sun reaches its *zenith* – the point at which it is vertical to the observer – twice a year over the equator and all points in the band enclosed by latitudes 23°30′ North and South. These two occasions are the summer and winter solstices, on June 22 and December 22, and the edges of the band are the Tropic of Cancer and the Tropic of Capricorn. This band experiences the maximum amount of the Sun's radiation because the Sun's rays are least oblique there, and there is the smallest amount of difference between the duration of night and day, which varies between 10 hours 50 minutes and 13 hours 10 minutes.

The least favoured zones are the polar ice-caps within the Arctic Circle and the Antarctic Circle, where the Sun's rays come at a tangent during the solstice days. The Sun's rays have their greatest obliqueness at these ice-caps, causing the maximum difference between night and day. The phenomenon of night and day taking place in a period of time greater than 24 hours becomes most pronounced towards the poles, where they last six months each.

On the two equinoxes – on March 21 and September 23 – day and night last exactly 12 hours each all over the globe, because the circle of illumination coincides exactly with a meridian.

It is thus apparent that only in the zones between the tropics and the polar circles, known as the *temperate zones*, is there that gradual changing difference between night and day which enables the year to be divided into four distinct seasons.

The duration of twilight varies with latitude and with the seasons. It is longer when the Sun's trajectory is more inclined in relation to the horizon. In the Sahara, twilight lasts a relatively short time because the Sun descends almost vertically to the horizon, especially in summer. The photograph (*right*) was taken in winter at Ounianga Kebir. The inclination is shown by the trajectory of the Moon and Venus, photographed at intervals of 10 minutes.

Information from isothermal charts

All the foregoing facts give a theoretical picture of thermal distribution on the Earth's surface. This is modified by geographic considerations such as the distribution of dry-land areas, water, vegetation, sea currents, and so on. To obtain an idea of the effect of all these influences on thermal distribution, annual and seasonal temperature charts are drawn, marked with *isotherms* which join all points corrected to sea-level having an equal average temperature.

Sea-level is taken as the base so as to compensate for fluctuations caused by altitude. Isothermal charts of the Earth normally give the temperature situation in January and July, and annual averages based on lengthy series of statistics.

Humidity

The *humidity* of the air – that is, its water vapour content – is caused by evaporation at the surface of exposed water such as oceans, seas, lakes, and rivers. Evaporation uses up a great amount of heat. To

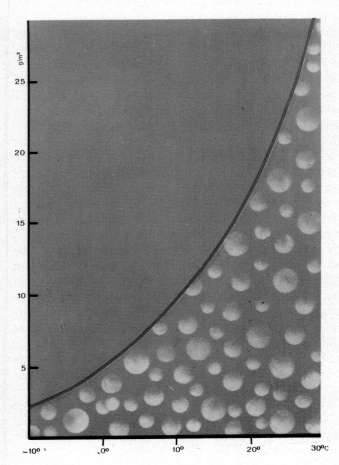

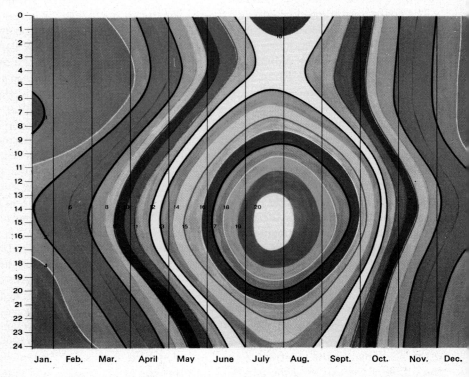

Above: An isothermal chart for Oxford, England, showing the variation of temperatures during a period of 24 hours (vertical scale) and over one year (horizontal scale). The cool temperate ocean climate shows appreciable daily fluctuations, with cool summers and mild winters due to the influence of the Gulf Stream.

Left: A graph plotting the volume of water vapour in the air in relation to temperature from 10° C below freezing point to 30° above.

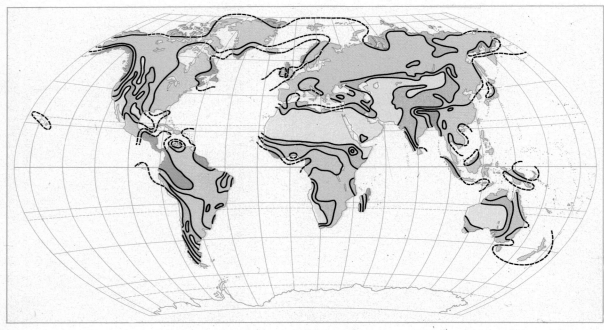

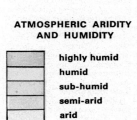

ATMOSPHERIC ARIDITY AND HUMIDITY

highly humid
humid
sub-humid
semi-arid
arid

A view of the desert landscape of Mauritania photographed in the morning. The light conditions, the blue, cloudless sky and the dry soil bare of vegetation indicate the extremely low relative humidity of the air. In some parts of the Sahara the humidity is the lowest recorded on the Earth.

evaporate 1 g of water at 15° C at normal pressure requires 596 calories, or 7½ times the amount needed to melt 1 g of ice. The Earth's regions that receive maximum insolation, the inter-tropical zones, are the most active in providing the air of the troposphere with water vapour.

Warm, dry air and a strong wind provide ideal conditions for large-scale evaporation. Thus the areas of maximum evaporation are the oceans between latitudes 10°–15° and 20°–30° in both hemispheres, because these are regions of dry air and constant winds. The dry-land areas of these latitudes are also the most arid, because evaporation takes away from the land a greater amount of moisture than it replaces through rain.

On the other hand, the amount of water that can be absorbed into the air at a particular temperature cannot exceed a certain limit which is determined by the temperature of the air. This is known as the *saturation point*.

Relationship of temperature and water content

Independently of other factors, the movement of large quantities of water through precipitation is prevented by low temperatures. In cold regions where the air is dry, precipitation is rare. The terms *absolute* and *relative* humidity are therefore misleading if employed without reference to temperature.

Physiologists consider that a relative humidity of 80% in air with a temperature of 15° C is the most that can be borne by a lightly clad person in calm weather. The same humidity at a temperature of – 20° C produces the sensation of an icy bath, while at a temperature of 30° C the atmosphere would be stifling. Meteorologists now therefore prefer to express hygrometric conditions of the air by the *dew point*, which is the saturation temperature of a volume of air at a constant pressure. At this temperature any increase in the quantity of water vapour in the air will condense in the form of dew.

Stability and instability of air masses

The *stability* and *instability* of air masses is an important characteristic since these are concerned in most weather phenomena. If a mass of dry air rises it cools at the *dry adiabatic rate*. If this rate makes it colder than the surrounding air, the mass will be heavier and will sink back to its former position. Such an air mass is stable.

If, however, the adiabatic cooling rate of the air mass is such that it is warmer than the surrounding air, it will rise. Such an air mass is unstable. These adiabatic heating and cooling rates both have linear gradients. Dry air cools at the rate of 3° C and saturated air at 1.8° C for every rise in altitude of 1,000 feet.

Condensation and related phenomena

Condensation is the transformation of water vapour into the liquid state, and is always caused by cooling processes. It takes place when air masses of different temperatures come into contact or when warm air comes into contact with a colder part of the Earth's surface. Although it has not been proved essential, the presence of *condensation nuclei* in the atmosphere plays a part in the phenomenon. These are solid microscopic particles, such as salt crystals, pollen and mineral dust, sometimes present in the air in concentrations as high as 150,000/cc. Condensation forms minute drops of water which, because of their microscopic dimensions, remain in suspension in the air. Clouds are made up of these droplets, their concentration ranging up to 1,500/cc.

Cloudiness varies with the seasons. Half of the Earth is almost constantly veiled in cloud, the least affected parts being the desert areas of the Sahara and Arabia, and the most affected, the northern parts of the Atlantic and Pacific oceans. The cloudy season in intertropical countries is the summer, while elsewhere it is the winter.

In stable air conditions in which turbulence is just enough to distribute the droplets in layers a mile or so deep, hazes are formed that cause grey, damp days of winter and autumn and stifling hot days of summer. If the droplets are distributed in strata only a few feet in thickness, fog is formed. This phenomenon is generally caused by direct contact of the air with a cold surface, which may be the ground, as in the case of early-morning mists that dissolve with the rising sun, or a mass of water as in the almost permanent barrier

that separates the warm Gulf Stream and the cold waters of Labrador along the North American coastline.

If condensation takes place in perfectly calm air and through direct contact, *dew* or *hoar frost* is formed. This is particularly characteristic of arid regions.

Left: The formation of a cloud at the summit of the Matterhorn. *Above:* Stagnant mists at the bottom of a valley in the Abruzzi area of the Apennines. In the first case, air rising up the mountainside in the morning cools adiabatically, creating a cloud at the summit. In the second case, the air comes into contact with cold soil in the early hours of the day. It cools to below the saturation point, forming a low-lying mist.

72

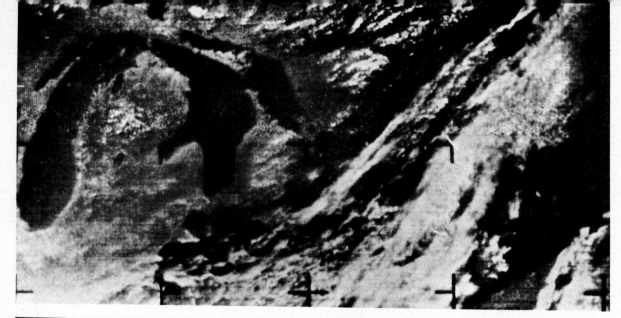

The upper photograph was taken at an altitude of 500 miles from a meteorological satellite. It shows the American great lakes, with the Appalachian Mountains on the right covered in thick cloud formed by masses of moist air from the Atlantic meeting the colder air of the continent.

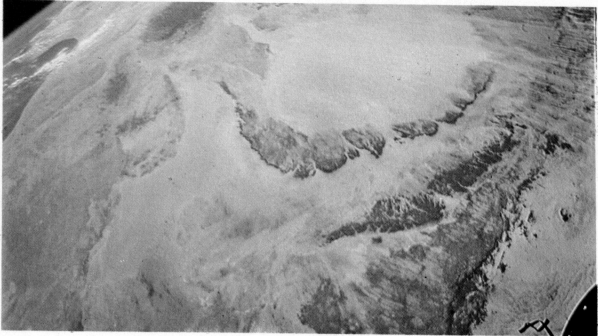

The Libyan sand sea seen from space. The dry areas appear brown because of the lack of water vapour in the atmosphere.

The 5-day isoneph (the line joining points that have 5 days of cloudiness a year) indicates the Earth's most arid zones around the equator. Pockets of greater cloudiness extend into the Amazon valley, equatorial Africa, and around the Atlantic coastal regions.

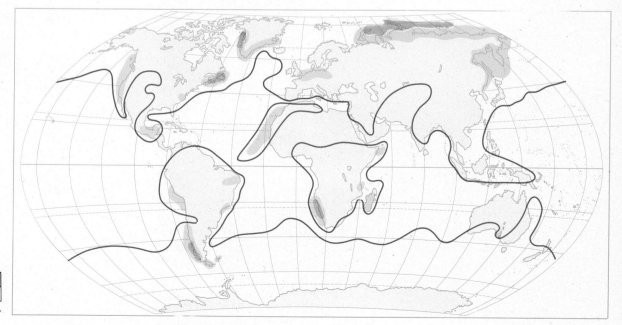

ANNUAL CLOUDINESS

80 days or more per year

40 days or more per year

five-day isoneph

Clouds are formed either by rising currents of air (in the case of cumuliform clouds) or by the cooling of a layer of air in the absence of rising air currents (stratiform clouds). Clouds are classified according to their height. *Above:* Small cumulus clouds over the Aegean Sea, at the same height as stratocumulus clouds in the background. *Below:* The ragged front of a nimbostratus, a low rain-bearing cloud. *Right, top to bottom:* High cirrus clouds (6 miles) made up of ice crystals; altocumulus; small mountain cumulonimbus.

Above: A gigantic cumulonimbus (thundercloud) in the sky of Oklahoma, photographed from an aircraft at 6 miles. Its anvil-shaped top, formed by the wind, reaches 8½ miles. Cumulonimbus is formed by powerful rising currents, which carry it to a great height where it reflects a glaring white light due to the purity of the atmosphere.

Condensation of atmospheric humidity in calm air and contact with cold bodies causes forms of precipitation known as dew (*below*) or hoar frost (*left*), according to the temperature.

Precipitation takes place following a process of coalescence in which microscopic droplets in suspension forming clouds collide and join together until they become large and heavy enough to fall at velocity (the diagram *above right* shows the drops greatly enlarged). This results in rainfall. *Above:* The monsoon rain from low-lying nimbostratus clouds as seen in India. *Bottom right:* Snow is produced by the transformation of water vapour into ice crystals at temperatures below freezing point. Snowflakes are formed in calm air through the aggregation of crystals in the shape of six-pointed stars. The crystals develop round a central nucleus.

Precipitation

Precipitation occurs when water droplets in clouds become heavy enough to fall to the ground. These droplets form by coagulation round ice crystals which are also present in the clouds, a process which continues until drops of 150 microns are formed. At this point the volume is further increased by coalescence of the drops as they meet in the process of their precipitation; the maximum diameter so reached is 5 mm, since beyond this size the drops break up as a result of falling at a velocity of 22 mph.

It has been calculated that for a drop to develop a diameter of 2 mm it has to fall for just over an hour covering about 3 miles. Since the average thickness of cloud is less than 2 miles, it is clear that to reach this size the drops' period of fall is prolonged, and this is caused by rising currents.

It has also been observed that the amount of rain unloaded from a cloud is often as much as 40 times more than the water contained in

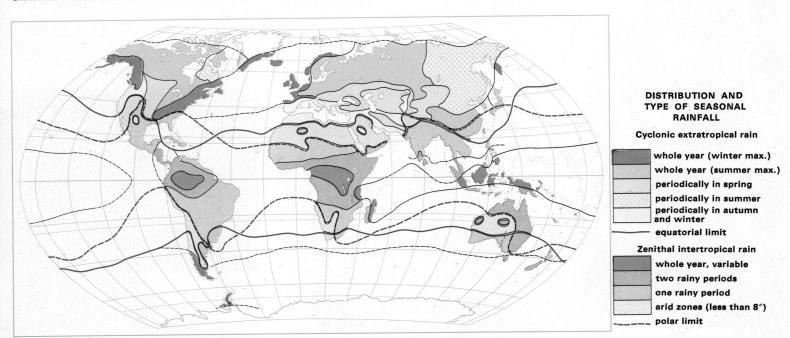

DISTRIBUTION AND
TYPE OF SEASONAL
RAINFALL

Cyclonic extratropical rain

whole year (winter max.)
whole year (summer max.)
periodically in spring
periodically in summer
periodically in autumn and winter
— equatorial limit

Zenithal intertropical rain

whole year, variable
two rainy periods
one rainy period
arid zones (less than 8″)
--- polar limit

the cloud. In this case, too, the cause is rising currents connected with the formation of the cloud, which carry unstable air masses upwards resulting in their condensation, increasing the humidity in the cloud. The base of a cloud is usually flat, being the level where rising air begins to condense.

Snow is an aggregate of ice crystals, which can form only if the cloud temperature is lower than freezing point. The actual mechanism by which ice crystals are formed and aggregated is still not fully known.

Rain distribution

The distribution of rain and snow throughout the planet is of great geographical interest. Snowfall is translated into millimetres or inches of rain, on the basis that 1 kg of snow gathered from an area of one square metre corresponds to 1 mm of rain on the same area.

As the rain chart shows, the areas of maximum precipitation are in general those situated in latitudes 10° North and South of the equator, where masses of hot humid air converge. But the highest rainfall occurs in another rainy region, the monsoon area of Cherrapunji, Assam, which has an average of 450 inches of rain a year. The rainfall there is increased by rising currents of air over the mountains.

From the equator to the poles there is a gradual decrease in precipitation, with a first minimum between latitudes 10° and 30°. The air in this zone contains very little moisture because, descending from the middle reaches of the troposphere, it is cool, although becoming compressed and heated.

Monsoon areas have some of the highest rainfalls on the Earth, particularly during the summer monsoon season. The rainfall is violent and concentrated into a short time, causing rivers to burst their banks. *Below:* A tributary of the Mahanadi River in Orissa, India, after a monsoon.

Outside the tropics there is a second area of maximum rainfall which is lower than the equatorial one. This occurs between latitudes 45° and 55°, and is marked by the convergence of rising air masses. Towards the poles there is a great decrease in precipitation, the air in these regions being cold and stable.

Air masses and fronts

The air of the troposphere is divided into masses that have their own individual characteristics. An air mass can be defined as a portion of tropospheric air, whose temperature and humidity variations in a horizontal direction are negligible.

Air masses develop their characteristics by prolonged stationing over regions that are morphologically similar – broad plains and ocean areas – and by being unaffected by atmospheric turbulence.

The air masses are identified by their region of origin. The principal air masses have the following characteristics:

Polar-continental originates in the northern regions of Eurasia and America. In the southern hemisphere, the ocean area in the high latitudes quickly modifies Antarctic polar-continental air masses into polar-maritime. In winter, the polar-continental air mass is extremely cold at its base and warmer above, making it stable and causing fine, cold and calm weather. In summer, the structure is reversed, making it somewhat unstable.

Polar-maritime is formed by the change of the polar-continental air as it moves over the ocean areas round the poles, producing a cool, humid and unstable mass. This air mass brings rain which is violent and heavy in spring, stormy in summer, and dense in winter.

Tropical-continental is found over tropical deserts such as the Sahara and the Australian Desert. This is a very warm and unstable air mass, but brings calm weather since it is very dry and far from its saturation point as a result of its high temperature.

Tropical-maritime is the most active of the air masses. It originates in the inter-tropical zone of the oceans and is affected by downward movement, making it warm, humid, and stable. It tends to shift to the higher latitudes so that its base becomes colder while the upper parts remain warm. This causes the formation of stratiform clouds over flat continental areas as it moves, and precipitations of rain and snow on high ground above which it has to rise.

The wandering air masses come into contact with each other along a plane of discontinuity known as a *front*. This occurs when two air masses having different temperatures, and therefore densities, are pushed towards each other. Fronts form in the areas of convergence brought about by the large-scale movement of the planetary atmosphere and, on a local level, at the fringes of two centres of high pressure.

Physical principles of atmospheric circulation

On a planetary scale the succession of types of weather generated by air masses, fronts, and related disturbances does not take place by chance, but follows a regular pattern over the various parts of the Earth. (There is, of course, a marked variety on a local scale.) This depends on a similar regularity in the circulation of tropospheric air, on which modern interpretations of climates are based.

The chief mechanical principle governing the atmosphere's circulation is the effect of the Earth's rotation on the molecules in movement. These molecules, if allowed to proceed without interference, would travel from the poles to the equator along a straight path. The increased speed of the Earth's rotation as the equator is approached produces the so-called *Coriolis force*. The moving air is deflected from its straight path by this and begins to form an eddy. The degree of deflection is in direct proportion to the angular speed of the Earth's rotation and the speed of the moving air, and varies according to latitude concerned. The deflection is to the right of the direction of motion in the northern hemisphere, and to the left in the southern one. It continues until about latitudes 15° North and South, where its effect becomes negligible.

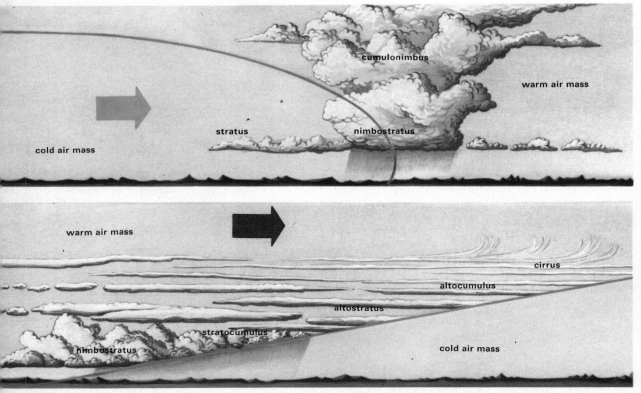

The upper diagram shows the meeting of a cold air mass with a warm air mass, which is dense and heavy. The cold air moves forward with a front indicated by the blue line, and wedges itself underneath the warmer air, which is pushed upwards causing it to condense and form rain clouds. The lower diagram shows a warm air mass passing over colder air and condensing as it rises into various forms of cloud according to the altitude.

The phases in the formation of a depression or cyclone. The frontal line separating the two air masses begins to undulate as a result of the colder air settling underneath the warmer air (*fig. 1*). The leading edge of the warm air mass is known as a warm front, and the leading edge of the cold air mass as a cold front (*fig. 2*). The warm air, pushed by the colder, intensifies the undulatory process. A low-pressure area is formed in the crest of this wave, which develops as the colder air pulls away, as indicated by the arrows (*fig. 3*). The next three phases mark the quicker movement of the cold front, which extends the area of low pressure formed in the crest (*fig. 4*). The cold front overtakes the warm front, forming a third type of front known as an occluded front (*fig. 5*). The low-pressure trough rotates in a counter-clockwise direction and produces rain (*fig. 6*). The trough finally subsides as normal pressure conditions resume.

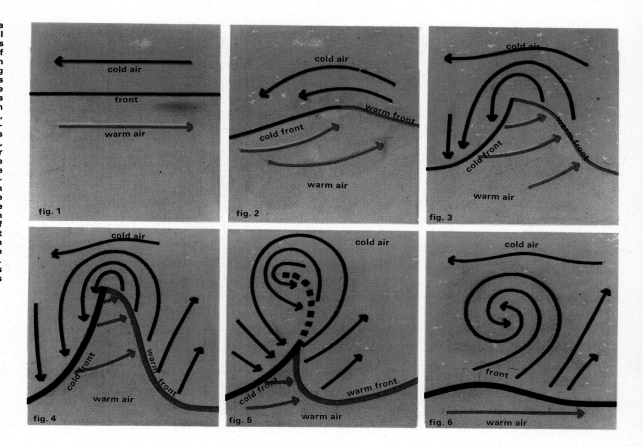

As a result, the circulation in the lower reaches of the troposphere outside the tropical zones is basically vertical, because winds are driven into a rotatory movement. Above an altitude of about a mile, where the friction is less, winds are no longer subject to deflection.

The pressure of the air is its weight. Normal pressure is equivalent to a column of mercury 760 mm high weighing 1,033 g resting on an area of one square centimetre. These values are correct at sea level at latitude 45°, but there is a slight decrease towards the equator and the flattened area of the poles. The pressure also decreases by 1 mm for every 36 feet of altitude as a result of decrease in the air's density. Meteorologists have evolved a more exact means of measurement, the *millibar*, which is equivalent to a force of 1,000 dynes per square centimetre. The pressure of 760 mm of mercury is equivalent to 1,013.2 millibars.

An area of low pressure, known as a *cyclone* or *depression*, is represented on charts by a series of concentric *isobars*, the pressure values of which increase from the centre to the edges. An area of high pressure is known as an *anticyclone*.

In both cyclones and anticyclones the air moves in a rotatory direction which, in the lower layers of the troposphere, is centripetal in cyclones and centrifugal in anticyclones. Thus cyclones suck in air from their outer edges and constitute areas of convergence, while anticyclones push air outwards and form areas of divergence.

The diagram shows the linear velocity of given points on the various latitudes caused by the rotation of the Earth. Because of this rotation, the paths of the air masses (which, as a result of varying pressure conditions, are directed, for example, from the pole to the equator) are deflected to the right of their direction in the northern hemisphere and to the left in the southern one. This effect, known as the Coriolis force, is significant in the lower layers of the troposphere and up to equatorial latitudes (where it dies out), and is the cause of the vortical movements of winds in zones outside the tropics.

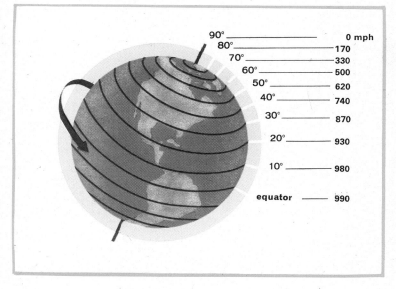

90°	0 mph
80°	170
70°	330
60°	500
50°	620
40°	740
30°	870
20°	930
10°	980
equator	990

Features of tropospheric circulation

The main feature of tropospheric circulation is the increase in vertical movement from the equator to the poles. There are three basic components: a vertical movement in which the air is displaced by less than ½ inch per second; a meridional one of about 6 feet per second; and a zonal one of 15 feet per second or more.

The circulation scheme functions in fixed zones of low and high pressure. At ground level in the equatorial zone low pressures prevail, in the tropics high, and in the medial latitudes of 50° to 60° the pressures are low again until the polar regions are reached, where the pressure values increase once more. Higher up, however, there is only an increase in pressure between the equatorial and tropical zones followed by a progressive decrease up to the poles. The decrease in pressure at altitude over the poles is more rapid than above the equator, so that at a height of about 3 miles,

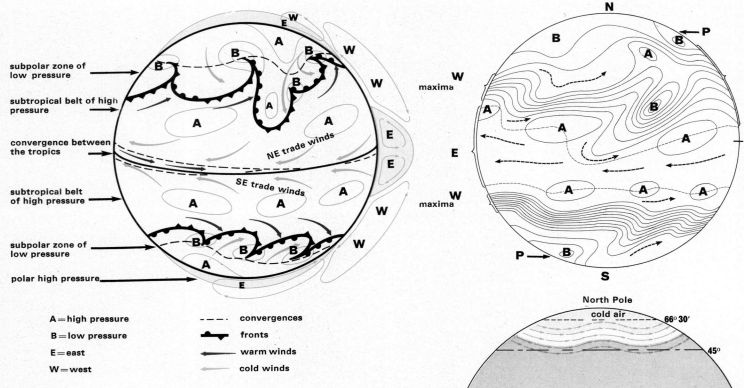

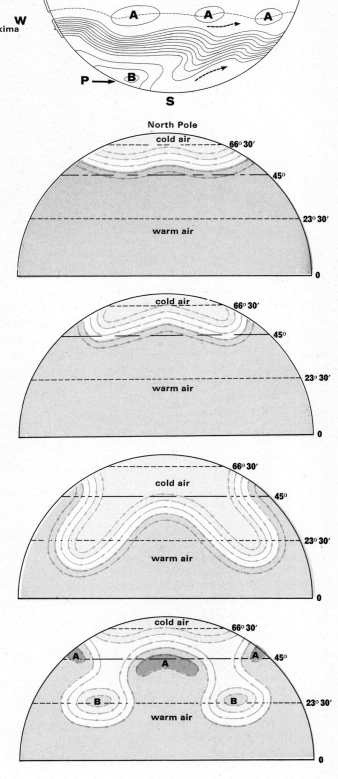

subpolar zone of low pressure

subtropical belt of high pressure

convergence between the tropics

subtropical belt of high pressure

subpolar zone of low pressure

polar high pressure

NE trade winds

SE trade winds

W maxima

W maxima

A = high pressure	- - - - convergences
B = low pressure	fronts
E = east	warm winds
W = west	cold winds

The diagrams above show the general circulation of the atmosphere at low and high levels in the troposphere. The four diagrams on the right show the meander cycle of the jet streams. These airstreams move at high speeds at the level of the tropopause. Their path undulates, and in the course of a few weeks the meanders become more marked until the loops are detached to form cyclonic and anticyclonic cells. The meandering movement of the jet currents appears to be connected with transitory meteorological conditions that occur lower in the tropopause.

between the poles and the equator, there is an inversion of the pressure situation as compared with the ground.

In the lower layers of the troposphere there is a general flow from the high-pressure tropical areas, which are characterized by divergence, towards the low-pressure areas of the equator. This flow of air constitutes the trade winds. From the same tropical anticyclonic areas there develops an airstream that goes towards low-pressure areas in the middle latitudes and forms westerly winds. Finally, from the polar ice-caps, with their high pressure, the air moves towards the middle latitudes to form a great convergence area.

At altitude, pressure distribution is normally such that easterly winds prevail in the equatorial belt, while in the rest of the troposphere winds are mainly westerly. Around latitudes 40° in both hemispheres at the level of the tropopause, the western airstream reaches extremely high speeds, creating the so-called *jet streams.* These jets were a major discovery of modern meteorology and many scientists believe they are the main motive force in air circulation. The jets do not follow set straight paths at a fixed speed, but wind like meandering rivers and sometimes split up into two currents. The jet that runs in the winter hemisphere reaches the highest speed, which may be as much as 300 mph.

There appears to be a close relationship between the jet streams and the origin of transitory cyclones and depressions, apart from those known to start through heat conducted from overheated or overchilled terrain, such as the summer Indian cyclone and the winter Siberian anticyclone. But fixed centres of action, namely the tropical anticyclones and the cyclones of the middle latitudes, appear to be due respectively to a mechanical raising or lowering of the atmospheric pressure at the edges of the jets.

Right: Lentisk trees in Sardinia distorted by the local prevailing wind, the mistral. This wind originates as it descends from a cold front in the polar regions and moves towards the Mediterranean, which is situated in a depression, shielded in northern Italy by the Alpine arc (left-hand diagram, *below*). This meteorological condition also causes the bora in Istria. Cold, damp air rises over the Alps (right-hand diagram) to create the föhn, a dry wind that is rapidly heated following its descent from the mountains and melts the spring snows.

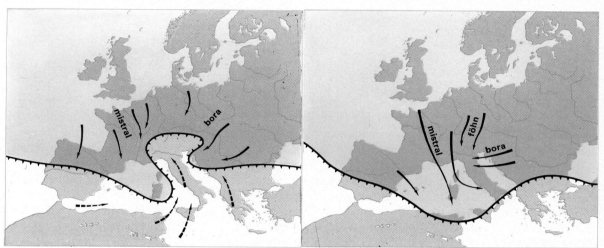

Effects of tropospheric circulation

The division of tropospheric circulation into two annular zones separated by a belt of tropical anticyclones is a simplification of the actual picture. The surface wind pattern is cellular in character, being made up of anticyclonic and cyclonic circulations round cells of high and low pressure.

The trade winds emerge from the cells as constant sea winds, which cover about 31% of the Earth's surface. They are dry because they are fed by high-pressure areas and directed towards warm zones, which raise their saturation point. They bring calm weather except when they have to surmount mountains or rocky coastal structures as in, for example, eastern Brazil, the Gulf of Guinea, Australia, and eastern Madagascar.

The equatorial cyclonic belt, situated constantly just north of the equator, is divided into convergence zones for the trade winds, each about 300 miles wide, and, alternating with these, cyclonic cells having sharp rising currents. Both cases provide suitable conditions for constant and violent rainy weather, in the former through dynamic convection and in the latter through rising currents.

Inter-tropical circulation, generally quite simple and uniform, assumes a different character in the belt between the Gulf of Oman and the Sea of Japan. In this vast area the winds in summer are south-westerly, moving from the ocean to the continent, while in winter they are north-easterly and move in the opposite direction. These are the monsoons, which bring much rain to the Indian subcontinent in summer but are dry in winter.

There is much controversy regarding the origin and characteristics of the monsoons. One theory is that the summer monsoon is merely the trade wind of the southern hemisphere which has been deflected by the Earth's rotation into a south-westerly wind; another holds that the monsoon is part of a large equatorial air cell, which assumes a westerly direction once north of the equator.

There is, however, general agreement that the pressure gradient between the tropical highs of the southern hemisphere and the continental depressions of Asia during the summer half of the year is the cause of monsoon weather in this part of the Asian continent. These pressure variations are of thermal origin and alternate seasonally, giving rise to the enormous anticyclone in the northeast in winter, and to the summer depression in Afghanistan, Baluchistan and Turkestan.

Disturbances in the equatorial belt

At latitudes below 20° and on the oceans disturbances develop that are almost a permanent feature, appearing as violent storms. Some of these disturbances begin in an unusual way and cause tropical cyclones, which are notorious for their violence. These take place during the hottest season, always at latitudes above 5° and near to continental land. Though not of large dimensions, they set up abnormally low pressure readings and create winds with velocities up to 150 mph. These disturbances move in a violent rotatory manner, but enclose in their centre an area of calm known as the *eye*.

These revolving storms are called *hurricanes* in the southern Pacific and northern Atlantic, *typhoons* in the western Pacific, *cyclones* in the Indian Ocean, and *willy-willies* in the Sunda Sea.

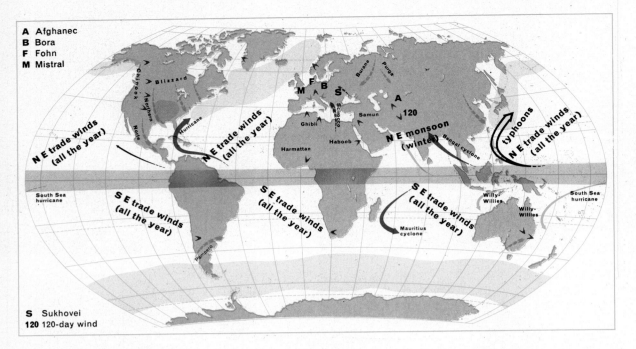

A Afghanec
B Bora
F Fohn
M Mistral

S Sukhovei
120 120-day wind

PERIODIC AND LOCAL WINDS

| | U.S. tornado area |

tropical cyclones:

	less than 2
	from 2 to 4
	from 5 to 10
	more than 10 a year
	equatorial zone free of cyclones
	max ·variability of wind-force direction

warm > descending wind (föhn)
cold > descending wind (bora)

warm wind of leading edge of tropical cyclones

cold wind from trailing edge

Extratropical circulation

Extratropical circulation is dominated by western winds. In the southern hemisphere, prevalently an aqueous zone, these are regular and constant, while in the northern hemisphere they are limited to a belt between latitudes 40° and 55° and along the western seaboard of the continents, to which they bring a cool, rainy climate. In Eurasia and parts of America these winds cannot affect the interior of continental areas, because they are pushed away by winter anticyclones and by the powerful convective currents of the summer depressions. From this point of view the large areas of continental dry-land regions are climatically autonomous, having continental climate characteristics with large temperature fluctuations. The main feature of extratropical circulation is its turbulence.

The development of the groups of disturbances in the temperate zone is due to the undulation of the polar front caused by the opposing thrust of warmer air. In each wave two fronts are formed: a cold one from the wedge of cold air lifting the warm air, and a warm one, generated by warm air rising above the cold air. In both cases, downward movements form cyclonic areas of heavy and abundant rainfall. Formerly, this process was thought to be responsible for the origin of these frontal disturbances. Now, however, they are thought to be caused by the undulations of the westerly flux.

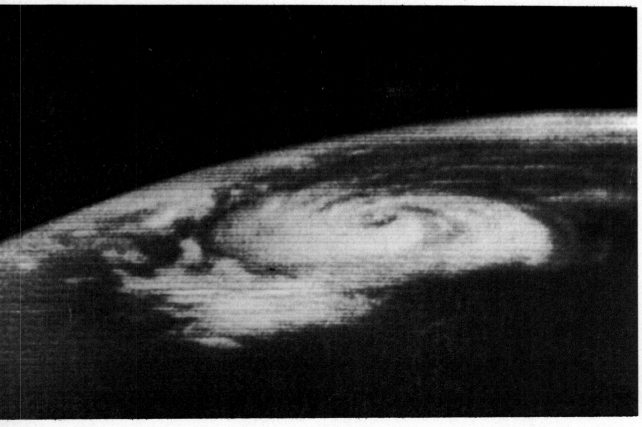

The eye of a hurricane about 150 miles from Cape Hatteras, North Carolina. Tropical cyclones are disturbances that form round a central depression in very warm and humid air masses. They measure up to 350 miles across and often reach land areas, where they dissolve, sometimes after causing great damage. Perfectly symmetrical, they generate winds that reach velocities of up to 150 mph at the edges, while the centre – the eye – remains calm.

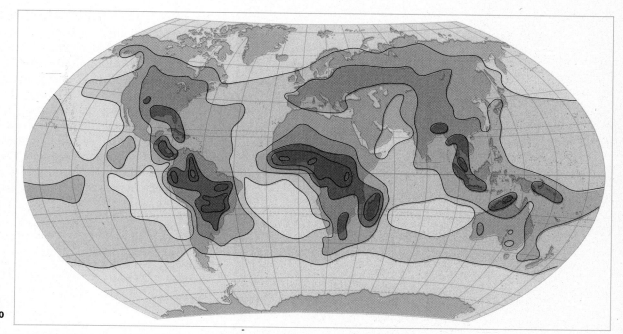

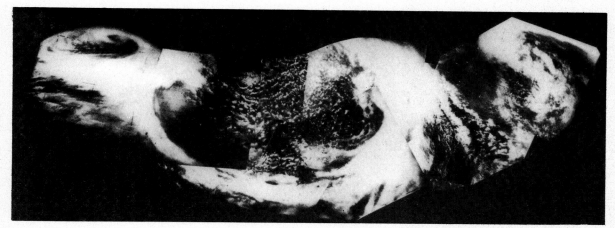

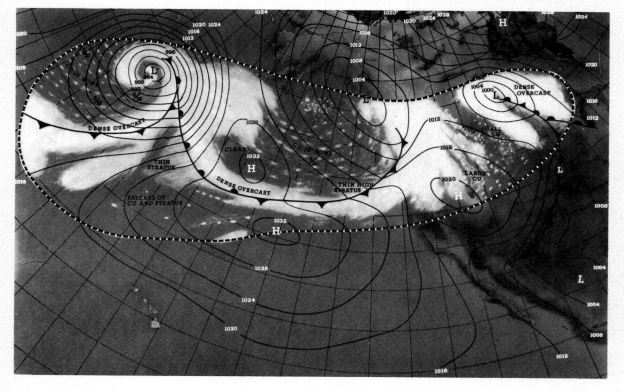

This series of photographs taken from a weather satellite and joined together affords a reconstruction of the meteorological conditions in all the vast region outside the tropics of the northern Pacific Ocean west of the United States. The situation is that of 20 May 1960. Isobars (in millibars) have been superimposed according to the cloud density to give a large-scale outline of cyclonic, anticyclonic, and frontal areas. Cloud cover is indicated as cumulus (CU) in rows, thin stratus, dense overcast, thin high stratus, and large and small cumulus.

The first signs of the approaching southwest monsoon in India. The phenomenon occurs seasonally as a result of winds from the tropical high pressure area moving into the Asian continental low pressure area.

The classification of climates

The prevalently zonal character of tropospheric circulation comprises a distribution of climates in concentric belts along the latitudes. The large-scale uniform movement of air masses within the tropics gives that region's climate continuity and uniformity along all points of latitude.

Outside the tropics the uniformity disappears and is replaced by fragmented atmospheric movements. Variable and local winds, characteristic of atmospheric circulation outside the tropics, produce wide differentiation in climate along the same latitude level of the temperate zones. Uniformity of climate and atmospheric circulation is once more restored in the upper latitudes.

Type	Conditions of pressure and wind		Precipitation
	Summer	Winter	
TROPICAL HUMID CLIMATES (Average temperature of coldest month more than +18° C.)			
Equatorial rainy	Intertropical convergences. Equatorial calms. Equatorial westerly stream.	Intertropical convergences. Equatorial calms. Equatorial westerly stream.	Rain at all seasons. Precipitation in driest month more than 2½ in.
Tropical with two rainy seasons.	Intertropical convergences. Equatorial calms. Equatorial westerly stream.	Trade winds	Zenithal rain. Aridity with minimal height of Sun above horizon. Precipitation in driest month less than 2½ in.
ARID CLIMATES (Evaporation exceeds precipitation)			
Tropical arid (tropical 'hot' deserts and pre-deserts).	High subtropical pressures. Dry trade winds.	High subtropical pressures. Dry trade winds.	Pure zenithal rain during one brief season.
Temperate arid ('cold' deserts and pre-deserts of temperate continental zones).		Continental winter anticyclones.	Pure summer rainfall.
MESOTHERMIC HUMID CLIMATES (Temperature of coldest month between 0° and +18° C.)			
Mediterranean	High subtropical pressures (eastern side of the anticyclone cells).	West winds	Dry summers, rainy winters. Driest month less than 1¼ in.
Sinic and Pampean.	High subtropical pressures (western side of the anticyclone cells).	West winds	Rain in all seasons.
Oceanic (extreme maritime).	West winds	West winds	Rain in all seasons, with maxima in winter.
MICROTHERMIC HUMID CLIMATES (Temperature of coldest month always below 0° C. Temperature of warmest month more than +10° C.)			
Danubian humid with warm summers (warmest month with average temperature about +22° C.); medium continental.	West winds	West winds and winter anticyclone.	Rain in all seasons with maxima in summer, snow in winter.
Sarmatic humid with cool summers (warmest month with temperatures between +18 and +22° C.); extreme continental.	West winds	West winds and winter anticyclone.	Rain in all seasons with maxima in summer. Long snow covering in winter.
Subarctic	West winds	Polar winds and winter anticyclone	Low in all seasons.
POLAR CLIMATES (Warmest month with temperatures lower than +10° C.)			
Subpolar	Polar winds	Polar winds	Low in all seasons.
Glacial	Polar winds	Polar winds	Low in all seasons.

ROCK EROSION

Physical and chemical action of water

The basic processes that shape the surface of the Earth externally can be listed as follows:

1) The *disintegration of rocks* which break up into fragments of all sizes, ranging from one ten-thousandth of an inch in diameter (particles of clay) to several yards (rocks brought down by landslides or broken up by chemical action).

2) The *transport* of such detritus by the action of gravity, wind, running water, the sea, and ice.

3) *Sedimentation* (both mechanical and chemical) of the separated particles.

Erosion caused by the disintegration and transport of rocks occurs mainly in sloping areas such as mountains. Where the land is flat deposition and sedimentation of rock particles are the predominant processes. These tend to level out land irregularities and help to build new land forms, such as desert or coastal sand dunes, lateral and frontal moraines of glaciers, and alluvial plains along the floors of valleys.

Rock erosion caused by forces that move particles of rock is a basic factor in the shaping of the Earth's surface. Erosion is affected by the structure of the rocks and by the amount of water present. Water can have a direct influence, as in the case of chemical erosion. Lack of water influences the efficiency of other agents, such as thermal fluctuations causing rocks to break resulting in the scaling-off of rocks in arid climates.

An example of the direct action of water is found in rocks that, having many fissures and cracks, absorb considerable amounts of water from rain. The liquid absorbed is often a saturated solution,

Water is one of the chief factors shaping the Earth's surface. It helps to break up rocks and carries away the detritus. *Above:* An Alpine torrent that rises in summer from a glacier and runs through a bed littered with detritus.

in which case the crystals multiply and exert pressure on the rock enclosing them.

Rock-mushrooms and perched blocks are the result of the combined action of water, which aids chemical attack, and wind, which bombards rock surfaces with solid particles undercutting the harder rocks above.

In the tableland regions of Colorado (Monument Valley), erosion has formed isolated masses (buttes) of a surface crust made up of bedded, arenaceous rocks resting on softer rocks. Detritus is scattered about the surrounding terrain to be removed by wind and water.

Freeze-thaw phenomena

A fairly widespread form of mechanical erosion by water is caused by intermittent freezing. This type of erosive action results from the increase in volume of water as it passes from the liquid to the solid state; this increase of some 9% exerts a theoretical pressure of about one ton per square inch. The alternating freezing and thawing of water, both in interstices of solid rock and in unconsolidated ground, causes the fracturing of the former and surface disturbance of the latter. In the case of rocks, fracturing leads to the accumulation of areas of detritus or the splintering of surface sections of calcareous rock into stone polygons. If the detritus is transported, the landscape becomes pitted with hollows, furrows, and small valleys.

When the freeze-thaw process takes place in unconsolidated ground it causes a phenomenon known as *frost-heaving*, which is common in Arctic regions. The freezing and melting of the ice within the soil causes the soil alternately to contract and expand so that some sections swell outwards and begin to creep downhill. This *creep* process, known as *solifluction*, takes place on slopes of 5° to 30° and follows a zig-zag progress. When the gradient becomes greater, large masses of soil break away from the hillside in sections to form a stepped or terraced structure.

Solifluction also affects masses of detritus of varying shapes and sizes situated on steeper slopes with gradients of up to 40°. The rocks become self-propelling and form flows which move as a mass. The larger rock-masses move more quickly than the surrounding soil, causing it to arch and roll into cumulus-shaped masses.

On terrain with only a small gradient, the process leads to the formation of grassy cushions which sometimes reach gigantic proportions, perhaps 30 feet high and 300 feet wide. These small hills have a nucleus of ice which grows constantly as a result of freezing water in the surrounding soil or nearby springs.

Sometimes surface areas of grass-covered soil break up into a

Two processes that are typical of regions subjected to continuous freezing and thawing. *Far left:* Grassy cushions which swell with the freezing of their water content. *Left:* The grid-like pattern of the soil in Spitzbergen. This is probably caused by the soil swelling as a result of freezing accompanied by the rolling-off of small rock particles that come to rest in the cracks round the swelling.

The alternating action of frost and thaw during the day, and particularly in spring, causes the slow downhill movement of grass-covered soil known as *solifluction* (*left*). Sometimes sections settle to form small terraces (*right*). In many mountain areas used for pasture, herds of cattle increase the terraced structure by using them as paths.

grid-like pattern made up of sections which have a regular polygonal shape. In flat areas these sections tend to be hexagonal, while on slopes with a gradient of up to 5° they are usually rectangular. These mosaic patterns are caused by movements of the soil accompanied by movements of the detritus content.

Permanently frozen terrain is commonest in sub-polar regions, where only a surface layer of the soil is exposed to frost and thaw. Underneath, the soil is permanently frozen, sometimes to a depth of many feet. This is known as *permafrost*.

The regions in which freeze-thaw phenomena occur, estimated to be one-sixth of the Earth's surface, are of two types:

1) The circumpolar regions in both hemispheres, with a marked increase in the lower latitudes, where the climate is of the continental, dry type.

2) Mountain areas, where free-thaw action varies according to latitude, exposure, and the effective level of the permanent snowline.

The permanent snow-line is the limit above which there is always some unmelted snow. It reaches as low as sea-level only above latitudes 80° North and 65° South. In the Alps, the permanent snow-line lies about 2 miles above sea-level, while in the arid tropical mountains it begins at about 3 miles. In equatorial areas, which are subject to abundant rainfall, the limit averages 2½ miles above sea-level.

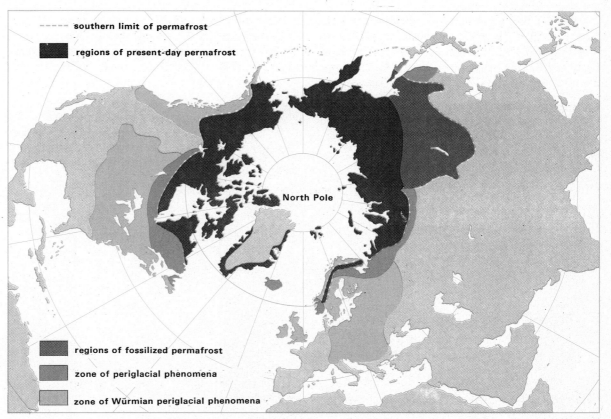

southern limit of permafrost

regions of present-day permafrost

North Pole

regions of fossilized permafrost

zone of periglacial phenomena

zone of Würmian periglacial phenomena

The map shows the present limits and extent of terrain subject to frost and thaw (*molisol*) and that which is permanently frozen (*permafrost*) in the northern hemisphere, as well as periglacial phenomena from the period of maximum glaciation during the Quaternary.

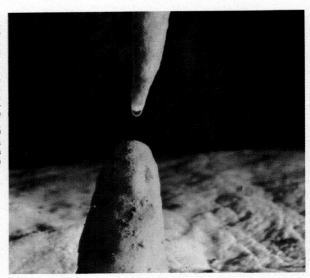

Water turns the calcium carbonate in limestone into calcium bicarbonate. On the walls of caves, the reverse process takes place; the bicarbonate becomes carbonate and changes back into a rock. Stalactites and stalagmites *(right)* are caused by the dripping of water in underground caves. *Far right:* The dissolution of calcium carbonate by water can cause the deposition of layers of clay in the cracks, hollows, and rocky surfaces of calcareous rock beds. These clays include iron oxide, which gives the red colour to soils often present in limestone areas.

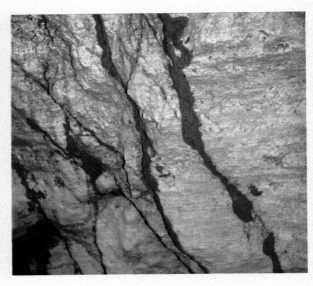

Erosion in karst regions

One-fifth of the Earth's land area equivalent to about 11 million square miles is eroded and shaped by the action of water, chiefly chemical in nature. This is the dissolution of carbonates and rock salts carried out by organic and inorganic acids present in the water, which involves the separation of part of the dissolved salt into ions. In this way limestones are dissolved. Their main component, insoluble calcium carbonate, is turned into the soluble calcium bicarbonate. The basic action of this process is expressed in the following formula:

$$H_2O + CO_2 + CaCO_3 \rightleftarrows Ca(HCO_3)_2$$

The reversibility of this reaction brings about the deposition of sediments of chemical origin, such as alabaster, pisolitic or oolitic limestones, and travertines. Deposits in the form of *stalactites* and *stalagmites* or similar encrustations found in underground caverns are where lime-rich water has percolated.

Although large amounts of calcium carbonate are left behind by the water, a far greater quantity is washed away to the sea, so that this chemical action constitutes true erosion. The land forms produced by this process are known as *karst topography*, from the Karst district of the Dinaric Alps in Yugoslavia.

The chief characteristic of this type of terrain is its arid surface. Its underlying regions are riddled by water which has entered into the rocks through cracks and fissures and this leads to the drying-up of surface water-flow. The aridity has not, however, prevented the growth of vegetation because the process of dissolution affects only the calcium carbonate in rocks. The other substances are deposited as decalcified clay which holds water, is fertile, and is favourable to both natural and cultivated vegetation. Generally the surface area of a karst has a pitted appearance because of the many cavities of different shapes and sizes caused by the subsidence of the underlying caves and grottoes dissolved out of the limestone by water.

The most common surface cavities are the *dolinas*, or *pots*, hollows ranging from a few feet to a hundred yards in diameter and of varying depths. It is not clear whether they are formed by surface erosion or by subsidence of the underlying ground. Collapse is thought to be the cause of deep gorges and broad plains called *poljes*. Some dolinas have a sink-hole at their bottom, allowing surface waters to discharge into the rocks below. Water may form underground rivers leaving *dry valleys* on the surface. These are quite common in the interiors of some karst regions. They are

An underground cave (Grotte du Dôme, Dordogne, France) with its ceiling festooned with large and small stalactites. Some of the stalactites have met stalagmites rising from the floor, forming stalactitic columns. Both stalactites and stalagmites are composed of layers of varying sizes.

A view of the Lessini mountains, which consist of great beds of limestone and show all the characteristics of karst. The rocks in the foreground have been subjected to physical and chemical erosion by water. The region has a cave system that has been explored to a depth of nearly 2,900 feet, one of the deepest known to speleologists.

either completely dry or contain a stream which suddenly disappears underground.

The subterranean passage carrying water is formed of well-like pools and tunnels. Where the water moves by gravity under normal conditions of pressure the structure of the passage is extremely varied, the dominant feature being the signs of mechanical erosion. Stalactites and stalagmites are found in some caves. Stalactites hang from the roof like giant icicles. They are formed by drops of water sliding from the roof down the stalactite to its extremity, depositing calcium carbonate particles. Stalagmites also are formed

A dolina in the Venetian pre-Alps. A layer of clay has been formed at the bottom which holds rain-water to form a pond. Slabs of rock have been strung along one of the slopes by local shepherds to mark out pasturage areas.

by deposits left after evaporation, but in this case the water falls from the roof of the cavern onto the floor, the stalagmites growing upwards at the point where the water falls. Stalactites and stalagmites cannot form in caves through which streams are flowing.

If the underground passages become completely flooded with water, circulation is caused by pressure, and the pools and tunnels are scooped out. The water-conduit may sometimes include a hump in its bed, which creates a natural syphon giving rise to intermittent springs.

As the chemical content of the water increases, there is progressive penetration of the internal parts of the karst, but the water does not always remain at the same level. If there is a blockage the water will seek another outlet, sometimes at a higher level.

Other features of karst regions include canyons probably caused by the collapse of underground caves. Sometimes such subsidence leaves sections of the surface intact to form natural bridges. Other canyons can be caused by other types of sub-aerial erosion.

Erosion by living organisms

Erosion of rocks by living organisms is another factor contributing to their disintegration. Most exposed rocks contain some moisture so that they can harbour algae, fungi and lichens, the last being a permanent union of the first two. Acids secreted by these organisms attack the rock to a depth of some millimetres, producing a microsoil which in turn provides the necessary conditions for other lichens and, later, mosses. Once these are established they open the way for higher forms of vegetation which, with roots, speed up the disintegration of the rocks by the acids they secrete and by the mechanical action of their growth, the pressure of which can reach over 200 pounds per square inch. Animals perform a

89

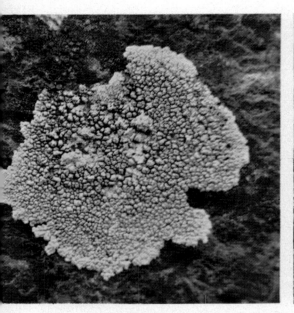

The 'geographical lichens', *Rhizocarpon geographicum* (*left*), break up silica rocks by emitting acids, used by the organism in its nutritive processes, and carbon dioxide, produced by its breathing. Mechanical erosion is caused also by shellfish (*centre*), which thrust themselves into rocks. Rock-dwelling *Lithodomus lithophagus* emit acid that attacks harder rocks. Worms (*right*) alter the soil by swallowing earth rich in organic residues and emitting it once more enriched with organic matter; this contributes to the production of humus.

secondary stage of disintegration by moving material which has already been eroded by chemical or mechanical action.

In ordinary garden soil this type of erosion is carried out by moles, mice, ants, countless types of insect and 133,000 types of worms, which digest all the soil content in the course of a few years. An acre of soil contains more than a third of a ton of micro-organisms which act to bring about the decomposition of organic matter.

How soils are made

Rock terrains are changed by the action of biological organisms into soil following physical and chemical processes of disintegration. Soil constitutes a covering of fine and mobile material in which vegetation grows by biochemical action. Soil formed by the decomposition of the underlying rock is known as *autochthonous*. In cases where the underlying rock has been weathered almost out of existence the soil is known as *parautochthonous*. Often the material is transported elsewhere and it then forms *allochthonous* soils, which are divided into those that have slipped down a slope (*colluvial soil*), those carried away by water (*alluvial*), by glaciers (*glacial*), or blown by the wind (*aeolian*).

Soil classification also distinguishes between *azonal* soils, formed from underlying rocks and not well-developed; *intrazonal*, which

are not fully developed (in some cases for non-climatic reasons, such as inadequate drainage); and *zonal*, regarded as mature.

The most important group of intrazonal soils is that formed by the *calciform* soils, which develop on calcareous or dolomitic rocks that are not very compact. They are rich in active calcium, and consequently are alkaline. Their chief drawback is their shallowness – about 8 to 12 inches and to prepare them for cultivation conifers are planted to hasten the disintegration of the underlying rock. The conifers produce an acid and corrosive humus.

Intrazonal soils also include waterlogged soils, formed by the presence of shallow fresh water. These are the peaty soils, which are distinguished according to whether they are formed in running or in stagnant water. Their chief characteristic is their accumulation of organic matter that neither decays nor ferments because of the extreme denseness of algae, water-lilies, mosses, and reeds, which prevent both aeration and the presence of the bacteria that cause decay. This provides the natural environment of the anaerobic microbe *Incrococcus carbo*, which carbonizes dead vegetable matter and turns it into peat.

Zonal soils can be classified according to their climatic characters. A widespread variety of soil is that found between the polar circle and latitude 46° N, a region which lies in the cool temperate zone. Its upper layer, known as the *leaching zone* or *eluvial horizon*, where

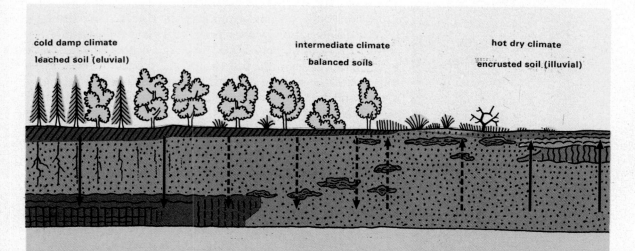

cold damp climate
leached soil (eluvial)

intermediate climate
balanced soils

hot dry climate
encrusted soil (illuvial)

A diagram showing the distribution of soils according to climate. In damp regions, infiltrating waters drag soluble elements downwards leaving a zone of leaching in the upper layers and a zone of accumulation at depth. In dry regions, water from depth rises by capillary action and evaporates at the surface, leaving crustal deposits. In intermediate soils, seasonal factors balance these movements.

Small strips of clay soil, cultivated in the Peloponnesus karst region, are formed by the chemical and physical action of water upon calcareous rock. The soil is very shallow and has a reddish colour owing to the presence of iron oxide and to its poor humus content.

Peat is formed in areas of stagnant water by accumulation of organic matter. An anaerobic bacterium, *Micrococcus carbo*, carbonizes the vegetable matter.

chemical changes take place, is poor in iron, calcium, and humus which all accumulate in a lower layer known as the *accumulation zone* or *illuvial horizon*.

These are characteristics of *podsols*, which are acid and on which mainly coniferous forests develop, with some broad-leaf forests according to the degree of acidity in the leaching zone.

In the temperate zone, between latitudes 40° and 30°, *brown soils* are formed in which the downward movement of mineral solutions during the rainy season is balanced by their return to the upper layers during the dry season. These are soils of slight or no acidity, and prairies or broad-leaf trees develop on them.

Warm climates cause a profound development of soils. In warm-temperate zones clay develops. This forms the *red soils* of the Mediterranean which are extremely poor in organic matter. The type of vegetation that develops on these soils thrives in conditions of drought and includes vines, olives, and almond trees, whose long roots reach the underlying rock.

In the tropics, laterite soils are produced, with crusts or hard shells. These appear in savanna lands as a result of leaching and take the form of clay rich in iron and in alumina.

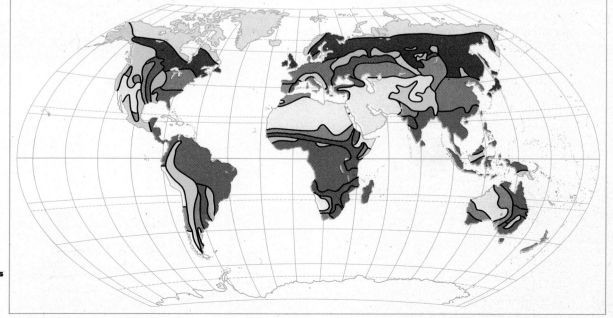

CHIEF TYPES OF SOILS

(according to Glinka, Marbut and Kellog)

- polar soils
- podsols
- brown earths
- red earths, laterites
- mountain soils
- prairie soils
- black earths, chernozems
- light earth
- desert earths

Sand dunes in the Mauritanian desert. The sand has been formed by the disintegration of the mother-rock which makes up the mass at the top left. In the foreground can be seen detritus showing the desert patina formed by iron and manganese oxides dissolved by water and deposited after rapid evaporation on the rocks.

silica. In deserts, the only sign of any process of chemical change in the terrain is a black shiny patina about a millimetre thick consisting of iron and manganese oxides, dissolved by rain or dew, and deposited on the surface as a result of rapid evaporation. In sub-desert regions, however, various soils are formed. If the underlying layer is not too deep, calcium and chalk rise to the surface to form crusts which support a sparse, steppe vegetation.

If rain is relatively abundant but confined to a short season, *chernozems* are formed, providing the most fertile soils in existence. Classic examples of these are found in the Ukraine. They are formed in a temperate continental climate that is moderately dry, and on mother-rock made up chiefly of *loess* (a type of loam) rich in calcareous matter. The fertility of these soils is due to the richness of the humus in the deep illuvial horizon. This humus comes from the organic remains of steppe vegetation which the soil recovers during autumn and which micro-organisms cannot destroy during the cold winter season.

Above: A laterite soil in the savanna region of Lake Rudolph, Kenya, inhabited by the Turkana tribe. The reddish colour is due to the pressence of iron oxide. *Far left:* The black soil (chernozem) of the steppes in the Ukraine. Its fertility is due to the accumulation of humus derived from the organic remains of steppe vegetation in autumn. The long, cold winter prevents micro-organisms from destroying it. *Left:* A brown soil in Thrace, Turkey, in which downward migration of soluble mineral components during wet seasons is balanced by their re-ascent during the dry seasons.

EROSION AND DEPOSITION

Transport of eroded materials by water

Rock materials loosened by erosion are carried away in a variety of ways. The material can be in the form of particles or large masses. It can be removed by streams and rivers, or from interfluvial areas. In the latter case, the areas between the river systems is gradually lowered.

An important form of erosion on interfluvial surfaces is the movement by percolating water which is present at depth, circulating in the soil's pores and interstices, and bearing away the particles dissolved in it. This phenomenon has already been noted in relation to karst regions. At other times, particles of soil are lifted and dropped again at a distance from their original location, a process known as *saltation*. Saltation is caused by the impact of rain-drops, falling stones or trees, the passage of animals or people, or changes in the volume of the ground due to intermittent frost.

These, however, are only some of the factors in the endless process of the transport of detritus from interfluvial areas. The process, obviously, is more concentrated in surface areas than deep down. It results in movement of the entire mass of detritus towards a lower level, a process known as *creep*, and has the two-fold effect of smoothing out the jagged profile and exposing the mother rock by taking away its protective mantle.

Water circulation on sloping ground. Above the impermeable rock-layer is a layer of unabsorbed water. The soil immediately above contains water drawn up by capillary action. The surface soil contains atmospheric moisture and is covered by a slight layer of newly fallen rain. The arrows in the underground water layer indicate the direction of flow of the water as it takes material in solution downwards. The upper arrows indicate:
e_1 evaporation of surface water and newly fallen rain
e_2 evaporation of capillary water
e_3 evaporation of underground water
e_4 evotranspiration through the trees via the roots and the leaves

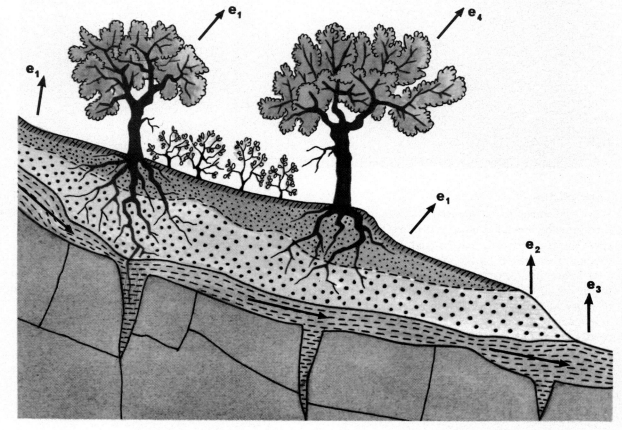

Along the steep slopes of this canyon in Yellowstone National Park, in the United States, the transport of eroded material reaches large proportions because of the friability of the rocks and the rapid removal of matter by the swiftly flowing torrent. The removal of detritus from the lower levels reduces the chances of vegetation taking root and thus robs the terrain of the protection normally afforded by this.

Landslides in unconsolidated rock consisting of moraine material that has not been cemented and has been attacked by the River Mallero, in Val Mallenco, Italy.

Landslides

When the transport of material involves large masses of rocks or earth moving in a solid block, the phenomenon is known as a *landslide*. The manner of formation and detachment of landslides, and the final form taken by the material affected, are as follows.

1) Those that move from areas of surface detachment created by fracturing or fissuring, or from contact planes or rock formations of different consistencies. These are slips of considerable masses. The accumulation of the material, generally in fragmented blocks, creates conical heaps of detritus and chaotic masses of material of various textures which can be overtaken by later slips.

2) Those that move as soon as they are detached. The most typical take place in unconsolidated material which has absorbed a large amount of rain; when the process (which can be a gradual one) is finished, the slope affected shows a terrace structure, while the material at the foot is bunched.

3) Those that do not offer any surface detachment area because they are caused by slow creep of the terrain which has been made plastic by rain, because they involve the total movement of various parts.

Run-off

The transport action of water is seen more directly in run-off that is not canalized, on interfluvial areas. Water from rain and snow

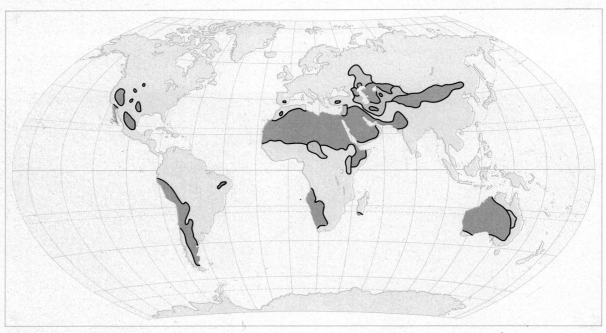

HYDROLOGICAL REGIONS OF THE EARTH

 arheic regions
 endorheic regions
 exorheic regions

In the high tablelands of the south-western United States erosion creates spectacular effects. The photograph shows Bryce Canyon, the steep slopes of which are composed of loosely cemented sandstone and have been cut by water, wind, and snow following vertical fractures. The unusual shapes are a result of the various planes of resistance to erosion offered by the rock.

does not run off completely from a surface area. The extent of run-off depends on the permeability of the rocks, climatic conditions, and their effect on evaporation and transpiration from plants. For a given terrain at a given temperature, surface run-off does not take place unless precipitation reaches a certain level; the greater or lesser permeability of the terrain affects only that part of the rainfall in excess of this minimum level.

Water from rain or snow which does not evaporate is not used by plants and does not infiltrate into the soil runs off over the surface in a series of innumerable tiny trickles which vary in size, position, direction, and flow according to the obstacles encountered. The greatest irregularities occur on steep slopes covered in vegetation. The total effect of the run-off is like a single thin layer of water 'washing' the surface of the ground. Its capacity for transporting material is limited to the particles of clay carried away in suspension or the grains of sand that are rolled away. Obstacles force the water constantly to deposit its transported material, so that the area is subjected to both erosion and deposition. In time, however, the effects of run-off show themselves as a wearing away of the ground, and a tendency to a reduction in gradients.

Run-off can also act in a quicker, more evident and harmful way on interfluvial areas of impermeable, fine-grained rocks with no vegetation. This is particularly so when precipitation is violent and concentrated and the angle of gradient steep, so that there are no obstacles to impede the run-off. Small furrows are formed at first which become longer and then ramify. They finally affect the whole slope from the foot to the summit.

Typical examples of this accelerated erosion are the Badlands of South Dakota where hurried deforestation brought about by such circumstances as the overpasturing of livestock has left the ground unprotected. In the United States the surface area rendered unusable by such erosion has been estimated at about 80,000 square miles, the total area affected being 230,000 square miles. Over 1 million square miles of land were threatened – nearly a third of the total area of the country.

Formation of torrents

Through the irregularity of terrain, the trickles of water running over a surface sometimes converge at one point, with a pronounced concentration of the effects of their mechanical action.

The unusual 'caps' on these rock formations are due to the upper layer of rock being more resistant to erosion than the softer rock underneath.

This convergence creates a channel which carries away the run-off, feeding it into other channels and eventually into the sea. The sudden loss of the water's force as it leaves steep ground causes it to deposit the material it has been carrying as an alluvial fan; the river spreading out in a fanlike shape at the channel's mouth. This type of run-off and the resulting shaping of the terrain is characteristic of torrents.

Transport and deposition by canalized run-off

The movement of run-off water cannot be smooth because collision with irregularities causes the water particles constantly to change their direction, producing eddy currents and turbulence. This consumes about nine-tenths of the run-off's force. The kinetic energy left transports material which has reached the channel by other means such as creep and immediate run-off.

The speed of the water-flow is an important factor in this process. It depends on the steepness of the channel bed, but varies from place to place inside the stream according to eddy currents and turbulence. At the surface it is reduced by friction with the atmosphere, and at the bottom with the channel bed.

This friction with the channel bed is important, because all transport of material except for floating matter is activated from the bed upwards. The larger alluvial materials are simply rolled along and become rounded in shape. This shape identifies rock deposits of river origin which lie in layers of alternating large material and finer material. In time, these deposits are cemented together by the presence of calcium carbonate to form conglomerates. In *breccias* formed by the cementing of landslide material, the component rocks are still angular.

The turbulence of a torrent also causes material to be plucked from the channel bed, but it more often acts to keep finer material in suspension. Greater energy is required to detach finer particles from the channel bed than is needed to transport them.

The transport capacity or the maximum density of detritus in a given volume of canalized water can be 50% greater than the volume itself. This situation occurs in turbid river currents, formed of particles rarely larger than three-hundredths of an inch in diameter which are borne in suspension during high-water periods, and in rivers which cross rocks that are easily broken up such as clays, sands, and loess. The greatest river of this type is the Yellow River which carries into the sea some 1,000 million tons of material a year carried from loess deposits inside China.

The kinetic energy of a water-course not used in carrying material removed from interfluvial areas may be increased locally by cas-

An avalanche slope and watercourse that drops down almost sheer slopes in the Rhaetic Alps, ending with an alluvial fan.

cades. Development of waterfalls into rapids is caused by their drop being reduced under the pressure of descending water, energy being dissipated in erosion. But in the case of the Niagara Falls which retreat at a rate of nearly 2 feet a year, the drop is maintained because the rocks are vertically bedded at the upper edge. If the waterfall is too high the edges of the drop are worn away more than the centre because the middle part of the water forms a fine spray and thus loses much of its erosive strength.

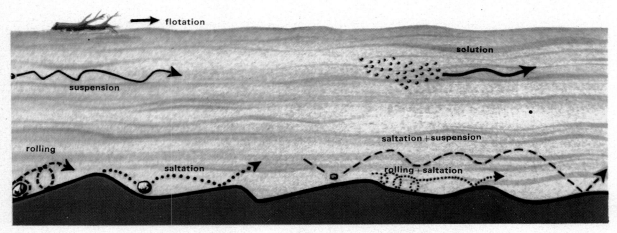

The diagram shows the various ways in which a course of water transports materials.

Shingle deposited on the bed of the River Vomano, Italy, during high-water periods. The shingle has formed islands the shape of which is determined by currents. River pebbles have a round shape and lie in layers, each containing rocks of different sizes and corresponding to successive high- and low-water periods.

The confluence of the White Nile and the Blue Nile at Khartoum, with the bridge joining the Sudanese capital to Omdurman. The picture was taken in September when the high-water period was receding. The waters of the White Nile (left) are thrust away and almost stemmed by the rushing current of the Blue Nile (right), laden with fertile mud which it has transported from the Ethiopian plateau and which gives the water its reddish tinge. The different colour of the two currents is a striking illustration of the different carrying capacities of the two rivers at this point. In January, the White Nile, laden with algae and vegetable matter accumulated in the marshy region of Sudd, progressively increases its carrying capacity, while that of the Blue Nile is reduced by 18%.

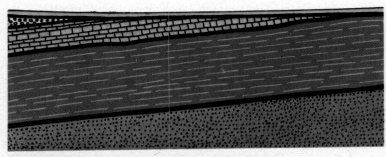

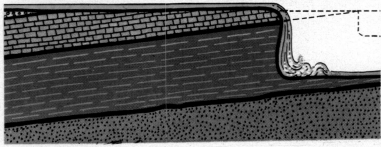

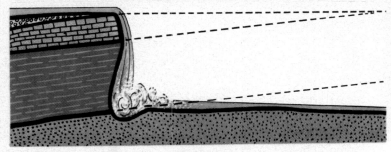

The Niagara River joins Lakes Erie and Ontario, which are separated by a height of 570 feet, part of which is the drop forming the Niagara Falls. The three diagrams show the geological structure of the region crossed by the river. The upper beds consist of hard limestone on top of soft schistose rocks which are easily eroded. These in turn rest on arenaceous rock. The first diagram shows the original geological structure of the region. The second diagram shows the structure 10,000 years ago, by which time the waters have almost worn away the schistose rocks, and the third diagram illustrates the present structure, showing a retreat of 7 miles from the site of the original drop.

Potholes and meanders

The material being transported by water acts as an abrasive through being whirled about by the turbulence of the flow. Examples of this type of erosion are *potholes*, roughly hemispherical in shape gouged out of the rocks in the river bed by the circular scouring movement of stones and other material within a restricted space. Potholes can also be formed at different levels on the channel wall, indicating the gradual stages in which the river cuts out its channel.

A further aspect of fluvial erosion is that of river bends, the sinuous windings of a river. Any bend in the flow is aided by centrifugal force, which displaces the main part of the current in the middle of the river towards the concave side, which it erodes. At the same time the slower current of the river laps at the convex side, depositing alluvial material eroded from the concave side.

The eroded concave bank is steep and the water there is deeper and more turbulent, in contrast with the less steep convex bank. The erosive capacity of a river is not diminished by these bends, some of which have been cut with some force through solid rock. *Meanders* are distinct from river bends, which resume a straight course after a short distance. The serpentine shape of a meander is formed when a balance is set up between the force of the water-flow and the resistance of the channel's walls. The speed of the water is such that it cannot bear away the materials obstructing

A giant pothole gouged out of the rock at the level of a former course of a river. The cavern was formed by the rotation of abrasive material by the current.

it, while the resistance of the materials is not great enough to make the river change its course completely.

The development of two meanders can result in their edges meeting so that the river by-passes the loop. Deposits eventually form a bank at this point, the effect of this being to isolate the former course of the river with water still in it, in the form known as an *oxbow lake*.

A meander in the River Semois, in the Ardennes plateau, Belgium.

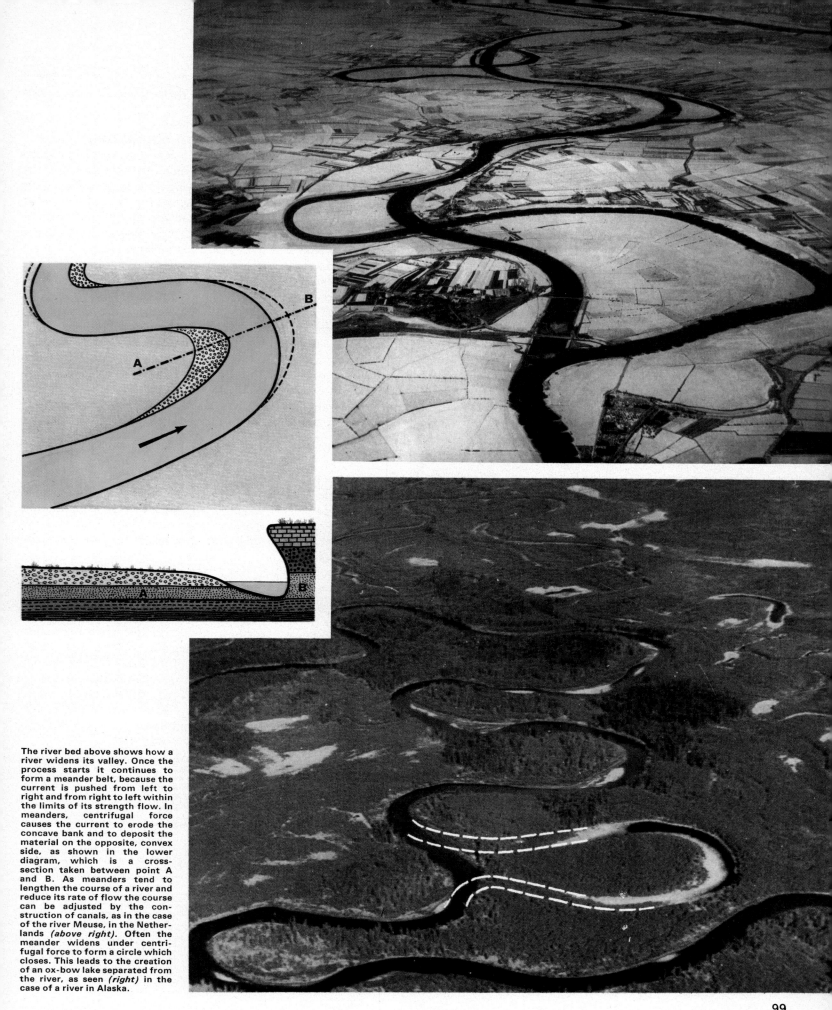

The river bed above shows how a river widens its valley. Once the process starts it continues to form a meander belt, because the current is pushed from left to right and from right to left within the limits of its strength flow. In meanders, centrifugal force causes the current to erode the concave bank and to deposit the material on the opposite, convex side, as shown in the lower diagram, which is a cross-section taken between point A and B. As meanders tend to lengthen the course of a river and reduce its rate of flow the course can be adjusted by the construction of canals, as in the case of the river Meuse, in the Netherlands *(above right)*. Often the meander widens under centrifugal force to form a circle which closes. This leads to the creation of an ox-bow lake separated from the river, as seen *(right)* in the case of a river in Alaska.

The equilibrium profile of rivers can be irregularized by changes in the sea-level, so that the river resumes its erosive activity along its entire course. The greatest changes in the sea-level in recent geological times have been caused by the melting of the Pleistocene ice-caps, as can be seen in the fjords of northern coasts. The photograph (left) shows a fjord in Greenland. The sea-level rose and then the land began to rise.

Deposition and the profile of equilibrium

Valley floors are usually flat and as a result are partially flooded during periods of persistent rain. Their structure is caused by deposition produced by the river flowing through them. This takes place when the river decreases in velocity as a result of the gentler gradient, and no longer has the force to erode its channel or transport all of the material it has brought from higher levels. Deposition of the large-scale type that helps to shape some of the main outlines of the Earth affects the entire course of a river to produce a *profile of equilibrium*.

In a water-course where available current-strength is used up in turbulence or in the transport of materials, there is a balance between power and load at every point. The idealized longitudinal profile of the river-bed from source to mouth forms a more or less smooth curve, steeper towards the source and gentler towards the mouth. When the river-bed is still young it contains many irregularities such as lakes, confluences with other rivers, beds of hard rock, and waterfalls. The river will theoretically smooth them all away by a combination of erosion and deposition, until the profile of equilibrium is reached.

Regressive erosion

If the base level of a river changes in height, the profile has to adjust itself to the new height. If the base level is lowered the river erodes; if it is raised deposition takes place. Both these processes start from the mouth and work backwards to form *regressive erosion* or *deposition*.

Variations in altitude take place at different periods and on various scales, and may considerably modify the local geomorphology. They can be caused by variations of the sea-level – *eustatic movement* – or by deformations of the Earth's crust. The results of the Pleistocene ice age are a notable example of this. The effect of glaciation can be seen in various regions, while the post-glacial isostatic movement of large sections of the Earth's crust resulting from the recession of ice-caps is a process that is still continuing.

The melting of Quaternary ice in the past 50,000 years has caused the sea-level to rise by about 500 feet, as can be seen in the morphology of the continental platform submerged under the sea.

Many rivers are born as mountain torrents. At the beginning of their course they are rapid and powerful in their capacity to erode. Gradually, by cutting deeper as they flow from the mountain to the valley, in successive phases, as shown in the diagram (below), they change their longitudinal profile and broaden their drainage basin. At the same time the gradient of the profile becomes less until it reaches 'old age', where it assumes its *profile of equilibrium*. Nearer the mouth, where there is more water and the material carried is finer, the river runs over an almost flat surface and consequently at reduced speed, and there is more deposition than erosion. This stage is reached when the base level, formed by the sea or a lake, remains constant. At the mouth of a river deposition creates alluvial cones. When the material deposited in these assumes vast proportions which cannot be moved by the water, the river expands to form a delta composed of many branchings-off of the main stream. An example of this is the Colorado delta (centre left).

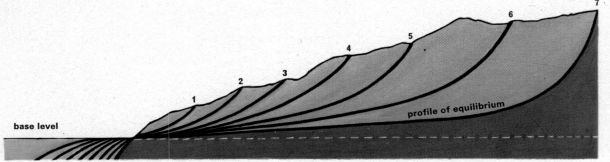

base level

profile of equilibrium

Below right: When rivers, by regressive erosion, 'eat back' their heads to beyond the watershed, they 'capture' the waters in another river-bed, together with the new surrounding structure created by this phenomenon.

Right: Aerial photograph taken over the Brecon Beacons in Wales. The rivers in the valleys are 'eating' backwards and will eventually take over the drainage basin of the river running from the reservoir at the top left of the photograph, and modify local hydrographic conditions.

Many river mouths have been changed into estuaries; these are really drowned valleys known as *rias*.

Similarly, large sections of the Earth's crust which were formerly under a thick layer of ice have gradually risen as a result of losing the weight that once held them down. In the Gulf of Bothnia, in Scandinavia, the surface area has been raised by more than 800 feet, and still continues to rise at a rate of about 2 inches every 5 years.

One of the effects of regressive erosion is *river capture*. As a river erodes back beyond its head, it may trespass into the course of a neighbouring river and partially or completely capture its headwaters. Entirely abandoned original beds become dry valleys.

Examples of this regressive erosion can be found in the southern Andes. The streams that once flowed down the western slopes were very steep and their heads were quickly eroded back so that their sources today are now farther to the east – sometimes as far as 125 miles – from the highest mountain crests on the border between Chile and Argentina, and the rivers now run into the Atlantic. In territorial disputes between the two countries, Chile is at an advantage as a result of this regressive erosion.

Rivers can change direction because of accumulations of alluvial material. Unable to wash away the accumulations, the river is forced to change course and run into the bed of a neighbouring river, leaving its own dry valley behind.

The formation of terraces

Terraced structures may be formed on the banks of a river by changes in the river's base level and the effects of regressive erosion. When the base level is lowered, the river cuts a new bed, starting from the mouth and working backwards. The former valley floor is left behind as a terrace. As the base level drops or the land level rises, a series of terraces is produced. Terraces are also formed by alternating phases of erosion and deposition. During deposition the river overruns its bed and then cuts a new channel in its own alluvium.

The terraces formed by continuous erosion consist of rock with a thin covering of alluvial material, while those formed by alternate erosion and deposition consist entirely of alluvium.

The formation of plains

Most plains are formed by fluvial deposition. The lessening of gradient, and consequently of speed of flow, which is responsible for the formation of flat plains and meandering, also produces alluvial deltas at the river's mouth, creating large and flat areas. If this process is carried out by a large river or by several rivers acting together, vast tracts of flat land eventually emerge. Sometimes the flood plain is enormous; the plain of the Mississippi River, below the point where it is joined by the Ohio River, stretches for nearly 500 miles. Vast areas along the Amazon, the Ganges, the Yangtse, the Hwang Ho, the Danube, and the Po are also liable to flooding.

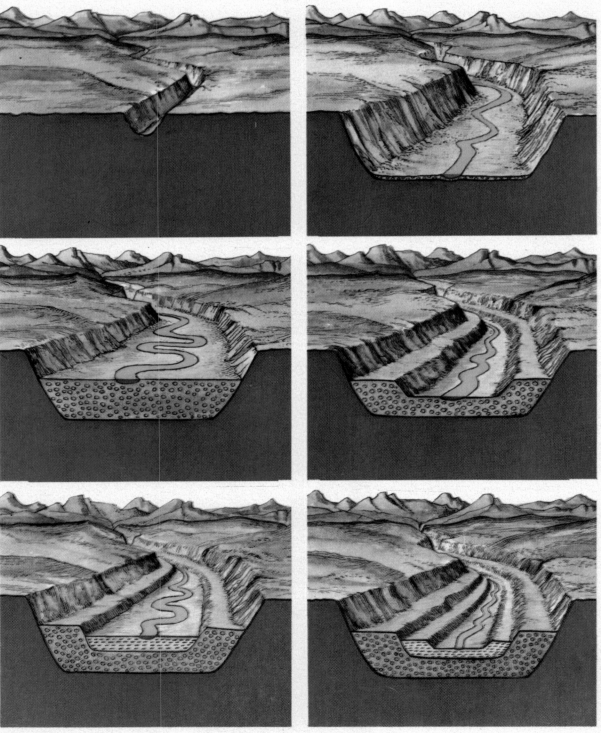

The sequence in which river terraces are formed is shown in this series of drawings. As a result of the base level being lowered, the river resumes its erosive activity and cuts itself another valley, leaving a terraced structure on the sides of the valley.

Right: The river Elbe near Bastei. As well as the original terraces isolated from the river in geologically distant times, there is a terrace of alluvial material formed during a low-water phase of the river, with erosion taking place in a narrower channel.

Below: The Diano valley in the southern Apennines is a vast plain situated between mountains formed first by lake sedimentation. Until Pleisticene times this huge valley was covered by a lake which dried up as alluvial deposits were brought down by the mountain torrents. The natural drainage of the water left large marshy regions on the plain for a long time. These were drained first by the Romans and again more recently. The plain today is perfectly horizontal, with the cultivated rectangles aligned in the direction of drainage towards the river Tanagro.

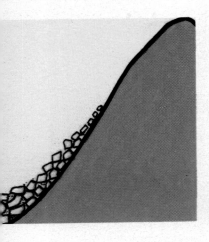

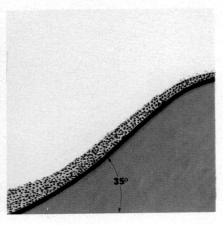

How a slope develops. The first phase is marked by collapse and landslide, in which large pieces of detrital rock move down the slope and gather at the foot. As the gradient is diminished the detritus becomes finer, and the slope takes on an S-shape. When the angle of gradient becomes less than 35° there are no further landslides, and subsequent development of the slope is due to the chemical and physical disintegration of the rocks.

Theories of erosion cycles

At the end of the 19th century, the American William Morris Davis depicted a geomorphological cycle as beginning with the emersion of land from the sea. A relatively simple river drainage system develops on the surface and becomes more complex as the land mass rises higher out of the sea. The erosion that shapes interfluvial areas and the linear erosion of river valleys are interdependent processes. The capacity of a river to erode depends on the quantity of detritus it receives from the valley walls, since this detritus absorbs the river's kinetic energy. The amount of detritus that can reach a river depends on the gradient of the valley walls.

The river channels of this first phase are known as 'youthful'. They are narrow, deep, and steep in the case of rapid emersion, and broad and shallow in the case of slow emersion. Subsequently the valleys become broader and ramify, reducing the height of the interfluvial areas which were originally high plateaux. At the landslide stage, the transport of detritus to the river gradually diminishes its erosive capacity. The slope then becomes less steep, and below a gradient of 35° landslides do not occur. The river regains its erosive power until it, too, reduces its own gradient and loses energy. This stage is known as the 'mature' stage.

As the valleys become broader and shallower all the surface irregularities are smoothed away, apart from some gently rolling areas, so that the surface area becomes flat and geomorphologically almost identical with the original land mass. The final result of this interdependent modelling is the formation of a *peneplain*, which is a surface still marked by channels, but on which all points are more or less at the same level. At most the area will have only gentle undulations. This is an 'old-age' structure, but it can be 'rejuvenated' by a new uplift of the land mass.

The Caledonian landscape of Loch Ness, in Scotland, is an example of an 'old-age' terrain. The area once consisted of a high mountain chain which emerged in Silurian times.

Other opposing theories were proposed, including that put forward by Walter Penck in 1924. He classified the forces at work as *exogenetic* (or *exogenic*), acting externally on the Earth's surface, and *endogenetic* (or *endogenic*), acting within the Earth and indicated by movements of the Earth's crust. The exogenetic forces cannot begin their work until the endogenetic ones have raised up a land mass for them to operate on.

In 1960, J. T. Hack put forward his equilibrium theory, which related the morphological aspects of a territory to the existing dynamic equilibrium of the various forces taking part in the morphogenesis. The most recent theories on the origin of relief structure tend to be based on analytical palaeontological research, which indicates that tectonic and erosive processes occur simultaneously with crustal deformations and climatic crises.

Below: The three phases of an erosion cycle: 'youth', 'maturity', and 'old age'. These mark the progressive flattening of a relief structure with the formation of alluvial plains and the successive modification of the coastline on which a deltaic promontory is formed. Erosion has left an inselberg (island-mountain) in the interior of the peneplain. An entire uplift of the whole region would restore its former characteristics and erosion would begin again. *Right:* Stone Mountain in Georgia is an inselberg of granite left standing above the flat Piedmont.

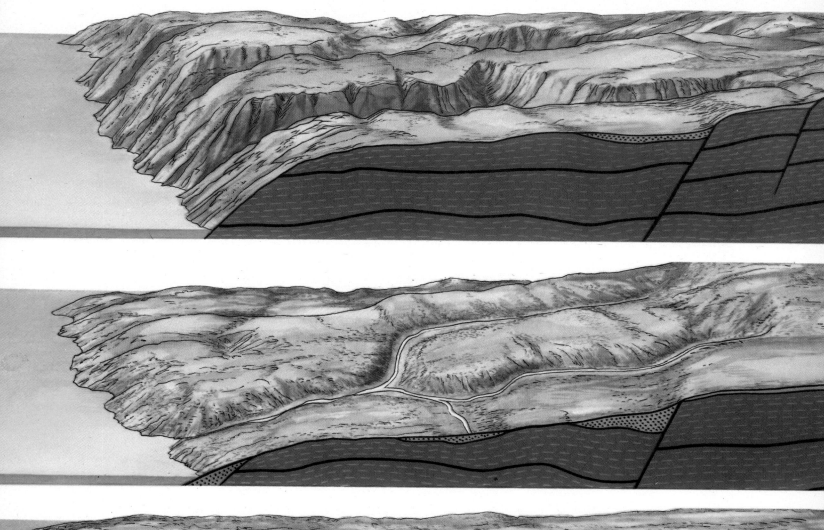

Above: A panoramic view of the Bernese Alps. The landscape is a typical example of glaciation and its morphogenetic action. This is limited to a few areas of the Earth, in temperate zones situated above an altitude of 10,000 feet. Present-day glaciation is the residue of the Pleistocene ice-spread, the recession of which can be seen in progress in the Bernese Alps. The ice-spread once covered vast areas of the Earth, as is still the case in the ice-sheet of the Antarctic (*below*).

Glacial morphogenesis

Some of the most striking aspects of climatic morphogenesis are those seen in glacial regions, which are remarkable for both the effects and the extent of ice action that took place during the Pleistocene period and still takes place today. Some 6 million square miles (10%) of the dry-land area of the Earth's surface are covered by ice. The volume of this is about 8 million cubic miles, equivalent to about 98½% of the total volume of fresh water.

The ice mass is particularly concentrated in the Antarctic, in Greenland, and in the mountain glaciers of temperate and tropical zones. During the Pleistocene ice-expansion – its latest but not the only phase of the Quaternary ice age – glaciers covered a surface area of about 17 million square miles, so that modelling by glacial action has affected a further 10 million square miles of the dry-land areas of the Earth.

Sea-ice

Sea-water, because of its salinity, freezes at $-2°$ C. Freezing can take place only when external temperatures drop to $-5°$ C in calm waters and $-10°$ C in choppy seas.

The first phase is marked by the formation of numerous floating ice-crystals, which give the water an oily appearance. These crystals then agglomerate to form slabs known as *pancake ice*. These join together to form the *banquise*, the average thickness of which is about 6 feet because the ice-covering, being a poor conductor of heat, prevents the underlying waters from getting colder. The banquise is propelled by the wind and by currents, and breaks up into large blocks (*floes*) which are separated by deep channels (*polynia*). This is how pack-ice is formed. Its jagged surface is the result of the mechanical action of waves and atmospheric agents, which break up and bunch the floes into hummocks.

The formation of a glacier

A glacier is a mass of ice in movement, and is formed by the accumulation of that snow which does not completely melt during the year. Thus it originates from above the permanent snowline.

In temperate and tropical regions glaciers are formed by *diagenesis*, the transformation of crystals of fallen snow whose density is less than 0·1 g/cc. The crystals are first turned into granules with a density of 0·6 g/cc by melting in exposed areas, the water in the interstices re-freezing with consequent expulsion of air.

The formation of a snowfield, a mass of compact snow, follows a similar process, with the formation of compact ice (density 0·8 g/cc) in which the granules are flattened into laminations. In the mountains of Europe the process takes from 60 to 100 years, and in the polar regions up to 300 years.

Types of glacier

The continental ice-sheets known as *ice-caps*, which are typical of Greenland, Antarctica, and certain Icelandic regions, are relics of the Pleistocene ice-spread, with an average thickness of about 6,000 feet, but reaching nearly 14,000 feet in some places in the Antarctic. Glaciers fed by these ice-caps often reach the sea, where the ice is broken off in large pieces which float away as *icebergs*.

Another type of glacier branches out to cover plateaux, hollows, and rock masses. The Mount Rainier glacier in the United States is a classic example of this, and there are others in the Norwegian Alps; hence its description as *Scandinavian*.

Large valley ice-streams coalesce to form the *Himalayan* type of glacier, examples of which are not confined to the Himalaya, but can be found also in the European Alps. The physical state of the ice is intermediate between plastic and viscous, and prevents the two streams from blending. Instead, there is a superimposition or

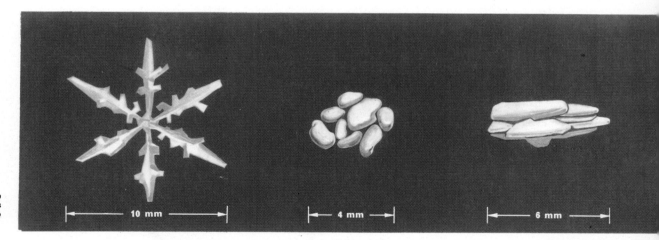

The successive phases of the transformation of snow crystals into grains and subsequently into the laminated ice of a glacier.

| 10 mm | 4 mm | 6 mm |

The southern edge of the Arctic banquise in the seas around Greenland breaking up as a result of the ice melting during the summer season.

An aerial view of Spitzbergen, showing the flattened relief modelled by the ice-cap which once covered the entire archipelago and is now limited to an ice-cap which flows with fan-shaped snouts into the valleys.

Below: A steep glacier marked with crevasses reaches out into the sea in a Norwegian fjord. In situations like this, which are very common in northern regions and particularly in Greenland, icebergs are formed by sections of the glacier being broken off by the sea.

juxtaposition, with each of the two streams preserving its own individual characteristics and adapting itself to the same bed. Himalayan-type glaciers reach large dimensions. The Siachen glacier in the Karakoram covers more than 450 square miles and several glaciers are as much as 45 miles in length.

In non-polar mountainous regions the commonest type of glacier is the *Pyrenaic.* This is a hanging glacier rising from large cirques carved below the crest of the mountain or on its slopes. Glaciers of this type are simple structures.

The *piedmont* or *Alaskan* type was, during the Pleistocene, the normal type of glacier, reaching out from mountain regions. Such glaciers emerge from their valleys and spread widely on a plain or on the sea beyond the mountains. There are few examples left today; they include the Malaspina, Bering and Alsek glaciers in Alaska, and the San Rafael glacier in southern Chile. This type of glacier requires a considerable supply of ice, which is available only in humid sub-polar regions high above the permanent snowline.

The movement of glaciers

Glaciers move only when the gradient of the glacier and the thickness of its constituent ice have a certain relationship. For a gradient of 10° the thickness must be 50 feet. The behaviour of the ice is intermediate between the plastic and the viscous state.

The movement of glaciers as a whole appears to take place along non-convergent lines, making it possible to calculate the exit point of any object trapped in the ice once its point of entry is known. This was exemplified by the famous prediction of the glaciologist Fobes, who forecast the time (with an error of only one year) and

An iceberg in the Stephens Strait, Alaska, detached from one of the massive glacier snouts which reach to the sea.

the spot where the bodies of the climbers who had fallen into the Bossons glacier (Mont Blanc) in 1820 would re-emerge from the ice. The bodies appeared on 15th August, 1861.

The study of the movement of glaciers is highly controversial and has stimulated many conflicting theories. So far the problem has mainly been approached experimentally, from the point of view of internal flow in a longitudinal direction, ignoring the possible effects of attrition and the behaviour of ice-flow relative to the floor and sides of the valley.

Morphology of glacial surfaces

In conditions of special stress (gradient irregularities, expansion zones on the bed and at the snout), glaciers tend to break apart and split into *crevasses*. In temperate zones the depth of these is generally less than 150 feet because of the greater plasticity of the ice, but in polar glaciers, in which the ice is much more viscous, considerably deeper crevasses are formed.

The surface of a glacier is severely contorted as a result of the ice-mass adapting itself to the contours of the bed and of the action of deposited detritus, which slows thaw or the irradiation of heat. The surface is further modelled by fusion processes. Rivulets and small torrents cut out gullies more than a yard deep with gradients of about 30° which wind like small meander belts, each marking the outcropping of a layer of ice. They often collect in semicircular pools shaped by the whirling motion of the water. If they reach the rocky bed, the detrital material which they carry scoops out cavities known as *glacial potholes*. Melting creates temporary lakes and mushroom-shaped blocks of ice, formed by the protection against thaw afforded by the rock mass on which the ice rests. Near the snout of the glacier, melting produces *ice-cones*, pinnacles of ice topped by a layer of fine glacial sand from the bed.

The Aletsch glacier in the Bernese Alps, formed by the confluence of several glaciers. The largest examples of this type of glacier are found in the Himalaya, where some reach 45 miles in length. The Aletsch glacier is the longest in the Alps – 15 miles.

collecting basin

3656 m
3689 m
259

limit of permanent snow

crevasses

medial moraine

ablation basin

relative surface velocity

snout

glacial torrent

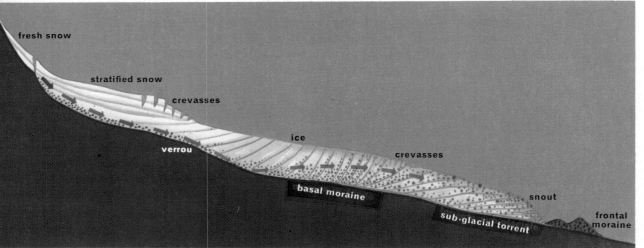

fresh snow

stratified snow

crevasses

verrou

ice

crevasses

basal moraine

sub-glacial torrent

snout

frontal moraine

Above: A typical alpine glacier, the Gauligletscher in the Bernese Alps. The various parts of the glacier named also indicate the process that provides its dynamics: the collecting basin above the snowline, the crevasses marking steps in the floor (verrou), the ablation area, the snout, and the glacial torrent. The velocity of various points on the surface is indicated by arrows. The fastest movement is at the centre.

Left: Long profile of an Alpine glacier. The arrows indicate the line of the maximum flow-velocity. When the verrou is passed, this line rises and assumes an inclined S-shape. As a result, the ice-layers tilt upwards almost to a vertical position and fall again towards the snout. This conformation causes detritus to be raised from the bottom and deposited as a frontal moraine.

Below left: This photograph, taken near the snout of the Lobbia Alta glacier in the Adamello, Italy, shows the blue blistered veins marking the direction of stratification of the ice, which forms a compact mass detached from its bed of rock with water gathering in the resultant crevasses.

Aspects of glacial deposition

Both the surface and the interior of glaciers carry a large amount of detritus of varying volume and size, which has either fallen into the glacier from the neighbouring slopes or been dragged out of the bed and ground up by the action of the glacier.

The accumulations of such material are situated along the sides of the glacier. Known as *moraines* they are deposited during stationary or regressive phases of the ice-flow.

Among the most interesting types of moraine are the *drumlins*, which are deposited by ice-sheets in the lowlands.

Top left: The crater of the Beeren volcano on Jan Mayen Island acts as a collecting basin for a glacier which runs through a gap in the crater's rim. Because of the high speed of the glacier's flow resulting from the steepness of the slope, the ice is fractured by many crevasses.

Top right: Crevasses and medial moraines in the Morteratsch glacier.

Centre right: The snout of the Balmaceda glacier, Argentina, reaching the sea. This is a frequent occurrence in northern and southern regions of the earth where the snowline can be as low as 3,000 feet. The recent retreat of the glacier has left a perfect morainic arc through a gap in which the glacier's melt-water reaches the sea.

Bottom right: The large medial moraine of the Morteratsch glacier. In the foreground can be seen large lateral moraines which run along the entire length of the glacier and are formed by detrital material from the side slopes.

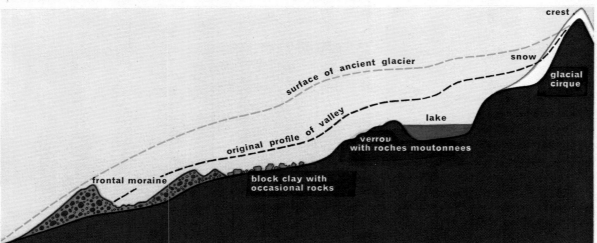

Labels on diagram: crest · surface of ancient glacier · snow · glacial cirque · original profile of valley · lake · verrou with roches moutonnees · frontal moraine · block clay with occasional rocks

Above: A gorge in northern Italy through which the River Adige emerges out of a valley into a plain. As the present landscape shows, a large glacier occupied the valley during the Pleistocene period; its snout stretched as far as the low morainic hills in the background.

Longitudinal profile of a glacier valley after the retreat of a glacier which has become a small patch of ice in what was once the collection basin. The profile shows the characteristic steps, which at the head of the valley are hollow and contain lakes. Erratic rocks and fine clay soils in blocks are littered about farther downhill.

They are elongated hills or ridges of clay with or without a rocky core. They are shaped like half an egg, the long axis parallel to the flow of the ice, with the thick, steep end facing the direction from which the ice came. Other deposits, called eshers, lie in long chains. In Sweden, where they are called *osar*, they stretch for several hundred miles, and the consistency and disposition of their material – rounded pebbles and shingle – seem to indicate that they were transported by glacial meltwaters.

The Aldman, a tributary of the Saskatchewan River, in Canada, runs over a plain covered by clay deposits left after the retreat of the great Pleistocene ice-sheet period which modelled the region. Wind transport of this fine, light soil formed the loess deposits in the Mississippi valley.

Right: Rocks bearing characteristic glacial striae. The rock surface, rubbed smooth by the action of moraine detritus dragged across it by the glacier, carries drawings by Iron Age people depicting episodes in their daily lives (Valcamonica, Italy). *Far right:* Moraine detritus in the Val Malenco Mountains, Italy. The two boulders have been rounded by glacial action.

In front of present-day glaciers the disorganized paths of waterways of glacial origin form a characteristic plain of deposition (*sandur*) covered by sands, mud and mire. These are later flattened by the action of the wind, which blows away powdery detritus to deposit it elsewhere, forming characteristic layers of loess. Examples of this can be found in the Mississippi river basin, in central Europe, on the Sarmatic plain, and in eastern China, where layers of loess date from the sandur of the Pleistocene.

Glacial erosion

Apart from deposition, glacial action also carries out a process of demolition known as *abrasion*. The marks of this action can be seen in many forms, such as the rounded rocks that outcrop in groups and, resembling the shape of sheep, are known as *roches moutonnées*. They show scratches (*glacial striae*) where the ice-mass moved past them. They may form part of the valley slope which is rounded and U-shaped. The direction of the striae marks the direction of the former ice-flow.

Another result of glacial action, especially in the case of severely fractured rocks, is the detachment of blocks from the lower sections of the *roches moutonnées*, thus making their lower slopes the steepest. Glacial striae occur also in morainic pebbles, of different hardness. The presence of such pebbles in loose rock accumulations is firm evidence of glacial action.

Large scale erosion beneath the ice-sheets gives rise to large plains and high plateaux, known in Swedish as *fjell*. Their surfaces bear rounded rocks, moraines, and other forms of accumulation, together with hollows scooped out of solid rock often filled with water. Examples are the plains of northern Canada, Sweden and Finland.

An aerial view of the Alps: a succession of valleys excavated around the Mont Blanc massif (centre) by glacial erosion. A good idea of past glaciation can be obtained by imagining these valleys filled with glaciers. The whole picture represents an Alpine zone which underwent one of the most intense and extensive actions of glacial morphogenesis during the Pleistocene period.

This landscape in Banff National Park, in the northern Rocky Mountains of Canada, shows typical aspects of glacial morphology.

Below: Lyse fjord in south-west Norway is a valley excavated and modelled by a glacier. The depth of fjords gives rise to the belief that glacial erosion took place on a massive scale in past geological ages at depths below sea-level.

In mountainous surroundings, the characteristic element of glacial modelling is the shape of river valleys, both in their longitudinal and transverse profiles. The head of a glacial valley is usually a *cirque*, a huge hollow scooped out of the mountainside, having a flat floor and surrounded by sheer walls giving it the look of an enormous armchair. The cirque is the collecting basin that starts a glacier. The cross-section of a glacial valley is U-shaped, giving it a trough-like look. These classic forms, however, may be modified by subsequent geological processes. The longitudinal profile of a glacial valley usually shows a series of steps, the vertical faces of which slope downwards towards the valley. The steps are hollowed and contain either a lake or a bog. Tributary valleys usually hang over the main valley, sometimes at a considerable height.

The formation of the longitudinal profile of glacial valleys and cirques can be explained by the longitudinal movement of glaciers.

Mechanical, chemical, and biochemical actions wrought by the sea all contribute to the modelling of the littoral regions of the Earth's dry-land areas. *Above*: The coast of northern California, near the border with Oregon. The mechanical action of waves has isolated groups of islets in the sea where there once stood a promontory which marked the limit of a crescent-shaped beach. As can be seen, various kinds of flotsam are left on the beach by the waves.

THE SEA

Salinity

The morphogenesis of sea-shore regions is determined by mechanical, chemical, and biochemical processes activated by the physical properties of the sea. An important feature of the sea is its salt content, which averages 35 parts per thousand. The salt is mainly in solution, the commonest form being sodium chloride, which is present in a quantity of 27.213 grams per litre.

The other important salts contained in sea-water are magnesium chloride, magnesium sulphate, calcium sulphate, potassium sulphate, calcium carbonate and magnesium bromide. Traces of 49 of the 92 naturally occurring elements are found in sea-water. Many of these are only found in appreciable quantities in the remains of aquatic animal and vegetable matter; for instance, vanadium is found in holothurians (wormlike, limbless echinoderms), and nickel in molluscs. Gases present in solution include oxygen, nitrogen, and carbon dioxide; these are partly absorbed directly from the atmosphere, and partly produced by organisms during their vital processes of absorption, synthesis and assimilation. Sulphuric acid is found in some seas lacking oxygen in solution, as in certain zones of the Black Sea where its presence causes skin inflammation in bathers and prevents the existence of fish-life.

The origin of salinity in the 'washing-away' process wrought by fresh water applies only to continental lakes and seas such as the Aral Sea, the Caspian, the Great Salt Lake and the lakes of the African Rift Valley. Here the waters contain a preponderance of carbonates as in rivers. This origin cannot be ascribed to the salinity of the open seas, which consist mainly of chlorides and sulphates. Marine salinity is believed to have originated in the release of chemical substances during the progressive cooling of the Earth. The arrival of fresh water, from rivers and melted ice, causes local modifications in salinity, but adds to the mineral content of the seas.

The areas of greatest salinity are located in the tropics around latitude 20°, while the waters of the equatorial region generally have below average salinity. The highest salinity in the open sea occurs in the Red Sea, where values of 41 parts per thousand have been recorded. The Baltic Sea has the lowest salinity (7·8 parts per thousand). In the Mediterranean salinity increases from west to east, as a result of an increase in aridity and evaporation. Salinity also affects the density of water, which in the sea averages 1·06; but this density can also vary with temperature – colder waters are denser than warmer ones. This determines certain movements of ocean waters, such as the exchanges between waters of different temperatures and salinity, cold waters and waters of high salinity tending to sink.

Sea-water temperatures

The temperature distribution on ocean surfaces is chiefly zonal in character, with the warmest seas situated in the tropics and the coldest in the polar regions. The warmest sea is the Red Sea, particularly off the coast of Eritrea where the temperature reaches 35° C.

In low latitudes of the Atlantic Ocean, the temperature is very

The washing-away of mineral salts from the land by fresh water has only a slight effect on the salinity of the seas and oceans. This process, however, enriches the salt content of endorheic lakes such as those in the African Rift Valley. *Right:* Salt deposits left by waves on Lake Manyara.

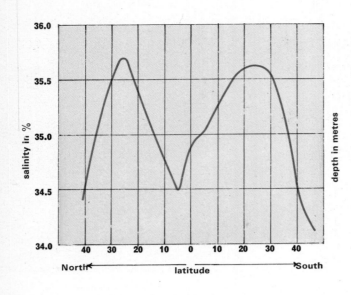

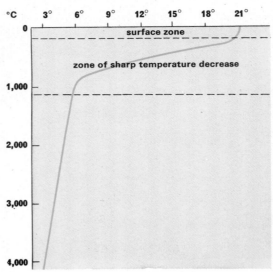

Far left: The salinity of oceans generally varies with latitude. Near the polar regions it decreases as a result of the melting of ice, which contains no salt. The decrease found in equatorial zones is due mainly to the large rivers, fed by the heavy rains of this region, which flow into the ocean there. Left: Variation of average temperature with depth. On the basis of thermal variations, salinity, and consequent phenomena present up to depths of 1,000 metres, the water-mass is often divided into two layers, like the atmosphere; the upper layer (down to 1,000–1,300 metres) may be compared with the troposphere and the lower layer with the stratosphere.

much lower than expected in the eastern part, while in the western sector the reverse applies. An opposite situation occurs at higher latitudes. Thus, there is a difference of 15° C between the sea temperatures off Florida and Newfoundland, but only 5° C difference along the coasts of Europe in the same latitudes. Ocean currents, especially, and the influence of dry-land areas – both on coastal seas and on the continental shelf – alter the regularity in zonal distribution of temperatures and accentuate the seasonal fluctuations, which in the open ocean and at medial latitudes do not exceed 10° C.

The temperature variations at depth are much more regular. From 13,000 feet deep the temperature is of the order of 1° – 1.5° C at all latitudes, probably as a result of the arrival of polar waters at the surface, which, being colder, sink to a lower depth.

The influence of external thermal conditions ceases at about 650 feet; below this depth the temperature decreases rapidly to about 3,000 feet; at 1,500 feet it is already half the surface value. Below 3,000 feet the temperature decreases more gradually. A problem that remains unsolved is why the temperature increases in the abyssal trenches. In the Mindanao Trench (34,580 feet) the

temperature is 2·7° C. This may be due to orogenic activity, vulcanism, or seismic conditions.

In inland seas the temperature of deep water is stabilized at that of the water at the sea-ocean threshold. At 13,000 feet in the Mediterranean the temperature is 13° C, the same as at 1,300 feet in the Strait of Gibraltar.

Other characteristics of sea-water

The transparency of sea-water is extremely important for life forms that can live only at depths up to 650 feet; the Sun's rays cannot penetrate below this depth, and the process of photosynthesis cannot function. (At great depths other forms of organic life exist with different vital processes.)

The *colour* of the sea varies from blue in warm waters (phytoplankton and zooplankton being almost absent) to green in cool waters. Generally, any other colorations, such as the red tide of the Florida coast, the Red Sea, the green of coastal stretches, and the milky whiteness and the phosphorescence common in tropical seas, are caused by organisms floating in the water.

An aerial view of the sea near Guadeloupe showing islets and coral formations. Inside the coral rings the water is emerald-green in colour; this is due to the shallowness of the water and the local characteristics of the sea floor. The blue colour of the sea is due to the dispersion by the water of the short-wave (violet and blue) radiation from the Sun. The intensity of colour depends upon the sky colour, the temperature, depth, and salinity, and the presence or absence of organic or inorganic particles.

The waves of the sea are usually caused by wind. The mechanics are illustrated in the diagram *(below)*. In deep water, the movement of the water particles is oscillatory. They travel in a circular path, returning to their point of departure after each oscillation. This movement also affects the underlying water but in a progressively decreasing way down to a depth equal to half the length of the wave, beneath which the water is calm. When the water in oscillation touches bottom near the shore, the rotational movement is disturbed; as a result the upper part of the wave travels faster than the lower part, which is slowed down by coming in contact with the bottom. Breakers produced in this way may be spectacular, like those on the island beaches of the Pacific and particularly Hawaii *(above right)*, where the regularity and the length of the waves provide ideal conditions for the sport of surfing.

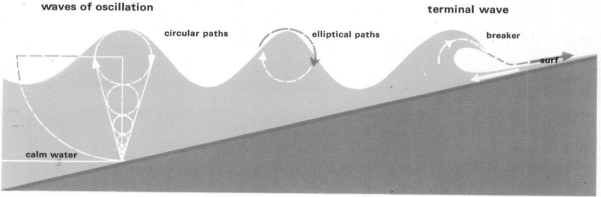

waves of oscillation terminal wave

circular paths elliptical paths breaker

surf

calm water

Waves

Waves caused by the wind or by cataclysms that act mechanically on the water mass, such as earthquakes and submarine eruption, have an oscillatory motion. Every particle of water set in motion completes an almost circular orbit, progressing slightly in the direction of the propagating force. The diameter of the orbit decreases with depth and, in the case of the deeps of the high sea, becomes imperceptible at a depth of half the length of the wave. The average height of waves during storms is normally less than 15 feet and heights of 30 feet are quite exceptional.

There are, however, waves of much larger proportions caused by catastrophic events. Typical of these are the *tsunamis* caused by earth movements beneath the ocean floor. The length of the wave in these cases may be 100–125 miles. The velocity is directly related to the depth, thus enabling forecasts to be made of when the wave will reach the shore. The tsunami that was unleashed on 4 November

1952 by an underwater earthquake with its epicentre near Kamchatka took only 4 hours 16 minutes to travel 2,700 miles between the epicentre and Hawaii, which it struck at a speed of 434 knots with waves 60 feet high.

The height of a wave may increase as it strikes the coast. As it reaches the shore, the circular path of the water-particles becomes elliptical, and the lower part of the ellipse is flattened. This causes the rear part of the wave to accelerate and push against the crest, which in turn accelerates and then breaks. On a shore of uniform gradient, this occurs when the wave's height-depth ratio averages 1:3. The breaking produces a violent movement of water onto the beach.

Waves are a powerful force in shaping littoral areas. To the great force of the water itself must be added the effect of rock and sand particles being dashed against the cliffs and shattering them, and the tremendous suction caused by undertow, which drags away the particles so dislodged.

A reef situated near a coastline breaks the oscillatory movement of waves and reduces them to foam. The impact of the waves depends, apart from their size and speed, on the effect of return waves and the amount of exposed rock passed by the waves as they approach the beach. Their erosive capacity depends on the amount of impurities carried. When a wave carries sand particles picked up from a shallow bottom, it can cause considerable erosion.

Above: The rocky coastline of the Scottish island of Arran. The shores are very steep and contain many inlets. These influence the direction of the wave movements.

The rocky coastline of Tasman Head, Tasmania, whipped by waves. The destructive action of waves first attacks cracks in the schistose rocks where the material is softer and easily removed. In the foreground, a block that has been undermined from the foot of the cliff.

Tides

The tides are caused by the gravitational attraction of the Sun and Moon. The directions of these forces are constantly changing as the Earth rotates. Their effect is to cause the level of the sea to rise and fall rhythmically, with two complete cycles a day along most coasts. Certain coasts (the Gulf of Mexico, the Java Sea, the South China Sea, the Sea of Japan, and, in Europe, the Gulf of Bothnia and the Gulf of Finland) experience only one cycle of tides per day. Along Pacific coasts and off the western Deccan both types of tides occur at various times.

The amplitude of the tide in the open ocean is less than 30 inches but along coasts having a wide continental shelf and deep narrow inlets it is much greater. The greatest amplitudes are located in the Bay of Leaves, Labrador, and the Bay of Fundy, Canada, where the difference between high and low tide reaches 60 feet. Only two seas show a negligible tide swell of less than 4 inches, the Baltic Sea and the Black Sea. Regular continental coastlines exposed to the oceans have an average swell of between 3 and 6 feet.

The tide consists of a vertical oscillation of sea-level. This phase is followed by horizontal movements known as tidal streams, which sometimes reach high velocities (16 knots in the Moluccas and 10 knots in the Gulf of Morbihan in Brittany where the tidal

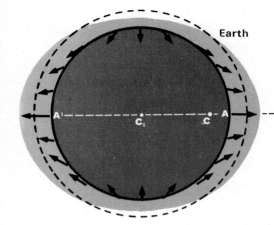

Earth

Moon

238,857 miles

The tides, according to G. H. Darwin, are the result of the Earth and the Moon working as a single mechanism and rotating round a centre of gravity at C (about 2,800 miles from the Earth's centre C_1). The Moon's gravitational attraction on the hemisphere of the Earth exposed to it causes high tide at A. The process is repeated in the other hemisphere away from the Moon (A_1) as a result of centrifugal force. The tide is higher when the Moon's force of attraction is supplemented by that of the Sun, a situation that exists when the Sun and Moon lie in the same direction from the Earth.

amplitude is just over 15 feet). The delay of about six hours between the tides of the Ionian and Tyrrhenian seas (where the amplitude is less than 1 foot) causes 5 knot currents in the Straits of Messina which form the famous whirl-pools of Scylla and Charybdis.

The most important morphogenetic effect of tides is the erosion of the two banks of a river during the ebb and flow. This results in the river mouth being constantly cleared of its deposits and sediments and becoming an estuary. When tidal action is exceeded by the process of sedimentation, the estuary becomes a delta.

Currents

The complex variety of this type of sea-water movement is caused by physical differences in the water mass of the ocean, especially its density. Between latitudes 45° and 50° south and at latitude 60° north there is an upper layer of warm water about half a mile deep. Beyond these latitudes towards the poles, and at greater depths, the water is colder. These differences promote first of all an exchange along the meridian of water masses with different temperatures, and further impetus is provided by the wind. This is evident in the surface circulation of the Indian Ocean and in

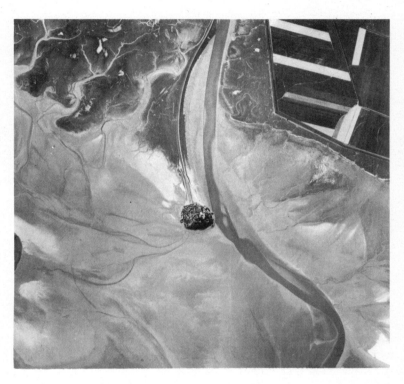

Above: The amplitude of tides varies from sea to sea, and reaches higher values in gulfs and inlets. The flat expanse of the Bay of St. Michel (France), surrounding the medieval monastery on its rock, spans about 6 miles when the tide goes out. This aerial photograph shows the effects of both fluvial and marine currents.

High and low water in Anchorage Bay, Alaska. The indicator structure records a tide amplitude in this case of 33½ feet. In some parts of the world tides can reach as much as 65 feet (e.g. the Bay of Fundy between New Brunswick and Nova Scotia).

119

Low tide at Cannemore, Scotland, leaves large areas of beaches dry, and strongly conditions life forms on shore.

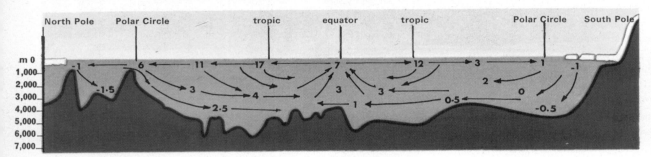

A cross-section of the Atlantic Ocean showing the exchange system of currents between the surface and the bottom. In the sub-polar regions water with low salinity, which is cold and heavy, moves downwards and causes the warmer equatorial waters to move outwards along the surface. In this way a circuit is formed with polar waters moving towards the equator and equatorial waters moving towards the poles.

the tropical zone generally, where there is a marked correspondence with tropospheric circulation. Water that is displaced horizontally is replaced by water rising vertically from lower depths, which itself is displaced by deep horizontal displacements moving in the opposite direction to those at the surface.

The characteristics of the Humboldt current in the Pacific and the Benguela in the Atlantic, which both originate in Antarctica, are due to their deflection away from the continental land masses by the effects of the Earth's rotation. The negative thermal phenomenon produced along the shores causes condensation at sea, while the land remains extremely arid, producing deserts such as those in Chile, Peru, and southern Africa (Namib). The cold waters which rise to the surface are rich in organic life, providing sea birds with an excellent diet; consequently there is an abundance of guano on the islands along the coast of Peru.

Littoral morphogenesis

Waves and currents along coasts are the chief modelling agents of the sea-shore. They are aided by others from the continental land mass, such as water running into the sea. The effect depends on the rock structure of the shore, softer rocks being most affected and harder rocks standing out as headlands.

The battering-ram effect of the waves followed by the suction forms *falaises*, cliffs with a gradient varying from 15° to the vertical in which caves are scooped out or natural arches formed. The destruction of the cliff by the sea's onslaught forms a platform

Below left: An inlet on the falaise coast of Victoria, Australia. The movement of waves and their undertow have isolated this stack consisting of horizontal rock beds, so that what was once a cave has become a sea arch. *Below:* The Needles, Isle of Wight, England, are the remains of a promontory made up of tilting beds of Cretaceous chalk eroded by the sea into a series of stacks.

Above: The falaises of Étretat, north-east of Le Havre, France. The calm, shallow water reveals the wave-cut platform left by the retreating cliffs and on which detritus accumulates. The erosive action of waves working at the foot of falaises and the consequent collapse of the overlying rocks cause the cliffs to retreat. *Below:* The island of Groix off the coast of Brittany, France. Wave action has removed the soil and surface rocks to reveal the underlying rock.

of abrasion in the formation of which chemical and biochemical processes also take part. This platform is distinct from the continental shelf which is the edge of the continent submerged by the sea.

The loose material collected is carried away by the waves and shore currents. The waves leave pebbles in a line parallel to the beach, the lower pebbles resting against the higher ones, while shore currents leave the pebbles in a series of arcs. The beaches are formed by sedimentation. This is a process carried on constantly by the waves of the sea, which can both erode and construct features along the coast.

Material deposited by shore currents before they reach the land forms *offshore bars*. These deposits may be left when the current loses speed as a result of passing over rocks or a submerged bank. The offshore bars are gradually transferred to the land by the action of the waves. If the bar is complete it may enclose a stretch of water known as a *lagoon* or *sound*. Spits sometimes form out from an island and grow shorewards, eventually producing an island linked to the land that is known as a *tombolo*. Monte Argentario in the Tyrrhenian Sea is joined to the coast by a triple tombolo.

The action of the sea tends to produce a regular coastline by smoothing away capes and projections and filling up inlets. On the other hand the sinking or rising of land areas along the coastline and changes in the sea-level can produce *marine transgression*, involving partial submergence of continental land, or *regression*, bringing about emersion of submerged land.

Different types of submerged coastline include the Dalmatian coast of Yugoslavia, which is formed by the sea infiltrating a continental zone affected by major folding; and the coasts of Brittany and Cornwall, where *rias* are caused by sea penetration into river valleys. A ria coastline is not to be confused with one indented by *fjords*, which were modelled by the Quaternary glaciers. Fjords are found on the western coasts of Norway, Scotland (known as *lochs*), Canada, Alaska, southern Chile, and southern New Zealand.

Coastlines that have emerged as a result of vertical dislocations of continental land masses, or of regressions of eustatic origin, may reveal the remains of the shore platform formed by erosion or deposition and previously submerged. The alternation of transgression and regression, typical of Quaternary palaeogeographical processes, shapes coastlines on which falaises, raised beaches, and platforms are all found.

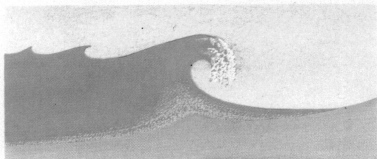

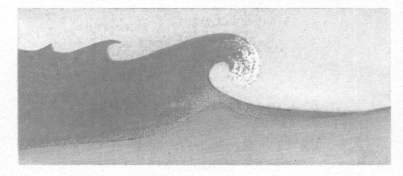

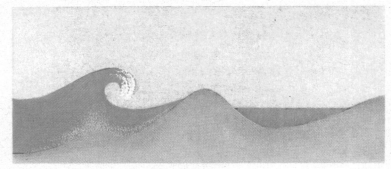

The action of organisms in marine modelling

Corals and algae are important as constructive agents in marine modelling. The basic structures they form are the *barrier reefs* and the *atoll rings*. These structures are situated in surroundings where the conditions necessary to keep these organisms alive exist or have previously existed: a water temperature always exceeding 18° C, a depth of not more than 120 feet, constant submersion, high salinity, an abundance of nutritive material, and limpid, clear water.

An aerial view of the coast of Greece with a typical deep inlet. The extreme fragmentation of land surrounding the Aegean Sea and the irregularity of the coastline are the result of a marine transgression of this tectonically unstable land.

These are all conditions typical of warm seas, which are usually situated in the tropics and are not affected by cold currents or made murky by deposition of detrital material. The structures abound along western oceanic coastlines (Brazil and eastern Australia), in the central Pacific, and in the Red Sea.

The barrier reefs are built by corals living below low-tide level, because they live in symbiosis with microscopic algae (*Zooxanthella*) that need a great deal of light for photosynthesis. Their constructions are extended by certain calcareous algae (*Lithothamnion*) which, when located in a cool and moving sea, thrive in the coral colonies.

Lithothamnion constitute the upper part above the water surface of coral barriers or atolls. The next level, exposed at low tide, consists of dead corals on which small colonies of still-living corals thrive. An atoll sometimes has small islands inside its ring-shaped lagoon, the waters of which may be deep; the lagoon bottom is of sand with pinnacles of coral sprouting upwards to within 10–50 feet of the surface.

A likely explanation of coral-reef formation is that proposed by Charles Darwin, who suggested that since the reef-builders flourished only in shallow water and the height of the barrier or atoll was greater than the maximum depths at which these animals can live, these structures are accounted for by progressive subsidence of the rock base on which the reefs originated.

Left: An atoll in the Tuamoto Islands showing part of the internal lagoon which itself harbours numerous coral structures. The surrounding ring is formed of sands of coral origin accumulated as a result of wave action. *Right:* An atoll in the Society Islands seen from great altitude.

This view of Mount Kilimanjaro is a fine example of the close combination of the physical and organic world. Below the snowline, at a height of about 15,750 feet, zones of prairie land, forests, and savannas follow one another. In the savannas live animals such as giraffes with forms developed through thousands of years of adaptation to their surroundings.

PLANT AND ANIMAL LIFE ON THE EARTH

The physical factors which have helped to mould the surface features of our planet are not the only influences at work; living organisms also play their part. Many rocks, such as limestone, have their origins in organic life. But what of the more obvious and immediate effects on the landscape of living organisms? Their distribution over the face of the Earth is clearly an important influence on their activity. All organisms need water, warmth, and light to carry out their vital processes and these are all provided in various degrees by the climates of the Earth, which determine the adaptations and distribution of life.

Of course, animals are less dependent on climate than plants, since they can move about. Their independence varies according to the range of their activity. Animals that live permanently in the soil (worms, ants, and certain mammals) are more closely bound to

their habitat than are more highly evolved animals such as mammals and birds. Living at the surface, these are able to look for food over large areas. Plants are more directly conditioned by the weather, and by the soil they live in. Each species is adapted to live in a particular environment which has precisely the right combination of temperature, humidity, and sunlight for its optimum growth.

Plants

Plants make their food by the process of *photosynthesis*. Carbon dioxide is taken from the air to form sugars from which proteins are formed. Photosynthesis occurs only in the light and is affected by temperature. Within limits, it takes place faster with increase in temperature. Another activity found in plants is respiration, a breathing process which is the reverse of photosynthesis in that sugars are broken down to carbon dioxide. This continues day and night, and its rate also is governed by the temperature. It is therefore apparent that large increases in temperature can prove harmful to plants since they will lose more carbon than they can afford. In fact, plant species have a *thermal optimum*, a temperature range in which they grow most comfortably. The thermal optimum is the most important factor which determines the distribution of plant life. For a plant in a cool temperate climate, the optimum temperature is around 15° C. For those of the tropical regions, the figure is between 30° and 35° C, while for desert plants it may be as high as 50° C. In the northern Siberian and American forest zones, optimum is about 7° C, and if the temperature exceeds this level it has no beneficial effect on the plants.

The carbon dioxide content of the air is an important regulator of photosynthesis. Indeed, scarcity of carbon dioxide can limit the rate of photosynthesis even though light and heat are abundant. The carbon dioxide content of the air varies according to the

Above: Mount Elbert (14,430 feet), in the Rocky Mountains, is the highest mountain in the State of Colorado. In the foreground, flowers of the carnation family are in bloom. At a higher level, in different soil, stands a coniferous forest, and beyond that lie the mountain slopes with their sparse vegetation.
Below: The loss of leaves in autumn is an adaptation for conserving water in winter. This picture shows a typical Pre-Alpine environment during the shortening days of autumn.

125

environment; for example, like the atmosphere, it is low in mountain areas because the air is thin. But carbon dioxide levels are high in zones of dense vegetation near the ground, where the content is constantly replenished by the decay of dead organisms. This explains the extraordinary luxuriance of vegetation in rain forests even where the light intensity is low.

Water is the basic element of life. Biochemical reactions occur in aqueous media, and the entire structure of organisms is designed to maintain an adequate water content in their cells and tissues. For plants, water is a supporting medium as well as a transporting one; it keeps them upright. Plants constantly lose water to the air through their leaves and this water loss increases as the temperature rises; it is regulated to a great extent by the water-vapour content of the air. Most plants therefore wilt and droop in dry weather.

Plants replenish their supplies by drawing water in through their roots. Climatic extremes which increase transpiration or alter the availability of water in the soil can cause spectacular adaptations such as reduction of leaf area, thickening of cuticular membranes, and the secretion of resins. Leaf fall is itself an adaptation to an environment in which the year is divided into seasons. Leaves

fall in winter in temperate regions, when coldness reduces the humidity of the air.

Nothing is more important to the plant than the soil it grows in. To provide themselves with a supply of water plants prefer a fine-grained soil, such as clay. Besides, the colloidal part of soil acts as a reservoir for mineral salts, including nitrates, phosphates, and sulphides for making proteins, and potassium, calcium, and magnesium. The last two are needed to make chlorophyll. The plant also requires traces of other substances; attempts to introduce South African fodder plants into Australia failed because the necessary trace of copper was lacking in the soil.

The growth of the plant and the onset of flowering are also influenced by climate. The length of the day has a profound influence on the development of flowers. Some plants bloom only if the daylight length is more than 15 or 16 hours; others will bloom only if the day is less than 11 or 12 hours long. Naturally these plants cannot be transplanted to an environment different from that to which they have become adapted. A typical example is tobacco which requires not more than 11 or 12 hours of light daily. If transplanted to more temperate latitudes it blooms only in autumn, just when frost might kill it.

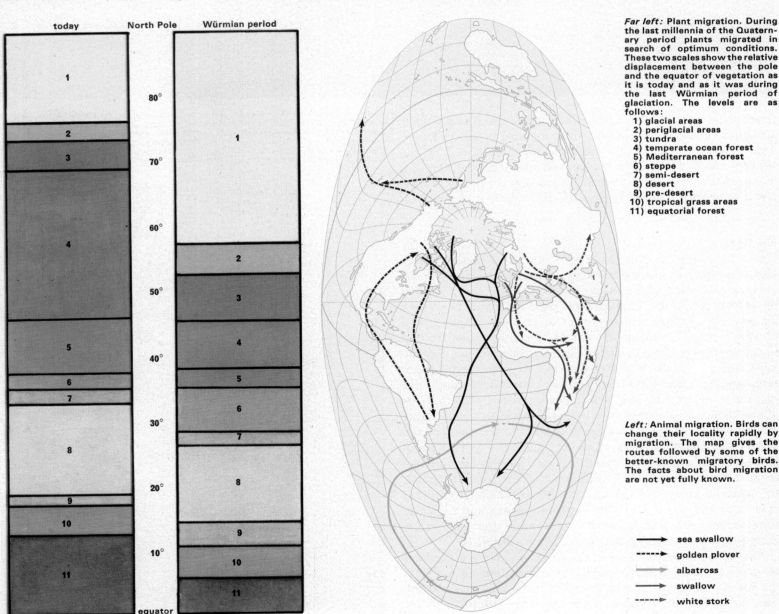

Far left: Plant migration. During the last millennia of the Quaternary period plants migrated in search of optimum conditions. These two scales show the relative displacement between the pole and the equator of vegetation as it is today and as it was during the last Würmian period of glaciation. The levels are as follows:
  1) glacial areas
  2) periglacial areas
  3) tundra
  4) temperate ocean forest
  5) Mediterranean forest
  6) steppe
  7) semi-desert
  8) desert
  9) pre-desert
  10) tropical grass areas
  11) equatorial forest

Left: Animal migration. Birds can change their locality rapidly by migration. The map gives the routes followed by some of the better-known migratory birds. The facts about bird migration are not yet fully known.

sea swallow
golden plover
albatross
swallow
white stork

Animals

Animal cells can exist between 0° and 45°–50° C and the optimum range is between 5° and 25° C. Primitive animals are largely confined to the Earth's warm zones because they cannot stand the cold. If there is a cold season they spend it either in the soil, which forms their natural habitat, or as eggs, larvae, or chrysalids. Many animals, however, must be mobile in order to avoid being caught by predators.

Mammals and birds keep their body temperature at a fairly high level, and, within certain limits, are unaffected by thermal fluctuations. Some of them survive temperature changes by having a reserve of fat which produces more heat during the cold season, or a growth of fur or feathers which conserves body heat.

Excessive heat is harmful only in places where there is no vegetation to provide shade; in such cases animals may move deep into the soil or into ravines to take refuge from the sun. The problem of water is less important for animals than it is for plants, since in most cases their skins are a protection against excessive transpiration. Exceptions are certain lowly organisms which breathe through their skin and many molluscs which protect themselves against water loss by a secretion of mucus or by living in shells. Mammals with sweat-glands are the most exposed to dehydration. These are helped by certain physiological adaptations such as the excretion of nitrogen in the form of solid crystals and of uric acid rather than aqueous urine; and most of all by their mobility which makes it possible for them to travel to distant water-supplies.

Above: In the steppes of Anatolia (Asia Minor) the temperature difference between night and day is extreme. Sheep are protected against the cold nights by a thick covering of wool. In the day, they graze in such a way as to escape the full effect of the Sun, producing the characteristic alignment of flocks in that area. *Below left:* The ostrich is a typical wandering animal of open spaces, steppes, and semi-deserts. It is the largest living bird, and, though it cannot fly, it can run as far as any four-footed animal. *Below right:* A nest of redstarts awaiting food from their mother.

Left and centre: Adaptation to a particular habitat is linked with the need for food. This depends directly or indirectly on vegetation. A water snake (*Natrix natrix*) fights with a salamander (*left*); a mongoose seizes a cobra (*centre*). *Right:* The spread of the domestic goat, with man's help, has been responsible for far-reaching changes in the Earth's plant covering. The destructiveness caused by the eating habits of these animals led to deforestation of entire regions in northern Africa and the Middle East. The photograph shows goats eating a juniper tree on the Atlas Mountains.

Biological associations

Plants and animals are for the most part associated in groups that share the same territory. This association is dictated by their need for food, light, warmth, and humidity. Many animals depend directly or indirectly on certain plants for food. *Herbivores* (plant-eaters) are directly dependent on them, while *carnivores* (flesh-eaters) who live by hunting herbivores are in indirect dependence. Thus a particular plant will probably be found to have certain animals in association with it. Associations are in dynamic biological equilibrium. The destruction of this balance may lead to the extinction of some members of the association and even of the association itself. When men chop down forests they kill not only the plants but also numerous dependent animals as well.

Distribution of living creatures

A number of problems arise in interpreting the distribution of life on the Earth today. First of all, the list of living species is far from complete. Secondly, though the list has been drawn up on the basis of direct observation of the distribution of living creatures, it does not help us find the causes of this distribution. Neither does it explain why certain organisms are not found in areas that seem to be perfectly suitable for them. For example, deciduous forests are found to the north of New York, but do not exist along the Canadian-American border on the Pacific seaboard where the climate and soil are identical. The reason for this lies in the past. On a geological time scale the Earth has only recently emerged from a great climatic crisis, that of the Pleistocene glaciation. This was a real catastrophe from the biological point of view; the colossal climatic change completely upset the ecological balance of the moderately warm Cenozoic period. Faced with such a change, plant life had the choice of extinction or migration.

The latter was often prevented by natural obstacles such as mountain ranges and seas. According to the theory of evolution, however, plants and animals of today are the descendants of those in past geological times. The present-day distribution is thus not the result of an on-the-spot evolution and some migration, but of flights, exterminations and mass exoduses, and partial and incomplete returns.

The means by which organisms spread have remained the same. Animals move elsewhere when their food runs out. For plants, and for animals whose powers of movement are limited, changes in distribution take place through the wind, sea currents, and the agency of living beings such as man. The wind is a most important agent for pollination and seed dispersal in many plants.

Among other things, sea currents affect the distribution of coral barrier reefs. These normally develop between latitudes 32° 30′ N and 30° S. If the temperature were uniform these barriers would develop along all continental coastlines. Yet they form only along western coastlines washed by warm currents; the eastern coastlines have no reefs.

Water currents operate in a mechanical way also, simply carrying small plants and animals on so-called 'floating islands'. These include the well-known ones at the mouth of the Danube, which harbour complete biological associations. These are borne southwards by the currents of the Black Sea, often reaching the Bosphorus. Other well known 'floating islands' occur in the Mississippi delta and float far into the Gulf of Mexico.

Animals help the distribution of other organisms in two ways: either by sheltering parasites or, as in the case of woolly animals, by harbouring larvae or seeds. Plants of southern Africa colonized Australian territory through the importation of sheep to that continent. Darwin once noted that a small piece of earth on a partridge's tail contained the seeds of 82 plants.

A coral along the coast of the Red Sea. Colonies of this form of animal life develop only in littoral zones of continents washed by warm currents. This is one of the many forms of distribution of living organisms brought about by marine currents.

Man's appearance on Earth was a most powerful factor. By domesticating animals for his own needs, and by growing plants for food, he revolutionized the biogeography of his own planet. Man often changes the distribution of plants and animals quite accidentally. Plant and animal life from all continents have colonized regions of Europe, often simply because they were transported there by chance in the cargo of ships or aircraft. For example, 527 kinds of plants not native to the area have been identified in Port Juvenal, near Montpellier. Of these, 86% are from parts of the

Mediterranean and 7% from America. Port Juvenal is used for laying out raw imported wool, so in this case sheep gather the seeds and man transports them.

Man also plays a destructive part. Though this is often dictated by the need to eliminate harmful organisms, it is sometimes irrational and senseless. Man has already caused the extinction of the bison in Europe, and the almost total extinction of whales in the Arctic and of the large penguins in New Zealand. He also causes great changes when he adapts nature to his own advantage. The

The green spaces in the map show the present regions where camels are found (camels and dromedaries in Africa and Asia, llamas and related animals in the Andes). The brown areas show where fossil remains have been found. This distribution indicates that the camel originated in North America and migrated in the direction indicated by the arrows until, following the Quaternary glaciation, it disappeared altogether from its original birthplace. The dromedary *(above left)*, a relation of the true camel and found mostly in the mountains of central Asia, was introduced by man into the desert and semi-desert areas of northern Africa. *Left:* Llamas in the Peruvian Andes.

Man represents one of the most destructive forces in the animal world. Bison were once plentiful on the American prairies and whales in the oceans. Both are now enormously reduced as a result of being hunted and butchered. *Right:* A bison in Banff National Park, Canada. *Far right:* Whales being skinned and gutted before being processed at Iquique, Chile.

Below: A representation of the dodo, a bird that survived into historical times, but finally became extinct. It lived in a land lacking in natural enemies, and had no means of defence. Its extinction took place around 1650 when the old biological equilibrium was upset by the introduction of new competing animals to the island. *Bottom:* The map shows the barrier lines hindering the expansion of species between Australia and the old continent, according to Wallace and Weber.

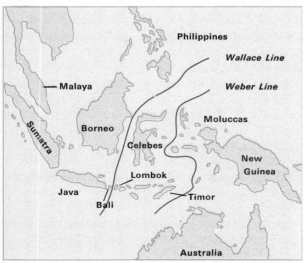

opening of the Suez Canal, for example, led to the migration into the Mediterranean from the Red Sea of a species of pearl-bearing oyster, and to a migration in the other direction of marine fauna and flora.

The appearance of vast tracts of water as a result of hydro-electric schemes has enabled vegetation to flourish once more on land previously denuded by artificial deforestation and progressive aridity.

But what happened before man came on the scene? Past distribution (as found in fossil remains) shows that living things have always migrated. We have seen that the great climatic changes that took place in the geological past could explain the causes of many migrations, as well as the extinction of many species. But the explanation of the climatic changes themselves must wait for a deeper comprehension of the behaviour of the Earth.

What paths did these ancient migrations follow? The most accepted theory today is that of the 'permanence of continents and oceans'. The study of geology has revealed the presence of continental shields that have not been invaded by the sea for upwards of 200 million years and on which, therefore, flora and fauna have had the opportunity of evolving *in situ*.

Massive earthquakes and upthrusts of the Earth's crust have undoubtedly occurred many times in its history, and caused the sea to invade new areas and recede from old ones. Disappearance of oceans would link two or more continental land masses. This is the view expressed by the theory of continental bridges. Biogeographers have often theorized about the existence of vast inter-oceanic bridges linking primordial continental land masses. These connections have not yet been confirmed geologically, but, in principle, they do not run against accepted theory. The only actual links which make up such inter-continental connections today, and which are known to have provided a migration path, are the isthmuses of Panama and Suez, and the Bering Straits.

Although bridges are hard to find, obstacles or barriers, it seems, are not. Wallace's Line, which runs between the Philippines and the Moluccas, Borneo and the Celebes, and Bali and Lombok in the south-east Asian seas, separates the biological environments of Asia and Australia. The Weber Line, which is situated more to the East, has also been suggested as marking this separation.

131

NATURAL LANDSCAPES OF THE EARTH

The variables associated with the formation of surface features (*morphogenesis*) and of soil (*pedogenesis*) at a local level have given our planet an infinite variety of landscapes. In the course of a man's lifetime, only changes of detail take place. Changes affecting the Earth as a whole occur over a geological time-scale, the minimum duration of which is a thousand years. As a result of the extreme slowness of these changes, an analysis of the surface features of the Earth is valid for a long period of time.

The climatic conditions also may be considered constant within limits; climatic types tend to be distributed in parallel zones according to latitudes, but are modified to a considerable extent by the distribution of land and seas.

THE LANDSCAPE OF THE RAIN FOREST

Climatic characteristics

The rain forest landscape is found in the hot, humid climate of the Equator in the zone extending between latitudes 10° North and

The forest in southern Togo, showing three typical levels of rain forest vegetation. The upper level is occupied by trees that seek the Sun and grow to about 160 feet; their trunks are bare and topped by clumps of branches and leaves. The intermediate level has trees of between 50 and 100 feet high. The lowest level consists of shrub and other forms of vegetation that have adapted to a humid environment in which light is almost absent.

5° South. It is a region of intertropical convergences and equatorial doldrums. The climate also exists in zones situated at latitudes 15° and even 25°, the limit being marked by the regular occurrence each year of a dry season, which, even if only a brief one, is incompatible with the typical equatorial climate.

Insolation is considerable and constant, so that the average annual temperature is about 25° C, with seasonal variations between 1° and 2°. The variations depend more on changes in cloudiness and rain conditions than on variations in the inclination of the Sun's rays. The highest temperatures are in fact recorded during the minimum rain conditions of the solstices.

The daily variation can be as much as 15°, but discomfort from chill at night and heat by day is caused not so much by the temperature, which seldom exceeds 32° in the day, as by humidity. Anomalies in the typical temperature pattern are the considerable variations, both daily and seasonal, caused in the Amazon region by southerly winds, which lower night temperatures to 10° C from 30° C during the day, and in the Guinea belt of Africa by incursions of a north-easterly wind called the *harmattan*.

Rains are abundant everywhere and distributed throughout all the seasons. The average rainfall is about 80 inches a year. It is slightly higher in the South American region, where the rains arrive through the great gap between the high plateaux of Brazil and Guyana and the Orinoco basin in the form of masses of very humid tropical maritime air. Rains are much less (45 inches) in the African region, which is sheltered from the very humid air masses in the east by a high plateau.

The cloud cover (cumulus and cumulonimbus) in certain constant areas indicates the persistent high humidity of the atmosphere, which is near its saturation point. Generally, this humidity develops in the morning hours and precedes severe storms; there are up to 150 storm days a year. This is especially true of coastal zones; inland, rainfall of longer duration is more common, lasting up to several days, but not always accompanied by storm conditions. Days of rainfall rarely exceed 325 a year.

Geographic distribution

In the South American region the rain forest covers the Amazon basin and continues along the Atlantic coasts of Brazil from Salvador to the southern margin of the Serra do Mar. To the West, on the Pacific coast, the forest stretches from Chimborazo to the Panama isthmus, and then follows the Atlantic coastline as far as the Yucatán peninsula and continues in a fragmented way into the Antilles.

In Africa, the rain forest occupies a large belt on the west coast along the Gulf of Guinea, Sierra Leone, and Ghana (mangrove forest). It resumes at the Niger delta, and continues to the mouth of the Sanaga where it expands inwards as far as the western boundary of the high plateau with its lakes, including Gabon and the central Congo Basin. The islands of Mauritius, Réunion, and the Seychelles and the eastern coast of Madagascar are also affected by the rain forest.

In Asia, the forest runs along coastal stretches (India, Burma, Indochina) to form the typical monsoon jungle. It also covers the valleys and lower slopes of Malacca, Sumatra, and the Philippines (where it is less intense), and Borneo, the Celebes, and the neighbouring archipelagos.

Rain forest areas of Oceania include New Guinea and several stretches of the north-eastern Australian coast, Melanesia, the New Hebrides, the Fiji Islands, and Samoa.

An aerial view of the Amazon forest in the Peruvian region crossed by the Ucayali River. The picture was taken in November when the river is fed by waters from the slopes of the Andes and becomes swollen and muddy, filling up former abandoned meanders.

Pedogenesis and morphogenesis

The continental regions in which rain forests are found are mainly situated on tablelands occupying the ancient pre-Cambrian platforms. Since the Palaeozoic, these platforms have been subjected to gentle, rigid-type crustal settling, leading to a morphological uniformity in the form of immense, almost flat depressions. Nevertheless this morphology is, even in its details, the result of a particular morphogenesis connected with climate, and in this sense it is present in those pericontinental and island areas that have a well-defined relief structure. The chief phenomenon is the rapid and profound chemical decomposition of rocks promoted by humidity and by constant high temperatures.

Kaolinite is the basic product of this decomposition. The mountain slopes are covered by a red clay, whose thickness varies between 6 and 20 inches and in which liberated iron oxides form aggregates that make it relatively permeable. This permeability aids the infiltration of water and thus accelerates decomposition at depth.

The soil in the forest has three horizons: the upper one varies in depth, but is very much leached and demineralized so that it is light in colour. The intermediate horizon is rich in iron oxides, making it red in colour. The bottom horizon is rich in kaolin, and therefore whitish in colour with a few red stains.

The depth and the high viscosity of the soil cause frequent large-scale landslips, making it almost impossible for steep rain gullies to be formed. The soil stays relatively damp and, in practice, saturated. The excess of water produced by precipitation removes itself partly by large-scale evaporation and partly by pouring off locally as a film of running water which, with creep and land-slip, is responsible for the slow transfer of fine-grained detritus to the base of the slope. This detritus is deposited quite abruptly on flat ground, forming groups of hemispherical caps that are sometimes eroded rapidly on one side like the *lavakas* of Madagascar.

River action is severely limited by the absence of large detritus carried in suspension. The rivers cut themselves wide beds down gentle gradients in areas covered by a mantle that has been deeply eroded, but they have difficulty cutting into any rock out-cropping. Their course is interrupted by rapids and cascades; this is a characteristic of equatorial waterways and is due mainly to the water's inability to erode the *knick points* (breaks in slope) and drops left by the vertical dislocations of large sections of the African and Brazilian platforms during the Tertiary.

A morphological phenomenon that stands out among the gentle undulation that marks rain forest areas is the 'sugar loaf' structure.

A 'sugar loaf' mountain near Pedra Azul, Brazil. These structures are typical of the landscape near Rio de Janeiro and in El Salvador (reduced rain forest areas). They are the remains of a former relief structure formed by the raised margin of inland high plateaux. Erosion caused by intense water run-off, together with high temperatures, shapes these structures of old crystalline rock.

This is not typical of the equatorial region alone, but is characteristic of the whole intertropical belt. The sugar loaf is a rocky mass bare of vegetation, with steep slopes (35° to 55°) and a convex peak. It seems to be caused by differential erosion in rocks of varying compactness.

Vegetation

Because of the rapid and deep-ranging disintegration of the terrain, the soil lacks nitrates, phosphates, potassium salts, and calcium, which are all dissolved and carried away by the large drainage system. As a result, below a depth of six feet the soil is poor and unsuitable for the support of vegetation in the normal way.

The establishment of the luxuriant vegetation which does exist is the direct result of the conditions of heat and humidity; these promote extremely intense bacterial activity on the surface, so that the very slender layer of humus, enriched by nutritive matter circulated by the water, can support a considerable mantle of vegetation. A remarkably large number of species are to be found, and in some parts of the Amazon region as many as 10,000 have been counted.

The absence of a rhythmical seasonal climate means that there is no seasonal pause in vegetable activity. With a few exceptions the renewal is continuous. Tree trunks do not show the annual growth rings characteristic of the temperate zone, and the rain forest is always green.

The different sunlight requirements of the species cause vegetation to be stratified into different levels. Trees more than a hundred feet high tower above the rest of the forest, their trunks long, smooth, and bearing no projections until they reach their summit, which is tufted with branches and leaves. They are exposed to a considerable degree of light, wind, and consequent rapid and considerable evaporation, so their leaves are smooth, thick, and shiny on the upper side, sometimes being covered with waxy material. The lower sides are furry and opaque. The succeeding layer of vegetation rises to a height of about sixty feet, and the lower level consists of sparse, shrubby vegetation with small narrow leaves.

The darkness hampers the growth of herbaceous vegetation on the ground; the impenetrability of rain forests is caused mainly by creepers that climb the trees. The trees are also colonized by groups of *epiphytes* (plants that thrive above ground level on other plants, without being parasitic). Parasitic plants are less common, while *saprophytes* (plants that feed on decaying organic matter) are even rarer. The lack of light causes flowers to bloom near the tops of trees, and reduces their size. Pale colours are prevalent; but the taller trees, many epiphytes, and the lianas have strikingly coloured flowers of great beauty, including many of the orchid family.

Root structures also show noticeable aspects of adaptation to soil conditions. The roots are limited in their growth by the shallowness of the soil-layer. Many of the plants therefore have roots that are small and superficial and sometimes even adventitious. The mangroves send down aerial roots from overhanging branches which become true roots and start off a new tree.

Left: Lake Ossa, which is situated near the mouth of the River Sanaga, in Cameroon, is surrounded by one of the most beautiful rain forests in Africa. There is almost daily rainfall, with an annual average of 160 inches. The small palm tree in the foreground grows in a reduced section of the forest.
Right: A road through the rain forest of Guinea shows the red laterite of the soil; this is produced by the chemical decomposition of the rocks. The region's high humidity and high temperatures are responsible for this widespread decomposition.

The western slopes of the Owen-Stanley Mountains, which form the backbone of the long south-eastern strip of New Guinea. Almost all the surface of this large island is covered by thick vegetation. Some inland areas have rainfall exceeding 240 inches a year.

Because of their economic value, ebony, palisander, and mahogany are the best known trees. The palms in ocean environments yield oil and wine in Africa, and sugar and coconut in Asia. Among the musaceous plants the best known is the banana tree, and of the graminaceous the bamboo and sugar-cane. Other trees include the cinnamon, pepper, clove, and the well-known orchidaceous epiphyte vanilla. Edible tubers include the sweet potato and taro. *Euphorbiaceae* produce manioc, a staple diet for many indigenous dwellers of the forest regions, and *Hevea brasiliensis* yields rubber. Other trees of great importance in world trade and industry are those producing cocoa and coffee.

Fauna

A census of the fauna living in the equatorial region is far from complete. Information gathered in the Barro Colorado reserve in Panama reveals some 20,000 species of insects and 464 of mammals. A large number of species included in this count are also found in tropical areas outside the forest, suggesting that the forest may represent a place of refuge for these animals from the encroachment of man.

Climatic conditions seem to have increased the rate of development and reproduction of these animals. The result of this faster succession of generations is a more rapid rate of evolution of a

The rain forest has few mammals, but is rich in insects, especially brightly coloured butterflies and ants. *Far left:* The giant ants of the Amazon forests. *Left:* A python of the Indonesian forests crushes a rodent before devouring it.

135

large number of species which do not possess the organic means to regulate their temperature. Adaptation shows itself in either an increase in size, as in certain reptiles (giant tortoises, boas, pythons, anacondas), insects (butterflies, beetles), and spiders, including the deadly poisonous ones; or a decrease, as in the case of many birds and mammals (elephants, Malay tigers, antelopes, and some bovines). Another consequence of the high temperature and humidity is the almost total absence of amphibious creatures.

The distribution of vegetation at various levels provides a basic support in the forest environment, while the network of lianas facilitates movement and migrations. There is a corresponding vertical stratification of fauna, particularly from the quantitative point of view. There are few vertebrates at ground level, and these are chiefly birds; the mammals are mainly apes of the anthropomorphic type. Rodents and certain carnivores are also numerous, while there are relatively few reptiles. Insects are present in great number and variety at all levels, including exotically coloured butterflies, often very large, and the ubiquitous termites which nest in the trees or live in symbiosis with certain epiphytes.

TROPICAL LANDSCAPE WITH TWO SEASONS

Climatic characteristics

Between latitudes 5° to 10° and 15° to 20°, both North and South of the Equator, the climatic year is divided into a wet and a dry season. The amount of precipitation on the equatorial drainage area can exceed 60 inches per year, but in the tropical area it is about 25 inches.

The first storms in the northern hemisphere take place towards April, and during May and June the rains increase in intensity; they diminish in July and August, near the time of the equinox, when the warning signs of the rainy season appear in the other hemisphere. The rains thus follow the zenith of the Sun, and can be forecast fairly accurately. The Equator is the area having the greatest degree of disturbance arising from intertropical convergences, and the duration and intensity of the rains diminish farther from it.

Average annual temperatures are about 23° C; seasonal variations are about 5°, while the diurnal variation is negligible. The hottest period occurs just before the rains, when it is most humid, and is marked by storms. The dry season is, like the desert weather, dry and windy.

Geographic distribution

The areas in which these climatic conditions occur are covered by the typical form of vegetation of the savanna and are located for the most part in two regions of South America. The first lies north of the Amazon Basin in Venezuela, Colombia, and Guyana, and the second in southern and central Brazil and in the adjacent regions of Bolivia and Paraguay. In Brazil there are the *campos cerrados*, which are tree forests, and the *campos limpios* or *campinas*, which consist only of graminaceous plants.

There is a similar distribution in Africa in the great Sudanese belt and another smaller one in the zone that runs from Angola to Mozambique and Botswana. A large part of the Deccan, inland Burma, Indochina, and the northern coastal zone of Australia are all savanna regions, as are the western coast of Madagascar, much of the Antilles, the Yucatán peninsula, the Mexican lowlands, and the western coastal regions of Central America.

The River Uaso Nyiro, which crosses the savanna on the north-eastern border of the Nyanza plateau in Kenya. This picture, taken in May, shows the river swollen from water accumulated on the plateau in the rainy season.

Above: The western slopes of Madagascar, in contrast to the eastern slopes which are covered by rain forest, have a savanna-type vegetation. This is often broken up into graminaceous zones due to degradation brought about by grazing livestock or by deforestation. The photograph, taken in February, during the rainy season, shows the landscape to the west of Tananarive. The houses of the village are built in red clay, and the village lies in a hollow near rice paddies. Rice was introduced to the region by peoples who came from the monsoon regions of Asia.

Below: The shape of these residual relief structures in the central savanna plateau of Cameroon is due to the type of erosion operating in tropical regions. The slopes always have the same angle of gradient, and their progressive retreat leaves these rounded rock masses isolated on a flat or gently rolling countryside.

The presence of savanna regions in the eastern African highlands is unusual. These regions lie astride the Equator or on high plateaux where temperatures are often below the typical averages of savanna regions.

Pedogenesis and morphogenesis

The results of the alternation of a dry and wet season are seen at the outset in pedogenesis, which stops during the dry season and is most active during the rainy one. Pedogenesis in these areas entails almost total leaching of the basic components of the soil, with the formation of kaolinite and the precipitation of less soluble constituents, particularly unhydrated haematite. The latter accumulates at the foot of slopes or underneath a light covering of clay, forming the typical shields of reddish lateritic crust that cannot support any vegetation. The only exceptions are the more persistent marshes and swamps, where black and fairly fertile soils, known as 'black cracking clays', are formed.

The most characteristic aspect of the morphological evolution of this climatic environment is the great power of erosion of run-off waters during the rainy season. The slopes affected by this run-off erosion are worn away evenly to produce large rounded relief structures such as 'sugar loaf mountains' or *inselbergs*. In the dry season rivers are reduced to a trickle or disappear completely; in the rainy season they become extremely swollen. The result is a reduced capacity for linear erosion, because of the presence of coarse material suspended in the running water. On the other hand, the enormous seasonal differences in transport capacity assist lateral erosion of the river bed.

137

The baobab is a typical tree of the African savanna landscape. Adaptation to a regime of one dry and one wet season is seen in the baobab's development of a reservoir system for storing water inside its wood. The root development of this tree, which is always large, is very extensive, being equivalent to the branch structure exposed to the air. This picture was taken during the dry season.

Vegetation

This falls into two categories, according to seasonal rainfall and the water content of the terrain: deciduous forest and savanna.

A herd of buffalo in a pond in Ceylon formed during the rainy season.

The deciduous forest region is situated at the outer edges of the equatorial belt, where the dry season is no longer than four or five months and the annual amount of rain exceeds sixty inches. As the dry season grows longer and rainfall diminishes away from the equator, the deciduous forest gives way to the savanna, except in strips bordering rivers, where a type of rain forest persists.

The savanna consists of graminaceous vegetation, the tallest being elephant grass (*Pennisetum benthamii*), which is up to fifteen feet high. Trees grow either singly or in small clusters; they are never very tall and leaf development is slight. Their trunks are usually very thick because of the formation of sponge tissues for storing water during the dry season. Typical of these are the baobab and the bottle tree, the latter growing in Australia. Other adaptations to drought conditions can be seen in the reduction of leaves to spines or scales, which grow sideways to present as small an area as possible to the sunlight (as in the case of the eucalyptus) and in the appearance of a waxy covering and secretion of oil to reduce evaporation. Umbrella acacias and *Euphorbiaceae* are also characteristic trees of the savanna. Vegetation can also take the form of low shrubs known as *dry forests*, which are spiny bushes with contorted branches growing along the ground.

Landscape of the monsoon areas

The typical monsoon area extends along the western coasts of the Deccan, Burma, and Malacca, along the eastern coasts of Indochina, over the great Ganges-Brahmaputra delta, and the northern Philippines. This area also has a year divided into two seasons, but the rainy one is much more concentrated than in the savanna, and rainfall levels can reach values recorded in rain forest regions. In these areas some of the highest levels of rainfall on the Earth are recorded; Cherrapunji, in Assam, had 475 inches in 1931. The monsoon area is also a forest region. The forest, known as *jungle*, differs from the rain forest only in the distribution of deciduous trees and vegetation, indicating a seasonal pause by the vegetation during the dry season. A typical spontaneous plant is the teak tree.

Unlike the rain forest region, the monsoon region provides a considerable quantity of vegetable products of great economic importance. Rice is the chief of these, a spontaneous graminaceous plant of the Ganges delta. Also grown are cotton, jute, camphor, and tea, which in its wild state grows on a tree about thirty feet high. The environment of the bushy and herbaceous savanna, being dryer, can grow certain cereals such as sorghum and millet, though only on a subsistence basis, and maize, which originated in Central America. Pineapple and tobacco are also grown; tobacco, which is a variety of the coffee plant, was discovered in Central America and introduced to Europe in 1559.

Fauna

The fauna of both the savanna and the monsoon zones consists mainly of *ungulates*, such as giraffes, zebras, various species of antelopes, and buffalo. Elephants, rhinoceroses, and (near water) hippopotami roam through the tall grass, and lions and tigers are also found in these regions. Reptiles are also numerous and spend the dry season in a state of lethargy. Birds include birds of prey, some non-flying species such as the ostrich, and, in the marshes, many waders. The countless species of insects include termites and locusts, the latter being extremely damaging to local agriculture.

Above: Rice paddies near Madras in December. Although rainfall in monsoon regions is very high, the growth of vegetation is determined more by the alternation of dry and wet seasons. Rice is the most widespread of the many plants of economic importance that grow in these regions. *Below:* A herd of gnu grazing in the huge crater of Ngorongoro, in Tanzania. The crater's rim protects the hollow from masses of humid air during the rainy season, thus weather in the crater is always warm and dry, and this has led to the creation of steppe land with ample room for a large number of herbivorous and carnivorous animals typical of African landscapes with two seasons. The inside of the crater's rim is covered with vegetation typical of the savanna (the other side is covered with rain forest vegetation). The picture was taken in June in the rainy season. It shows the masses of clouds that hang over the rim without penetrating the inner area.

LANDSCAPE OF ARID REGIONS

The most noticeable external feature of the arid regions is the periodic disappearance of vegetation caused by the extremely low rainfall, or the rapid evaporation of any moisture in the ground.

The arid regions have two well-defined environments: the tropical environment, affected by the subtropical anticyclonic cells and forming warm deserts and pre-deserts in which frost is rare during the winter season; and the temperate environment, which forms cold deserts and pre-deserts in which frost is normal during the winter season. In tropical regions rainfall of the order of 20–25 inches a year is not enough to provide continuous vegetation. In temperate zones, however, eight inches may be enough for vegetation to grow even on slopes with a small angle of gradient. In both cases wind is an extremely important climatic factor. The term *pre-desert* denotes an area in which vegetation, though not continuous, is enough to be a key component of the landscape. Pre-deserts are usually classed as steppes, though as well as having continuous vegetation the steppe is also subject to a vegetative cycle with two periods of pause, while pre-deserts have only one.

Climatic characteristics

The warm deserts are the hottest regions on the Earth (Azizia, in Libya, 58°C; Death Valley, California, 56.6°C in the shade). At noon the temperature in the Sun can reach 70°C. This is one of the effects of the dry air and cloudless skies, which favour insolation and at the same time permit the rapid loss of heat by the ground after the Sun sets, which causes the very marked diurnal variation of up to 40°C. Annual variation is of the order of 20°C inland and less than 7°C in the coastal zones not affected by strong or constant winds. Average annual rainfall figures have no real significance, since precipitation is extremely irregular. In some areas of the desert there may be no rain at all for a period of years; for instance, some parts of the northern Chilean desert receive no rain for twenty years or more. Other deserts may have torrential rainfall, as in the Thar desert in north-west India, where the annual average is five inches, but where thirty inches can fall in two days.

The cold deserts and pre-deserts show the same general climatic characteristics as the warm ones, but on a smaller quantitative scale. There is one clearly defined cold season in both hemispheres, but seasonal temperature fluctuations are much higher in the cold deserts of the northern hemisphere: for example, Ulan Bator in Mongolia, at an altitude of 3,750 feet, has 17°C in July and –28°C in January, while Santa Cruz in Argentina has 15.3°C in January and 5.4°C in July.

In the cold arid zones average annual precipitation figures have more significance because of the greater regularity of rainfall: eight inches a year is the most common annual average. The equatorial limit of the hot arid zones can be set generally at the 18-inch isohyet, while for the cold arid zones of Eurasia it is the 12-inch and in America the 16-inch isohyet. The arid regions cover about 26% of dry-land surface area of the Earth.

Geographic distribution

Warm deserts and pre-deserts are situated chiefly along the western coastlines of continents which are subjected alternately to the seasonal action of the trade winds and the subtropical anti-

cyclones. The Earth's greatest desert is the Sahara in Africa, which covers an area of three million square miles. It is bordered roughly by the 18th parallel in the south and runs from the Atlantic coast to the Red Sea, interrupted only by the narrow strip of the Nile valley. It continues under a different name across the Arabian peninsula, through a large part of Iraq, the southern part of the Iranian plateau, and the great plain of the Indus (the Thar desert). This is the Earth's most extensive and homogeneous desert belt. Also in Africa the coast of Angola as far as Benguela is an arid zone, as are the Kalahari desert in south-western Africa and the Eritrean and Somali coastal regions.

In North America arid zones cover a large part of central and southern California, and the basins of the Colorado River and the Rio Grande. In South America the warm deserts and pre-deserts extend along the Pacific coast from Guayaquil down to Peru, and as far as Coquimbo in Chile. On the landward side of the Andes the deserts cover the area between the Salado and Colorado rivers in Argentina. The Great Australian Desert stretches from the Murray River basin to the Indian Ocean.

Cold deserts are normally situated well inland; where they are near oceans they are placed in a mountain basin inaccessible to ocean winds. Asia has the most extensive zone of continuous cold aridity. This runs from Anatolia and covers the Aral-Caspian depression and Iran, and goes as far as the border of Manchuria. Turkestan, Tarim, and the Gobi are its greatest desert areas. Patagonia is the only cold desert area of South America.

Pedogenesis and morphogenesis

The climatic conditions in arid zones reduce or eliminate the possibility of any soil formation. Salt precipitations such as sodium, boron, and potassium are the only substances that can be dissolved during the rare rainfall and they are present in the form of crusts on the surface of the ground. They are totally absent from true deserts, and are found only in pre-deserts.

The chemical and mechanical disintegration of rock manifests itself as flaking and by the transformation of the rocks into sand in regions with high temperatures and low humidity. The rocks also have a characteristic black varnish, the colour of which is due to manganese oxide, which was formed by the action of lichens which apparently became extinct 5,000 years ago.

The erg north of Fort Flatters, in the Sahara, with its characteristic hillocks formed by clay modelled and polished by the wind-borne sands.

The particular morphological characteristics of deserts and pre-deserts can be listed as follows:

a) Large surface areas with longitudinal gradients of between 1° and 5° and transverse ones of nil. They are the typical escarpments cut out of rocks that tend to break up into sand, and are called *pediplains*. The character of this land is stressed by the absence of any rolling ground.

b) Residual relief structures (inselbergs, 'sugar loaf' mountains, etc.), which are very common because of the efficacy of erosion.

In sub-desert areas, precipitation causes the formation of a layer about eight inches thick, known as *sheet-flood*, which becomes rapidly laden with fine detritus and then becomes a mud flow capable of transporting rocks up to eight inches in diameter. These flows end up in a *wadi*, a temporary torrent that runs through a variable gulley with a wide rocky bed.

Wind action

In true deserts the wind is the basic morphogenetic element. It shapes the terrain in three ways. The first, *abrasion*, is the bom-

Erosion in the Guadalupe Mountains, in Texas, which are situated in the State's western desert area.

bardment of rock surfaces with particles of sand carried in suspension by the winds. Abrasion attacks clay surfaces, shaping them into hillocks or gulleys with parallel but unstable crests. Wind action also produces gently concave surfaces on rock masses.

The second is *deflation*, which is the transport of material less than about half an inch in diameter. This results in selection of detritus, and a layer of pebbles (sometimes called *reg*) is left on the ground. Deflation can also form hollows of various dimensions in the ground, caused by the disintegration of rock surfaces periodically moistened by rain and dew and by flanking. These hollows have highly saline mud (*playa* or *bahada*) at their bottoms.

The third way in which the wind shapes the terrain is *accumulation*. This forms dunes (*erg*) in areas where the sand is very fine and loose, and shapeless accumulations in areas where there is a partial cover of vegetation. Dunes are crescent-shaped or longitudinal; in cross-section they have a gently sloping side to windward and a steep side to leeward. The crescent-shaped structures are formed by the wind blowing round the edges of the dunes, where it meets less resistance than at the centre, so causing them to move. Longitudinal dunes, typical of the Great Australian Desert, and also found in the Sahara, are believed to be caused by a wind blowing on compact sand masses. One theory is that the wind scoops out long gaps between sections of the sand to form valleys lined by long, almost uninterrupted, chains of dunes; these are a useful route for desert caravans. Another theory attributes longitudinal dunes to the combined action of a low-intensity prevailing wind and an occasional wind of greater intensity.

Vegetation

The opportunity for the development of vegetation in arid regions is conditioned by the size of the surface material (though vegetation can take root inside the cracks of rocks) and the system of rainfall. Vegetation, if it grows, will adapt itself to the prevailing conditions. Generally, in areas where rainfall lasts for at least several weeks of the year, the absorption of water is relatively deep, and it stays in the ground for some time. In these

Top: A residual structure in the flat landscape of the Mauritanian desert. *Above:* An inselberg of granitic rock in the Sahara, with visible signs of intense abrasion caused by wind-blown sand. *Below:* The curious needle-rocks of Sisse, in the Tibesti Massif of northern Chad. These are the remains of a relief structure that was destroyed in past geological times when the local climate was different from today's. The rocks were modelled by the characteristic action of desert erosion.

An erg in Mauritania. In this vast region of the Sahara the wind builds crescent-shaped dunes, which move from 15 to 50 feet a year. Their shape is due to the action of the wind blowing round the edges. The windward slope is gentle and is subject to erosion, which is weakest at the centre.

areas permanent xerophytes such as the *saxoul* are the chief plants. These are the leafless trees found in the pre-deserts of the Aral-Caspian regions, with their branches and trunks contorted into bizarre shapes. Species of *Artemisia* (wormwood, sage-brush, mugwort), which have small deciduous leaves, are also found. All the plants have very deep roots to enable them to reach water.

In areas where the moisture is close to the surface of the ground, plants develop a mass of surface roots, or have a reservoir capacity of hundreds of gallons, as in certain cacti. These plants can also stand temperatures from 15° to 20° above that which would kill off any others.

In fine-grained, well-drained soils considerable quantities of hard graminaceous plants (*Stipa tenacissima*) grow, or dicotyledons such as the broom, as in the sandy regions of the Sahara, the Great Australian Desert, and Argentina. Rainfall of 15–20 inches a year enables the *Spinifex* genus to thrive, spiny shrubs represented mainly by acacias and mimosas which grow in a relatively continuous covering in the Australian desert.

Adaptation to environmental conditions involves the reduction of foliage to small scales or spines. Leaves present their edges to the sky to reduce the surface of evaporation. They also produce oily or waxy secretions to prevent excessive transpiration. Herbaceous and some bushy plants usually disappear during the dry season, though their roots stay alive.

The number of plants which can provide food for man is very small. The chief one is the date-palm, a native of the hot deserts of Asia. There are also some graminaceous plants such as esparto grass, used in the manufacture of good-quality paper.

Above: A caravan of camels owned by Ghilzai nomads in the pre-desert regions of southern Afghanistan, on the border of the Registan desert. The soil has a few sparse artemisia shrubs, one of the plants best adapted to arid conditions. Left: The common yucca (Joshua tree), a characteristic liliacea that grows in the Arizona desert. Far left: Some desert lizards become inert below a temperature of about 15° C. The two shown here are the *Uromastix hardwickii* of north-western India. Below: Spiny shrubs in the Mojave desert in south-eastern California. These plants adapt themselves to desert conditions by growing scaly or spiny leaves which reduce transpiration. They also have very far-ranging roots to catch all the available moisture. This type of structure also helps the plant to withstand wind erosion of the soil.

Fauna

Desert-dwelling animals show various forms of adaptation as a result of the scarcity of food and water, and exposure to intense heat in zones without shade.

Birds, reptiles, and some rodents have no sweat glands and excrete uric acid in crystals instead of urine to prevent loss of water. Many animals, including mammals such as gazelles and camels, replenish their water supply from moisture contained in food or produce it by their own metabolic processes, as do most of the insects. The camel can withstand a loss of 13% of the water contained in its bloodstream and an increase in its body temperature of up to 5° C.

However, the fauna of arid regions is poor. There are a few reptiles which spend most of the year in a state of lethargy, and some carnivores (coyotes, pumas, bears, cougars). The Asian desert also has many domestic animals, which include oxen, sheep, goats, horses, and camels.

SUBTROPICAL LANDSCAPES

The three sub-types

The term *subtropical* is used here mainly in a topographical sense to indicate those zones that are relatively close to the tropics, though it is inadequate to describe the climatic conditions and the landscape forms connected with them. In fact the milder aridity of these areas, which are affected peripherally by the permanent tropical anticyclones, is found in only one of the three sub-types into which the subtropical landscape can be divided – the *Mediterranean*. In the other two sub-types, the *Sinic* (Chinese) and the *Pampean*, the amount and regularity of rainfall are governed by conditions of atmospheric circulation outside those areas.

The three sub-types have four seasons in their climatic year (as do all the temperate regions), and a fairly standard annual average temperature of around 16° C. There are noticeable annual fluctuations, with summer temperatures rising above 25° C in the hottest month, and winter ones of about 8° C (somewhat lower in the Sinic zone), but always above zero.

The pause period in vegetation is also governed by average winter temperatures, unlike tropical zones, where seasonal temperature contrasts are slight and the pause depends on the system of rainfall alone. Another climatic element shared by the three sub-types is the variability of the weather. This is the zone where air masses from the poles and the tropics begin to come into contact with one another, so that the formation of fronts and disturbed areas is a fairly frequent phenomenon.

The Mediterranean sub-type

The climatic year of this sub-type is marked by the alternation of a cool season of the temperate oceanic type, with considerable rainfall and some days of frost, and a summer of an almost desert type, dry and with high temperatures. Average temperatures for the cool season are around 5° to 10° C; the summer ones are between 21° and 25° C. The amount of rainfall varies, according to location, from 15 to 25 inches a year, and snow is absent or very rare at low altitudes. Precipitation is concentrated in the winter season, and is intermittent. Clear periods are quite frequent and even in winter about half the days are clear. The summers are dry with clear skies, bright light, and high insolation. The characteristic warmth of the Mediterranean Sea, which maintains a temperature of 13° C, determines the formation of cyclonic cells during winter, resulting in convergences and very active fronts. Rainfall can be heavy, but during summer the tropical anticyclones bring about dry conditions.

Apart from the Mediterranean area, these climatic characteristics are also found in the Cape region of Africa, central Chile,

A citrus grove at the foot of Mount Etna in Sicily. The snow-capped summit of the volcano rises in sharp contrast to the typical Mediterranean landscape with its evergreen vegetation, orange trees, and cypresses. The picture was taken in March, the month marking the end of the rainy season.

central California and its southern coast, and southern Australia – areas covering about a seventh of the Earth's dry land area.

Summer evaporation continues for several months and acts in such a way that the soil can conserve only capillary water in its deeper horizons. Only rivers with drainage areas of several thousands of square miles and with terrain rising to at least 1,500 feet can maintain a flow of water throughout the year. Many rivers dry up completely during the summer, but the concentration and violence of winter rainfall may turn them suddenly into torrents.

The long summer period of evaporation hampers the growth of vegetation with short roots and the development and yield of various plants. As a result, there is a scarcity of humus (which in any case decomposes rapidly because of the heat) and a serious and constant tendency for soils to be eroded by run-off, since any protection afforded by vegetation is hazardous and temporary. The most typical soil is the *terra rossa*, formed by dehydration of the terrain over a long period, followed by precipitation of iron hydroxides.

Lower slopes are more or less immune to the processes of disintegration, but when higher forms of vegetation become established, chemical disintegration increases. Run-off assumes an important role in transporting materials. Water-courses, because of their periodic flooding, have an extremely high capacity for linear erosion, and in areas where the lithological structure is not too compact, their beds become planes of erosion and accumulation.

Vegetation consists basically of a typical forest formation with

Right: The Bay of Monterey at the centre of California's Mediterranean area. In the foreground stands a typical cypress of the region, a tree that can withstand salinity and is used to afforest coastal areas. *Above:* Gigantic cacti are common in the chaparral, a shrubland found in semi-arid regions of the south-western United States and extending also into southern California.

trees of medium size having permanent leaves which are thick and small. They are mainly evergreen and show marked signs of *xerophilous* adaptation – that is, capacity to survive conditions of drought. The characteristic shrubland is known in Spain as *tomilla*, in Italy as *macchia*, and in France as *maquis*. Being a reduced form of vegetation, it is replaced at its limits by woody labiates such as thyme, lavender, and sage: all of which are *suffruticose* (shrubby) and aromatic plants.

Types of vegetation vary from region to region. In the Mediterranean area the characteristic tree is the olive, a native of Lebanon; with it are found evergreen oaks, the umbrella-pine (*Pinus mediterranea*), the cypress, and numerous other fruit trees including the fig and almond. Shrubs include the wild olive, the laurel, myrtle, prickly oak, and juniper, as well as a number of labiates and *Ericaceae*. Growing on higher ground are rhododendrons, azaleas and box-trees in bushy thickets, and in the shrubland of the East, *Orchidaceae*, camellias, and wistaria.

Another typical plant is the vine, a native of the Caucasus, while the various *Rutaceae* of the citrus genus (comprising lemon, orange, lime, and mandarin) are all natives of tropical Asia, only fairly recently common in irrigated zones of the Mediterranean. Besides these plants, the Cape of Good Hope region also has *Protaceae* with furry leaves in its shrubland. California has bushy *Ericaceae* and *Rosaceae* associated with trees of the oak genus, all with evergreen foliage and known as chaparral, and, in the dryer regions, thickets of mimosa associated with cypresses. Central Chile, being a transitional zone between the desert climate in the north and the oceanic one in the south, has a shrubland consisting mainly of prickly bushes. The vegetative cycle of most of the plants, except the cacti and *Bromeliaceae*, stops during the dry season.

Far left: The pines of Aleppo, a typical variety found in the Mediterranean, provide a backcloth for the ruins of ancient Olympia in the Peloponnesus. The sun, the wonderful climate, the close links between land and sea, and the varied and animated morphology combine to give a picture of the Mediterranean that is typically Greek and has become an inseparable part of an unmistakable civilization. *Left:* In the Mediterranean area, waterways are usually torrential because of sudden and violent flooding; they have a powerful erosive action on slopes. The picture illustrates the effect of this erosion in the mountains of Epirus.

147

Above: A landscape on the island of Shikoku, Japan, with terraced rice paddies laid out round a village and natural vegetation growing on the upper slopes of the hill. *Below:* An autumn view of the Arkansas River. The climates of both the Mexican Gulf area of North America and of Japan are regulated by humid tropical air masses in summer and cold, dry continental air masses in winter.

Australian vegetation has unique characteristics because of the processes undergone by the climate during the Quaternary, and the isolation from the conditions of the other continents. In Australia's Mediterranean climate area the prevailing plant is a myrtacea of the *Eucalyptus* genus. Some varieties of this, such as the *karri* of the south-western region, reach heights of two hundred feet. The trees are set far apart and the leaves grow with their edges uppermost, forming forests that cast little shade.

Economically, the Mediterranean region's most important forms of vegetation are corn, which originated in southern Syria and Palestine; flax, which once provided the raw material for cloth worn by the region's ancient peoples; and hemp, which came to the region from central Asia.

The Sinic sub-type

The Sinic sub-type is distinguished from the Mediterranean by its greater annual temperature variation, the result of the fairly low winter values. In China and Japan temperatures average 2° to 3° C, resulting in fairly frequent, though brief, periods of frost. Summer temperatures are slightly higher than in the Mediterranean sub-type, reaching 26° C in July. The amount and regime of rainfall are also different. The Sino-Japanese area (like the south-eastern area of North America and the Gulf of Mexico, which are two other aspects of this sub-type) is affected seasonally by humid tropical air masses in summer and polar air masses in winter. As a result, the rainy season is in summer rather than winter, and precipitation is high; from 38 to 58 inches a year, with minima occurring in September and October in America.

The resemblance to tropical soils, which exists in the Mediterranean sub-type, is more marked in the Sinic sub-type with its argillaceous soils. The terra rossa is mainly fine-grained and in it dehydrated iron hydroxides are found, together with clays in the form of kaolinite. There is extreme leaching of the soil's upper horizons.

Linear erosion by water and accumulation of alluvial detritus, much greater than in the Mediterranean sub-type, cause rivers to alter their course, and the obstacles presented by heavy deposition form river-beds of considerable width.

Vegetation presents many complex forms as a result of the high humidity and the climatic hybridism. Coniferous and highly hygrophilous, deciduous, broad-leaf forests grow beside plants that show signs of xerophilous adaptation. The bamboo can be regarded as the basic plant of the Sino-Japanese area, but magnolias and some *Lauraceae* (cinnamon, camphor, and cryptomeria) are also common. The sub-forest is rich in *Orchidaceae*, wistaria, *Cameliaceae*, and many epiphytes. In the American area, pines and cypresses predominate, and oaks, magnolias and cedars are also found.

The pampean sub-type

This is found only in the southern hemisphere. From the climatic point of view there is an interesting relationship between the annual thermal conditions and the regime of precipitation which brings about a mantle of vegetation that is quite different from that in the other two sub-types. Average summer temperatures are around 22° C, but winter ones stay at about 10° C, so that the area is warmer than the other two sub-types. Rainfall averages about 25 inches a year in Australia and South America. The maxima occur in summer, though the winter is not completely dry. In south America an important phenomenon is the *pampero*, a violent, dry south-westerly wind. Similar climatic conditions are present in the vast southern African plateau known as the *Hoogeveld* and are also found in the river basins of the Murray and the Murrumbidgee in south-eastern Australia.

The Paraná River, before it flows into the Uruguay, runs through territory almost bare of vegetation, which is the first sign of the vast pampean landscapes to come.

The characteristic aridity of this sub-type results in grassy vegetation, with only a few trees growing mainly by rivers. The South American area is the best-known example with its *pampas*, enclosed areas of graminaceous vegetation that merge into regions of sparse bushy thickets consisting of xerophilous shrubs. Arboreal forms as endemic species are relatively rare. In South America the characteristic tree is the ombu, and in the Australian area the eucalyptus associated with certain prickly acacias.

All subtropical areas are transitory ground for fauna, so that apes, bears, wolves, and boars can be found sharing the same territory. There are some highly characteristic forms of bird life, such as the Japanese heron, Chinese golden pheasants, and Californian peacocks and quails. Only the Australian fauna is radically different from that of other areas, because of the isolation of the continent; it includes marsupials and the *Ornithorhynchus*, species that have become extinct elsewhere.

A view of the pampas in the State of Buenos Aires. The subtropical areas in South America have less precipitation than those in the northern hemisphere.

LANDSCAPE OF OCEANIC CLIMATES

Climatic characteristics

The basic climatic element of this type of landscape is its maritime quality, determined by oceanic air masses brought to the continents by westerly winds. This climatic zone is thus located on the western coastal zones of continents from about latitude 40° towards the polar circles. Summer temperatures are never very high, averaging about 18° C, and fluctuations are on a reduced scale because of the high atmospheric humidity. There are brief spells of warmer weather when the passage of a temporary disturbance holds back oceanic air masses and replaces them with continental or tropical air masses. The low temperatures make growing cereals such as rice or corn difficult. Winter temperature averages between 3° and 7° C, and fairly lengthy spells of frost are not infrequent.

Precipitation is determined both by the high humidity of the atmosphere and by the orography. Where there is a predominance of flat land, as in western Europe, the amount of annual rainfall is little more than that in the southernmost regions of the Mediterranean – between 20 and 30 inches a year. Where coastal areas are rimmed by mountains, as in Norway, North America and Chile, the average is higher and sometimes exceeds 80 inches a year. Rainfall is evenly distributed throughout the seasons, with a slightly larger amount falling on coastal zones in winter. Snow falls for about 15 days a year on the plains, but does not lie for long because of the relatively high temperature.

The south-western sector is more affected by warm, humid ocean winds. Snow lies for only about four days in the year, but on higher

The coast of Pontevedra, near the north-western tip of the Iberian Peninsula, has an oceanic climate typical of coastal zones.

ground (the north American coastal chain, the southern Andes, the Scandinavian Alps, and New Zealand) snow can lie to a depth of 30 feet.

On the plains, precipitation is mainly cyclonic in origin, associated with the formation of large and persistent frontal zones.

The Rhine at Schaffhausen, in northern Switzerland. In Europe, oceanic climates are found deep inland because there are no obstacles to atmospheric circulation. In North and South America and in Oceania, oceanic climates are restricted mostly to the coastal zones.

Above: Scotland's Grampian Mountains and Rannoch Moor, a heather moor scattered with lakes and bogland. This is a typical oceanic-climate landscape, but is also influenced by polar air masses. Morphology, soil type, and vegetation are basically the result of glaciation during the Quaternary. *Right:* Deer in Bushey Park, near Hampton Court, by the River Thames, in England. Although the landscape has been taken in hand by man, this combination of deer, meadows, and large trees stands out as one of the most typical examples of an oceanic climate in the British Isles. *Below:* The giant sequoias that grow in the forests on the western slopes of the Sierra Nevada, California. The high precipitation of this part of the mountain chain exposed to oceanic influences makes possible the growth of this enormous coniferous tree, which represents one of the world's oldest forms of vegetation. Some sequoias are as much as 3,000 years old.

The development of weather is slow and cloudy conditions and rain last for long periods, but the amount of precipitation each day is limited.

Geographic distribution

The characteristics of this type of climate are present throughout the British Isles, and the Atlantic seaboard of the Iberian peninsula, France, Belgium, and the Netherlands, from the mouth of the Douro to that of the Rhine. The area extends into France as far as a line joining the western border of the Champagne district to the Massif Central, while the vegetation typical of this climate continues farther, reaching the Saône valley and the Moselle valley, as far to the north-east as Lübeck, and including all Jutland and the Norwegian coast as far as Trondheim.

In the North American area the climate is restricted to the coastal zone between California and the Queen Charlotte Islands. In South America the oceanic climate affects southern Chile, and in Oceania, Tasmania and New Zealand.

Pedogenesis and morphogenesis

The high humidity and relatively low temperatures cause severe, rapid biochemical changes in the terrain, but chemical decomposition and leaching processes are not as vigorous as in the humid tropical areas. Their effects are, however, just as far-reaching, because their action, not being frequently interrupted by pause periods, proceeds in a uniform and homogeneous pattern.

Humic soils derived from the decay of vegetation and peat are common. In zones nearer to the polar limits, erosion and accumulation by glaciers of the Quaternary have had a major effect in re-forming and re-orientating soils. Lean soils rich in rock detritus are common in Scotland and Scandinavia.

The greyish-brown soils certainly represent the best of this series and are those on which the primary mixed forest of evergreen and deciduous vegetation first took root. They support a rich and active agriculture producing a variety of crops.

Vegetation

The original vegetation of this area was a mixed forest of ever-green and deciduous plants with a prevalence of oaks, together with lindens, elms and beeches. The forests have been extensively removed in historical times by human settlement in these areas, which are now among the most densely populated in Europe. Coniferous trees chiefly occupied the western side of the highlands North of the 60th parallel.

By contrast, along the rainier North American coast a very rich forest of spontaneous growth still stands. In northern California the dominant tree is the famous *Sequoia gigantea*, which averages ten feet in trunk diameter and is the tallest tree known. It grows on the slopes of the coastal chain of the Rocky Mountains and gives way to pines and cedars in the internal zone of the forest. Farther north grows the Douglas fir, which provides the best working wood lumbered on the Pacific coast. It often grows with the Canadian red cedar.

On the South American coastal zone the forest is denser, but the trees are commercially less valuable. On moderately high ground evergreen broad-leaf trees grow, including a variety of beech. The undergrowth consists of heather and myrtle plants. Tasmania and New Zealand have evergreen beeches, broad-leaf conifers, eucalyptuses and a wealth of ferns which grow up to 40 feet high.

FOREST AND PRAIRIE LANDSCAPE OF TEMPERATE CONTINENTAL CLIMATES

Continental climate in a temperate zone

The basic characteristic of these landscapes is the continental type of climate, with its large temperature fluctuations. An area of dry land in a temperate region large enough to give rise to a continental element in the climate occurs only in the northern hemisphere between latitudes 40° and 65°. Continental air moves towards the eastern seaboard, so that the polar-maritime air mass has difficulty in reaching this zone, being diverted by westerly winds. Thus the influence of oceanic air masses on eastern continental coasts in the northern hemisphere is small. These coastal areas are also washed by cold currents, and temperatures and precipitation decrease gradually with distance away from the coastline and from south to north. As a result, the climate falls into two categories: a colder, drier northern zone, which is labelled sub-arctic, and a southern zone, which is further subdivided into two regions – the more southerly with a long, hot summer and the other with a long, dry winter.

The first of these subdivisions is the *Paduan-Danubian* sub-type, with the so-called *maize climate*, because this grain crop is best cultivated there. The second sub-type may be called *Sarmatic*, and has a *spring wheat climate*, so-called because the length of winter hampers the growth of other cereals.

Geographic distribution

In Europe this type of landscape occupies the upper Po valley and all the inner Balkan region where the rivers run down into the Danube, much of Poland, eastern Germany and southern Sweden.

In Asia, the areas affected are northern China and Korea, a narrow zone of mid-western Siberia on the 55th parallel, as well as

The White Mountains (New Hampshire), the northern section of the Appalachians. The relief structure, consisting of rounded ridges left by the Quaternary glaciation, has been covered by forests of broad-leaf trees and conifers. In spite of the proximity of the Atlantic Ocean, all New England is subject to a continental climate because of the general atmospheric circulation to the east and the influence of the cold Labrador current.

A panorama of the Monferrato hills near Alba, Italy. This region, like most of the Po valley, is subject to a continental climate with long hot summers and long periods during which air masses remain stationary. This produces clear blue skies, although storms make summer the wet season of the year. The length of the summer provides farmers with much scope for cultivation, as can be seen in the many cultivated rectangles planted with grain, forage crops, and fruit trees. The soil is basically calcareous, alternating with sands and clays.

south-eastern Siberia, mid-western Manchuria, and northern Japan.

In North America, it is located in the territory east of the 100th meridian as far as the Atlantic seaboard, between the 40th parallel and a line from latitude 50° North down to Lakes Winnipeg and Superior, and then up to Quebec. All these regions are in the spring wheat climate; those to the south are in the maize climate.

Characteristics of the Paduan-Danubian sub-type

The most salient feature of this sub-type is the long, hot, humid summer season. Average temperatures in the warmest month in Asia and North America range from about 25° to 27° C, and in Europe from 21° to 23° C. The humid air hampers cooling at night, so that daily temperature variations are negligible. The formation of cold fronts due to the meeting of tropical-maritime and polar-continental air masses can lead to sudden violent storms which reduce the temperature.

There is a two-hundred-day gap between frost periods. The only long season is the summer, which is warm and favourable to agriculture. Winter is marked by frequent and sudden changes in the weather and temperatures can be as low as −4.5° C. Warm winter temperatures are often accompanied by cloud, humidity and fog.

Precipitation averages about fifty inches a year, but dry years are not uncommon, and have been responsible for some of China's great famines. Rainfall is a summer phenomenon, being caused almost everywhere by convection currents. The rainfall is heavy

and squally, followed by long clear periods. As a result, although summer is the rainy season, it has more fine, clear days than the winter dry season. The winter is also the dry season in eastern Europe and the mid-eastern United States. Japan and Korea, however, are affected by the winter monsoon.

Slightly less than half the winter precipitation is snow. Snowfall is associated with cyclonic conditions so that the number of snowy days (from 20 to 30 a year) and the duration of the snow-covering (from 10 days in the south to 60 days in the north) as well as its thickness are all limited.

Characteristics of the Sarmatic sub-type

The Sarmatic sub-type has a particularly short summer; because of the high latitudes, it is also a cool one. Average temperatures in the warmest month range from 18° to 21° C, with considerable variations from region to region. Warm and cool periods alternate, owing to polar-continental air masses, and temperatures reach 30° C. The greatest temperature fluctuations occur in the Asian region. This is also true of winter temperatures: the Asian and American areas have winter averages of −10° to −20° C in the coldest month, while in Europe the average is around 0° C or a little below. The winter is the longest season in all the regions.

Because of the prevalence of polar-continental air masses the winter is dry. Formations of fronts lead to precipitation, mainly snow. The thickness of the snow cover is about 40 to 60 inches.

The Danubian-type landscape shows less sign of human settlement than the Paduan. The left-hand picture is of a hill in the Morava valley in Serbia. Trees are few, not only because of man's activity, but also as a result of soil conditions. A field of oats grows at the foot of the hill. Sown in spring, it was already ripe by June, when the picture was taken. The right-hand picture shows the region south of Poznan, Poland. The low hills with their gentle slopes are covered in loess, fine-grained clays left after glaciation and carried by the wind, making the terrain highly fertile. Agriculture has taken full advantage of this, and only the tops of the hills have any natural vegetation left. The continental climate, with its severe winter, makes it possible to cultivate only spring wheat, which is here, in September, seen ripened and partly harvested.

It snows for 60 to 80 days a year, and snow lies for about 120 days.

Most precipitation falls in the short summer. The annual average is low – 20–30 inches. It is lower in the American and Asian areas than in Europe, which is open to the westerly maritime air masses. Squalls are not as frequent as in the Paduan-Danubian regions, because precipitation is caused by fronts, rather than local convective currents.

Pedogenesis and morphogenesis

The variety of local climatic, morphological, and pedological conditions brings about an alternation of forest and prairie. From a purely climatic point of view, prairies indicate rainfall of less than 20 inches a year, falling mainly during long hot summers, which are followed by a brief severe winter. But in the immense American and Eurasian plains herbaceous vegetation develops more easily than arboreal forms because the terrain, composed of alluvial, aeolian, or glacial soil, is more favourable for the former.

The formation of the forest soil is marked by the relative slowness with which parent rocks disintegrate. Only the mechanical action of roots has any effect on fissured or schistose rocks. Leaching is on a moderate scale, occurring mainly in the winter. The humus formed is less acid than the podsols and also less rich in calcium than rendzinas. The formation of the humus is helped by the high summer temperatures, enabling considerable bacterial activity to take place together with a large mobilization of nitrogen.

Clay formation is pronounced, and iron precipitates in small formations of limonite that give a brown colouring to the soil. The dehydrated oxides of the terra rossa do not appear. Calcareous parent rocks form brown fine-grained soils, rich in clay, silica, and colloidal iron, highly plastic and impermeable. On crystalline and silica rocks rich soils are formed through permeable concretions of limonite and silica.

The transport of material in solution is negligible, and run-off is important only in winter or after a particularly rainy period. Solifluxion has a greater effect, especially on the brown fine-grained soils and in winter, and on movements of large detritus. Taken as a whole this climatic area cannot present any pronounced curves in its morphological profile as it evolves. The end result is always peneplanation.

In the prairies, pedogenesis results in fertile, dark soils, at the other end of the scale to the podsols. There are two stages of evolution: neutral soils rich in humus, potassium, and phosphates, known in America as *prairie soils*, and the chernozema, which are more widespread, covering the Eurasian plains between south-eastern Russia and south-western Siberia, as well as part of southern Siberia and northern Manchuria. In North America they cover the plains of Saskatchewan and Alberta, and south Texas.

The forests

The broad-leaf, deciduous forest develops and flourishes because the supply of water is assured by the even distribution of rainfall throughout the seasons and by the arrival of rain brought by tropical-maritime air masses.

The species represented in the forests of these regions are relatively few, and are usually dominated by one tree which gives the forest its name, such as beechwood. The forest has plenty of light because the trees are set far apart and there is no great undergrowth.

The most common trees are the beech (found in the cooler

regions), the chestnut, and the oak (more common in the warmer regions). Others include the birch, hornbeam, alder, hazel, maple, ash, walnut, elm, and linden. Poplars and willows grow near rivers or where there is plentiful supply of water. An important tree in the American area is the hickory, valued for its hard, elastic and waterproof wood. The climate associated with the Paduan-Danubian zone is known in America as the *oak-maple-hickory climate*, because of the spread of these three trees. Climbing plants of this area include the hop, convolvulus, ivy, and wild vine.

A greatly limiting factor on fauna is the winter frost, which leads to the almost complete absence of reptiles and amphibians. Several animals adapt by developing fatty tissues (as with some rodents), storing winter provisions (squirrels and ants), or hibernating (moles, marmots, bears, etc.). Most birds migrate in winter because food is difficult to find.

The prairies

The absence of arboreal forms from prairies is due partly to the stratification of the soil into a moist upper layer, an intermediate dry one, and a deeper one in which the moisture reappears and which contains the underground water. Only the autumn rains are capable of soaking into all the layers of the soil. Winter precipitation occurs mainly as snow, and summer rain is almost totally absorbed by the roots or by evaporation. The spring thaw is wasted in run-off at the surface, because the lower layers are still frozen and thus impermeable. The underground water deposits are too deep to irrigate the upper levels through capillary action. In these conditions only herbaceous vegetation with root systems more extended at the surface than at depth can develop.

A temperate-continental forest, showing its variety of vegetation highlighted by the various colours of the leaves in autumn.

The prairie consists of perennial graminaceous plants, with bulbous roots which develop each spring. Colours are varied in the flowering season, but during the pause period at the end of the

Elk in the Lama valley (Wyoming) east of the Yellowstone National Park. The snow-mantle during the long winter in this region of the Rocky Mountains covers the prairies, which here alternate with strips of forest. The existence of animals like the elk inside the restricted areas of national parks is assured by emergency winter supplies of forage provided by man.

Cattle round a well in the Kansas prairie, the westernmost part of which lies in the Rocky Mountains and becomes an arid steppe area. The absence of trees over vast tracts of continental regions is basically due to particular characteristics of the soil, created by a climate that has a hard, dry winter. Any rainfall always stays on the surface of the ground and is absorbed by graminaceous plants with roots that do not grow very deep. Only autumn rainfall succeeds in soaking into the ground to any great depth. In winter, the upper and lower soil levels are separated by a frozen intermediate layer which is impermeable. Cattlemen obtain water supplies by sinking wells into underground water deposits.

summer the prairie has a desolate brown appearance due to the decrease of rain and the persistence of relatively high temperatures, which dry up the surface layers of the soil.

The fauna of the prairie adapts the rhythm of its annual biological cycle to that of the vegetation. Most of the animals take refuge in underground lairs once the vegetation dries up. Herbivorous rodents form the largest group of animals (75% in the Sarmatic grasslands), and consume about half of the available grass. The spring sees myriads of insects reach their adult stage. Their vast numbers are soon reduced by insect-eating mammals and birds. The wide open spaces are a good hunting ground for beasts of prey and large, fast-moving mammals. In winter they migrate in great herds towards the forest or the more arid, but persistent, pastures of the south.

THE SUBARCTIC LANDSCAPE OF THE TAIGA

Climatic characteristics

The subarctic climate, characteristic of areas covered by the great coniferous forests, is described by the Yakut term *taiga*. This extends between 50°–55° and 65° North. In Lapland, Canada, and Siberia it sometimes extends as far as latitude 70°. Only the northern hemisphere is affected by it.

The northern limit of the subarctic climate corresponds to the 10° C isotherm of July, which follows the northern limit of arboreal vegetation. Its characteristics are a long winter and brief intervening seasons. Summer temperatures are variable, ranging from 14° to 19° C as an average for the warmest month. But this variability is small compared with the fluctuations in winter, which can be as high as freezing point on the Atlantic coasts and as low as −50° C in Verkhoyansk in the heart of continental Siberia. There is a warm season of 50 to 75 days, with temperatures always above zero, from June to the middle of August, but polar air masses can produce sudden frosts.

The duration of sunlight in June reaches 18 hours at 60° and 22 hours at 65°. The length of twilight is also considerable. Daylight persists until the Sun is 18° beneath the horizon, so that in the northernmost sectors of the region there is enough light to read by at midnight.

Winter is the dominant season, and arrives suddenly after a fleeting autumn. In August, temperatures go down to below zero; rivers begin to freeze in September. Navigation on Canada's subarctic lakes becomes difficult by October. The constant frost lasts for seven months; from December to March, in the most continental territories, temperatures several tens of degrees below zero are normal. It is the severe winter that is responsible for the great annual temperature variations, which are never less than 23° C and are sometimes greater than 65° C. The long days of summer are matched by the long nights in winter: at latitude 60° the day

Taiga. A view in summer of a landscape in Alberta, Canada, with Mount Eisenhower in the distance. The conifers extend to about 6,500 feet.

Fir logs in the Finnish taiga ready to be floated downstream when the ice melts. In subarctic countries, coniferous forests are one of the few economic resources.

to a depth of three feet, and the melting waters have a considerable leaching effect. The decay of organic matter is limited owing to the lack of bacterial activity at low temperatures. As a result an acid humus is formed, which contributes to the separation at depth of calcium from hydrated oxides of iron and aluminium. This is the process of *podsolization*, which occurs with greater effect on gentle gradients (between 5° and 10°).

The podsols are characteristic of these cold regions and are the poorest of the agricultural soils. Demineralization due to leaching gives them their grey ashen colour and creates a deep horizon – known as the *B horizon* – where all the minerals gather from the upper layers. The local vegetation has adapted to this structure by developing a twin system of roots: the upper roots exploit the top humus layer and the lower roots reach the B horizon. The sharp-pointed leaves of the trees have a spread up to three times greater than broad leaves and live for longer than a year.

lasts only 5¾ hours; at latitude 65°, 3½ hours. The severe cold is bearable because most winter days are fine and clear with no wind, and the air is dry.

Precipitation is low because of the low humidity of the air, the width of the continental areas involved, and the high pressure of the anticyclones, which cause winds to blow away from the interior of the continental area towards the oceans. Annual precipitation is about 15 inches in the internal zones and 20 inches in the outer regions. Precipitation is concentrated in the summer season: for example, in Siberia, summer precipitation is 58% of the total, winter only 10%. Precipitation is accompanied by storms (five to ten a year); in winter they occur as snowstorms. Snow lies for up to seven months, and to a depth of 35 inches.

Pedogenesis and morphogenesis

Soil-formation processes resume after the thaw. The alternation of thaw and frost throughout the day causes an intense process of disintegration in rocks. The thaw eventually affects the soil down

The taiga

The coniferous forest is by no means uniform throughout the whole zone, and as the climate becomes more severe northwards, trees become smaller and grow farther apart. In contrast to the equatorial forest, that of the taiga is made up of far fewer species of trees. About 75% of them are needle-bearing; the rest are birches, poplars, willows, and alders. The dominant tree is the fir, spruce, or pine, according to the region.

Undergrowth is poor and sparse because of the perpetual shade, and consists of a few herbaceous plants with small roots, and woody bushes with long roots – junipers and myrtles, where there is enough light; in the darker regions only lichens, mosses, and some fungi are to be found.

The taiga is the region of the otter, ermine, mink, pole-cat, marten, Arctic hare, beaver, and sable. Reindeer, elk, and caribou with their enemies – the bear, the wolf – are the most conspicuous forms of fauna. There are numerous insects but they are active only in the warm season.

Autumn in the forests of the Canadian North (Yukon). The colour is due to the leaves of the birch, a typical tree of the subarctic region which grows among conifers. The vast forest area is crossed by the Alaska Highway, which joins Alaska with Canada.

The Haines Highway, marking the border between Canada and the southern part of Alaska. Although this region is 7° below the Arctic Circle, its altitude gives it all the Arctic characteristics, with temperatures in summer (when the picture was taken) not rising above 10° C and with long, hard winters. Vegetation consists of short trees, bushes, mosses, and lichens. Thaw and frost are responsible for modelling the landscape, as can be seen by the slopes in the foreground. The characteristic shape of the mountain in the left background is due to glacial action.

THE POLAR LANDSCAPE OF THE TUNDRA

Climatic characteristics

Regions with the temperature of their warmest month lower than 10° C are regarded as having a *polar climate*. These are mostly located inside the polar circles, so that their climatic characteristics are influenced by the duration of the polar day and night. At the polar circle the period of sunlight varies from 24 hours at the summer solstice to zero at the winter solstice. The prolonged absence of insolation (and this is also true of its prolonged presence, but for a different reason) brings about a continuous loss of heat from the ground, so that the year's lowest temperatures are reached just before the vernal equinoxes (21 March in the northern hemisphere and 23 September in the southern).

The 0° C isotherm for the warmest month marks the limit between two sub-types of landscape: the tundra and the glacial. The latter is determined by the permanent presence of ice, and has been described in an earlier section.

Temperatures in the warmest month range from 0° to 10° C. Two of the four summer months may register temperatures below zero, with consequent frost. Fog is common along coastal areas, and can last for several days. Summer temperatures in the tundra vary little from region to region, but winter ones show considerable variations: for example, in the Siberian tundra they are about –37° to –40° C far from coastal areas, while in the American zone they are –27° C along coasts and –32° C in the interior. The duration of frost is never less than nine months anywhere.

Precipitation is between ten and twelve inches a year and is concentrated in the short autumn and summer seasons as rain or sleet. In winter, precipitation takes the form of fine needles of snow, which fall in a dense, dry drizzle like grains of dust. It has been calculated that from 75% to 90% of the tundra regions are free of snow-cover throughout the year.

Winter weather exhibits noticeable variations. In some years, because of the prevalence of high-pressure conditions, the weather is clear and calm and very cold; in others severe cyclonic disturbances accompanied by violent storms occur.

Spring appears suddenly and lasts only a few days. Autumn is longer and perhaps the worst season because of the high humidity

The tundra landscape often merges with that of the ice regions in the north. In the fjords of Greenland, where the tundra is the only form of vegetation, projections of ice break away and form icebergs. (Picture taken in summer.)

The coast of Greenland along the Igaliko fjord, with the tundra and the meadows covered in their summer verdure. The funeral monument is a relic of the Vikings.

of the cold air. The intermediate seasons are the stormiest. Summer is more settled, with cloudy skies and mists.

The tundra landscape is almost exclusively characteristic of regions inside the Arctic Circle washed by the Arctic Ocean, including part of Iceland, stretches of the Greenland coast, and many islands ringing Antarctica.

Pedogenesis and morphogenesis

Soil formation is promoted by the disintegration of rocks through the action of ice. Generally, tundra regions are covered in a layer of glacial detritus, each fragment being about four inches.

The most evolved forms of soil have a very thin upper layer of humus that is decomposed only to a limited extent; a sub-layer of about four inches of grey soil, not altered into a full podsol though completely leached; and a deep layer of greyish-blue soil, which is semi-fluid during the warm season and increases in volume during frost, producing the small periglacial reliefs known as *pingos*.

The modelling depends on the effectiveness of glacial action. The most common form is the gentle slope with few gullies or traces of linear erosion. The profile of gradients is rectilinear, in accordance with the uniform size of the detritus which shows signs of progressive dislocation caused almost entirely by solifluxion. Run-off,

though not altogether absent during the warm season, has only a negligible effect because of the low precipitation. The detritus appears to undergo a reduction in size to enable it to move down even gentle slopes. This leaves the upper slopes open to further ice action and a process of demolition that leads to peneplanation.

Vegetation and fauna

Vegetation as a whole is very poor. Much of the area is covered in a thin carpet of mosses and lichens interspersed, when conditions allow, with heather or graminaceous vegetation and with dicotyledons or thickets of dwarf willows and birches (which form the arboreal vegetation of the tundra and are never taller than three feet). The season is very short, and does not enable the plants to go through their whole cycle. Some small woody plants on the heathlands, such as the rhododendron, keep their leaves for several years; and nanism is another form of adaptation to the severe temperatures. Another reason for the poor vegetation is the low quality of the soil, which is lacking in essential nutritive matter such as nitrogen.

The most decisive factor against vegetable growth is the aridity of the terrain, which is perpetually frozen at depth and thaws out only for six to twenty inches near the surface for about two months; in coastal areas, soil temperature is never higher than 5° C.

Where the ground is permanently frozen deep down, sparse woody bushes grow; on moderately exposed slopes facing South that are not too dry or humid, there are brief stretches of prairie lands with graminaceous vegetation and dicotyledons; on steeper slopes with poor soil that is arid by the end of the summer, only lichens grow; on gentler slopes where water has the chance of soaking into the soil, sedge and peat bogs develop. On northern slopes the lateness of the thaw prevents the development of vegetation altogether, resulting in rocky deserts with patches of permanent snow that never quite become ice.

Such poor vegetation can afford only a wretched existence for any fauna in a region where food must have a high energy content and where hibernation is impossible because of the presence of permanently frozen soil. Plant-eating insects are rare, though mosquitoes are plentiful during the short summer. Reindeer graze on lichens, as do the musk oxen, if they fail to find any grass on the rare prairie. Carnivores include the Arctic fox, which lives on rodents, but most of the animals of this region are omnivorous, even getting food from the sea by venturing onto the sheet ice.

Musk oxen in the Thule region of Greenland. These cattle are typical of the tundra landscape, and live almost entirely on lichens.

MAN ON THE EARTH

The function and scope of human geography

Physical and biological phenomena contribute in varying degrees to the creation of different types of environment on the surface of the Earth; but, fundamental though their study is, they represent only one aspect of general geography. The study is only complete when we add to it the scientific description of human environments and their distribution throughout the world: this is the role of *human geography*.

Since the purpose of geography is to describe the varied and changeable face of the Earth, it is evident that human geography is of basic importance, since it shows the wide range of man's effect on the face of this planet both now and in the past.

Man acts according to his environment; nevertheless, the interdependence between man and his surroundings is different from that between animals and their environment. More complex factors enter

At the end of the monsoon season large crowds gather at Chowpatty, on the shores of the Indian Ocean near Bombay, to celebrate 'coconut day'. Tens of thousands of people are drawn to this small area to take part in the performance of religious ceremonies and ancient rites. It is one of the many religious demonstrations so typical of India, a country whose enormous population creates many problems.

into man's activities; he is not willing necessarily to accept things as they are and, because he has the power of reasoning, he does not allow his actions to be governed by the idea that life is no more than a struggle for existence. Consequently, he behaves in a way that is, by animal terms, abnormal. But although man uses his technical knowledge to change the conditions in which he lives, he cannot free himself from the demands made by his environment. Even his most unnecessary actions can be traced back to precise determining factors within the geographic sphere. Just as physical geography involves the sciences of geology, climatology, and geomorphology, so the study of human geography involves all the other sciences of man, such as physiology, psychology, ethnology, sociology, and economics.

Evolution of the human species

The origin of man is a recent event in the history of life on the Earth. The science of *palaeontology* traces the succession of life which spans hundreds of millions of years. Through the study of genetics we can now recognize the exact biological mechanism, based on a comparatively simple chemical code, by which characteristics are passed on, and we have learned how these develop by mutation into new ones. These will in turn be passed on to later generations.

Specific studies of the general problems of evolution, based on the theories of Charles Darwin, have made it possible to correlate the various experimental data provided by scientific research, producing a rigorous logical construction. The evolutionary process contains the secret of the polymorphism of living things, of their variability in time, and, within certain limits, of life itself. Evolution is an essential characteristic of living things, enabling them to adapt to changes in their environment. Man, like all other living things, suffers these physiological and biochemical changes on a time scale that is imperceptible in terms of one individual's lifetime, since they take place over centuries and millenniums.

It is not possible to say exactly when the first man made his appearance on the Earth, but it is generally thought to have been during the first part of the Quaternary era – that is, from about 500,000 to 1,000,000 years ago. Long ago though this may seem, it is an extremely short time compared with the duration of the geological ages that have seen the emergence, evolution, and disappearance of many fantastic forms of animal life.

In this relatively short period of time man has changed incredibly; he has reached that degree of intelligence which places him at the top of the zoological scale. From considering the great variety of the peoples of the Earth, it is apparent that man's evolutionary process, like that of any other living creature, has not followed a single direct line towards some pre-determined goal, but has branched out in many directions, producing contrasting results. One can see how the process of natural selection that regulates and determines the survival or extinction of living things has also affected the various races of man, some of which appear to be going through a phase of expansion, while others are clearly regressing or nearing extinction.

The anthropoids

According to certain classifications man is one of the *primates*, which are divided into three sub-orders: *lemuroids, tarsioids,* and *anthropoids*. The first two form the group known as the *prosimians*, while the anthropoids are divided into two groups, the *platyrrhines*, or monkeys of the New World, and the *catarrhines*, or monkeys and apes of the Old World. The latter comprise three family groups: *cercopithecids, anthropoid apes* (chimpanzee, gorilla, orang-utan, and gibbon), and the *hominids*, which have only one living genus – man (*Homo*).

Man is thus closely related to monkeys and apes, and this relationship is most clearly seen in the case of the anthropomorphs. But when man's evolutionary process is summed up in the expression 'man is descended from the apes', it certainly does not mean from the species living today, and particularly none of the four

Some races on the Earth today show signs of decline and are in danger of extinction. The Bushman of the Kalahari *(left)*, a hunter and food-gatherer of southern Africa, is one such example. He displays morphological characteristics that distinguish him from present-day man. Similarly, the Australian Aborigine *(below)* lives at a primitive cultural level, and has his own marked racial characteristics.

anthropoid apes that exist at present and which resemble man in several ways. All these apes represent the final stages of evolutionary processes which have taken place parallel with those of man. The origin of man must therefore be sought in remote times, in a group of primates, now extinct, who can be regarded as the first anthropoids.

Anatomical changes

The basic characteristic in the evolution of all the primates, and the most apparent, is the major development of the brain, in both its size and its powers. All vertebrates have a highly developed nervous system, rising in scale from a lesser to a higher degree, from fish to amphibians, reptiles, birds, and mammals. But in these groups the greater changes seem to have occurred in parts of the body other than the brain. The first stage in this series of change is marked by the development of the *tetrapodous* (four legged) state, followed by the acquisition of various anatomical structures connected with locomotion, offence, defence, and ornament. In the primates, however, the evolution of the body appears to have stopped at a comparatively primitive level. They still retain, almost unchanged, the primitive five-fingered joint of tetrapods. By contrast, the nervous system has reached a highly specialized level of co-ordination. In man, who is sharply distinguished from all other animals because his brain is the most highly developed, the process of evolution has attained its highest level so far.

Man's ability to stand upright is another important factor in his growth and development. In the light of present-day knowledge, some scientists believe that anatomical changes connected with man's ability to stand on two feet occurred before the brain developed. One of the consequences of standing upright would be that he would have to flex the base of his skull in order to retain his horizontal vision, and the development of his brain might therefore have been a result of this newly found power.

All the changes that occur during an evolutionary process are correlated to new structural formations; anatomical changes are generally interdependent, consequently the flexion of the base of the skull caused the extreme reduction of the face and the progressive disappearance of the prominent jaws in the human species.

Hypotheses on the development of man

In 1930 Eugène Dubois, discoverer of Java Man, formulated an ingenious theory to explain the development of the human brain by a simple change of inherited characteristics.

The number of nerve cells of the cerebral cortex in man is about 9,000 million. This number is pre-determined before birth, since the nerve cells are able to multiply only after they have gone through a series of changes and have passed through 33 successive and synchronous processes of division of an original *neuroblast* (special cell from which nerve cells are formed). In the anthropomorphic apes, the cortex cells vary from about 1,800 million to 3,000 million after 31 divisions of the cells. The two additional divisions of the cells during the embryonic development of man's brain are enough to explain the differentiation from that of the apes: they are the key to the formation of man. According to Dubois, the volume of Java Man's brain was about 55 cubic inches, and so he possessed about 4,000 million cortical cells, the result of 32 divisions. Therefore, Java Man was the intermediate stage between the apes and man today.

The theory is impressive, but it disregards the basic fact that,

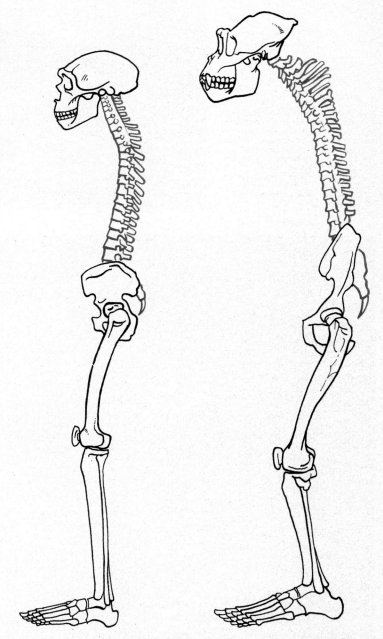

The skeleton of Neanderthal Man *(left)* compared with that of a gorilla *(right)*, an anthropomorph. The morphological differences are obvious, but the most important feature is the upright stance of Neanderthal Man; he probably marks the transition from a tree-dwelling form of life to a ground-living creature.

in considering the characteristics of the human brain in relation to that of apes, one must take into account not only the quantitative factor, but also the extremely complex one, difficult to resolve, that concerns the entire structure of nerve centres and co-ordination which is the basis of man's much higher mentality.

The origin of man's development is not to be found in chance circumstances acting on some primitive ape, but is in some way inherent in the very nature of the zoological group to which man belongs. This evolutionary process must be regarded, therefore, as only a part of the entire evolution of primates.

Palaeontological date

It is thought that man first appeared on the Earth in a certain region as the result of the evolution of a single line of pre-human forms. It seems improbable that various types of man made

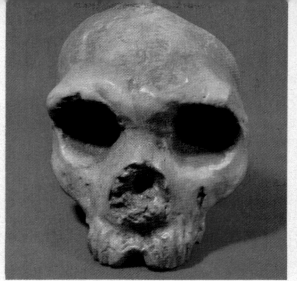

Neanderthal Man appeared about 300,000 years after Heidelberg Man. His fossil remains, which are relatively numerous, show that he was fairly widespread on the Earth at the beginning of the last Ice Age. *Below:* The skull of a Neanderthal Man found near Rome. *Right:* Two views of a Neanderthal skull found near Gibraltar.

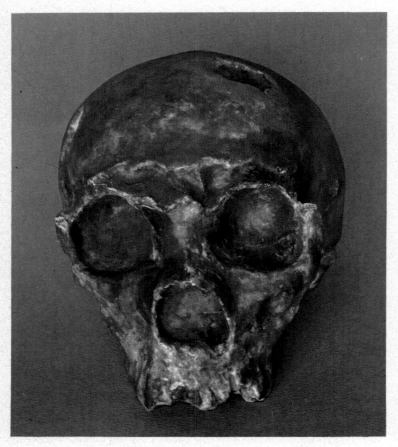

their appearance more or less at the same time in different regions as the result of parallel evolutionary processes. However, as is the case with almost all other species, the origins of man remain a mystery. This is not due to some chance factor which prevents us from finding the fossil remains indicating the first appearance of this new creature, but merely reflects a natural condition. When a new species begins to evolve it does so in very small numbers, which increase in subsequent generations. It is therefore highly improbable that the remains of these very few individuals will ever be found, though fossils of their later developments are fairly plentiful.

During the entire Tertiary era, long before man first appeared, apes had evolved into their various groups. In Africa, Asia, and Europe there lived many anthropomorphic apes, different from those of today, and with characteristics varying according to different trends of evolution. Perhaps the Proconsul group of Africa (in the lower Miocene) provides the best point of departure for an evolutionary process that might have led to the development of the human species.

One other group should be noted: the *Australopithecus*, which lived in southern Africa during a period difficult to date, but which appears to have been during the middle Pleistocene. Some believe it was during the whole of the Pleistocene and so the group was contemporary with the first men to appear on Earth.

The uncertainty regarding the age of these fossil primates makes it difficult to interpret their significance in the succession of life that led to the evolution of man. Even if today it seems a more likely hypothesis that the *Australopithecus* were a collateral, but sterile, branch of human evolution, they are nevertheless of material interest.

According to stratigraphic data, man appeared on the Earth at the beginning of the Pleistocene period. His remains have been found in Asia, Africa, and Europe; these were men who were still animal-like in aspect, with a small brain, deep-set eyes, a broad, flat nose, a jutting jaw, and no chin. However, they were able to fashion stone implements, to make fire, and possibly to communicate with one another. The most primitive of these was Java Man (*Pithecanthropus*), whom some do not accept as belonging to the human species, although very close to it.

Pekin Man (*Sinanthropus*), found near the Chinese capital, had certainly crossed over into the human state. He made stone tools, and lived in caves in which fires were kept alight. There are also signs that he practised cannibalism (a typically human form of behaviour involving magical and religious beliefs), evident in skulls with the base pierced as if to extract the brain. Both Pekin and Java Man probably belonged to the same species, and were not different types as their names suggest.

In Europe, more or less contemporary with Java Man, there lived a creature known today as Heidelberg Man (*Homo heidelbergensis*), of whom the only relic is a jaw indicating an extremely crude and primitive nature; in Africa there existed another form (*Atlanthropus mauritanicus*), which was very similar to Pekin Man, and of which there remain only the jaw and part of the top of the skull. Both Heidelberg Man and *Atlanthropus* were primitive tool makers, working in stone.

From these beginnings the morphology of man underwent very rapid changes and these were accompanied by a greater capacity for adapting to his surroundings and making even better tools. Relics of the primitive peoples who succeeded one another in Europe and in other continents during the first part of the Quaternary period are all too few until the appearance of Neanderthal Man. The

New types of man made their appearance in Europe during the upper Palaeolithic and represented the first real forms of *Homo sapiens*. *Right:* The skull of Grimaldi Man found at Mentone, who had Negroid features and was short in stature. *Far right:* The skull of Cro-Magnon Man from Les Eyzies, Dordogne, France; morphologically a more handsome man, and well-built. According to fossil finds, Cro-Magnon Man lived during the last Ice Age, hunting mammoth and other animals living in the northern steppes and forests of that era. A recent find of a man of the upper Palaeolithic (of the Cro-Magnon type) is that of Vladimir, Russia *(below)*. The picture shows the skeleton exactly as it was found in its burying place. The skeleton is not very different from that of a middle-European man and the body was evidently deliberately buried in funerary dress of ivory necklaces made from mammoths' tusks.

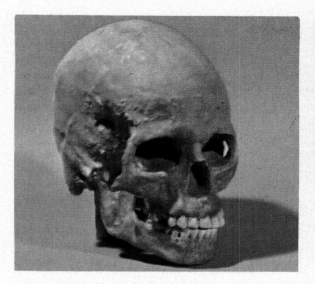
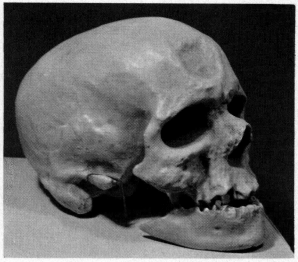
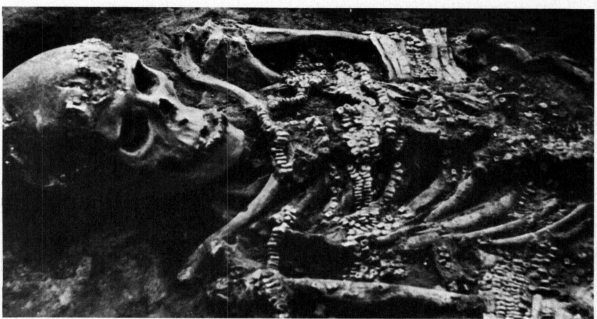

period between Heidelberg Man and Neanderthal Man was quite long – about 300,000 to 350,000 years – and although it has gone largely unnoticed in anthropological research, it saw the appearance and development of new and more highly civilized races.

Neanderthal Man lived in Europe, western Asia, and northern Africa during the third interglacial period and at the beginning of the Würmian Ice Age. About a hundred skeletons have been found, some of them in a perfect state of preservation. Sturdy but short, with a big head and a highly developed brain, they still had an animal-like look, although they had reached a reasonably good cultural level. During the last Ice Age, Neanderthal Man was suddenly replaced, in Europe at least, by new types of man with decidedly more modern features, so much so that they can be regarded, more or less, as *Homo sapiens* and as our direct ancestors. They were decidedly polymorphic, and already showed the first of the signs of differentiation between races which exists today. They included the little Grimaldi men who had marked Negroid features, and Cro-Magnon men of an athletic build and a capacious brain, certainly the most numerous, judging by the relics which have been discovered. The various finds in Předmostí, Oberkassel, Chancelade, Combe-Capelle, Placard, and recently in Vladimir (Russia), also reveal the existence of other, different types, though sharing the same high degree of morphological evolution.

The origin of *Homo sapiens* remains unsolved. Certainly he was not descended from Neanderthal Man, but sprang from a people who lived in regions and conditions that are still unknown – probably on the borders of the areas occupied by the Neanderthals. During the second interglacial period, before the disappearance of Neanderthal Man, Europe was inhabited by people who were very similar to *Homo sapiens*. They have left much evidence of their cultural activity, though skeletons are extremely scarce. Some of these, especially those of Swanscombe Man, in England, and Fontéchevade, in France, show oddly modern traits and are considered by some as the proof of the existence of an evolutionary line which might have led to the development of the *Homo sapiens* group of the Würmian Ice Age. Others, like those of Steinheim and Ehringsdorf in Germany and perhaps those of Saccopastore, near Rome, appear to date from before Neanderthal Man and may indicate his origin. Our information is too inadequate, however, for any definite conclusions to be drawn on these particular aspects of man's remote beginnings and the eventual relationship between the peoples of the second interglacial period and those of today.

One of the most eloquent pieces of evidence of Palaeolithic Man's spiritual activity, this skeleton of a youth was found in a cave in Arene Candide (Italy). Objects representing the dead person's possessions and which were an inseparable part of his personality were buried with him.

Nature of the earliest civilizations

From his very beginnings man has had spiritual and mental needs not found in other animals and which perhaps constitute the essence of humanity: the search for the supernatural, the sense, as yet vague, of abstract values that give worth and meaning to all things and all actions, such as courage, strength, happiness, and beauty.

Even *Sinanthropus*, so primitive in his appearance that his human nature appears to be in doubt, managed, perhaps for thousands of years, to keep his fire burning in the caves of Chu-Ku-Tien, and worked stone and bone, albeit crudely; it is possible that he was sufficiently mentally advanced to have mastered the complex reasoning process that provides the basis of the human condition.

The ability of these prehistoric men to improve both technically and spiritually is increasingly shown with the passage of time. Neanderthal Man, who was the artificer of the middle Palaeolithic and was a moderately skilful carver of stone and bone, had almost certainly achieved a relatively high mental level. Most particularly, we should remember that it was in his time that the burial of the dead was first put into practice, according to a ritual not very different from that of highly civilized people of historic times, such as the Romans and the Greeks. *Homo sapiens* of the upper Palaeolithic, also a hunter like Neanderthal Man, was seemingly on the same mental level and continued to develop these highly human customs and faculties.

From a strictly technical point of view, *Homo sapiens* was clearly superior, and was able to make different kinds of tools, both in stone and in bone, such as arrow-heads and spears, hatchets, scrapers, awls, harpoons for fishing, and even needles for sewing, complete with eyes for threading. He, too, practised the cult of the dead, and many examples of interment have been found.

But man of the upper Palaeolithic is clearly distinguished from all those that came before him because of his ability to express himself in art forms which even today fill one with astonishment and admiration. Murals, polychrome paintings, bas-reliefs, and statues provide a mass of evidence that shows us how this former hunter of reindeer had so highly refined his taste in shape and colour as to know how to choose and reproduce the main features of the living world of which he was part with impressive fidelity.

The first stages of human culture

The hunter of the reindeer age did not produce masterpieces only to satisfy a consuming need to create something of beauty. The art of this period was a form of magic: the representation of animals was in some way intended to make it easier to capture them. Often the animals are shown pierced with arrows, wounded, bleeding, or dying. The animal was symbolically slain and this rite gave the hunter the strength and courage, or perhaps the good luck, to bring him a good catch.

The kind of environment in which this man lived is shown in these early art forms. Animals, because of their importance to man as his means of livelihood, were a natural part of the geographic scene. Since Palaeolithic Man was bound more closely to his environment than is modern man, with his advanced technology, a correlation between habitat, flora, fauna and human culture can be established.

Palaeolithic Man's specific economy was basically that of a hunter, and his implements were limited to tools that made it easier for him to carry out the activities connected with hunting. However, these stone tools are the most lasting of the relics of prehistoric man, and they show a remarkable difference in the Mesolithic period – the transitional phase from the Palaeolithic to the Neolithic. This is because in this age, which began about 6000 B.C., definite cultures emerged with a well-defined geographical distribution. Only in more recent times do we see the evolution of a specialized technology, with the development of new tools and instruments to meet the needs of new forms of activity.

In the Palaeolithic and the Mesolithic, extreme variation of climate occurred, bringing about changes in the environment, and so of habitat; in this period of transition the first important and profound cultural differences begin to emerge. These become more evident during the Neolithic, when man was establishing

Left: Mammoth in the Rouffignac caves. The pictorial representation of animals to which man's existence was linked during the upper Palaeolithic has a double significance: it furnishes evidence of the intelligence and ability of prehistoric man, and conveys to a certain extent the the landscape of that time.

The coming of agriculture was linked not only with new forms of life and social relationships, but also new forms of technology, as can be seen by the Bronze Age mortar and pestle *(below)* from an archaeological site in the foothills of the Italian Alps. The reasons, characteristics, and date of the agricultural revolution are mostly unknown. From food-gathering probably evolved primitive agriculture, carried out by women, using digging sticks and hoes, as is still the case today in some underdeveloped African countries *(bottom).*

cultures that we can still recognize today in all their different aspects, because of the changes wrought by society on the patterns of industry which were inherited and progressively adapted to the particular needs of each culture according to its own environment and activity.

The domestic dog first appears in the Mesolithic, and man begins, during the Neolithic, to weave wool and other fibres, and to produce terra-cotta vessels, grow cereals, and bake bread. These activities seem to have taken place in communities in western Asia and northern Africa, and were generally associated with environments that were unforested areas, but in which the climate and the nature of the soil were favourable, with irrigation, to a rapid rotation of crops. Man's artistic talent found new directions, at least in those areas where the possibilities of new economic activities robbed life of its character which, in the Palaeolithic period, held religious and magic qualities.

As a result of finds in prehistoric sites and comparative studies of various primitive cultures of the present day, knowledge of the evolutionary phases of human civilization has been greatly increased during the last hundred years. It has been noticed especially that, on the basis of their respective heritages, cultures can be classified to show a kind of historical progress in civilization. The poorer, simpler cultures are the most ancient; the richer ones are of more recent origin.

The first methods of classification were based essentially on economic activities and on the concomitant social forms. The best synthesis was produced by F. Krause, in 1924, who grouped the various economic stages in the following manner: 1) primitive food-gatherers and hunters; 2) more highly skilled hunters; 3) superior food-gatherers; 4) primitive agriculture, together with the first forms of livestock breeding (pigs, etc.); 5) horticulture; 6) plough farming and cattle-breeding; 7) nomadic pastoralism (starting with goats and sheep and later including the ox, horse, and camel).

Other classifications were based essentially on the social and spiritual elements of the cultures, also presupposing an evolutionary principle that governed the history of civilization, understood as an identical and automatic succession of spiritual and material phases for every human group.

The formation of the races

A human race can be defined as a group of individuals or peoples with similar characteristics, conditioned by hereditary factors. The only characteristics that can be used to form a classification of races are those which are passed on through heredity; mental characteristics, which can be influenced by the social environment, cannot be taken into consideration. Similarly, nationality and language must be discounted, because these are not often basic characteristics of ethnic groups, but are rather related to changeable political conditions. The characteristics most commonly used to classify races are the shape of the head, height, bodily constitution, the colour and type of hair and eyes, the colour of the skin, the shape of the nose, and blood groups.

The information of the different races, living and extinct, comes within the general framework of the evolution of all living things and can equally well be explained by presupposing that man sprang either from a single source of pre-hominids, or from many populations with different origins; at all events, the races were subject to the same laws that governed the rise of an infinite number and variety of animals and plants during the long life of this planet.

It seems more probable, however, that humanity sprang from a single source· which itself arose from the evolution of a single stock of primates now extinct; all known human forms have, or have had, physical and psychological characteristics so similar as to make it extremely difficult to believe that they could have evolved along separate lines. Like all living things, man is subject to mutations that introduce new characteristics into the heredity of humanity, and it is from the particular redistribution of these new characteristics throughout the various populations that the different races came to be determined. Thus, in the case of man, geographical isolation can lead to the existence of societies that are inimical to each other, and, taken together with the political consciousness that arises from the creation of different nations, can determine territorial and linguistic frontiers. Nations of different ethnic groups who interbreed, forming eventually a homogeneous population with its own characteristics, encourage hybridization.

The pictures on pages 168–171 show the physical differences between some of the many different races of the world, and some aspects of their ways of life. Each group shows its own individual culture, and one of the first distinctions between them is their manner of dress. Cultural elements and their style of dress together form an integral part of their personality.

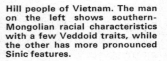

Hill people of Vietnam. The man on the left shows southern-Mongolian racial characteristics with a few Veddoid traits, while the other has more pronounced Sinic features.

A family in Samoa showing the typical characteristics of the Polynesian race.

Right: An Aizo man of southern Dahomey: as in many Guinean populations, he has features typical of Africa's forest-dwelling people, such as the broad, flat nose. *Far right:* A girl of Massaguet, Chad, showing both Sudanese Negro characteristics and those of the desert tribes of the Sahara, which in many regions have strong Arabic influences.

Women of the Wahgi river valley in the mountains of northwestern New Guinea. They belong to the Papuan mountain race, which often shows physical differences from the Papuans of the coastal regions, where recently there has been an influx of Melanesians. These people, having interbred with pygmies of the interior, can be regarded, morphologically, as members of the Negroid races.

Right: A Potosi Indian showing Andean features (Spanish-American). *Far right:* An American Indian of the Xingú river, of Amazonian origin.

Left: A marriage between two young Indians. *Bottom left:* Women on Iran's north-western border with Turkmenistan, where the population is mainly Turkish speaking (Turkomans); despite certain Mongoloid characteristics they are classified as Europeans. *Below:* A Lapp woman of Hammersfeld. The Lapps have very individual characteristics, and many ethnologists regard them as a race apart.

Right: Afghan man, a nomad with purely Indo-European features. *Far right:* Arab woman of Jordan. The Semites today are spread mainly throughout northern Africa and can be classified as of European stock.

Right: Slovak woman with the characteristics of Slavonic people who live chiefly in eastern Europe. *Far right:* An old Dane of Skagen, a representative of the Nordic race of Europe.

Right: Provençal girl of the Mediterranean race. *Far right:* A Pennsylvania American.

THE PEOPLING OF THE EARTH

Nature of early populations

Within the short period of time which has seen the emergence and the spread of the human species throughout the Earth, man has made considerable progress in adapting to his environment very quickly. By environment is meant all those factors that condition man and, especially as regards prehistoric pastoral civilizations, have had a very restricting effect on him. Climatic changes, with their succession of glacial and interglacial periods, had a fundamental effect on how the Earth first came to be populated. They resulted in a variable number of individuals living in certain regions, while other areas became uninhabited once the ice spread to them. Others which are barren and deserted today were once peopled, such as the Sahara, which still shows signs of a fairly dense human habitation in former times.

The reasons for the survival and multiplication of the human species can be found, broadly, in the way that man has adapted himself to new habitats by methods that were progressively evolved by the various cultures, and it is by following the path of these that we can trace the history of how the Earth came to be populated.

The history of man on the Earth is full of gaps, and clashes between institutions and different ways of life, sometimes to the detriment of the weak and the advantage of those made strong by new cultural discoveries with the power to increase man's potential for expansion by breaking pre-existing static and closed conditions.

Rock drawings of animals which today live much farther to the south. They are evidence that people lived in the Sahara before it became the arid desert it is today, as a result of changes of climate after the Ice Age. This is one of the best documented examples of how changes in natural conditions affected the Earth's early human populations. The picture shows elephants carved on rocks in the Ahaggar Mountains (Algeria). The lively hunting scene is similar to scenes that take place in more southern regions of Africa today where the elephant has its natural habitat.

Before the European colonization of Australia, the continent was inhabited by about 270,000 aborigines, spread throughout the region with an average density of about one man for every square mile. The cultural level of these people, although not the same throughout the Australian continent from a strictly ethnological point of view, can be compared with that of the hunters and gatherers of the Palaeolithic, and provides a comparison with the distribution of prehistoric man. The Australian aborigines could be descended from Java Man. In any event, they probably reached Australia across dry-land 'bridges'. Their isolation on the continent cut them off from any new racial elements, so that they represent a very ancient race that is dying out, like their close relatives the Tasmanians, who are now extinct.

Above: In a space cleared in the equatorial forest by fire, a Suya woman of the Xingú region in the Amazon plants maize. It is the most rudimentary form of agriculture, and needs much space, because new fields must be released every year. For this reason, regions where this form of culture is practised are thinly populated, being occupied by small groups of people who are without the means for demographic growth. In the case of the Amazonian populations, however, ancient cultural forms that have been hidden away in the forests have thus been able to survive. *Below:* A farming village in Anatolia near the heights of Alaca Höyük, the ancient Hittite centre. Its origin is linked with the first Bronze Age civilizations based on agriculture and animal husbandry, and which led first to density of population in limited areas and subsequently to urbanism. *Right:* The site of La Nasa, one of the prehistoric settlements of the Bronze Age in the foothills of the Veronese Alps. It stood on a rocky spur at the confluence of two valleys. A house built in recent times stands on the spot. The small terraced fields were probably cultivated by the ancient inhabitants. The present landscape shows signs of considerable change wrought by recent exploitation of agriculture and forest.

173

The tropical zones seem to have been the most favourable areas for the early populations. According to the latest archaeological finds the cradle of humanity might have been in Africa. From this region, in the course of hundreds of thousands of years, the earliest men might have crossed into Eurasia. In the middle and upper Palaeolithic, the zones open to human habitation become wider and extend northwards to the edges of the old glaciers.

Population density in the upper Palaeolithic can be estimated by the comparative method based on data concerning primitive cultures founded on hunting and harvesting which have survived to our own day. In 1788 the population of Australia was about 270,000 and was spread over an area of three million square miles (one inhabitant for every eleven square miles). The pygmies in the African equatorial forests needed three square miles per person. In the North-West Territory of Canada last century there was one person to every eighty square miles.

During the Neolithic, the agrarian culture that spread throughout Europe brought about a major development in population. This seems to have been a resumption of a trend that slowed down during the Mesolithic, probably as a result of difficult and unstable climatic conditions following glaciation. According to research carried out in France, it is calculated that about 10,500,000 people lived on French territory between 2600 and 1200 B.C. Estimating the average life span in those days to be 25 years, this means that the average population numbered about 200,000. How populations were distributed during pre-history can be deduced by examining the population densities of certain African regions where Mesolithic agrarian cultures have survived to the present day.

Migrations of mankind

The distribution of people throughout the Earth was the result not only of the simple increase of individual groups in one territory, but also of migration and the conquest of new territories, made possible by man's ability to adapt to the most varied environments. Often the conquest was dictated by a population growth exceeding the limits of its living space or its natural resources.

The oldest migrations are mostly a mystery, but traces of them do exist in the geographic distribution archaeological finds which often show the actual routes followed by the migrants. This is particularly true of the period ranging from the Neolithic to the Iron Age.

Migrations that took place in comparatively recent times are less difficult to interpret. They can be of different types: conquest of lands for colonization; a wish for greater prosperity; the necessity to escape from invasion by an alien people; the search for new sources of natural wealth, such as precious metals. Many of these migrations are now dimly remembered, like those of the movement of the Indo-Europeans and the Polynesians. For others, there is the evidence of history, as in the case of the Anglo-Saxons who occupied England, the Slavs who infiltrated into the Balkan region, and of the Arabs, Mongols, and Turks. The Greeks and the Normans moved to new lands where they left many traces of their colonization.

Names of rivers, mountains, and inhabited areas are useful in reconstructing the paths taken by the more recent migrants when the evidence of recorded history is lacking. Another pointer is the linguistic relationship between groups of people separated in time, as well as the spread of customs, rites, and social institutions.

Sometimes the migrations were determined by religious causes, as happened with the exodus of the Huguenots from France, the Circassians from the Caucasus, and the Jews from Egypt. In the case of the Huguenots their migration was not without its economic consequences. They were skilled, industrious people and their arrival in new countries saw the rise of new industries. The same can be said of the Greeks who left Asia Minor in the early part of this century, spreading the cultivation of tobacco and carpet-weaving.

There have also been mass migrations, such as the invasions of the Barbarians; infiltration by small groups, as happened with the peopling of America by the Europeans; migrations of organized groups and of individuals; spontaneous migrations and forced ones, as was the case with the Negro slaves brought to America from Africa, political deportees from Russia to Siberia, and British convicts to Australia.

In ancient times the number of people who moved from one country to another, for whatever reason, must have been small. In

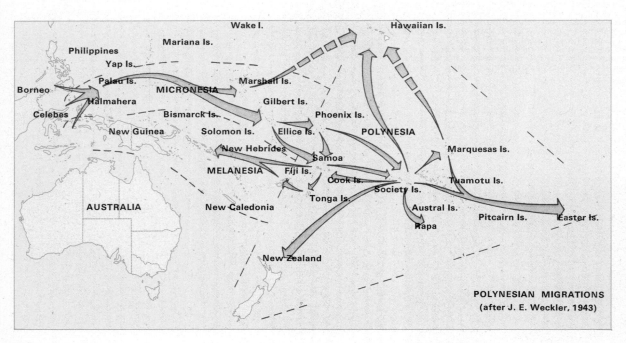

POLYNESIAN MIGRATIONS
(after J. E. Weckler, 1943)

The known and probable migrations of the Polynesian peoples according to J. E. Weckler. It shows that Polynesia was populated by people of Asian origin, some of whose cultural elements spread to the Pacific coasts of South America. An inverse process might also have occurred, from South America to Polynesia, as suggested by Thor Heyerdahl's expedition on the raft *Kon-Tiki*, which drifted on the Humboldt current; however, it seems that Polynesia was not originally populated by migration from the South American continents.

The Fulbe, a Sudanese people descended from mixed Libyan and Negro stock, are distributed throughout western Africa. They are basically pastoral, and according to many ethnologists they inhabited the Sahara in ancient times, where they left rock carvings showing herds of cattle.

some cases the invaders profoundly changed the country they invaded. In others, they were absorbed into the local populations, as were the Lombards in northern Italy. These early migrations were almost always carried out overland, following set paths or convenient routes through the countryside.

The great geographic discoveries that brought to light countries with sparse populations gave rise to emigration over the oceans.

This at first took place in an unplanned and disorganized way, often for the mere sake of adventure or conquest. There later followed the occupation of territories and efforts to colonize them. It is not easy to calculate how many Europeans moved to America. Between the 16th and 18th centuries it is thought they numbered about six million, of whom two to three million were from Spain, two million were Anglo-Saxons, French, and German, and one million

Left: A poster of 1858 invites new immigrants to the upper Mississippi valley and especially to the territory of Minnesota, which became a State of the Union in the same year. The new city of Nininger needed mechanics, merchants, and people of all trades and professions, and the poster gives directions for reaching it by rail, or by the Mississippi river boats. Right: A print of 1866 shows an episode in the great migration which brought the whites to conquer the American West. One of the innumerable caravans of settlers reaches the foot of the Rocky Mountains.

EUROPEAN EMIGRATION OVERSEAS IN THE 19TH CENTURY

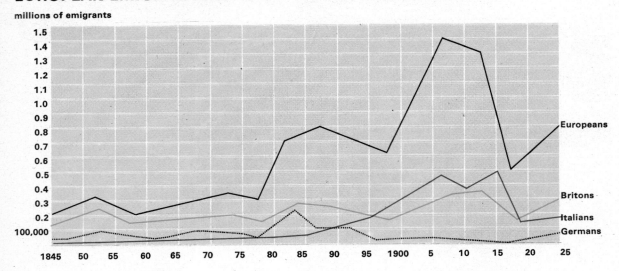

millions of emigrants

Europeans

Britons

Italians

Germans

Portuguese. Since male emigration predominated, the Europeans created, especially in Latin America, a class of half-breeds. Africa, too, contributed to the peopling of America, and the period beginning with the first landings in Cuba and Hispaniola in 1503 and lasting for over three centuries saw from six to eight million Negroes transferred from one continent to the other.

Immigration from Europe was particularly high from 1800 onwards, after the end of the French Revolution, with the improvement of sea transport and the abolition of slavery. Between 1801 and 1935 an estimated 70 million people migrated, most of them Europeans, of whom 47 million settled permanently in the New World, chiefly in North America (28 million). Anglo-Saxons, Scandinavians,

and Germans were the predominant group in the earlier period; people from southern and eastern Europe were the chief immigrants of the second period. Later the migrations eased, but did not die out altogether. This expansion of Europeans into the New World has had no parallel in history. For 400 years, from the end of the 15th century to the end of the 19th they dominated most of the world's countries and seas. America was occupied and subdued, Australia become a British colony, the Pacific islands were politically taken over, as were a large part of Africa and three-quarters of Asia. Many of these countries later won their independence; nonetheless, migrants from Europe swarmed all over the Earth, bringing European languages to America, Australia, and parts of Africa.

During the last century, Indian migrations, especially from Malabar, were on a large scale. Indians crossed the Indian Ocean to work for European employers in sugar-cane plantations. They preserved their individuality in the new country, as well as their customs and way of dress. The photograph shows an Indian religious festival being celebrated on the island of Mauritius, near a sugar factory.

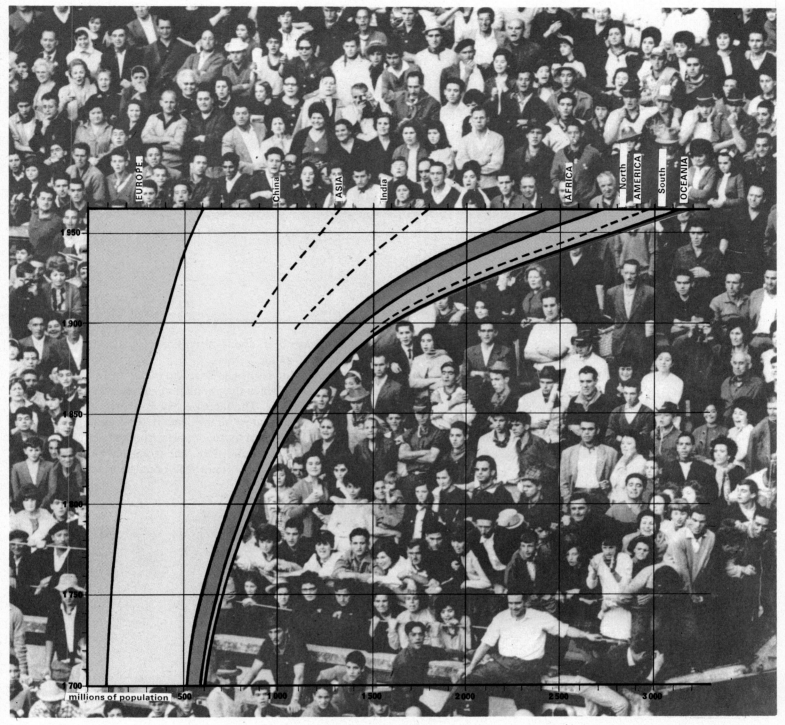

The growth of human population in the five continents from 1700 onwards. The rate of growth increased rapidly with the advent of industrial civilization.

This expansion by the Europeans profoundly changed the ethnic and anthropological map of the Earth; so much so that often the native populations with whom they came into contact disappeared in a short space of time, either because of the introduction of new diseases or by the ruthless waging of war. The products of tropical countries began to flow in great quantities into Europe, which in turn exported its manufactured goods and thus initiated an exchange of these for raw materials on a large scale. New forms of plants came from America to Europe, such as maize, potatoes, and tobacco, and found favourable conditions for cultivation, while in new lands big herds of cattle and sheep were built up.

Migrations of a certain importance have taken place, and continue to do so, even within the limits of single continents. In Asia, the Chinese tend to move to more southerly zones, such as Thailand, Singapore, and Indonesia, and today about 11 million of them live outside China. They choose countries that are less densely populated than their mother-land, or else devote themselves to trade in heavily populated areas. In Africa, migrations of considerable proportions take place in the southern part because of the demand for labour in the mining regions of the Transvaal. In Europe, too, there is migration from country to country. The main countries of origin are Italy, Poland, and Spain, with Germany,

177

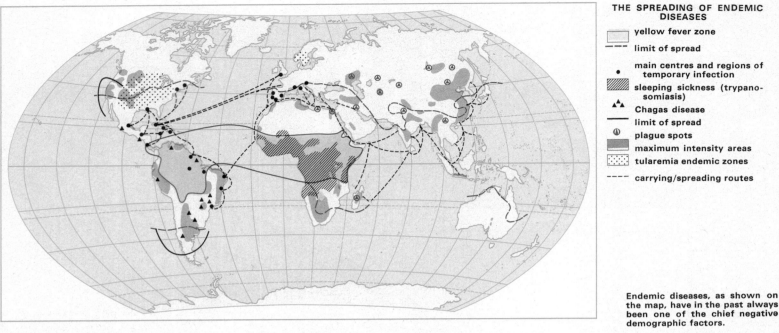

Endemic diseases, as shown on
the map, have in the past always
been one of the chief negative
demographic factors.

Switzerland and France as the destinations. In this case, because of the lesser distances involved, the changes are only temporary.

Growth of world populations

There are no exact statistics of the number of men who peopled the globe in ancient times, and there were no links between the Mediterranean world and eastern Asia, America, and Australia. By a very approximate calculation, the total world population is thought to have been about 50 million around 8000 B.C. and 100 million by 1000 B.C.

By the beginning of the Christian era the figure of 160 million can be accepted, from which the population has risen to over 3,000 million in our own day. The increase has not been a steady one; at first the population grew slowly and it took almost a thousand years until A.D. 900 for it to double. Another 800 years passed before it doubled a second time, but from that time onward the rate of increase was more rapid; the population redoubled in the

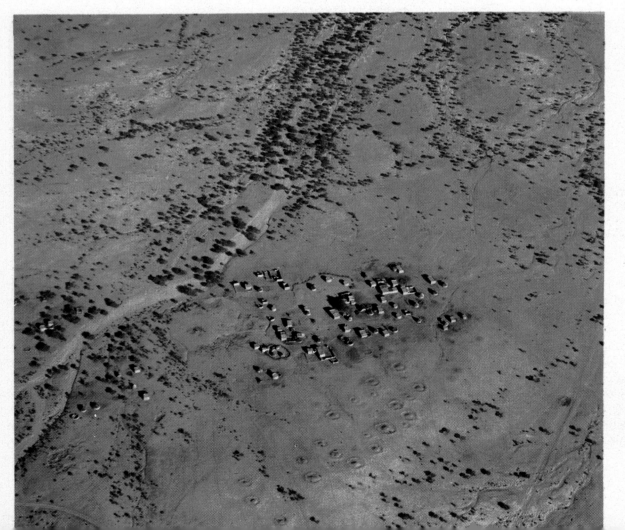

The uneven distribution of people throughout the Earth can be seen in these two pictures. A small village in the savanna south of Khartoum, Sudan, near the White Nile. *Opposite:* The centre of Chester, England, with its industrial suburbs.

next 150 years, from 1700 to 1850, and again within a hundred years, from 1850 to 1950.

Today, the increase is continuous and shows no sign of slackening. Each day 140,000 human beings are born, making a total of 52 to 54 million every year, so that by the end of this century, if not sooner, world population may exceed 6,000 million. The increase is due mainly to the fact that, following the vast improvement in standards of hygiene, the mortality rate has decreased, with a consequent prolongation of the average life span. Improved economic and social conditions, and the development of agriculture, which can now provide food for more people than in the past, are other positive influences.

But the increase is not always steady. In many instances the growth-rate is noticeably influenced by negative factors, independent of man's will and for which it is difficult to find a remedy, being as they are natural calamities that affect all of mankind.

Such disasters include earthquakes, volcanic eruptions, floods, and famines, which in the past were a very serious threat to mankind. In Europe such calamities are now comparatively rare, but in 1846–1847 more than a million people died in Ireland as a result of a blight that destroyed the potato crop and thus robbed the people of their staple food. More recently, dreadful famines have struck India and China.

Epidemics and plagues have also taken a heavy toll throughout the ages. The epidemic of Spanish influenza which broke out in 1918 was a fearful example, greatly weakening Europe after the First World War and claiming twenty million victims. In tropical countries cholera is the greatest scourge, and malaria kills about two million people every year.

Other negative factors are wars and conflicts between nations. The First World War (1914–1918) claimed thirteen million dead on the battlefield, equivalent to 0·7% of the human race. But if the civilian casualties are added to this figure, as well as the consequent reduction in the birth rate, the total is more like 35 million.

The increase in population varies from region to region, so that the relative importance of continents has altered over the years. For example, Asia had 67% of the world's population in 1800, but now has only 57%. From the beginning of the 18th century Europe has slightly increased its share (from 19% to 22%), but America much more so (from 2% to 13%), while the population of Africa, remaining the same in terms of numbers, has been reduced from 18% to 8%. Even the order of importance of European states has been disturbed; whereas in the days of Louis XIV the population of France made up 20% of Europe, it is now less than 8%.

The index used to evaluate the variation in the number of inhabitants, both throughout the world and in individual countries, is called the *movement of the population*, and is calculated from statistics of births and deaths of specific countries. In order to make comparisons, calculations are based on relative data rather than on absolute figures; the annual number of births and deaths per thousand is first ascertained, then the difference between the birth quotient and the mortality rate is calculated, to obtain the increase quotient, which gives the excess of births over deaths. This increase quotient averages about eighteen per thousand throughout the world, but is very high in some countries outside Europe, such as Venezuela, Mexico, and other Latin American countries. In Asia, too, it is higher than average, whereas in Europe, and in western Europe especially, it is much below.

Distribution of man today

There is a considerable disparity in the distribution of the Earth's inhabitants. Great contrasts exist between sparsely populated and densely populated areas. If Antarctica is excluded, some 750 million people live on 2% of the Earth's land area and another 750 million occupy 4%; thus nearly one half of humanity lives on 6% of the dry-land area. The Old World carries the greater share, with 86% living in Asia, Europe, and Africa and only 14% in America and Oceania.

Density of population in given areas

Equatorial islands such as Java, Barbados, and the Antilles have an extremely high population density. In Malta the population increase within a limited space has resulted in a density of 3,000 inhabitants per square mile. In the Tonkin delta it is estimated

that in an area of 6,000 square miles some eight million people are engaged in agriculture. Leaving aside these exceptional concentrations, Eurasia has a density of a hundred inhabitants to the square mile, and this is due to three great concentrations of population which exceed 250 to the square mile.

These are:

1) Eastern Asia – in central China; that is to say, the districts bordering the Gulf of Chihli, Chekiang province, and along the Yellow and Blue rivers. This zone extends into Japan (except for the island of Hokkaido) and the western coast of Korea. The Chinese are mainly farmers; in the South, rice is the chief crop, with wheat in the North, together with many other crops, such as tea and soya, and mulberry (for breeding silk-worms).

2) The coastal zones of the Indian peninsula and most of the Ganges basin, where the humid climate is favourable to the cultivation of rice. The population is concentrated mainly in villages or small hamlets rather than in large cities.

3) Mid-Atlantic Europe (central and southern Britain, north-eastern France, Belgium, Holland, West Germany) and part of Italy (the Po valley and Sicily). This zone is much more discontinuous.

The two great Asian regions have been heavily populated since ancient times and the natural conditions lend themselves admirably to agriculture: the alternation of rainy and dry seasons, due to the monsoons, favours the cultivation of useful crops, especially rice and other cereals. Animal husbandry, however, is rather limited, because it requires considerable space for pasture and grazing; for the same reason transport is also carried out by man without the aid of animals. China, a country of loess plains and of hills crossed by rivers which have left considerable layers of alluvial deposits, was especially suitable as a site for human settlements. Farming techniques underwent great development and the land was divided into many small plots.

Conditions in Europe are quite the opposite: the action of man is the determining factor. The Atlantic climate, mild in winter, with even rainfall throughout the year, is particularly favourable to the growth of woody plants, so much so that forests had to be cut down to win space for the cultivation of crops; this gradual process led to a similarly slow increase in population. The high population density is a recent phenomenon, beginning in the second half of the 18th century, and is connected more with industry than agriculture, especially in areas near iron and coal deposits.

There are other zones in the world, which are not so extensive, but which have high concentrations of population; these include:

4) The island of Java, which has the highest population density in the southern hemisphere. Here the population began to grow as soon as the equatorial forest was cleared and the inhabitants began to cultivate rice, maize, and potatoes, and Europeans established plantations which found favourable conditions in the volcanic soil.

5) Egypt, which has been densely populated since ancient times, because of the high fertility of the alluvial soil deposited every year by the Nile. The population is concentrated in the delta and along the valley of the river; the desert areas are inhabited by a few nomads.

6) The eastern region of the United States, especially from Massachusetts to New Jersey, the first area to be colonized. The population is much denser between Boston and Washington D.C., and near the shores of the Great Lakes, though it is also increasing to the west. The development of industry is favoured by the richness of the sub-soil, and the high density is due largely to immigration from Europe.

7) The Antilles, especially Cuba and Puerto Rico, are well-populated because the fertile soil and the humid climate are suitable for tropical cultivation; this high density is comparable with that of Java.

8) Southern America reflects many aspects of the African environment in its population. The density is highest along the periphery, with the highest values occurring between Rio de Janeiro and Sao Paulo. The territories that border the Rio de la Plata also have higher than average densities, because of the great richness of the farming soil and the advantages of maritime trade.

The valley and the delta of the Nile have been, since ancient times, among the most densely populated areas in the world. *Right:* Old rural settlements in the Nile delta. As can be seen, no inch of space is wasted if it is irrigated by waters of the Nile. *Opposite:* The avenues of New York City, which run the length of the island of Manhattan. Owing to the development of skyscrapers, this zone has the highest population density in the world.

Main influences on the distribution of mankind

A map showing the various densities of population reveals also the many factors, both physical and human, which influence its distribution. Different factors act in a positive or negative manner to prompt the population to settle in a particular region. In the geographic sphere, a characteristic area of attraction is the sea, either because it makes trade easier, or because a living can be made from fishing, or because the climate is more moderate. These advantages have attracted large populations to some coastal areas. On the other hand, coasts which are rocky or barren or perhaps provide an easy path for an invading force are not favoured.

Rivers have always been important zones of attraction in arid or semi-arid regions. Because of the possibilities opened up by the irrigation in the broad valleys of the Nile, the Tigris, the Euphrates, the Indus, and the Ganges, the world's first great civilizations were able to develop, based on agriculture and the exploitation of a soil that has remained unchanged until the present day. Rivers have always been important, too, as natural traffic lanes, especially in temperate lands such as Russia, Germany, and North America, and in the equatorial regions (where the soil is covered by vast tracts of rain forest). Man settled along their banks, and in modern times they have become vital arteries carrying the life-blood of trade and industry.

The geological constitution of the soil is another factor of importance. According to the various structures of the land (calcareous, volcanic, alluvial, etc.), the population varies for three main reasons: 1) the different agricultural possibilities; 2) the varying stability (landslides, etc.); 3) the varying permeability.

Man has been attracted to the sea since pre-history, especially because of the resources offered and often because of the better living conditions found in certain coastal regions. *Above:* Bonifacio, in Corsica, where houses extend along the sea-front and where most of the people earn their living from the sea, rejecting the harsh and barren hinterland. In many islands, however, the native populations have in the past shunned living close to the sea to escape malaria and to avoid being exposed to the danger of attacks by marauders.

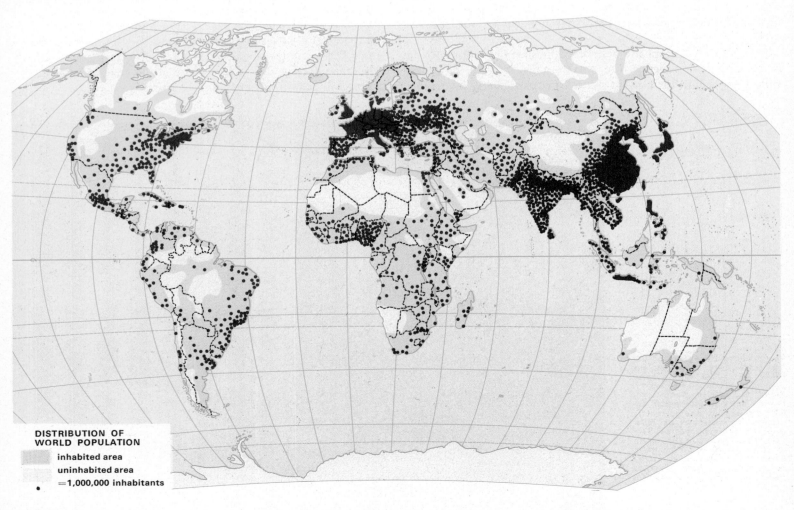

DISTRIBUTION OF
WORLD POPULATION

inhabited area
uninhabited area
• =1,000,000 inhabitants

Rivers have always been areas of attraction for human settlement. This is due not only to the many possibilities they offer to the needs of humanity (such as the irrigation of arid areas, like the Nile Valley), but also because they provide excellent natural highways for commerce and other activities. Such a river is the Rhine (*above*), with its easy navigability and well-defined course. Already, as it comes out of Lake Constance, the Rhine passes one of its many urban centres – in this case the medieval town of Stein, consisting of closely packed houses clustering round a castle.

The type of terrain is also important. This influences first of all the climate; with gradual increases in altitude there is a small-scale reproduction of the process that takes place in approaching the poles. With the decrease in temperature, there is less chance of successful cultivation, and, therefore, nothing to encourage human settlement. In Europe, the populations tend to concentrate in the lower plains and valleys where suitable agricultural areas are found, and the density of population tends to decrease with altitude.

In tropical regions, however, populations prefer higher altitudes (from 6,500 to 10,000 feet), especially in the vast high plateaux of eastern Africa and South and Central America. They avoid the low-lying regions and plains, which are often covered in impenetrable and unhealthy forests. The low-lying areas of Canada and Siberia are also sparsely populated, as they are too cold and damp and are covered in snow for much of the year. In Europe, only one inhabitant out of every 200 lives above 3,000 feet, but in Africa almost a quarter of the population lives at an altitude greater than 3,000 feet.

The distribution of man on the Earth varies according to altitude. *Right:* A Nepalese village in the Baghamati valley near Katmandu. In the distance rise the snow-covered peaks of the Himalayas between Gosainthan and Everest.

Valley floors (the one above is the Durance, France) are always sought by man because they are more convenient for communications, settlement, agriculture, animal husbandry, and trade. Man also lived at altitude in former times for strategic reasons, as is often shown by the presence of a castle, and tended to avoid the valleys which in those days could be unhealthy and unstable owing to stagnant waters and flooding. *Below left:* Arcidosso, in Tuscany, Italy. Often these centres acted as areas of attraction, bearing out the theory that human beings are often motivated by artificial pre-existing factors in that they tend to gather in regions that are already populated. *Below right:* The village of Langadia, in the Peloponnese: an example of how population tends, in mountainous regions, to increase on slopes that catch the sun.

184

The natural resources of an area, such as mining or industry, must also have been among the reasons that led people to settle in certain regions.

The extent of the inhabited world

In his dispersal throughout the Earth, man has made his way as far North as the 78th parallel, to Greenland, land of the Eskimos, and as far South as the 55th parallel, to Tierra del Fuego in South America. But it is not everywhere that man can find sustenance. He settles in those areas which at least afford the minimum conditions essential to a permanent way of life. These are known as *ecumenical zones*, from the ancient Greek word meaning 'land that is known and inhabited'.

There is no definite line of demarcation between the inhabited and uninhabited zones; in order to hunt and fish and to find new pastures, man often moves beyond the limits of his own region, especially during a favourable season, into places where he lives for only limited periods and which are known as *sub-ecumenical zones*. Near the polar ice-caps the Tungus of Siberia and the Eskimos of America lead a nomadic life, moving from place to place in their search for food. In the deserts and steppe-lands of the Old World, the Bedouin of Arabia, the Tuareg of the Sahara, and the Kirghiz of western Asia lead a nomadic pastoral life and move from one oasis to another. In high mountain zones, sub-ecumenical areas consist chiefly of pastures lying between those of the upper, uninhabited levels and the lower plains and valleys.

The zones near the poles that are not habitable both because of the long, dark polar night and because no economic activity is possible are known as *anecumenical zones*.

The limits of the inhabited world

The northern limit of the inhabited world can be drawn with sufficient accuracy. Starting from the Bering Strait it first follows the Asian coastline; it then cuts across the Taymyr peninsula, which juts far to the north and makes navigation difficult, excludes Novaya Zemlya, but takes in the islands of Spitzbergen (latitude 78° North), by-passes the Jan Mayen Islands, and takes in Iceland. In Greenland, the inhabited area is located on a small part of the eastern uplands and much of the western coast as far as latitude 78° North (the Etah region, discovered by Ross in 1818 and inhabited by about 200 Eskimos).

A United States base is situated near Thule and has a few satellite posts to the north. The line then cuts through Baffin Land, excludes the Boothia Felix peninsula, and follows the American coast as far as the Bering Strait.

This limit can vary from one century to another depending on the exhaustion of fishing and hunting grounds and the exploitation of useful mineral deposits. A well-known example of this variation is the European population of eastern Greenland. The Normans, helped by winds and ocean currents, reached Iceland and then sailed on to Greenland, which they found uninhabited. Eric the Red colonized it in about 984. Later, for reasons that are not clear, links with the motherland became fewer, and the colony, which had become prosperous and had grown to 2,000 inhabitants, disappeared.

Only in 1721 was Greenland once more populated by Europeans. The population is now about 35,000 but it is difficult to say how many of these are Danes, as they have interbred with the Eskimos, who are the major population group and practise hunting and fishing.

The population of Spitzbergen (Svalbard) is also of some interest. This group of Arctic islands has never been populated by Eskimos, perhaps because the intervening distance of the sea is too great. The Dutch settled there in the 17th century and built a whaling station. Later the islands became Norwegian territory (1920). They are not really suitable for permanent settlement because they consist of desolate mountains, but are inhabited because of their deposits of coal. The inhabitants now number about 2,600 (Russians and Norwegians) and all work in mining, except for about 30 hunters and fur trappers. Because of the better climate (influenced by the Gulf Stream) it is estimated that in Europe more than half a million people live inside the Arctic Circle, while in America areas in the same latitudes are almost completely uninhabited.

The southern limit of the inhabited area of the Earth is less clearly defined. Starting from the most southerly of the three islands that form New Zealand and going eastwards, there are the islands of the Antipodes which are uninhabited, though the Kermadec Islands, Tuamotu, and Easter Island are all inhabited. The southern tip of South America, Tierra del Fuego, is inhabited, as are the Falkland Islands and South Georgia. So, too, are Tristan de Cunha and St Helena, between the southernmost tips of South America and South Africa. The uninhabited islands of the Indian Ocean are Kegúelen, St Paul, and New Amsterdam.

Conditions in Antarctica make it impossible for permanent human habitation and the sea provides the necessities of life rather than the land. This region contains the world's greatest desert, formed by a high plateau at an altitude of about 10,000 feet with enormous ice-covered areas, bigger than Italy, interrupted by high mountain chains. Exceptionally violent storms make any human settlement difficult even in the coastal areas.

Permanent settlement nearest the Antarctic is at Tierra del Fuego, in Argentina, where Ushuaia, the world's most southerly city, stands. Even so it is situated at only latitude 54° 49' South, which shows the more severe climatic conditions that inhabitants of the southern hemisphere have to face. The city was founded in 1868 by a Protestant mission, and has about 4,000 inhabitants, mostly people of Tierra del Fuego. Puerto Williams has been established farther south on the Chilean island of Navarino, as a naval base with about 350 inhabitants. A similar settlement in terms of latitude is Grytviken, a whaling station in South Georgia with 1,500 inhabitants, at latitude 54° 17'.

Peri-ecumenical and anecumenical areas

For some years now, because of the ever increasing importance of flights over the poles, meteorological stations have been set up to give warning of changes in weather conditions. There are stations in the Canadian and Soviet Arctic (ten in Novaya Zemlya, five in the Northern Territory, six in the islands of New Siberia, etc.). Bases have also been established in the Antarctic, as support for military stations and to prospect for mineral wealth. These can hardly be included as ecumenical regions of the Earth, being isolated outposts where man obtains his means of survival from outside. The meteorological stations and bases are detached from the inhabited and uninhabited regions and it would be more apt to describe them as *peri-ecumenical*, or *fringe areas*.

Apart from the uninhabited regions of the poles and elsewhere, which together make up about one-ninth of the Earth's surface area, there are others at lower latitudes, which although they have been occupied by man are not particularly habitable. These are known

Deserts are uninhabited zones within populated areas and they occupy about the same amount of the Earth's surface as the polar regions. Man's struggle to conquer these barren wastes goes on unceasingly, either because of the continual growth of the population or because modern techniques offer greater means of exploiting the natural resources of these regions. Israel is in the forefront in this campaign. *Above:* An experimental plantation in the Negev desert. *Below:* Ushuaia, Tierra del Fuego, is the world's southernmost town. It is at a latitude equivalent to that of Danzig in the northern hemisphere, showing that the limit of the inhabited polar regions in the southern hemisphere is at a much lower latitude and that this is due not only to the limited extent of the Earth's surface, but also to the harsher climate.

The American Antarctic base at McMurdo Sound, with fuel drums in the foreground.

as *internal anecumenical zones*, and include:

1) The deserts, which in the northern hemisphere form an almost continuous belt from the Sahara across Arabia to the Gobi; in the southern hemisphere the area they occupy is discontinuous (the Kalahari in Africa, the Western Australian Desert, the Atacama Desert in Chile). An essential element in human life is water, which not only satisfies thirst, but is also a necessity for plant and animal life. Where there is a subterranean store of water which rises to the surface, as in the case of oases, life is possible. Where there is no trace of water whatsoever, existence is ruled out. The largest uninhabited areas that are completely without water are in the western Sahara Desert, in the Libyan Desert, in Arabia (especially in the Rub' al-Khali), and in the Gobi Desert. Deserts in the cold countries are also uninhabited and unfit for permanent settlement, such as the vast areas of Siberia, North America (Labrador), and Tibet.

2) Equatorial forests, which, because of the climate (high humidity, heavy rainfall, and high temperatures throughout the year, with minimal variations) and because of biological factors (extreme parasitism), are highly unsuitable for permanent settlement. Conditions are particularly bad in the basins of the Congo and Amazon rivers and in the larger of the Sunda Islands (Borneo, Sumatra) where man can settle only along the banks of certain rivers or in some clearings of the forest.

3) The higher elevations of mountains, which form perhaps the greatest barrier to human settlement. As the height increases, the area of cultivable land diminishes and the climate becomes more and more unsuitable for agriculture. Great uninhabited areas exist in the Alps, the Andes, and the Himalayas, and especially in Tibet. The highest limit at which human settlement is possible varies from the equator to the poles, as does the permanent snowline, but it is also influenced by local factors. Thus the highest inhabited areas are not located at the equator (where there is maximum precipitation in the form of rain), but in the zones to the north and the south. In Tibet, Buddhist monasteries are situated at heights of up to 16,000 feet. In the Americas, the highest villages inhabited by shepherds are located in Peru at an altitude of nearly 17,000 feet, while cultivation ceases at 14,000 feet. There is mining at greater altitudes.

Demographic capacity of the Earth

It is only necessary to look at a map of the population of the world to see how unevenly distributed it is, with almost incredible densities in some regions, while in others, just as well endowed by nature, the population is very small. As a whole the Earth, which may seem to be overpopulated, could accommodate in terms of space and food a far greater number of people.

187

Brisbane, a city of the newest continent, is almost entirely peopled by Europeans from the last stage of exploration for new uninhabited lands.

The problem of determining the number of people that could live on the Earth, once all the planet's resources were available, has only recently been taken up by scientists. Such a calculation has a number of variables, such as the varying needs of people living in different climates and the possibility that new techniques may increase production. On the other hand, in the last few years, our knowledge of the climate and the soil throughout the planet has become much broader and more accurate. The work of Köppen has been of great importance in classifying the Earth's climates.

The German geographer Albert Penck (1858–1945) first attracted the attention of scientists with a paper in which he regarded the relation between man and his environment, in man's need to feed himself, as 'the main problem of physical anthropogeography'. He examined Köppen's eleven climatic regions and calculated that the Earth could accommodate 7,689 million inhabitants. He attributed to each climatic region a population density that could be adequately support by its productivity; for example, in the warm, humid climate of the rain forests he gave an average density of 520 inhabitants to the square mile, in the periodically dry climate of the savana he quoted 230, and for a temperate climate 260. He was thus able to calculate what the population of the separate regions would be, and he considered that while in the present day about 70% of the world's inhabitants live in the temperate zone and 30% in the tropical regions, about 62% of the world's potential population would have to find their livelihood in the tropical zone and only 38% in the temperate zone. Europe and Asia, which at present hold 80% of mankind, could sustain only 25%, once the world population maximum was reached. South America would progress from 3·5% to 25% and Africa from 7% to 29%.

At about the same time (1925) an Austrian, Alois Fischer, was considering the same problem. He tried to determine how much of the Earth's area, as cultivable or grazing land, was required for each individual, bearing in mind his various needs and that productivity depends on the industry of man and increases with the degree of civilization of a group of people. He assessed also the capacity of individual political units to support their populations, differentiating between their natural resources and their dependence on external aid. Obviously, the distribution of population is not entirely governed by the productivity of various regions, and there will always be transmigrations that preserve the balance,
even when the limits of local capacity are exceeded. Fischer's research, allowing for this, aimed at working out a population index for each state, and providing a basis for determining in what way it would be possible to reduce tension in the economic field by a better distribution of population and labour. His calculation of the total world potential population was 6,200 million, somewhat lower than Penck's figure. Differing totals were put forward later (1937) by W. Hollstein, who calculated that the Earth's alimentary capacity could support 13,300 million inhabitants.

Although these various figures do not agree with one another, it is evident that the Earth's population will reach saturation point in a few decades, and the exploitation and development of land must be considered in a rational manner. According to these estimates, Europe is about to reach its population limit, and Asia is not far behind, while other continents have much greater areas at their disposal. However, these areas are not very suitable for population by people of white racial stock, and may have to be reserved for coloured populations. In the course of its evolution, through thousands of years, mankind has developed into diverse types, not only from the physical or somatic point of view, but also from that of climate; man must be able to acclimatize to his new environment if he migrates.

However, there are greater opportunities to make use of territory that hitherto has been little exploited. In Canada, for example, the introduction of a variety of wheat which matures 30 days sooner than other varieties has made it possible to cultivate a zone 60 miles wide. Bigger harvests can be gathered by improved agricultural techniques, including the use of hybrids, better fertilizers, and machinery. In deserts, greater use can be made of deep deposits of water. Even the energy provided by the wind and the tides is beginning to be harnessed, while nuclear energy has been exploited for some time. The use of sea algae, the cultivation of herbaceous vegetation, not in soil but in water-solutions containing all the minerals necessary for a plant to grow and bear fruit, and the use of certain foods (especially sugar) in special processes of fermentation have all been suggested. With all these possibilities in mind, a German economist, F. Baade, in 1961 gave a much more optimistic forecast on the Earth's potential population capacity: he placed it at from 30,000 to 38,000 million, about ten times the present figure.

Collective farming in China: this method laid the basis for the modernization and industrialization of agriculture, an urgent necessity not only for over-populated countries, but for the Earth as a whole, which has shrunk alarmingly in its resources in the light of the recent sharp increase of the population.

This farm in Normandy is a form of settlement dictated by its environment and by the manner in which people earn their livelihood – in this instance by agriculture and the breeding of livestock. With its separate buildings, each having its own function, the farm is typical of a settled community.

INHABITED ZONES

Settled tribes and nomadism

To say that man is either a sedentary or a mobile animal is a conventional way of describing his different reactions to his environment. Really, the problem must be seen as the constant effort by man to achieve conditions of life that satisfy his personal needs, which vary according to the area and time in which he lives. When man settled down he achieved a new form of permanent occupation of the land which laid the foundations of his progressive civilization. The habit of permanent settlement (a phenomenon born with the first agrarian civilizations of the Mesolithic and the Neolithic) is today deeply rooted in him. Moreover, it has become an almost indispensable condition of life on a planet which is becoming overpopulated, and in an ever more highly organized society which necessarily surpasses the limits of local groupings (such as clans, tribes, or nations) characteristic of past civilizations.

Man's decision to settle down is first signified by his occupation of a geographic area in which he develops his personal vital interests such as economics, politics, and religion. Here he takes up residence, which is more or less permanent according to the continuity and intensity of his own interests in that region. Such habitation has always had, especially in the past, the character of a form of dedication to territorial possession and is a visible confirmation of that ownership.

Man does not exercise an entirely free choice as to where and how he will live; human settlement depends to a great extent on the environment, becomes a living part of the landscape and so must take different forms. However, the manner of life, and the extent of the area occupied, is determined also by the individual needs of the people living there – by their social ties, which may be those of the family, the community, or simply formal – that is, an artificial community (as in a modern city, for example) as distinct from an indigenous community (as in a village).

190

The next consideration must be the resources of the area in which they are settled, in relation to their activities. Thus the greatest concentrations of population are usually attracted to areas of limited extent (bearing in mind, however, the possibility of displacement): in wider areas, settlement is likely to be temporary, or else the community is split up into smaller units for practical and economic reasons.

At the present time, more than half of the world's inhabitants live in towns with over 5,000 inhabitants. In 1800 these town dwellers represented only 7% of the world population. This implies that in general, in relation to the increase of the urban population, forms of life and economy progressively need less space. At the same time changed means of communication, and economic collaboration between different zones reciprocating one another's needs, have brought about a different kind of partnership of man, and a greater stability to existing settlements. It is in just such a way that a city like New York, where 12 million inhabitants are concentrated within a few square miles, has economic, cultural,

Australian Aborigines of Arnhem Land. These people hunt animals and gather food over vast areas, and have no fixed home. They take advantage of rocks or caves as refuge from the intense heat.

The social ties that form the core of human societies, and the relationships between these and the environment, are shown in different ways in the two pictures on this page. In the little village of Ossau in the lower Pyrenees *(right)*, the dwellings gathered round a church (in the past round the castle, now ruined) imply many different, natural links with the neighbourhood, suggested by the layout of the village and the cultivated fields. This is also true of the Zulu dwellings *(below)*, which form an enclosure in the surrounding landscape to fence in the livestock.

social, and political relations which have world-wide ramifications.

However, it must not be forgotten that cities (and modern cities especially) represent the most highly developed forms of human settlement and have reached a standard of organized civilization by a long process of social, economic, and political development.

The simplest forms of dwelling, the tent and the hut, date from the early history of man, and each represents the way in which he gained his livelihood – the first, by nomadic animal husbandry, the second by primitive agriculture.

Both ways of life are followed today: the first in a way that has not changed in thousands of years; the second, somewhat more developed even in its primitive form, is much richer in social ferment (the first commercial centres and organized cities grew from agricultural villages).

Nomadism

Nomadism is a way of life rooted in antiquity, and by its very nature is dependent on mobility. It has its origin in the interdependence of man and animals, in a society where animals were the chief source of wealth. Nomads have to keep moving in order to find fresh pastures for their flocks or herds; they spread over wide areas, extending to zones where vegetation is scarce, such as the wild regions of the north and the steppes of central Asia.

A different type of nomadism is that which originated with the settlement of farmers, who cultivated crops and domesticated animals such as sheep, a certain source of wealth compared with the hazards of an exclusively agricultural economy, or of a precarious

economy in danger of attack by predatory nomadic peoples, as had happened often in the past (as, for example, the invasion of Central Asia by the Mongols).

Three types of temporary dwellings used by nomads practising hunting and food-gathering. *Above left:* Shelters made of leaves by the Ituri pygmies in a forest clearing. *Above:* A primitive shelter made by Australian aborigines. *Below:* A construction of woven straw made by the Caragia Indians of the Amazon during the seasonal migrations when they hunt for fish along the banks of the Araguaia.

The nomadism of hunters and food-gatherers

By an extension of terms, people who hunt and gather their food are also nomads. The hunting nomadic people who have survived include the Bushmen of the Kalahari, in Africa, although they have been reduced in numbers by the infiltration into their territory of the Bantu and of Europeans. Bushmen hunt animals, and have to search for sources of water. The Australian aborigines have similar characteristics and they, too, roamed over wide areas of the Australian continent, before the coming of the European, hunting animals such as the kangaroo, or fishing along the coasts. The pygmies of the Congo and other parts of equatorial Africa are also a nomadic hunting people. All these people are also food-gatherers, and seek fruit, roots, etc. They have no fixed homes, but live in temporary shelters – in the case of the pygmies these are made from leafy branches and situated in forest clearings.

Hunting nomads also include the prairie Indians who once followed the herds of bison. Today they lead a sedentary life inside their reservations. Their former nomadism was linked with the migrations of the herds and thus was different from that of other people who practised a more erratic form of nomadism. This is also true of the hunters who live in cold regions such as Siberia and Canada, because the seasonal cycle imposes a more regular rhythm on their activities, while the long winter makes it necessary for them to have fixed settlements to shelter those members of the community who do not take part in hunting expeditions.

The makeshift dwellings of these people consist usually of poles

At the end of the summer (from 5 to 20 September) large caravans of Ghilzai nomads come down from the higher zones where they have spent the hot months and spread across the vast plains of south-western Afghanistan with their flocks.

pushed into the ground to form a conical framework which is covered with animal skins or matting, such as the *tepees* of the American prairies. The *toldo*, consisting of vertical poles set up in parallel lines and covered in skins, was once quite common in the Patagonian steppe land.

Pastoral nomadism

Pastoral nomadism today is connected chiefly with the raising of sheep, goats, camels, horses, and reindeer. These animals are the determining factors of nomadism, understood as movement from place to place (at more or less intermittent periods) by entire families with all their goods and chattels. Originally each type of nomadism corresponded in general to the type of animal being raised, and each culture must have been influenced by a different environment, according to the distribution of the various kinds of animals. Today, however, camels, sheep and goats are often raised together, as happens in the arid and semi-arid zones of Asia and Africa. Three main areas of pastoral nomadism can be said to exist: the northern reindeer zone; the steppes and prairies of central Asia, where at one time camels and sheep as well as horses were raised; and the goat, sheep, and camel region of the Iranian plateau and south-western Asia, where there are close similarities to the pas-

toral nomadism practised in Africa.

In south-western Asia nomadism probably developed, at least in the Iranian plateau, from the great nomadism of the horse-breeders of central, Asia where it is a cultural phenomenon with its roots in prehistory.

Above right: Nomads on the move: their way of life is inevitably one of constant insecurity, governed by their animals' needs. *Below:* Thousands of tents form this unusual encampment of pilgrims in the plain of Arafat, around Mecca, during the spring ceremonies. Mecca is not only the spiritual centre of Islam, it is also the geographic centre of pastoral nomadism in the semi-arid and arid regions of the Old World. This is no coincidence: nomadism has certain psychological characteristics which are typical of a Moslem believer.

MAIN REGIONS OF PASTORAL NOMADISM IN AFRICA AND ASIA

- northern reindeer region
- steppe region of central Asia (horses, camels, sheep)
- semi-arid and arid tropical (camels, sheep, goats)

Distribution of types of tent used by stockbreeding nomads:

- conical, framework of poles
- Turko-Mongolian, pointed or rounded roof
- Arab-Tibetan, quadrangular dome-shaped, framework of poles.

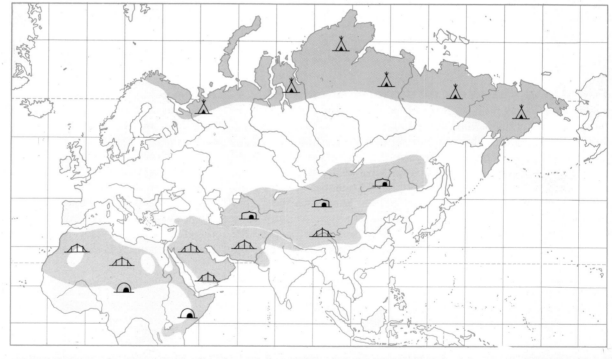

Tsetserlig is a centre consisting half of permanent dwellings and half of *jurta* (tents). It is situated on the road that crosses Mongolia, 250 miles west of Ulan Bator, on the slopes of the Khangai Mountains. The site was originally occupied by a monastery and today it is an important trading and livestock centre which attracts nomads belonging to new collective groups, common in socialist countries.

Forms and character of pastoral nomadism

Today it is rare for any group of people to live an exclusively nomadic form of life without exploiting some agricultural resources. In the humid regions which do not suffer from periods of drought, nomads practise a form of agriculture from time to time; they plant cereals which have a rapid vegetative cycle, such as barley, and return to the place at harvest time. The tent is still the only form of dwelling for these people. Often they own land that is fertile enough to warrant a less summary type of cultivation and cannot be left untended; in these cases, only part of the nomadic group move on with the animals in search of pasture; the rest stay behind. Some groups may keep on the move for most of the year, but still remain within a short radius of cultivated oases they may own or use for trading purposes. All nomadism in the Sahara and Arabia is connected with ownership of oases and wells, so that in most cases the way of life is really semi-nomadic.

The group that is left behind to tend the crops lives in permanent dwellings which are furnished and equipped according to the level of prosperity obtained from the crops. The nomads on the move live in tents that have to be carried from place to place and therefore must be easy to dismantle and light to carry. These tents are made from skins or wool, with a framework that is usually

An encampment at the foot of the Hindu Kush in western Afghanistan. A flock of sheep is seen in the foreground. These animals are the main base of the economy of this small group of nomads led by a *rish safid* (elder). The group has pitched its tents for ten days (20–30 August) before migrating south. The small craters are wells connected with subterranean canals, which indicate the proximity of an oasis and of an inhabited centre, essential conditions for nomads who are faced with the need to obtain water and to trade their animals for foodstuffs and other consumer goods.

of tamarisk wood or, more rarely, of bone. Carpets are the most common form of furnishing. Bedouin tents are made from the wool of sheep or camels that has been spun and woven. Several tents are pitched together to form an encampment with an open area (*merah*) in the middle where the herds are kept to prevent them from being stolen or attacked by other animals. In central Asia, where the climate is of the continental type, tents are bigger and more comfortable, such as the Turkish-Mongolian bell-tents known as *jurta*. These are made to withstand the rigours of winter and consist of a wooden framework covered with felt and leather; they are anchored to the ground to prevent them being blown away.

The nomads know every inch of their territory and use every scrap of vegetation that grows on it, both the grass of the steppes and plants which spring up after a sudden fall of rain. In their travels they have to take several things into account: they must always be near wells or oases; they must carry provisions with them, and they must look for employment as carriers of goods produced by settled tribes. The latter, in exchange for animal products, supply them with dates, barley, tea, and sugar.

Pastoral nomadism can be classified in various ways, according to the following criteria: whether the nomads consist of small groups of two or three tents or of large encampments; whether the movement is within a short or wide radius, and whether it is continuous or confined to a certain time of the year; and according to the type of animal raised.

The herdsmen of the Sahara who wander over large territories follow the meridian of the Sun, possibly to take advantage of zenithal rainfall, or else to profit from the meagre winter rains associated with the low pressures of the countries round the Mediterranean. In the latter case they stay in the coastal regions until the harvest of the cereals, helping the local farmers during the threshing. The movements of nomads in winter are usually of a greater range than in summer, because the weather is not so oppressively hot and they do not have to spend so much time sheltering from the Sun.

Women and children of the great Ghilzai tribe of Afghanistan. Their tent is made of woven sheep's wool, and its shape is much the same as can be seen from Tibet to Iran and from Arabia to Morocco.

In the Near East, the 'fertile crescent' has always attracted nomads. This is the area of steppe land at the edge of the Syrian and Arabian deserts, where the nomads find a refuge during the hottest months. In central Asia and on the Iranian plateau the most common forms of nomadism are based on the different temperatures of the plains and the mountains, the latter offering better conditions in summer with cooler temperatures.

Nomadism is now in decline everywhere. There are many reasons for this: the decline of the caravan trade, the use of mechanical vehicles for crossing deserts, the reduction of the feudal rights of the nomads over oases, military operations during the Second World War, the use of machinery for threshing grain, and the

Nomads arriving at their summer pastures (July 20) on the coastal plain of Lake Wan, eastern Turkey, at an altitude of 5,600 feet. These nomads spend the winter in the valley of the Tigris (1,000 feet) where they practise some agriculture, so that they might be described as semi-nomadic.

The winter base of a group of Uzbeks in the Surkhab valley. The picture was taken at the arrival of the group from their summer pasture in the mountains. These semi-nomadic people raise camels and karakul sheep along the northern slopes of the Hindu Kush.

discovery of huge petroleum deposits found in Arabia and in the Sahara. Another reason is the government policy of setting up public works aimed at attracting nomads to a settled way of life and eliminating the many passive aspects implicit in nomadism.

Transhumance

While people who carry on a nomadic way of life spend all or most of their time travelling from place to place, in transhumance only some groups of herdsmen accompany their herds, leaving the rest of their families behind in permanent settlements where agriculture is carried on in the immediate vicinity and to which the herdsmen return after long intervals. Another feature of transhumance is the exploitation of certain defined pastures at seasonal times of the year. These grazing grounds are auxiliary to, and usually separated by, cultivated areas of woodland.

Transhumance is of ancient origin, and occurs in the greater part of the Mediterranean regions (the Atlas Mountains, the Pyrenese, the Alps, the Apennines, the Balkans, etc.). In the Mediterranean area it mainly affects sheep, which can live in the open

A Libyan nomad ploughing a field at the edge of the desert.

Sheep resting near the Piacenza region of the river Po, pictured in October when the animals come down from the Apennines to the Paduan Plain.

without having to be penned. The shepherds live in primitive dwellings. In winter pastures, they build huts of bracken and at night the flock is kept within wire enclosures. On summer mountain pastures, the flocks are kept inside stone pens with a simple shelter for the shepherd. Formerly, sheep were taken to pasture along sheep-tracks, but now they are carried in specially fitted trucks from the winter grazing grounds in the plains to the summer mountain pastures, and vice versa.

Research has shown that transhumance occurs not only in Mediterranean countries, but in all continents and at all latitudes from the Equator as far as latitudes 50° North and South; for many regions, however, information is too scant for a definitive classifica-

tion. However, six distinct types of transhumance can be made out:

1) Normal transhumance, by far the most frequent form in Mediterranean countries. It involves the use of mountain pastures in summer and those of the plains for the rest of the year. The radiation centres from which the flocks set out in the spring are often close to the winter pastures, though in the Apennines they are midway.

2) Inverse transhumance, in which agricultural areas are located in the mountains, near the summer pastures. When at the end of the summer season the grazing grounds are used up, the owners of the flocks have to look for new pastures for the winter, and find them in lower regions. This occurs, for example, in the Mari-

Left: Wooden houses in a *yayla*, the summer residence of shepherds in the arid interior of Anatolia at the edge of the forest of the plateau. *Right:* A farm in North Island, New Zealand, which provides summer pasture for livestock that has come from the coastal plains. As well as a fenced area for the flocks, there are living quarters for the shepherd and a building for tools and livestock products.

time Alps. This type of transhumance is also common in the Balkans.

3) Winter, or tropical, transhumance, in which as a rule the flocks go to higher grazing grounds in autumn and come down again in spring. This is characteristic of those tropical regions where seasonal temperature fluctuations are not great, but where rainfall is of greater importance. The winter is dry, creating a shortage of pastures for the animals, while in the rainy summer season the pastures flourish. This type of transhumance takes place in the Andes, Patagonia, and eastern Africa.

4) Small-scale transhumance, as in the Maritime Alps, for example, where the climatic conditions make it possible to keep animals on the mountains all the year round; they are moved in winter to lower regions of the same mountain area. A similar type has lasted for centuries in the Pyrenees, where it has led to special agreements between French and Spanish livestock owners.

5) Partial or mixed transhumance, which occurs when agricultural cultivation is so far developed that it leaves less room for pasture in the plains in winter, so that local pasture is no longer adequate to feed livestock, which has to be partially fed with fodder brought from outside the area. Often the areas allotted to the livestock are fenced off, and sometimes byres are built to house the animals. This has happened, on a large scale, in the open country round Rome, in Greece, and in other Mediterranean countries.

6) Complex transhumance, which includes cases in which there are intermediate grazing grounds between the winter and summer pastures where the flocks feed for a period during their migrations. The combinations of these can vary widely from region to region.

Summer mountain pasture

The removal to summer mountain pasture is different in character from transhumance, and must not be confused with it, because the grazing grounds are not distant, but are usually at different levels on the same mountain slope. However, limited though the movement is, it requires adaptation to quite considerable changes of altitude. Another difference is the greater importance of dairy cattle in this type of grazing, as compared with the goats and sheep of transhumance. For the most part the chief industry in these

Left: A herd of cattle in their summer mountain pasture near a small glacial lake on the Little St Bernard Pass. *Above:* Alpine herdsman's living quarters, which are lived in on a temporary basis and surrounded by fields of potatoes. *Right:* Another herdsman's house in the Alps, with its roof made of tiles from local schistose rocks.

Right: One of the most primitive forms of dwelling: a hut resembling an empty nut-shell or a bird's nest. This is the *kraal* or *manyatta* of the Turkana herdsmen who live in the vast savanas of northern Kenya, south of Lake Rudolph. The framework is made of sticks and covered with dried dung and mud. *Far right:* A simple structure does not always signify a low cultural level, but reflects the way in which people make use of the materials that are readily available in their immediate surroundings.

mountain pastures is the production of cheese and butter. The herdsmen's quarters are therefore better constructed, either as detached dwellings or grouped together to form temporary villages.

To use the grazing grounds to the best possible advantage, the herdsmen migrate with their cattle according to the season, following a timetable which has been determined for centuries and is only slightly revised when weather conditions are particularly bad. Having spent the winter in the villages, where the animals are kept in comfortable byres and fed on hay gathered during the summer months, the herdsmen set out in the spring for the grazing grounds (or fallow land) half-way up the mountain; these are mostly privately owned. The buildings are of masonry or of masonry and wood, and are usually two storeys high, the lower floor being the byre for the animals, with a room for the herdsman, and the upper

floor a hayloft. Some form of cultivation is also carried out in the fallow land surrounding these buildings, such as the growing of potatoes and other vegetables. After a fortnight or more, the herdsmen drive their animals farther up the mountain to the higher grazing grounds, where the land is generally communally owned or belongs to public organizations. The upper limits of these pastures are reached by mid-July. By the end of September, or earlier if weather conditions are poor, the herds begin to come down towards the permanent villages, stopping occasionally at the intermediate grazing grounds. In the higher grazing grounds, at altitudes ranging from one to one and a half miles, buildings used to shelter both men and animals are fairly large, according to the importance of the pasture area.

The main building has many rooms, housing the dairy, where milk, cheese and butter are processed and stored, and provides accommodation for the herdsmen. There are also cattle-sheds, and store-rooms. These buildings are mostly of masonry and wood, with roofs of slate, slabs of rock, or zinc sheeting.

Classification of dwellings

Man's living quarters can be classified according to different criteria. Factors to be taken into account include the type of activity predominant in the life of the person who has built the house; the length of time for which the building is likely to be of use; the type of material used in its construction; the relationship between it and neighbouring houses; and differentiation between scattered dwellings and those in centralized areas.

If they are judged according to the types of activity connected with them, without giving a full classification, they can be broadly divided into the following categories:

1) Dwellings of people who gain their livelihood exclusively from fishing. This class includes the igloos of the Eskimos, the dwellings of the herring fishermen of Norway and the cod fishermen of Brittany, and the coastal habitations of southern Asia, which in some cases are built on poles. Typical fisher-folk dwellings are also to be found along the great rivers of Africa and in many other parts of the world.

2) Dwellings of people who obtain their living from forest regions, such as the log cabins of Canada and the wooden huts of the Alps, Finland, Siberia, the Ivory Coast, and certain regions of South America.

3) Dwellings of pastoral people. In this category the type of housing depends on the method of rearing, and the needs of, the livestock. There can be many different types of shelter as well as the nomads' tents and the temporary huts of the summer mountain pastures, which have already been discussed; there are the dwellings

The pictures on these two pages show only a few of the many different types of dwellings found in different parts of the world. The types vary according to climate, the activities and needs of the inhabitants, the material used in their construction, and other environmental factors.

Left: Huts made from coconut-palm leaves at Dhanushkodi, a fishing village in southern Madras, India.

Below: Houses made of blocks of basalt quarried from the mountains of Kurdistan. The roof serves as a threshing-floor and as a working area for the women.

Above: Cells carved out of the erosion cones at Cappadocia by Byzantine monks during the Middle Ages. A form of cave-dwelling, this was a perfect adaptation to local conditions.

Right: Enclosed dwelling – a house typical of mountain-dwelling people of the Hindu Kush.

Top left: A sampan, or houseboat, characteristic of the rivers of the monsoon region of Asia. *Above left:* Houses at Monschau, Germany; rural dwellings adapted to urban conditions, but with only slight modifications to the old buildings. *Above right:* Small modern houses occupied by Greenlanders at Umanak. *Below:* Fishermen's houses at Mykonos in the Aegean Sea; the small windows and the white walls are designed to keep the interior cool. *Right:* Longleat House, Wiltshire: a stately home which stems from an urban and civilized concept of living.

of farmers who prefer to raise cattle rather than farm the land, as in the Po valley (Italy), Denmark, and New Zealand, and also the great ranches or *estancias* of Argentina, where cattle live chiefly in the open.

4) Dwellings of people employed mainly in agriculture. These can vary considerably according to whether the form of agriculture is primitive, traditional, or more or less specialized. Besides living accommodation, the farmer's house in this category almost always has other buildings in which to store they products of the fields and their by-products, such as a large cellar for keeping wine cool or a shed for storing hemp.

If, instead, dwellings are evaluated according to the length of time that they are likely to be required, they can be classified in a different way. There are then: temporary shelters, needed for only one night, such as those of food-gathering people who are satisfied with shelters made from leaves; temporary dwellings, such as the tents used for some weeks by nomadic shepherds; seasonal dwellings, occupied by herdsmen practising transmigration, or semi-permanent dwellings occupied for some years, such as the huts of African Negroes who abandon their villages once the land has become infertile through excessive growth of the same kind of crops. Lastly, there is the type most common in advanced countries, where the permanent dwellings are rebuilt from time to time, but are occupied by several generations.

Many kinds of materials are used to build these houses. The Eskimos use snow and ice to build their igloos. In Siberia, Canada, Scandinavia, Finland, and Alpine areas, wood is often used in the form of logs or planks, while the houses, to minimize the risk of fire, are built detached from each other.

Other useful raw materials include blocks of peat (in Poland and northern Germany); bricks of mixed mud and straw, baked in the sun (in the black-earth regions of Russia), or dried mud (in the poorer Mediterranean regions, especially in Egypt, where clay

Above: Huts providing living accommodation, and small buildings used as granaries by the peasants of Bobo, Upper Volta.

Right: Inside a fortified village *(qala)* of Iran. Agriculture and livestock breeding are practised together. The inner enclosures are for the animals and are overlooked by the cell-like living quarters.

can be mixed with straw and used to cover a wooden framework). In regions where quarries provide suitable building material, such as limestone or granite, stone is the main material. Roofs, also, are made from a wide range of materials; in the rainy equatorial regions, leaves are used as well as branches or any other forest vegetation. In the steppes and in the grassy grain-growing regions, reeds or thatch may be used. Where wood is plentiful, planking is used. Wood has the advantage of being an elastic material and can bear heavy loads of snow; this type of roof is built with a sharp slope so that the snow runs off easily. Where there is plenty of clay and the climate is dry, as in Egypt, terraced roofs of mud are built with a supporting wooden framework. In mountain areas, stone slabs are used. In tablelands where there is clay soil, and most houses are brick-built, roofs are usually tiled.

Rural dwellings

Rural dwellings are adapted to meet the needs of the farmer and the agricultural worker and so vary from place to place.

Many factors have to be taken into consideration; first there is that of function – that is, the structure of the house and the arrangement of its rooms, in relation to the type of rural life in which it has its setting. Then there are geographical features which have different effects, such as humidity, climate, and whether or not water is readily available. Historical influences also play a part, because frequently the buildings meet the needs of the past, but are not adapted to modern conditions. Economic and

social influences (for example, the system of ownership and tenancy, etc.), and ethnological problems (which persist even after the population has migrated from one part of the world to another) have also to be taken into account.

Classifying according to function, six different types of rural dwellings can be distinguished in Europe, of which four are uniform (that is, single buildings under one roof) and two consist of groups of buildings. These main types are:

1) The simple house with only one room. A common form in the past, it is now found in Europe only in Albania, and Sardinia, more often as a temporary dwelling. (Outside Europe, it is found in Egypt and in southern Asia.). In earlier times, animals lived under the same roof as man, but later sheds were built for them.

2) Houses with adjoining rooms. Usually these are a kitchen, bedrooms, a stable, etc. They are common in northern and central France, in Belgium, and in certain parts of central Germany. They are also found in Russia.

3) Houses with communicating rooms. This type is common in the Netherlands, north-west Germany, and Lorraine.

4) Multiple-storeyed houses. These are the most common type of dwelling in Italy, and house both peasants and farmers. The peasants occupy the ground floor, where the stable, cellar, kitchen, and tool store are also situated; the upper floor is the living area and is often reached by an outside stone staircase. Houses with two storeys are found in the Balkans and in northern Turkey, where the upper floor overhangs the lower, which is used for stabling and storage.

Top left: A Dutch house with a water-mill. *Top right:* A Breton house. *Right:* A farmhouse of an agricultural inspector in the Black Forest.

5) Courtyards, in which the houses are either situated round a walled yard or themselves form an enclosed area. These houses are usually quite spacious, and nearby are stables, haylofts, tool-sheds, and buildings for processing and storing products, such as drying sheds for tobacco. This type of house is found in the Po valley, northern France, western Germany, Bohemia, and Spain. It also occurs in central Asia, especially as a means of protection in stock-breeding areas.

6) Detached houses built round an open area. These resemble the previous group and are typical of livestock farms and ranches. They are found in the Swiss Alps, northern Germany, and parts of northern Italy and Britain.

It is interesting to look into the characteristics of rural settlements; the arrangement of the buildings is relative to the landscape, reflecting their agricultural function, and is influenced by the natural surroundings, social conditions, types of cultivation and ethnic considerations. In hilly country, dwellings are likely to be scattered, as is also the case where there is a large number of springs. In regions where the soil is calcareous, buildings tend to be clustered together round deep springs. Where the climate is cold and damp, houses are built in groups to form villages. Conditions of insecurity and exposure to attack also oblige farmers to group together for defensive purposes. This occurs in coastal regions, where the enemy can land on the shore, and in open areas exposed to the danger of invasion, as on the fringes of the steppes or the deserts. On large estates, rural dwellings are for the most part concentrated in large villages, either because land-owners can more easily avoid their property being taken over by the peasants, who, living on the land they cultivate, might be prompted to lay claim to it, or because farm labourers living in villages or towns can find employment more easily than they would if they lived in isolated areas. On the other hand, in those regions that are reclaimed and in which colonies are set up either by the state or by large owners, scattered dwellings are predominant.

Systems of cultivation and types of crop also have an influence on the type of rural settlement. In the past, especially when crop rotation was carried out by collective farming, this led to over-crowding. Later, with the division of the land into smallholdings, housing became scattered, with dwellings situated in the heart of the property and often enclosed by hedges. The *bocage* of Brittany is a typical example. Intensive forms of cultivation, such as orchards, vineyards, and citrus groves, require more attention from the farm worker and therefore the houses are farther apart, while extensive cultivation is for the most part practised by peasants living in villages.

Isolated, scattered, and centralized dwellings

From a geographical point of view, a classification of considerable importance is that which makes a distinction between isolated houses, distant from each other, and localities where houses are either scattered over an uncontrolled or an unsettled area, but are near each other, or where they are in central areas such as a village or city. There are, of course, many intermediate forms.

A farm in Walloon Belgium showing the house, stables, hayloft, and storage sheds, which overlook an inner courtyard. This is a typical example of isolated dwelling, which in its basic lines depends on the nature and the size of the property, as well as the type of farming carried on.

Left: A farm in New Hampshire with silos in the background.

Below: A Brazilian fazenda in Paraná. The farm is isolated in woody surroundings and, as in all parts which are being colonized, it represents the first element of change in a natural landscape.

Above: A castle at Verrucola in Tuscany, Italy. In the past, towns developed with the castle, church or monastery as the focal point.

A fortified village near Meshed, Iran. This form of settlement consists of numerous dwellings, typical of the open arid regions of the Iranian plateau, and ruled by the landowner. Despite the structure of the village, the inhabitants have no community or family ties and are entirely dependent on the landlord for employment. This corruption of a primitive social structure is a consequence of the system of land ownership.

A large sugar-cane plantation in Jamaica. The houses of the plantation workers are part of a design which recalls that of circular African villages.

In marshy regions land needs to be drained and this is achieved through a system of parallel ditches leading to a river, as in this zone near Bangkok. This results in houses being located along the banks of the river, which is also a communication route, and to the division of plots of land into parallel strips.

5) Embankment villages, with houses lining roads bordering a river or canal. The roads are on top of the embankment while the houses are situated lower down, at the foot of the outer wall. These villages are usually located on reclaimed land and are sometimes known as Flemish villages, not only because they are found in Flanders, but also because they reflect conditions prevailing in the Low Countries.

6) Heaped villages, with their houses massed together in an irregular pattern, without any formal plan, round a square or a castle, and separated by narrow winding streets. These villages show conditions of the past and are found in Europe and northern Africa. Villages with the houses shouldering one another lend themselves best to defence and, having narrow streets, offer much shade in summer. At the same time their population density is high.

7) Round villages (*Runddörfer* in Germany), with the houses radiating from an open centre, which is usually accessible through one entrance only. This open space provides grazing ground and night shelter for cattle and sheep. A similar form of round village, but with huts instead of houses, is the African *kraal*, designed for defensive purposes, indicating that similar social conditions can inspire similar forms of settlement in different types of people.

8) Radial villages, with roads radiating from a central nucleus, and thus promoting communications between the centre and the periphery.

9) Insular or peninsular villages, built originally for defensive purposes on an island or a spit of land at a time when there was little security against possible attack from outside.

10) Coastal or seaside villages, arising from the growth of an inland town, when, with improved conditions of security, the building of roads and railways attracted population. These villages are built along the shoreline and earn their livelihood from fishing and trade, or from tourism during the summer months.

This classification takes in most villages of flat countries. In hilly or mountainous areas, where the morphological features of the region are the governing factor, the site of settlement is of paramount importance. The links with the physical environment are much closer because all the available land must be put to the best possible use. Classifications within this category (that of location) include valley-floor villages, bridge villages, basin villages, hillside coastal villages, terraced villages, mountain or ridge-top villages, peak villages, spur villages, and mountain pass villages. In mountainous regions, vital factors that have to be taken into consideration include exposure and the need for a sheltered position (especially if the wind is strong), as well as the land formation.

Whatever the transformation wrought in the past by rapid development, natural disasters, or wars, a village as a geographical entity typical of a basically agricultural society shows far more definite changes today, due to industrial development and town-planning. *Above:* The ruins of Eski Dogubayazit in Armenia, near Mount Ararat. The village, established in the 18th century round the citadel of a Kurdish Pasha, was partly destroyed by the Russians in 1914 and subsequently devastated by earthquakes. It was abandoned and re-built in the plain of Ararat near the frontier road linking Turkey and Iran. *Below:* Industrialization in the Po Valley has disturbed the pattern of the old centres and created new forms of habitation, raising many small agricultural villages to the rank of cities.

Urbanism is primarily the product of an agrarian social system in which concentration of population, brought about by new and particular social and political institutions, is made possible by the exploitation of the resources of the river-banks, which put agriculture on a firm economic base for the first time in Asia. The map shows the distribution of cities between 1900 and 1400 B.C., together with the distribution of villages, which formed the first step towards urbanism.

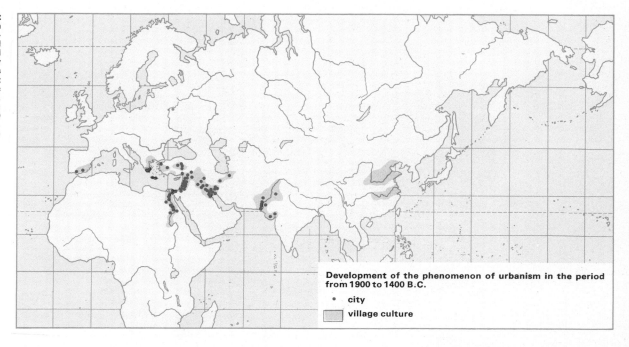

Development of the phenomenon of urbanism in the period from 1900 to 1400 B.C.

• city

▨ village culture

Urbanism

The creation of cities is without question the most radical of the changes wrought by man on the landscape. A preliminary classification of cities could be given according to the degree of the departure from the limits set by the original natural conditions. At the two extremes could be placed the village, closely tied to its physical environment, on which it depends and to which it gives the first forms of social organization, and the megalopolis, which is predominant, with its tentacles spreading over the landscape.

A constant element in urban growth, from ancient times to the present day, is the creativity of an organized society aimed not so much at the settlement of a number of families, as the setting-up of a religious, civil, political, and commercial system for a whole community within an entire region.

Whether a city is born and grows in response to some sort of historical destiny (that is, as an inevitable result of political, religious, and social factors) or according to strict geographical laws (determined by topographical conditions, natural means of communication, suitable environment, etc.) is no longer a controversial topic. Vidal de la Blache was the first to establish that in different measures both theories, considered in conjunction, could explain the origin and the development of a city. Exceptions

The diagram *(right)* is a plan of Ur (4000 B.C.), the first city to have all the characteristics of urbanism, such as the fortified wall, palaces, tombs, and living quarters. Symbolically the topography was in conformity with a particular social hierarchy, enclosed within a 'sacred perimeter'. The map *(far right)* shows the quarters of Mohenjo Daro (4000–2000 B.C.) in the Indus valley. The density of the houses and of the streets is one of the earliest indications of the tendency to urbanism which reached its peak in the first industrial age.

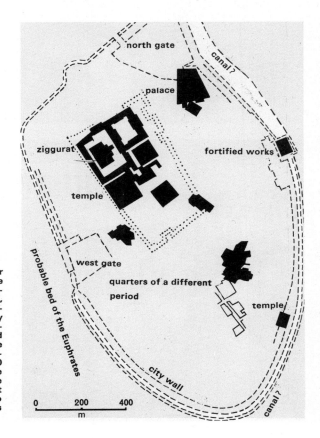

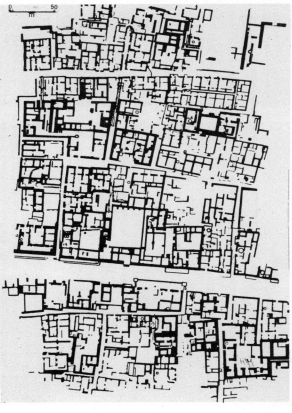

213

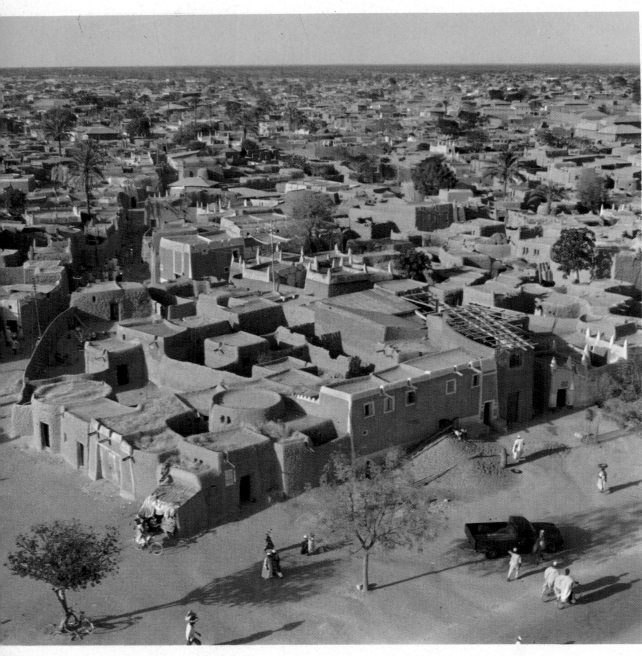

Kano, an example of an African city on the fringes of the Sahara, which flourished as a commercial centre at the time of the great trading exchanges between black and white Africa and developed under Arab influence.

The Acropolis, centre of the ancient Athenian city, served as the fulcrum for an urban society that lasted without a break for centuries.

Aigues-Mortes in southern France, a typical example of a fortified medieval city *(bastide)*, was planned by a group of Genoese architects in the 13th century. It is laid out geometrically, and appears to be modelled on the Arabic pattern.

are those cities which were deliberately created out of nothing, in surroundings chosen more for political reasons than geographical ones (Brasilia, for example); but it is true also that there are places so well endowed geographically as to be the sole justification for the creation of a city and the rebirth of a new city on the same site at the end of a historical cycle.

The fact remains that the fate of a city, independently of the causes of its foundation, is tied to complex geographical, political, economic, and cultural influences. Often only one of these factors, such as the change of a political border, the advancement of a coastline, or the discovery of coal deposits, can predominate over the others and bring about a sudden halt or speed up the development of an urban centre. Some cities go into decline and others grow and prosper, but today urbanism, which had its inception in the 18th century, is of particular interest and is of ever-increasing importance.

The powerful appeal of industry, which in the more economically and politically advanced countries has been growing for the past 150 years, has brought about a serious depopulation of the countryside, accompanied by a large increase of city population, the consequences of which are reflected in ways of living, in social customs, and in the culture of hundreds of millions of people.

215

Teheran, which until the 18th century was still a village of shepherds at the foot of the Elburz mountains, has developed since becoming the capital city of Iran, taking on a modern structure based on Western ideas.

Below: An aerial view of a crowded quarter of Zanzibar, with the small houses lying in cheerful chaos, without relation to any rational plan.

Urban centres

The characteristics that distinguish cities are extremely complex and it is not always easy to make this distinction. Sometimes numbers are taken as a criterion, with all centres having a population exceeding a certain figure considered as cities. But in countries of former civilizations, as in most of Europe, even centres with only a few hundred inhabitants can bear a strong imprint of urbanism. Another distinctive feature can be the density of the buildings, although this is not an adequate standard, as even in heaped villages it is possible to find a heavy density of population. Political, economic, and cultural factors also have been taken into account, as well as the network of communications converging towards a focal point. But the most important consideration is the existence of a complex economy based on an activity that stems chiefly from trade and industry.

The most striking feature of a city is that it is not a homogeneous body; as well as residential quarters there are industrial and commercial areas with buildings for cultural use (schools, libraries, museums), for entertainment (theatres and cinemas), for sport (stadiums), for defence (barracks), for social needs (hospitals, hostels, convents), for administration, etc. The city, therefore, is not merely an overgrown village, but has its own functions and is the highest expression of a civilization. The different activities go on at the same time, but it is possible for one of these to be pre-eminent. Therefore, one can differentiate between agricultural cities, industrial cities, commercial cities, mining cities, resorts, military cities, religious cities, seats of learning, and political cities.

To explain the conditions which have influenced the rise and growth of a city it is necessary to take into consideration the physical

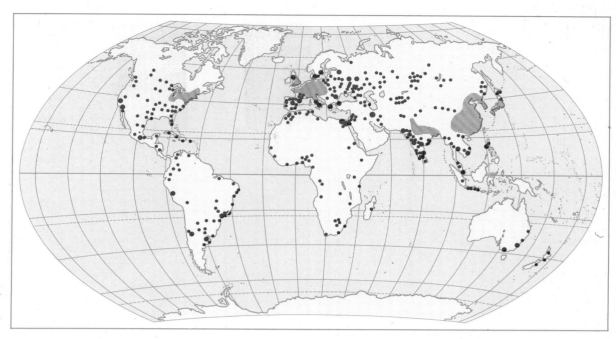

MAJOR URBAN AREAS
OF THE WORLD

░░ densely populated zones

Isolated cities:

● more than 1,000,000 inhabitants

• 100,000 to 1,000,000 inhabitants

features distinguishing the general situation of a city from the local position. The general situation concerns the vast geographic horizon that surrounds the urban centre, while consideration of the topographical site shows how the city was able to spring up in a particular place. The site therefore explains the origin of a city; the favourable situation explains its subsequent development. In some cases the geographical situation and the topographical position are equally favourable – for example in the case of Constantinople, which is situated at the crossing of land and sea routes and was established on a small and easy-to-defend peninsula

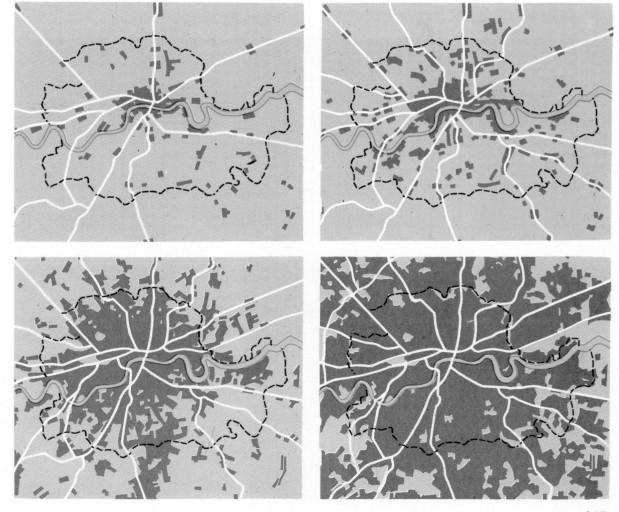

Four successive phases in the urban development of London around its old centre on the Thames, and following the lines of the old Roman roads. In 1660 the city had 450,000 inhabitants; in 1750, about 750,000; in 1862, 3,222,500 (2,808,500 in the county area); and in 1971, 7,379,014. To a great extent the development of the world's largest cities is due to industrial expansion during the past hundred years.

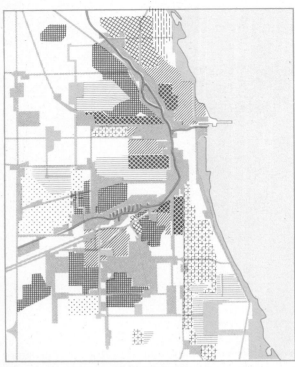

Far left: The diagram relates to Chicago, but it could apply more or less to any industrial city where immigrants always tend to live in colonies with their compatriots, to counteract, both practically and psychologically, the disruptive effect wrought by industrial urbanism on the spirit of the community. Left: Isochrones, lines of equal distance in time from the city centre, show the rhythm of life as well as the efficiency, or lack of it, in a city with only one major centre.

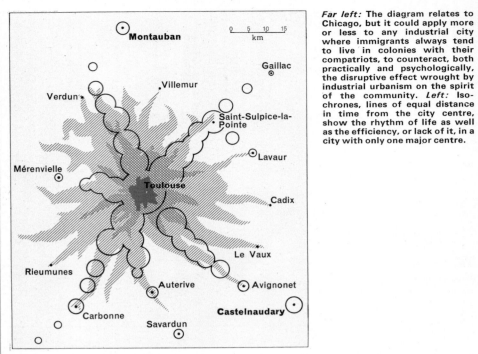

Ethnic segregation of Chicago immigrants
(according to Halbwachs-Baulig)

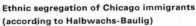

Czechoslovaks		Swedes	
Jews		Germans	
Italians		Mixed population	
Negroes		Parks and avenues	
Poles and Lithuanians		Industrial and railway zones	

Isochrones for the city of Toulouse (France)
(according to J. Coppolani)

city centre

Zones from which the centre can be reached in:

less than 30 minutes by bus

less than 60 minutes by bus

○ less than 60 minutes by rail

The flow of rural immigrants towards cities is not always fully absorbed. This, basically, is the origin of the *bidonvilles*, or shanty towns, where the immigrants set up temporary residence in conditions which do not come up to the standards of modern city life. This state of affairs is typical of countries going through the first phase of rapid uncontrolled industrialization, and also of those countries with a poor economy in which a city comes into being that has features quite extraneous to the economic and social structures of the country. This is the case in Beirut, as can be seen from the photograph *(left)*, which shows the chaotic jumble of shacks that has sprung up on the margins of a residential area.

Night view of the fast motorways on the periphery of San Francisco.

Below right: A freeway in Los Angeles; this big Californian city has an urban structure of areas of varying density of population distributed over a wide region, so that we speak of it as a city-region. Motorways for fast traffic are the chief means of communication: the motor-car is almost the only means of transport in this city, even for local journeys by businessmen to and from their place of work.

Below: The great arteries of communication, both road and rail, which reach or leave the city at different points, provide the first indication of the range of action in which the city itself operates and the measure of the relationships which it promotes and fosters with the outlying areas. The complex development of roads and railways which cross each other near Fort Worth in Texas, a modern commercial and industrial city, is a striking example of this.

near the Golden Horn, which constitutes an ideal natural harbour. In other cases only the geographic position is favourable: this is true of New York in regard to North America, the Atlantic, and Europe, while its topographic site is unfavourable and restricted so that the city could develop only from north to south along the island of Manhattan, between the estuaries of the Hudson and the East rivers. The city was obliged to find more space by building skyscrapers and had to be connected by bridges and subways to its suburbs in Long Island and Brooklyn. Similar cases include Genoa and Algiers.

Cities can also be classified according to their population. Thus one can differentiate between rural cities (with 2,000 to 5,000 population), small cities (5,000 to 20,000), medium cities (20,000 to 100,000), and large cities (over 100,000). Cities with more than 100,000 inhabitants tend to take on particular characteristics in their system of building, communications, and economic life. In the 1960s there were 1,272 cities in this category (not including about 40 centres which form part of larger cities), with a total population of about 530 million, or about one sixth of the entire world population. Of these, 122 had between 500,000 and 1,000,000 inhabitants, and about a hundred are 'millionaire cities'.

Millionaire cities

Some urban centres with over a million inhabitants come into a separate category and are known as *millionaire cities*. In 1972 there were slightly more than one hundred, and they are increasing all the time. Mammoth cities, with greater attractions than neighbouring regions, are of ancient origins (Babylon and Rome are prime examples), but these great centres declined and by the mid-17th century not even the most prosperous cities – Paris, Naples, and Constantinople for example – had more than 500,000 inhabitants. With the arrival of the industrial era and the improvement of communications, which led to a relative decentralization and a broadening of the extent of urbanism, higher standards of living contributed to the development of larger cities.

By degrees the farm labourers are leaving the land and are being attracted to industry. The desire for a more comfortable way of

Oxford became a university city in the 13th century and acquired an unmistakeable identity with its dignified college buildings, libraries, and playing fields. The city also has important industries which gave rise to the development of modern buildings on the outskirts (which can be seen in the distance). These are separate from the old city, which has been left intact.

A view of Miami, Florida, which, because of its mild climate lasting throughout the year, developed as a holiday resort. The high standard of living is in relation to the demands and power of leisured classes of the industrial cities of the North.

Above: Vancouver, principal city and port of western Canada, developed as an outlet for the vast and rich region of the Canadian Pacific. It is a centre of industry and trade connected chiefly with the agricultural, mining, and timber products of the vast provinces of the interior.

Left: Johannesburg, the modern South African city that developed as a result of the mining of the region's mineral deposits. The slag heaps are partly visible in the background.

222

life also encourages the drift from the countryside. Gradually the city is infiltrating the neighbouring areas and absorbing the population, which is becoming an integral part of the city. London reached the million mark in the first decade of the 19th century; Paris about 1840; New York, which now leads the millionaire cities, about 1850; Berlin about 1870; Philadelphia, Chicago and Petrograd about 1880; Vienna and Moscow about 1890; and Rome in 1925.

The greatest number of millionaire cities is at present found in Asia, where there are about forty. An estimated 240–250 million people live in millionaire cities, about one-twelfth of the total world population.

A feature of millionaire cities is that few people live in the central area, which is reserved for business offices, while in the suburbs the number of inhabitants increases to such an extent as to create serious housing and transport problems. Traffic problems assume great importance, with much emphasis being given to underground railways and subways, which occupy the minimum surface area. The large cities consume enormous quantities of food every day, and the constant provisioning with foods such as milk, meat, fruit and vegetables adds to the traffic problems, and requires special organization.

Many millionaire cities have four definite types of zones:

1) An ancient part (the Acropolis in Athens, the Campidoglio in Rome, the Île de la Cité in Paris, etc.) which originally had a religious function and with the passage of time acquired political and administrative functions.

2) A business or commercial zone, such as the City in London, in which the number of residents steadily decreases with the opening of new business centres, so that the area becomes practically deserted after business hours.

Right: Manchester with its satellite cities, which suggests the term *conurbation* to British geographers. *Far right:* London's satellite cities, situated outside the administrative boundaries of the capital, but dependent on it financially, economically and culturally. These 'new towns' form part of a broad plan aimed at creating a well-spaced-out urban region, avoiding overcrowding, but in which the inhabitants enjoy the amenities of city life.

Below: Los Angeles shows a number of advanced methods of dealing with population problems such as the shopping centres, which are possible only in cities built on an open plan and having fast motorways.

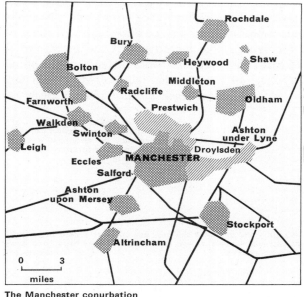

The Manchester conurbation

▦ towns of the conurbation

▨ outskirts of Manchester

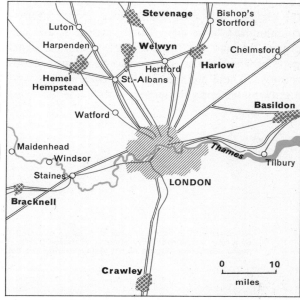

London and the New Towns (satellite cities)

═══ roads ─── railways ◈ new towns

223

3) An ever expanding residential area that is often uniform and monotonous, but occasionally enlivened by parks, squares, gardens, monuments, etc.

4) An industrial area which in recent times has been spreading to the suburbs and where the population steadily increases.

Conurbations

Cities can spread like ink-blots over their neighbouring regions. Cases such as Rome, which expanded over a very sparsely populated area and did not merge with other centres, are rare. However, it is quite common for smaller inhabited centres to exist near large cities, for example a coal-mining area, and this leads to the simultaneous development of several centres without any one of them reaching any dominant level above the others.

Recent times have seen the establishment of satellite towns near such cities as London and Stockholm, with all the amenities of the city, so that their inhabitants do not need to travel to the neighbouring large city. These satellite towns are built round a central nucleus and form a single economic district, the various parts of which are interconnected by a dense network of roads and railways. These are spoken of as *conurbations*, and they illustrate a growing tendency for large centres to merge.

The size of the population of conurbations is always difficult to establish because the main city's influence extends quite far into other centres. Some of these may be absorbed into the conurbation while others may retain their autonomy. Where there exist conditions favourable to the population living not only round a centre, but over a large area, such as the coal-mining region of the Ruhr, the Osaka-Kobe-Kyoto triangle, and the West Riding of Yorkshire with its wool textile districts of Leeds and Bradford, a conurbation of cities is formed which gives rise to a heavily populated area where the urban landscape clearly predominates over the agrarian one.

The city of the future

The process of urbanization, so intense and dramatic today, is inexhaustible. The enormous increase of the human race will impose, with ever-increasing urgency, forms of densely populated and organized settlement, and we have seen that density and organization are two characteristic features of urban settlement. It must not be forgotten that the process of urbanization, with its twofold characteristics of the constriction of nature and of the individual, constitutes the most developed and civilized form of social life to which all men spontaneously aspire, in their constant search

Opposite page: The deliberate planning of satellite towns makes it possible to apply new solutions to population problems. This has been done in the Apsley Estate, Nottingham, by adopting a circular layout which has escaped the monotonous structure of straight roads found in so many cities; the school is situated at the centre. ▶

Cumbernauld in Scotland was built as an overspill for Glasgow and is one of the best examples of a new town in Britain; it has the busy feel of a city, yet without the menace of motor traffic. *Left:* Terraced houses, shops, and blocks of flats have been designed in various designs by many architects. *Right:* Aerial view showing the complex road system.   *Cumbernauld Development Corporation*

for ever better conditions of life on the material and spiritual level. The large cities of the present day are undergoing frantic and sometimes disorganized expansion, so that the pattern of tomorrow's cities must be the spur to a more rational redistribution plan for both dwellings and activities. The city-region is already emerging, based on the planned exploitation of space and the reasoned control of the relationships between human settlement, productive activity, and ways and means of communication.

The preoccupation of sociologists and politicians to stop the flight from the countryside is now an anachronism, because people cannot be forced to stay tied to one fixed set of conditions far removed from the living standards that a city can offer. Nevertheless, the motives behind this preoccupation remain valid if the flight from the countryside results in the ever-increasing size of cities, and is not controlled by territorial planning which takes into account the harmonious development of the social and economic framework as a whole.

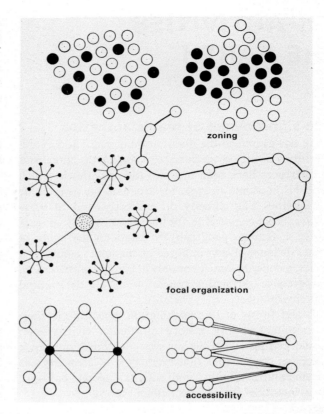

zoning

focal organization

accessibility

Right: The diagram shows some of the basic conditions that planners will have to allow for in building cities of the future. These conditions can be observed in present-day cities, which are going through a critical period with new needs arising all the time. They take into account several factors involved in the integration of cities and regions and the correlation between residential functions and economic activity. The first of these factors is the zoning of the typical elements of urban economy and life (shops, housing, cultural and entertainment centres, etc.). The second is focal organization or the interrelation between groups of urban concentration. The third is accessibility, the distance in terms of time of every point in the area from a certain type of activity or service.

MAN'S ACTIVITIES ON THE EARTH

Geographic significance of man's activities

So far this book has examined the distribution, spread, and evolution of human forms of life on the surface of the Earth. Numerous and repeated references have been made to the activities in which man engages in his constant struggle to dominate his geographic environment, activities that directly or indirectly, and in varying degrees, have been responsible for the great variety of geographic landscapes. Human geography is based on the study of man's continuous defiance of laws imposed on him as a member of a biological species, a defiance aimed not only at his own preservation, but at the progressive rational exploitation of all the natural resources of his environment.

The methods and forms of this exploitation constitute in their development in time the very history of human civilizations; their various and complex distribution over the Earth makes it possible to trace the connections that every type of economy has with its environmental conditions and with the social, political, and ethnological factors of the various human groups.

The specific task of economic geography is to determine all the reciprocal influences and actions and reactions between the geographic environment and man in his economic activity, and to identify and describe geographic-economic types and regions.

The different stages of economic development

Economic geography comprises the synthesis of information obtained from a very wide range of studies, including ecology, climatology, pedology, technology of commerce, and statistics. The growth of economics has occurred in different ways from country to country, so that today on the Earth, side by side with peoples that are extremely advanced at the technological and economic level, there are others anchored to primitive and archaic ways of life. Between the tribes of food-gatherers and hunters of the Amazonian forest and the organized and prosperous communities of developed countries there is practically the entire spectrum of human history, and yet the physical distance between the archaic and the modern forms of life can be covered in a few hours.

This disparity of economic, technological, and social development leads to a rough classification of underdeveloped, developing, and advanced countries and regions. An elemental factor of this classification is the *industrialization index*, which is the ratio of the number of people employed in industry to the total working population of a country. But to determine the stage of development of a country other factors have to be taken into account, such as income, literacy, education, the turnover of consumer goods, the press, social security, and medical facilities.

These factors, together with complex geographical and historical considerations, social organizations, and the tools and methods of production, are responsible for the various economic systems functioning throughout the countries and regions of the world. These systems, on which human activity is so dependent, form an environment in themselves or an intermediate stage between man and his natural environment.

The major economic systems

The major economic systems have been classified as follows:

1) Spontaneous or free-enterprise economy mechanisms, in which production, consumption, and exchange are allowed free rein according to the law of supply and demand, without any intervention on the part of the state.

Every geographic landscape carries signs to varying degrees of the forms of human activity and the general economic level of the people living in it. *Below:* A Swiss landscape, part of central Europe that has been transformed and exploited for centuries. There is industry as well as agriculture, as can be seen from the factory at the right of the picture. Note the perfect geometry of the fields, which has been achieved by means of machinery.

Above: A factory situated next to a peasant village south of Teheran. As frequently occurs in Middle Eastern countries, the industrial factor is one that has been forced, and it contrasts with the rest of the surroundings, where agriculture is still practised with archaic methods (this is seen *top right* in raising water for irrigation near Madras, India). The slowness with which some people, defined as backward in an economic sense, assimilate modern forms of economy can also be caused by certain typically human factors, such as religious attitudes which encourage passivity and detachment from human activities as a virtue. This is found in India where the picture *(right)* was taken, showing young disciples following their holy man.

2) Mechanisms imposed by groups such as trusts, monopolies, cartels, and pressure groups, sometimes in favour of a free-enterprise economy.

3) Different types of state-operated economies, with intervention by the government. This intervention, which is sometimes carried out to enforce the laws of free enterprise by means of taxation, financial policy, protectionism etc., is greatest when the state owns the means of production and consequently controls the planning of the entire process of the economic development of a country. This occurs in socialist countries.

4) An important role is played today by economic unions, which are supranational in character. These seek to harmonize their economies within a zone that includes different countries having similar economic systems. Examples of these are the European Economic Community (EEC), the eastern European Comecon, and the European Free Trade Association (EFTA). Sometimes international agreements in this field affect only certain spheres of industry, such as coal and steel, as in the European Coal and Steel Community. Countries may also see their common interest con-

verging in economic and political structures that often take the shape of federations or other types of union.

The two opposing economic conceptions, represented by free enterprise and socialism, and enshrined in the political doctrines of the two major blocs vying for world leadership, are tending to lose their characteristically rigid outlooks in the face of the need for an ever more rapid and pressing development of productive techniques. Thus, in the socialist countries a gradual process of revaluation of the concept of profit as an incentive is taking place, while in free-enterprise countries intervention by the state in the form of moderating or planning is often necessary to redistribute income, or to develop productivity by means of structural reforms. The inevitable evolution of technical progress seems to be leading to both a levelling of ways of life and a merging together of the economic systems.

Underdeveloped countries are particularly receptive to the call for more evolved forms of economic structures in which they can make their own choices within the framework of their historical, social, and economic traditions. However, there still remain great

Top of page: Harvest time on a large ranch near Moose Jaw, Saskatchewan, Canada. This is the North American grain region where extensive agriculture is practised with modern machinery and techniques. The use of machinery in various stages of cultivation is necessary in these vast areas to keep agriculture at a competitive level with other forms of economy. In contrast with this picture, there is the ancient method of threshing, used in Roman times and still used by the Kurds in a village in eastern Turkey *(left)*. In this case the difficulties of extensive agriculture are aggravated by physical conditions, the region being situated in the Armenian mountains near the border with Iran, an arid area with severe winters.

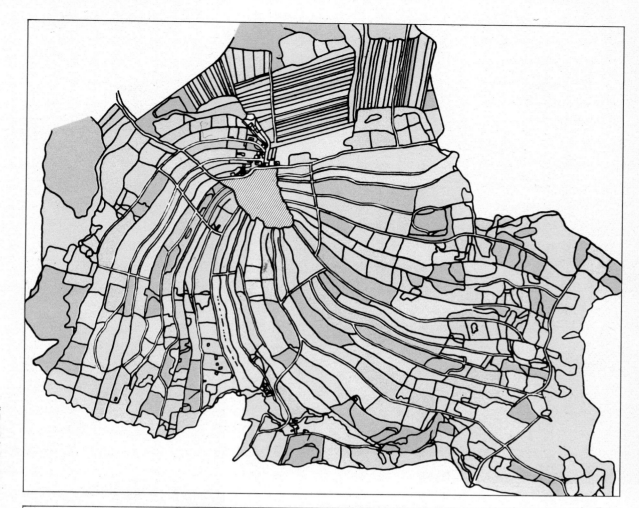

Economic systems play a basic role in creating, moulding, and differentiating geographic facts. The example shown in the two diagrams *(right)* is particularly enlightening: they show the subdivision of fields round a village in Czechoslovakia before and after the introduction of collectivization under the state's economic system. The first diagram shows the minute subdivision of properties and the multiplicity of crops in each of the properties. The second diagram shows a broader subdivision into large areas growing the same crops and using mechanization. The small parcels of land round the village are individual smallholdings owned by the peasants under the collective-farm system.

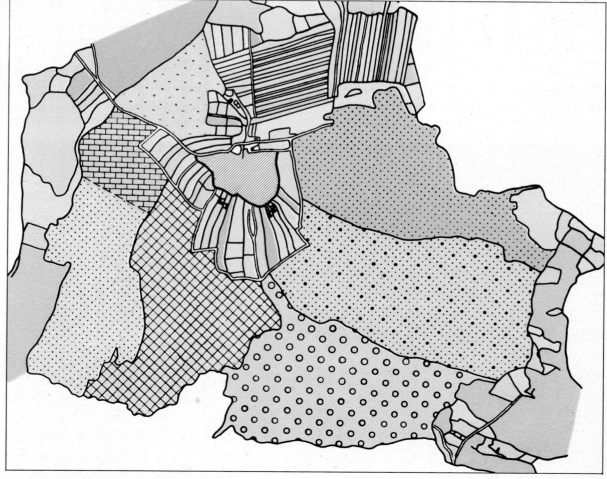

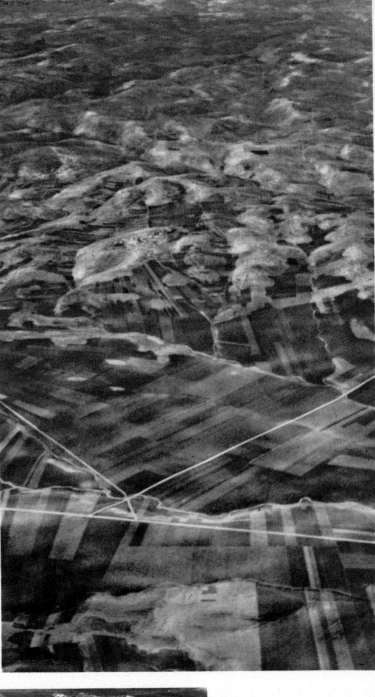

gaps in economic development, which will continue to exist for many years, because this is a process that has really got under way only in recent times and is at present confined to a few areas of the world.

Food problems

The serious picture of world hunger, which was revealed fully for the first time by the Food and Agriculture Organization's report

Above left: Landscape in the Veneto, Italy, where the subdivision of fields, the construction of roads, and the situation of the houses reveal an exploitation of the soil on the part of a free-enterprise system. Typical is the landlord's villa situated in its own parkland and surrounded by land worked either by tenant farmers or sharecroppers. *Left:* A co-operative village *(moshav ovdim)* in Israel. The circular layout of the houses round a centre that has schools, shops, offices, etc., and of the outlying cultivated fields was inspired by modern town-planning ideas put forward by R. Kaufmann. Differing from a *kibbutz*, which is a centre of communal production and consumption, the *moshav ovdim* allows the members to use their own initiative in production, while marketing is done on a co-operative basis. State intervention is also responsible for works of colossal scope, such as the development of pre-desert and desert regions. The picture *above* shows newly ploughed fields on the border of the Negev desert.

The underdeveloped conditions of countries in arid tropical zones can be improved by public works on a national scale that can be undertaken only by the state, almost always with the help of developed countries. *Right:* A canal created by the construction of the Adraskand Rud dam on the western slopes of the Hindu Kush of Afghanistan. The dam was built with American technical aid, and is aimed at reclaiming new lands for agriculture and persuading the nomads to find their place in the changing economy of the country.

in 1960, marked out the underdeveloped areas of the world. The boundaries of these areas include much of Asia, Africa, Oceania, and South America, where the economy is dominated by a primitive form of agriculture and, in some regions inhabited by small communities, by nomadic livestock raising, the gathering of spontaneously grown food, and hunting.

Whatever may be the reason for the technical backwardness of these regions, which are otherwise quite highly developed at the civil level, the gap they have to bridge, not only to meet their most immediate needs for a rapidly growing population, but also to develop their economy, is enormous. The extension of markets to economically depressed areas is one of the most clearly felt interests of countries with a high productive potential. It is because of this that aid programmes play such an important part in the political economy of advanced countries, constituting the starting point for solving the problem of the undernourished millions.

Most tropical countries (the majority colonies or former colonies) remain in conditions of underdevelopment. These conditions are expressed crudely in terms of food production, which the map shows on a comparative scale.

ASPECTS OF UNDERDEVELOPMENT OF THE TROPICAL COUNTRIES

Agricultural underdevelopment:
Calorie availability per inhabitant
less than 2,200
from 2,200 to 2,500
about 2,700
more than 2,700

Industrial underdevelopment:
power coal consumption
less than 5% of U.S. consumption
from 5 to 10%
more than 10%

Commercial underdevelopment:
—— in the dollar area
—— in the sterling area

231

THE EXPLOITATION OF NATURAL RESOURCES

Primitive food-gathering, hunting, and fishing

These are practised by people, now few in number, living mainly in areas where the influence of western civilization has been negligible. Today, primitive activities aimed at a mere subsistence level of living are practised by only a few isolated groups in tropical and subtropical regions in the rain forest or the savana, where wild life, still relatively undisturbed by the encroachment of colonialism, is plentiful. These regions are located in mid-western Africa, in certain zones of Malawi and Mozambique, and in South America, in the Amazon Basin and the Chaco. Other areas in which this form of life is practised in certain regions include, in Asia, the mountainous interior of the Indochinese peninsula and the highlands of Thailand, Burma, and Nepal; and in Oceania the islands of Borneo, the Celebes, and New Guinea. Ceylon has a very small group of aborigines, and southern Africa has its bushmen of the Kalahari, and these, with the aborigines of Australia, faithfully represent a way of life that is rigidly tied to forms of culture that were among the first to be practised by man.

At high latitudes, similar forms of life are to be found in the tundra regions and at the edges of the subarctic forests, where reindeer, caribou, and musk-oxen manage to survive and provide meat and hides for the sparse Eskimo population. In the southernmost areas of South America a few Patagonians live by primitive forms of hunting.

Primitive livestock breeding

Primitive livestock breeding is most commonly found in the pre-deserts, steppes, and savanas that cover vast areas of Africa and Asia. In these regions annual rainfall is usually less than ten inches, but there are others where it is as high as twenty inches, especially in Asia above latitude 30° North.

Man's ancient activities are today practised in their most primitive forms only by certain groups of people with cultures that have survived in areas where modern civilization has not penetrated. These primitive groups inhabit mainly the equatorial forest and Arctic regions. *Left:* Australian aborigines stalking their prey. *Above left:* A South American Indian wading from a river where he has just caught a fish with his bow and arrow. *Above:* Inside an Eskimo igloo where, next to the sealskins and the traditional implements, can be seen traces of a few signs of contact with industrial civilization.

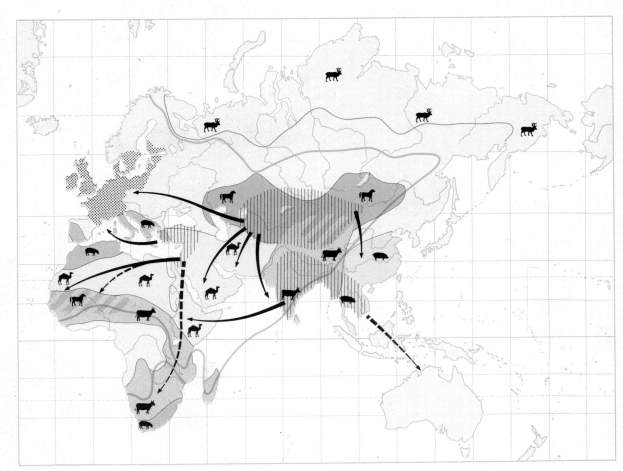

The spread of domestic animals first occurred in prehistoric times. Apart from reindeer-breeding in the northern regions and horse-breeding in central Asia, an animal-based economy is not peculiar to one pastoral age, but develops and co-exists with other activities. In particular, sheep, cattle, and pigs, though situated in different cultural areas, made their appearance in prehistory near centres that were basically agricultural and sedentary. *Bottom of page:* A herd of reindeer in migration in northern Scandinavia. Reindeer-breeding, as practised in Lapland, is almost identical to that of prehistoric times, and is a way of life considerably conditioned by the habits of the animals.

In the far north, primitive livestock breeding is practised in tundra regions of Alaska and Canada, the Scandinavian peninsula, and the Siberian North. Much of these territories is located inside the Arctic Circle where there is little evaporation and where the modest rainfall could produce good grazing land if it were not for the severity of the climate and the brevity of the vegetation period. Man's organized life is therefore conditioned by his capacity to raise caribou or reindeer.

In tropical and subtropical regions, in northern China and Mongolia, the animals that best meet the needs of man are sheep, goats, cattle, buffalo, and camels. From these the primitive livestock breeder obtains his sustenance, directly or indirectly, in the shape of clothing, coverings for his transportable dwellings, fuel, milk and its derivatives, meat, hides and skins, and bones. Horses, asses, and camels, which are also kept by sheep breeders, usually represent the only forms of transport for the nomads in their long migrations in search of new grazing grounds.

In many zones of nomadic livestock breeding population density is the lowest in the world. The system of property and its ownership is regulated by traditional laws imposed sometimes by tribal

groups on the grazing grounds. In other cases the territories belong to the state and were handed over to military tribes in the past who were made responsible for their defence.

In arid regions the ownership of wells is of major importance. Their use is regulated by laws that are often very intricate, and which, in the Near East and northern Africa, are based on Moslem law. Pastoral ownership, which comprises the collective use of grazing grounds by the tribe, becomes individual when agriculture is practised on the soil. Nomadic livestock breeding, which in its many natural forms is the result of a highly specialized way of life, is practised as a complete and exclusive activity only in very rare cases today. Some nomads in fact have exchanged contacts with sedentary people. Today, despite the inertia of the people, the most primitive and closed forms of nomadic livestock breeding are more subject to change. A contributing factor to this is the prickly question of nationalism, which has placed many barriers in the way of the great migrations and the traditional routes of the nomads in search of pastures and water supplies.

The action of some governments to eliminate or reduce nomadism with campaigns encouraging them to settle has had scant success, even if it has often succeeded in ending the traditional nomadic

Above: A herd of goats in a wadi on the Ethiopian plateau. *Top:* A flock of sheep in the Tunisian Sahel. Sheep-raising, derived from the most primitive of pastoral forms associated with agriculture, has become an exclusive activity and nomadic in character in those arid regions where settled agriculture was always precarious in the past.

In the grazing grounds of the arid zones where there are no tribally owned wells, nomads obtain water from any neighbouring farming settlements by offering animal products in exchange. *Left:* A well in Afghanistan where nomad women draw water in leather buckets. The amount of water consumed is calculated according to the time worked by the horse.

methods of livestock breeding. In Soviet central Asia, China, and Mongolia, the socialist system of government has overcome the more obsolete social forms connected with nomadism and respecting in certain cases the natural requirements of livestock breeding by rationalizing seasonal grazing, operated perhaps in the fairest manner to place archaic forms of stockbreeding into the framework of a more modern economy. In the African savanas the opening of wells by government organizations is tending to change the nature of nomadism into a ranch type of stockbreeding.

Primitive agriculture

Agriculture is the result of action that was first undertaken, probably during the mesolithic and neolithic eras, following a period in which livelihoods were obtained by food-gathering.

The first operation involved in agriculture is the release of the soil from natural vegetation, to make it available for cultivation. The difficulty of this operation depends on the intensity and vitality of the vegetation. Every primitive rural collective probably began its agricultural activity by using fire to get rid of the natural vegetation. Although this gave added minerals to the soil in the shape of ashes, it only partly succeeded in its aim, and the vegetation soon returned. This practice is still common in some areas of the Earth, and is usually associated with large areas of low population density. The people retain primitive ways of life and know nothing about crop rotation.

Primitive agriculture is found in territories which have no cold season and where rainfall is high, in the rain forests, tropical forests, and savanas. The soils are mainly poor in quality. In zones where a dry season is followed by a wet one, infiltration water rises to the surface, frequently bringing with it aluminium and iron hydroxides, which form slabs of laterites rendering the soil barren. This phenomenon affects large areas in the tropics. Primitive agriculture is still practised in large areas of Central and South America and in Africa, Asia, and Oceania. The American zone is located in the forest region of Central America, in the Amazon Basin as far as the Andes, in Colombia, Ecuador, Peru, Bolivia, and a large part of the Brazilian *coatinga*. Maize is the

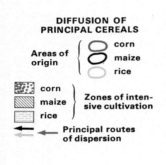

DIFFUSION OF PRINCIPAL CEREALS

Areas of origin
- corn
- maize
- rice

Zones of intensive cultivation
- corn
- maize
- rice

→ Principal routes of dispersion

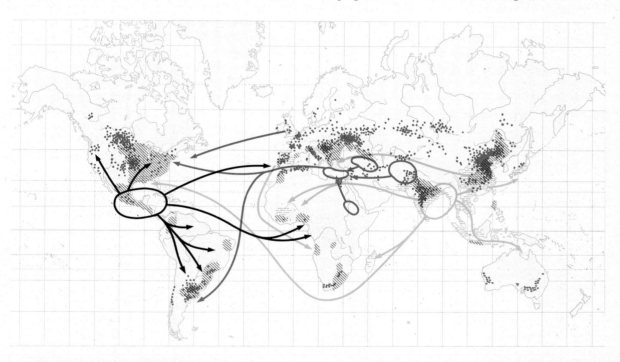

The first forms of agriculture, which consisted of replacing the natural vegetation of the Earth with vegetation of economic importance, were achieved by burning the natural vegetation. This practice is still common with some peoples. *Below:* Fire being used on savana land during the dry season to get rid of trees and shrubs on large areas and prepare them for sowing. The original vegetation will eventually grow again, but on a smaller scale.

predominant crop. In West and Central Africa there is a very large area contained in the savana south of the Sahara, reaching as far as latitudes 10°–15° North, and the Ethiopian plateau running into the Kenya Highlands and descending to occupy much of Mozambique, Zambia, and the northern part of Angola. The main crops in African primitive agriculture are millet, maize and manioc.

In nomadic agriculture the cultivators clear away the bush and forest and carry on cultivation for a year or more, during which time they live in huts near the cultivated lands. When the soil has been exhausted, the cultivators move on to new areas. This is a primitive type of agriculture very common in forest zones.

Itinerant agriculture is practised by cultivators with fixed abodes who travel into the surrounding area looking for cultivable land, which they eventually abandon to start work on new plots. This method of cultivation entails a progressive increase in distance from the fixed abodes. It is common in Central and West Africa, in the Yucatán peninsula in Mexico, and along the Amazon.

There is another type of primitive agriculture in which the habitations and cultivated land become stabilized in time, but where the techniques in use are still highly archaic, with the use of fallow land in rotation. Very little goes back to enriching the soil owing to the lack of organic fertilizers and ignorance of the appropriate techniques. This type of agriculture is practised in large areas of Africa, in the Andes, and in Central America.

Primitive intensive agriculture

Primitive intensive agriculture has many of the characteristics of primitive extensive agriculture in that it uses the same rudimentary techniques. But primitive intensive agriculture is

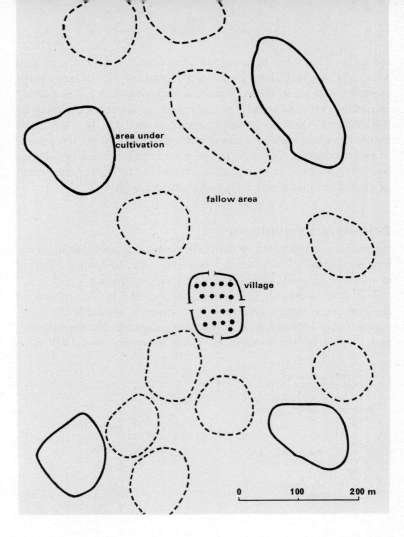

area under cultivation

fallow area

village

0   100   200 m

A savana region in Adamawa (Cameroon) planted with newly harvested (January) millet. Before sowing, the ground was cleared by fire, which failed to set light to a few trees. This is an example of itinerant agriculture, in which different areas of the savana are exploited from year to year. The system is shown in the diagram *(above)* taken from an aerial photograph of a region in the Central African Republic. The dotted lines show areas that have already been cultivated and where the natural vegetation is of reduced proportions.

A view of the agrarian landscape that lies along the northern slopes of the Middle Atlas Mountains in Morocco. The picture was taken at the beginning of March, and shows the alternate rectangles of ploughed land and land sown with wheat. Other parts have been left fallow or as grazing grounds. There is no trace of arboreal vegetation owing to the extensive cultivation of cereals, which need open areas. The characteristics of this landscape are its low population density and the type of land ownership which is aimed only partly at commercial growth of cereal products. The cultivation of wheat was introduced to the area chiefly by French colonists, and has not yet reached the advanced level of mechanization combined with the use of chemical fertilizers which is normally characteristic of large-scale grain cultivation.

Extensive commercial agriculture

This type of agriculture is almost exclusively based on the production of cereals. Modern means of cereal production use up-to-date mechanical methods and make plentiful use of chemical fertilizers; this requires considerable financial investment, large areas of cultivatable land, a minimum labour force, and extensive mechanization. The actual work of cultivation is limited to ploughing, sowing, and harrowing. Nothing more is done until harvest and threshing time.

Cereal-growing areas are located in regions of fertile soil and receive an average annual rainfall of between 10 and 20 inches; the distribution of rainfall throughout the year plays an important part, especially during the germination period. Hard-grained wheat is more resistant to drought than the softer varieties, which can tolerate excessively humid conditions, within certain limits. If the winter is mild, hard-grained winter varieties are used with autumn sowing and harvest in early summer. Where winters are severe, the softer varieties are grown, with spring sowing and an autumn harvest, as in Canada and the northern United States.

The large areas of grain cultivation of the world all have in common the widespread use of mechanized methods. The largest area in the Soviet Union for cereal cultivation surrounds the

241

Newly ploughed fields (October) in the Bekaa plain between the Lebanon and the Antilebanon mountains. Wheat is the chief crop as it resists the relatively arid climate of the region and is best adapted to the conditions of the reddish-brown soil.

Ukrainian capital of Kiev, and stretches eastwards as far as Omsk, and from latitudes 50°–55° North to the Caucasus range in the south. The chief varieties in the European zone are the hard-grained winter wheats; in Siberia spring-sown wheat is used. The *kolkhozi* are collective farms in which the workers receive a share in the profits; they cover several thousand acres. Even larger are the *sovkhozi*, opened in the virgin lands of Soviet central Asia, in which employees are paid a wage by the state.

The most important cereal-growing area of America is a belt beginning in the southern zones of the Canadian provinces of Alberta, Saskatchewan, and Manitoba and stretching south and south-west to Montana and North and South Dakota. Another important cereal-growing zone is located in Kansas, Oklahoma, northern Texas, and eastern Colorado. In the United States and

Above: Threshing of grain in western Anatolia, Turkey, the region's most agriculturally advanced area. *Left:* The Anatolian landscape is largely dominated by the extensive cultivation of grain. Trees are limited to small groups of poplars to give shade in the middle of the valley. Techniques of cultivation, especially on the plateau region, are still relatively primitive. Machinery has only recently been introduced and in limited quantities. In this area mechanization could greatly increase productivity. However, the conservatism of the farmers and the system of family ownership of land constitute a powerful barrier against progress and collective forms of cultivation.

Harvesting on a large ranch in the State of Washington. The widespread use of mechanical methods forms the basis of extensive agriculture in the great grain regions of the western United States. Farms are as large as 1,000 acres, though the number of employees is small, except during threshing time. The farms are isolated in the midst of vast areas of cultivated land.

Canada farmers grow hard-grained wheat varieties on farms of five hundred to a thousand acres. The size of farms is smaller in the central region of the United States. The number of people employed on these farms is generally small, consisting of the contractor and two or three men. The staff is increased only during harvest time.

In Argentina the cereal-growing area is in the province of Buenos Aires and extends west into neighbouring provinces. In Australia, the cereal-growing areas are located on the two southern extremities of the continent. The more important is the south-eastern one, which extends near the valley of the Murray and Darling rivers and has Adelaide as its centre. The other is centred on Perth and extends as far as the southern coast.

Intensive mixed agriculture

Intensive mixed agriculture originated in crop-rotation, which was one of the greatest advances made by man in the field of agriculture. This process enables soil to retain its fertility and limits its erosion. The system was subsequently organized to deal with

a wide range of adverse conditions that can strike at particular forms of cultivation. It also became possible to distribute work throughout the different seasons to meet the alternate requirements of cultivation and stockbreeding.

Mixed agriculture requires for its development land of good quality, and rainfall ranging from 20 to 60 inches a year, preferably occurring during the warmer months. The most important areas are in Europe and the United States, while smaller areas are situated in South America and South Africa.

In the European area, the main crops are wheat, beet, potatoes oats, rye, and leguminous and cereal types of cultivation that are most suitable, in the various individual environments, for animal foodstuff. Maize is an important crop in the Danube river basin. Permanent grasslands are fairly widespread throughout eastern Europe, and grazing land is more common in the Asian area. Wheat, beet, hemp, and sunflowers are the most widespread forms of cultivation in the Soviet Union.

Beef cattle and pigs are the main forms of stockbreeding in the European zone, and sheep in Asia. Dairy cattle are kept round

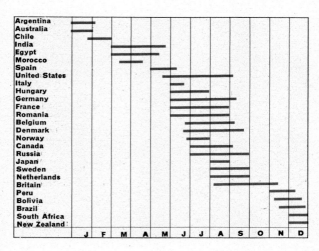

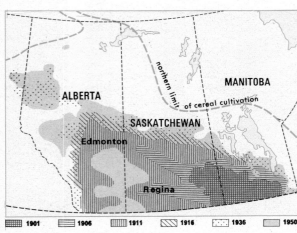

Far left: The harvest of wheat is an important stage in the work-cycle of extensive agriculture. The ripening of the crops varies from country to country and according to altitude. The diagram shows the harvest periods of different countries. Left: The map shows the progressive advance of cereal cultivation between 1900 and 1950 in the great plains of the Canadian West. This advance was made possible by the building of railways, which transported the products to the great marketing centres.

243

Mixed agriculture based on crop rotation is practised in temperate and humid climates. The landscapes produced are unmistakable and present a patchwork of fields growing different crops. Forage crops are an important item, especially in central Europe where stockbreeding is one of the main activities of agriculture. The cultivation of fodder crops *(right)* is one of the basic activities in this type of agriculture.

major European centres, and specialized forms of arboreal cultivation, such as fruit orchards and vineyards, constitute an important part of farming production.

European farms practising mixed agriculture vary in size; in the East they generally range from 75 to 100 acres. There are also many farms smaller than this, of about ten acres, operated by families. In eastern Europe and Asia the size of farms increases because of the co-operative structure of productive organizations; collective farms often have an area of thousands of acres.

Below: Crops growing in the upper Danube valley. Agriculture is confined to the valley floor not only because of the steepness of the hillsides, but also because of forestation. *Right:* Cultivated fields on the slopes of the Andes, with the Nevado de Huascaran rising above. Low walls line the cultivated rectangles, which are also bordered by poplars or hedges. The crops are alternated with fallow land, and stockbreeding plays an important part. The fields stretch upwards as far as cultivation is possible. The number of fields indicates that most of the farmers are smallholders, a common phenomenon in mountain areas.

Large fields bordered by lines of poplars are a familiar sight in the agrarian landscape of the Paduan plain *(right)*. The picture shows a certain variety in crops apart from the more extensive and predominant ones of cereals and forage. This variety is made possible by the Mediterranean climate. Agricultural villages are generally located along roads. Recently built farmers' houses indicate the presence of medium-size or small properties which are either owned or let out on the sharecropping system.

In the United States the area of mixed agriculture is located in the eastern states, the mid-West, and the South, with the exception of the Florida peninsula. Intense stockbreeding is supported by crops to provide fodder for livestock; maize in the northern part, in the so-called 'corn belt', as well as oats, clover and natural pasture. The main commercial products are wheat, tobacco, and cotton, in that order, going from north to south. Livestock raised in the corn belt is mostly cattle and pigs, often integrated with poultry establishments run on semi-industrial lines. The size of farms is about 200 acres, while in the area where tobacco is the chief crop, and, farther south, in the cotton belt, the average size of farms is around a hundred acres.

In southern Brazil and Paraguay there is a zone of mixed agriculture where the most common crops are wheat, tobacco, millet, and cotton, but where rice and sugar-cane are also cultivated in tropical plantations. Cattle and pigs are the chief types of livestock. Smaller areas are located in central Mexico and southern Chile. In these mixed farms of Latin America a substantial part of production is used for personal consumption, although the greater part is sold.

Other zones of mixed agriculture are located in Rhodesia and in the western part of South Africa, where the cultivation of maize, ground-nuts, and wheat and the stockbreeding of cattle, sheep, and pigs are frequently the basis of the farming economy.

Above: Farming landscape southwest of Toronto, where tobacco is the main crop. Farms here are medium-sized, being about 50 to 100 acres, and are evenly distributed throughout the territory. They are bordered by poplars. This is a specialized type of agriculture, with complex cultivation techniques, and requires such facilities as storehouses, which can be seen near the dwelling houses. *Left:* Mechanized potato harvesting on a farm in New York State.

Olive trees and vines are the characteristic features of the Alban Hills *(right)* near Frascati, in Italy. This is an example of mixed farming typical of the Mediterranean area. *Below:* The Pontine landscape at the foot of the Lepini mountains. This is basically open country where cereal and fodder crops are grown in rotation, as well as vines, fruit trees, and olive trees on the slopes. The plots of land are marked by roads that link the main highway with the various dwellings scattered about the countryside, and are only a few acres in area.

Mixed farming

This is a type of agriculture that is sometimes called Mediterranean agriculture, because of the area in which it is chiefly found. It is a form of activity aimed mainly at production for trading purposes, although there are still areas in which farm production is for personal consumption. However, the fundamental feature of this type of agriculture is the coexistence of extensive cereal cultivation with fallow land, extensive stockbreeding, and highly intensive forms of cultivation connected with horticulture, stockbreeding,

and tree cultivation, especially the olive, the vine, and fruit trees. Mixed farming is practised in areas with moderate rainfall, varying from 10 to 40 inches a year, but with particularly low rainfall during the summer months and a wide variation from year to year.

The largest area of mixed farming is located in the basin of the Mediterranean. In North America many examples of mixed farming are found in large areas of California. In the southern hemisphere examples are fewer and are located between latitudes 30°

Californian agriculture occupies a special place of its own in the framework of the United States economy, which has led it to specialize in certain crops best suited to the climatic conditions of the region. Many of the crops are of the Mediterranean type, such as citrus fruits, vines, and fruit trees, with the products destined for urban consumption. Irrigation is indispensable because of the relative aridity of the climate in the Californian valley regions situated between the two parallel mountain chains. The problem has been solved by using water from the Sierra Nevada through a system of canals. Irrigation agriculture in California, aimed at producing commercial crops of fruit, also extends along the Pacific coast of Mexico. *Left:* Irrigation of a vineyard in the Rio Sonora plain, Mexico. *Below:* Orange groves in the Santa Clara valley, California.

Right: Karst structures and aridity are features of Malta and they are reflected in the agricultural landscape, similar forms of which can be seen in other parts of the Mediterranean area. Cultivation is carried on mainly in dolines and hollows, bordered by sparse shrubby vegetation. The plots are enclosed by dry-stone walls built of limestone found in the ground. Most of the population lives in villages. The small white buildings in the fields are for storage and keeping farming equipment. *Above:* Hedges used as windbreaks and as barriers to stop the shifting of sand dunes in Agrigento, in Sicily. Tomatoes are grown between the hedges.

and 40° in Chile, in western South Africa, and in the West of Australia and the Murray river valley.

In the Mediterranean basin, autumn-sown cereals, mainly wheat and barley, are alternated with fallow land. Barley is also fairly common in Spain and Asia Minor and on the African coast. The vine and the olive are typical crops with summer and autumn harvests. Irrigation is fairly widely diffused, making possible a vast range of tropical and subtropical crops.

Stockbreeding frequently plays an important part in the agrarian economy of the Mediterranean area. The types of animals raised and their number vary. In some cases only enough animals are kept for the subsistence needs of the farming family; in others, stockbreeding may be an industry on its own. Stockbreeding has a greater share in the farming economy in areas where plentiful rainfall assures a good supply of forage crops. In these areas beef cattle and pigs are the chief animals reared, but dairy cattle are also kept in large numbers, particularly around heavily populated areas.

The agriculture practised in the Sacramento and San Joaquin valleys, on the central coast, and in the southern parts of California, show a wide range of farm types. In these areas there are uniform zones, often small in size, in which one type of crop predominates over the others, which may be pasture, forest, fruit, vines, olives, or cereals. The intensification of cultivation is based on extensive irrigation, the water being brought to the land by intricate canal systems or reservoirs. Hill regions are used for grazing cattle and sheep, the higher ground being used during the summer months, in which there is practically no rainfall. Agricultural activity in California is market-based, and the average size of farms is over 250 acres.

The difference between Californian agriculture, which has unique characteristics because of its highly specialized type of cultivation, and the Mediterranean type is due to the fact that California was comparatively recently colonized and was developed in conditions in which the population density was low. Thus it was

possible to put the soil to better use with the development of a system of irrigation.

In a category of its own is central Florida, where there is an important cultivation of citrus fruit and market-garden products. The uniformity of cultivation and the climate, marked by abundant rainfall in summer, make this zone unsuitable for mixed farming, but it can be classified as such because of its affinity with cultivation in southern California.

The limited agricultural zone in South Africa is occupied mainly by farms practising mixed agriculture with dairy-cattle breeding. The farms of the central region of Chile practising mixed farming are similar, as are most Australian farms. Those in the extreme south-west of Australia include dairy-farming, tobacco, market-gardening, and fruit. The Murray valley zone has extensive irrigation systems that enable farms to engage in fruit-growing, horticulture, stockbreeding, and rice-growing.

Tropical commercial agriculture

Tropical commercial agriculture, known traditionally as 'plantation agriculture', was first introduced into colonial territories. It was organized on extensive lines, and the type of farm developed from it was characterized by the cultivation of one dominant crop worked by a large labour force of slaves. Slaves were eventually replaced by labourers whose conditions were not much better than

The cultivation of sugar-cane in tropical countries was originally a colonial form of exploitation, in which the labour force was made up of slaves, on large plantations under the rule of European colonial powers. The English more than anyone else helped to spread the cultivation of sugar-cane in tropical areas of Central America, the Indian Ocean, and Melanesia, and the plantations of these areas had certain characteristics in common. The picture *(left)* shows a sugar plantation in Fiji, by the ocean, which often forms the background to this tropical crop. *Above:* The preparation of copra (obtained from dried coconuts) in Tahiti where the coconut palm, as in many islands of the Pacific, is the chief form of cultivation.

their predecessors. The colonial landowners continued to exercise their authority by means of a narrow paternalistic economy. The plantations retained their characteristics of vast areas and the predominant cultivation of a single crop, while financial investment remained modest. The cultivation of only one crop led to the impoverishment of the soil and erosion. This type of agriculture soon became prone to periods of crisis due to under-consumption and over-supply. It was from these negative factors that the need for diversification of crops arose.

After the Second World War, and during the process that saw the formation of new independent states, mechanized methods and higher wages were introduced. In new African countries, at least in those in which forms of neo-colonialism were less marked, there remained a close dependence of their economy on the former colonial power. In many Latin American countries a type of semi-colonialism continued to exist after the creation of new states, in the shape of vast companies, or new companies set up with foreign capital after the country concerned had won independence. Agrarian reform carried out by some governments had a drastic effect. In Mexico, for example, reform involved about 90 million acres,

almost all of which went to form the *ejidos*, village properties with the land parcelled out to individual families, with other land for communal use. In this case, as in other examples of land reform at present being undertaken in Latin America, the greatest difficulty arose from the lack of capital necessary to change the primitive areas into regions of intensive agriculture. The land reform carried out in Cuba is a special case, in which there has been a considerable effort to make large-scale investments, especially in the field of stockbreeding.

Almost all the zones in which tropical commercial agriculture is practised are situated in an area that extends from latitude 30° North to 30° South, and has a warm climate and abundant rainfall. However, intense insolation soon exhausts the organic matter in the soil, so that there is a tendency for tropical farming properties to expand into virgin territories – a kind of long-term crop rotation over a vast area.

In tropical climates sugar-cane, coffee, cocoa, tea, pineapples, sisal, and spices are widely cultivated, often in specialized forms. Bananas, coconut, and oil palms are also widespread, though often grown with other crops.

Left: An irrigation water measurer in cotton-growing territory in the Sudanese Gezira. The British introduced this form of cultivation to the land at the confluence of the two Niles, and cotton plantations are today the country's largest source of income. *Right:* Tea-harvesting in Taiwan.

The agave is a typical tropical crop; in Mexico this plant is grown to obtain sisal used in making textile fibre, while the variety known as agave maguey *(above)* provides the base for a very popular alcoholic beverage called pulque. *Right:* A *fazenda* in the middle of a large coffee plantation in the *terra roxa* region of Brazil's Paraná state. The organization of agricultural activities in the Brazilian coffee region is based on large estates.

Extensive stockbreeding

Extensive stockbreeding for commercial purposes did not generally evolve from primitive forms of stockbreeding, but was, in most cases, a purely independent and separate phenomenon. When the European populations emigrated to the new continents they found that conditions for carrying on any worthwhile form of agriculture were far from ideal: the land was too arid because of irregular or limited rainfall, so that any crops were exposed to high risks. But the large area of land available was highly suitable for the development of extensive stockbreeding.

Extensive stockbreeding is most widespread in North America, in Canada and the United States west of the 100° meridian, and in the northern part of Mexico. In South America it is practised on the plains of northern Colombia, the *llanos* of Colombia and Venezuela and the vast region of the continent to the south and south-east of the Amazon forest. Cattle is the main form of livestock kept in all the American zones except for Patagonia and a few other limited areas where sheep are kept.

In Africa, extensive stockbreeding is practised in the south, where colonization was least affected by pre-existing indigenous activities and where the most suitable environmental conditions prevail. In equatorial zones stockbreeding was always hampered by the tsetse fly. South of the Sahara, in Nigeria, Chad, and the Sudan, traditional native stockbreeding has recently been changing to commercial methods. In Asia it has already done so with stockbreeders north and east of the Caspian and Aral seas who raise cattle on the steppes of Kazakhstan and extend their activities as far as the borders of Mongolia.

There is a considerable amount of sheep-farming in Australia and New Zealand. These countries dominate the world wool market, being responsible for 70% of the world's total commercial production. Cattle are raised on the coastal zone of south-eastern Australia.

Conditions in which extensive stockbreeding is practised are generally arid, with annual rainfall usually less than 10 inches. Only in the central and northern part of South America and in New Zealand does rainfall reach a level approaching or exceeding 60 inches a year. The natural vegetation consists of prairies, steppeland, savana, and, in some cases, sparse forests. The most typical forms of extensive stockbreeding are to be found in the western prairies of the United States, the Brazilian *campos*, the Argentine *pampas*, and the Australian and South African grazing lands.

The typical establishment operating extensive stockbreeding is generally run to produce live animals or wool. The live animals are taken to abattoirs and refrigeration plants situated in large cities, if the animals are destined for meat, or else are sold for breeding or fattening.

Generally, the establishment or ranch occupies a large area of land, with a number of buildings including the house of the owner,

Extensive stockbreeding is a typical form of activity widespread in large territories outside Europe where, in the beginning at least, the European colonizers found only limited possibilities for agriculture. Stockbreeding developed particularly in the semi-arid and open regions of the Americas *(top,* Hereford cattle in the western United States) and in Australia *(above,* merino sheep in New South Wales), and was essentially speculative. Walls, fences, and other forms of land division often enclose the various sections of the large grazing grounds *(below).*

living quarters for employees, and storage facilities. The animals live in the open, and though the land area of these ranches is vast, it is fenced off in sections to provide a rotation of grazing. Wells are extremely important, and they are often fitted with windmills to draw the water. In some areas of the United States, 120 acres is barely sufficient to feed one head of cattle, but there are also grazing grounds of better quality where 25 acres can be enough. In the Chad 20 acres per head is considered exceptional, and the best Argentine *estancias*, in the province of Buenos Aires, often of several thousand acres, manage on six acres per head.

For sheep, the average capacity of Australian grazing grounds is six acres per head, while in New Zealand it is three-quarters of an acre per head; this shows the great difference in the quality of pasture land, New Zealand receiving a far greater rainfall than the arid regions of Australia.

The fact that extensive stockbreeding is practised on land that is not considered suitable to sustain an active form of agriculture explains why the population density is generally low.

Right: Cattle in the Esquel zone of Chubut (Argentina). In the Argentine pampas stockbreeding was the first form of exploitation practised by the Europeans. Subsequently, with the development of agriculture, stockbreeding moved to the west and south. *Below:* Penned cattle waiting to be taken to an abattoir in Sioux City, Iowa, where cattle are brought from as far as states west of Missouri. The vastness of the abattoir indicates the nature of extensive stockbreeding practised in the United States, where it is closely connected with the meat trade.

Intensive stockbreeding of the commercial type aimed essentially at dairy products has superseded the former subsistence-type stockbreeding in Italy. The transfer of livestock in spring to Pre-Alpine pastures is now limited to mountain areas near processing and marketing centres.

Intensive stockbreeding

Whereas extensive stockbreeding is aimed directly at producing meat and wool (and the livestock is kept in the open), in intensive stockbreeding highly developed techniques are used to produce animal products, including milk and its derivatives. Located near great centres of consumption, intensive stockbreeding for dairy purposes has led to the establishment of vast specialized areas. As well as milk and milk products, livestock feed is produced, and pigs and poultry are often reared.

The chief areas devoted to intensive stockbreeding are situated in northern Europe and in 'Anglo-Saxon' America. The south-eastern coast of Australia, the northern part of Tasmania, and New Zealand are other areas with concentrations of intensive stockbreeding based on dairy production. The climatic conditions required by this form of activity for the production of good forage crops are at least 30 inches of rainfall a year (or the aid of irrigation) and average day temperatures of over 20° C, but without excessively warm summers which tend to reduce milk yield.

The organization of establishments practising this type of stockbreeding varies considerably from region to region, but it is always based on breeds of dairy cattle that are the result of a long and careful process of selection. The Friesians are the leaders in this field, and the strains produced in the United States and Canada have enabled this breed of cattle to provide the largest amounts of milk, though the product does not have the same high fat-content as that produced by Jersey cattle. Other breeds commonly used in intensive stockbreeding are Guernsey, Ayrshire, and Brown Swiss cattle.

The great European zone of intensive stockbreeding includes much of the British Isles and Denmark, the northern part of France, Belgium, the Netherlands, Germany, Poland, Lithuania, Latvia, and Estonia. The zone stretches into the interior of the Soviet Union, where there are intensive stockbreeding establishments to the east and near large urban concentrations. The stockbreeding areas of Scandinavia are in the southern part of Finland, Sweden, and Norway, where they are found among the forests.

A modern cattle farm in New England where dairy produce is sold to the large city markets of the Atlantic zone of the United States.

Byres, haylofts, and sheds on a Cumberland farm during the winter season when the livestock is fed with supplies of fodder gathered during the haymaking season.

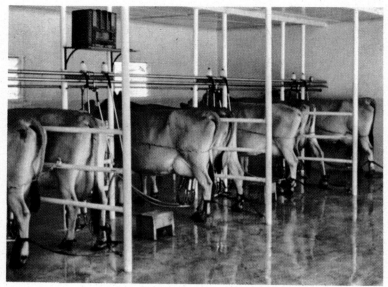

Inside a byre in a New Zealand farm, where stockbreeding is highly rationalized, as can be seen from the use of machinery for milking.

natural meadowland, and the rest given over to herbaceous cultivation such as artificial meadowland, maize, and oats. The land under forage crops is greater in Canada in regions with a severer climate. The number of animals per farm is about 25 cows, 40 pigs, and 150 chickens. Because of the greater use of machinery, the work involved in cultivation is carried out with a labour force that never exceeds two or three employees. Dairy farming, however, requires a constant labour force.

The dairy zones of Australia and New Zealand are particularly favoured by the climate, which enables vegetation to grow on the meadows throughout the year. Thus stockbreeders merely rotate their pastures, and do not go in for growing cereals or tubers. Operating in very favourable conditions, New Zealand dairy farms have developed an extremely active export market in dairy products, such as butter and cheese.

A view of the Dutch countryside, in which agriculture and stockbreeding are practised side by side as in other countries of central and northern Europe.

One of the characteristics of European intensive stockbreeding is the relatively small size of farms, often 35 acres or less; in Denmark many are only 10 to 15 acres. In these conditions much of the land is under potatoes, turnips, and beet, and grazing grounds are necessarily limited in extent. Much of the animal foodstuff is imported from abroad.

Because of the major development in transport systems in Europe a large quantity of milk and dairy products is brought to areas of large consumption. This supply has also led to the establishment of industrialized centres, situated outside the 'milk belt', which also produce milk and dairy products.

In addition to milk production other important products include butter and cheeses. The processing of dairy products is often carried out by co-operative organizations, whose functions also include the marketing of their products, as in Denmark and Holland.

The great American region of intensive stockbreeding includes the New England States, the St Lawrence valley, the States of New York and Pennsylvania, the Ontario peninsula, Michigan, Wisconsin, and Minnesota. There are about 500,000 dairy farms in this region. American farms are about 100 to 200 acres in area, and the ideal size, based on optimum conditions, is around 175 acres, with a third of its area under woodland and pasture, a quarter under

Commercial hunting and fishing

As well as trapping and fishing in inland waters and seas, there are also active industries involving the breeding of molluscs, trout, and other varieties that are fairly widespread in Europe.

Fishing assumes different forms according to the type of market. Coastal fishing, aimed at local markets, is frequently operated by family enterprises using out-of-date methods; deep-sea fishing, aimed at the inland market, requires an advanced degree of mechanization, storage facilities, refrigeration plant, adequate transport systems, and a complex organization that can be put into operation only by consortia or large commercial companies. Both these forms of fishing are for the fresh-fish market. Large-scale fishing also involves the processing of the catch (drying, smoking, canning), which is done by large companies.

Deep-sea fishing takes advantage of all the latest scientific knowledge of ocean conditions. It is known that fish gather in regions where the plankton is richest and in the greatest quantities; fish also like sunlight, so that shallower waters are preferred. These conditions reduce the total surface that can be fished successfully to less than 10% of the total marine area.

The largest area of deep-sea fishing is located in the north-western sector of the Pacific Ocean, which extends from the eastern extremity of the Soviet Union along the Asian coastline, Japan, and the islands of Indonesia, to continue into the northern basin of the Indian Ocean. The next largest area is in the Atlantic Ocean, extending from the Scandinavian peninsula, Iceland, and the British Isles down to the south as far as Finisterre.

The most economically important kinds of fish in the western Pacific sector are cod, salmon, herring, and crustaceans; in the northern sector the chief forms are salmon, halibut, and sardines, and, farther south, tuna. In the northern and eastern sectors of the Atlantic important varieties are cod, herring, mackerel, and anchovies, which are particularly abundant in the great banks of the North Sea and along the coast of Norway. The American western Atlantic sector abounds in herring, salmon, and cod, occurring chiefly off Newfoundland where the cold Labrador current, flowing south, meets the warm Gulf Stream, flowing north.

Commercially based hunting is practised in only a few areas of the world because of the extreme reduction of animals following the hunting by Europeans in colonial possessions of the most sought after species for their hides or ivory. In Africa hunting is mostly pursued for sport, with heavy taxes payable to the new African states; in some states, such as Chad and Kenya, big-game hunting constitutes an important form of revenue. Wild-life conservation is maintained by the establishment of several game reserves and parks throughout the continent (shown in the map below). *Above:* An elephant killed during a hunt in the Congo. *Left:* An antelope being gutted after being caught during a safari in northern Cameroon. The hide and the horns are trophies much sought after by European hunters.

Pulling in the trawl nets which have been laid out by the dinghy moored against the fishing vessel. The picture was taken off the Danish coast. *Below:* Oyster beds near Arcachon, France.

In the Arctic and Antarctic Oceans, whaling, carried out with the most up-to-date equipment, has led to the systematic destruction of whales. As a result, a series of international conventions has been signed by the interested states setting an annual limit to the number that may be caught.

The most important areas for inland fishing are located in the Scandinavian lakes and in neighbouring regions particularly rich in salmon. The great rivers of eastern Europe and Siberia are also excellent fishing areas, yielding sturgeon from which caviare is obtained. There is a large salmon-fishing industry in Canada. Fishing round China, the Indochinese peninsula, the Indian sub-continent, and the Sonda Islands is particularly important because of its valuable contribution to the dietary needs of an extremely dense population.

257

Left: Of all the activities concerned in exploiting the animal resources of the sea, whaling is the one that requires the most organized forms of industry, both for expeditions consisting of specially adapted vessels and for the processing of the catch. Whaling is carried out by large companies in those few countries where the whaling industry, now in decline (or at least greatly limited by international agreements aimed at the preservation of the species), is still practised. Chile is one of these countries, and has a whale-processing station at Iquique.

Far left: Cod being dried near Reykjavik, Iceland. Cod abounds in cold waters, and cod-fishing is the basis for a large fishing and canning industry. *Left:* The London fish-market of Billingsgate.

Deep-sea fishing boats at the quayside in Monterey, California.

Nets being pulled in from the sea on Kalkuda Beach, Ceylon, where fishing, almost exclusively coastal in type, is aimed at local consumption and neighbouring markets.

Commercial exploitation of forests

Forests have always constituted more a barrier to expansion and activity on the part of man than a resource that could be put to advantageous use. Man has always struggled to reclaim land from the forests, particularly in the temperate zones, to cultivate or to use as pasture for his animals or to break down the great barrier of vegetation that impeded communication.

The exploitation of forest resources depends, apart from the presence of commercially valuable material, on the accessibility of the forest area and the means of transporting the timber economically. The greatest forest areas utilized are in Russia, North America, and Africa. Then come southern Asia and South America, with Europe, Central America, and Oceania far behind.

The forests of the tropical zones consist of numerous forms of vegetation, among which the most valued are the denser hardwoods. But these do not float, and resultant transport difficulties limit their use. The most valued woods include mahogany from the United States and the coast of Guinea, cedar from Central America, teak from Indochina, and ebony from central Africa and Southeast Asia. In addition to the tropical forest zone, in the lower latitudes there are transitional zones where hard and soft woods grow together in forests. Beyond these, in both hemispheres, there is a forest zone in which the main types of timber are represented by the hardwoods such as walnut, American walnut, beech, and birch, used in furniture and utensil manufacture. The zone extends from the Mediterranean to the Baltic in Europe, to the United States on the American continent, and in the southern hemisphere to southern Chile, eastern Australia, and the southern tip of Africa. Apart from this zone there is the softwood region from Alaska to Labrador, from Scandinavia to Mongolia, and from Korea to Japan. The chief varieties of softwoods are fir, pine, and poplar, used for making wood pulp and building materials.

The demand for wood continually increases, and all countries try to conserve a minimum of forest covering. Legislation has set up organizations to regulate felling and look after the conservation of forests until the trees have reached a mature stage. In this way, some effort is made to limit the serious damage that indiscriminate felling has caused in the past, particularly in the more

A tractor pulls a large white fir trunk in the Cascade Mountains, Washington.

heavily populated regions. Serious soil erosion followed this felling, together with floods and often climatic modifications of the relief structure.

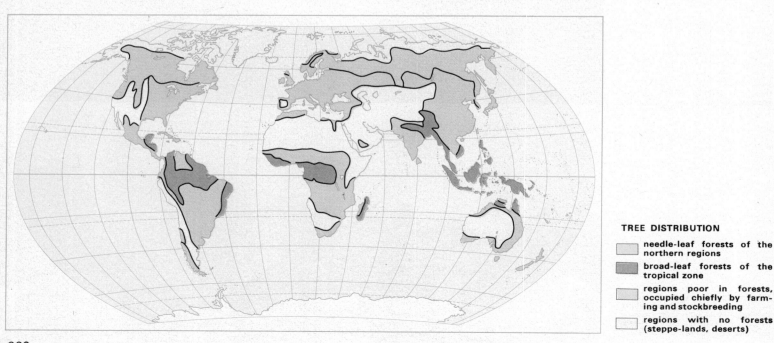

TREE DISTRIBUTION

- needle-leaf forests of the northern regions
- broad-leaf forests of the tropical zone
- regions poor in forests, occupied chiefly by farming and stockbreeding
- regions with no forests (steppe-lands, deserts)

Right: Forest exploitation in the mountainous hinterland of Port Moresby in New Guinea, where large industrial companies operate. In the past this form of exploitation in colonial territories led to the destruction of large forest areas, but today it is controlled everywhere by legislation aimed at preventing the indiscriminate felling of trees, which can prove harmful to the natural surroundings of the land concerned. Transport to centres where wood is processed and prepared for industrial use is carried out in countries which have suitable rivers by floating the trees downstream. *Below:* The floating wood arriving at a paper mill situated by an Ontario river. *Centre right:* Logs of Douglas pine being transported from the Chuska Mountains (New Mexico), where there is a large forest reserve owned by a wood-processing company. *Bottom:* A train loaded with timber from the Appalachian region approaching a large paper mill near the Great Lakes.

COMMERCE IN THE PRODUCTS OF THE SOIL

Exchanges between economic structures

The organization of agricultural trading has for a long time, even in countries with a free-enterprise economy, lost any relationship it had with *laissez faire* principles. This has been the result of certain aspects of supply and demand, determined by production limits imposed by natural conditions or by the agricultural structure of the individual countries.

The distribution of vegetation depends on morphological, pedological, and climatic conditions. These have a noticeable and limiting effect on cash crops and on some subsistence crops of the intertropical regions. This is significant because it is the intertropical regions that have the greatest number of countries with a backward economy, whose products are absorbed to a great extent by the developed countries of western Europe, North America, Oceania, and Japan. This phenomenon also occurs, in varying degrees, inside individual countries, such as the United States and the Soviet Union, where the territory is large enough to enclose a whole range of physiographic zones, and also in countries such as Italy, with regional imbalances in economic development.

In developed regions or countries, subsistence forms of economy were abandoned from the beginning of the process of development and resulted in a clear-cut division of the various tasks of production. This broke the traditional links between the city and the country, and built completely new markets for agricultural products,

with the creation, for example, of regions of exchange between territories that in former times had no mutual trade relations whatever. The degree of commercialization of agriculture depends on the amount of land cultivated. With an increase in area there is an increase in yield, especially with food products destined for trade. This underlines most clearly the difference between modern agriculture and subsistence agriculture based on smallholdings of 10 to 15 acres.

In underdeveloped countries, whenever there is an increase in agricultural production, it is usually absorbed by the producer. In

The farm produce market in Freetown, Sierra Leone, representing a short-range market created by urban demand for agricultural produce grown in the neighbouring countryside.

Opposite: Cocoa being shipped at Accra for consumption in developed countries, which in their turn provide industrial and manufactured goods. *Right:* Industrial products from developed countries invade the distant markets of Africa; the picture shows crockery being sold in a market in eastern Chad. *Far right:* The simplest form of trade: peasant women of Madagascar sell the produce from their smallholdings. *Centre:* Bananas from plantations on the coastal zone of Guyanas, in Eucador, are unloaded at a depot in Guayaquil before being sent to areas of consumption outside the tropics. *Below:* Large grain elevators dominate the cities of the Canadian wheat zone (the picture is of Indian Head, Saskatchewan). Advanced technology and suitable territorial conditions has given this region an even greater role in grain production, making it one of the few large-scale exporters of wheat.

the developed countries, however, the use of advanced forms of technology has made it possible to reduce the area under cultivation while maintaining and even increasing its yield. This process has led to the cultivation of certain crops becoming concentrated in a few countries possessing the most suitable conditions – countries exporting large quantities of wheat are Canada, the United States, Argentina, and Australia; and wool exports are now the field of Argentina, Australia, and New Zealand.

Supply and demand

Taken as a whole, the supply of agricultural products is substantially an elastic and short-term one, chiefly because of the varying seasonal availability of the products and the lack of any standard level of quality or quantity. It is true that uncertainty in supply can be remedied by taking advantage of 'geographic compensation' provided by the fact that the inversion of seasonal conditions in the two hemispheres makes it possible for products to mature all the year round at different latitudes. But this is not always satisfactory. Mediterranean-type products from Australia and South Africa reach the European markets in full summer, but their prices are higher because, owing to the smaller area of production, their quantity is clearly less than that supplied by traditional producers of the northern hemisphere in winter and spring. A scarcity of grain in western markets during the spring months could not be balanced by imports from countries in southern or eastern Asia because local consumption in those regions is very high and production completely absorbed by domestic markets.

Long-term supply is less elastic, since the production cycle of the individual products is by necessity long, ranging from several weeks to several years in the case of many trees. This inelasticity is increased by the limited availability of land due to the practice of agrarian rotation, and by the conservative attitude towards innovation of people who work the land.

Conversely, short-term demand is relatively inelastic when it concerns food that is a necessity even when its price rises. In the long term, however, demand is more elastic. Any improvement in the general standard of living causes a greater variety in diet and an increase in demand for industrial goods made from agricultural raw materials. It is evident that, because of their characteristics, supply and demand show a substantial inability to balance each other, and this is stressed by the behaviour of the producers.

Another factor that plays a considerable part in shaping trade in agricultural goods is the fluctuation of prices. The prices of most agricultural base products tend to come down in the long term for a number of reasons: increased supply, as has been the case with coffee when its cultivation was extended to Africa; ever greater use of substitute or synthetic products; the greater ability of monopolistic groups of importers to strike hard bargains with

Agricultural produce is made available out of season by use of greenhouses, so that many varieties can be supplied before their normal natural cultivation period. Greenhouse culture also makes it possible to grow produce that normally would not take to the surrounding climate. *Left:* Greenhouses in Guernsey, in the Channel Islands, where market-garden products, fruit, and flowers are grown. The selection and preparation of agricultural products destined for export are operations carried out with great care and only produce that will keep until it reaches the consumer is used. The creation of fruit-juice industries is a modern method of absorbing agricultural produce which successfully meets the problem raised by the perishable nature of fruit. *Top:* Table grapes for countries in northern Europe being inspected and packed in Crete. *Above:* Grapefruit arriving at a factory warehouse in Texas.

Cotton being shipped at Asunción, in Paraguay. Paraguay has very few textile industries and is forced to export a large portion of its production, which meets with competition from other cotton-producing countries of South America.

The negative effects due to surpluses in production which strike at underdeveloped countries are partly remedied by governments, often through international agreements which arrange for economic help in the form of aid being given to the countries concerned. The Food and Agriculture Organization contributes to this work and sends out many missions of experts to poor countries. *Above:* An FAO expert instructing local farmers in modern cultivation methods in Upper Volta.

Coffee for export being loaded at Santos, the port from which all Brazilian coffee is shipped. Coffee production in Brazil reached its peak in the 1930s to meet the rising demand, until overproduction was reached.

exporters, who are frequently disorganized and financially weak; and, in some cases, causes related to natural conditions. But price fluctuations with the greatest effect are those due to phases of expansion and recession that periodically affect developed economies and are known as *economic cycles*. These produce a periodic imbalance in the agricultural economies of individual countries, with the most serious repercussions occurring in the underdeveloped ones. Whereas in developed countries agriculture can be subsidized from sectors outside agriculture, in underdeveloped countries the economy is too dependent on agricultural products, which form the largest source of their national income.

Policies of stabilization and support

The adoption of stabilization policies to support agriculture, practised generally by importing countries and by the United States, now has a major influence on the scale and progress of trade in agricultural products and has cut off every functional tie between production capacity and supply and demand. As a result, large surpluses accumulate in the exporting countries: for example, in the United States and Canada, grain stocks exceed the total production of one year.

To meet these serious problems, which affect stability and economic development in individual countries, intergovernmental agreements have been drawn up with the following functions:

1) To improve trade exchanges through agreements between producing countries limiting production and exports.

265

The fluctuation of prices as a result of the constantly changing relationship between supply and demand has a major effect on the economy of countries which depend almost entirely on trade in agricultural products, as is the case with many former colonies, most of which cultivate one main crop and cannot adopt any policies to subsidize their agriculture for want of capital from other sources. Situations typical of this have struck at former colonial countries in Africa producing ground-nuts, and their economies have been safeguarded in many cases by the former colonial power with forms of compensation. These may be priorities granted in the supply of industrial products in exchange for the purchase of local agricultural produce. *Left:* Piles of ground-nuts at Kaolack, Senegal.

2) To prevent excessive fluctuation of prices and volume of trade, so as to favour economic stability both for the producing and the consuming countries.

3) To eliminate factors causing imbalance between production and consumption by means of long-term economic planning.

4) To adopt opportune counter-measures with regard to protectionist or preferential policies on the part of importing countries, thereby avoiding dangerous contractions in the market for primary products. The types of agreement signed in this field are: a) The multilateral contract that requires importers and exporters respectively to buy or to sell determined minimum quantities at a pre-arranged minimum or maximum price when the market price reaches or goes beyond the set limits. This type of contract operates in the international wheat market. b) Agreements to create buffer stocks of certain products in order to stabilize prices and make it obligatory to buy when the world price goes below a certain

minimum and to sell when it goes above a certain maximum. c) Agreements restricting exports to promote price stability for the products concerned.

As a further means of obviating the negative effects of the formation of surpluses in developed countries, a new form of commercial transaction has been introduced to supply base products to underdeveloped countries in the form of aid.

It is clear that problems relating to trade in agricultural products are expressed in different terms for underdeveloped or backward countries. Their transactions consist chiefly of exporting tropical products, about 85% of which are absorbed by Europe and North America. Market variations in these are fairly frequent and considerable, either through preferential treatment accorded to some products, through reduction of the percentage of agricultural raw material used in finished products, or, in the long term, through increase in production.

INDUSTRIAL ACTIVITIES

Interpretation of the industrial phenomenon

The term *industry* has been accepted in the technical and economic field as a convenient way of describing 'the activity of transforming primary products'. An examination of this definition is of primary importance for a correct interpretation of the events that, in the brief space of two centuries, have brought man from the age of the horse (as the fastest means of transport) to that of space travel, and have radically modified social, political, and economic structures, and in so doing have changed a large part of the face of the Earth.

The transformation of primary products has existed throughout the history of man on Earth, and the machine, understood as an instrument that increases the application of energy to the process of transformation, is as old as man. The history of technology is simply an account of the efforts made by man to break the impasse set up, in the scale of time, between the quantitative requirements of products to support him and the availability of the energy necessary to provide these.

The very slow rate of technological development up to the 18th century can be attributed to the persistence of artisan methods of production. Perhaps the very fragmentation of these methods, which for many centuries supplied the needs of a human society which had a social, economic, and political structure very different from the present day, provides a clue to reaching a correct understanding of the industrial phenomenon, as a form of rationalization of production, born from the need to have available much greater quantities of finished products, with a more uniform quality, than in the past. With such an understanding it is possible, on the one hand, to maintain the traditional acceptance of the term 'industry' as a 'type of production' and, on the other, to open up a vast horizon of motivation that may be observed by geographical as well as historical studies.

Above: A print, from *Bericht van Bergwerk* (1617), shows a foundry of the time.
Below: The blast furnaces of the Krupp steelworks at Rheinhausen.

The industrial phenomenon

The phenomenon of the 'industrial revolution', which began in the last quarter of the 18th century and continued throughout the 19th, may be regarded not so much as the result of the invention of machines, but rather as a radical upheaval of the social and economic structure.

The seeds of the industrial phenomenon can be seen as far back as the first discoveries of new territories. The broadening of man's knowledge of the world proved a powerful stimulus to scientific progress, while the discovery of new and more varied natural resources caused man to seek out new techniques to use them. The new discoveries also brought tremendous wealth from overseas territories to Europe, which was later to acquire that enthusiastic cosmopolitanism that was typical of the ruling classes of the 'age of light'. A powerful economic factor was to appear with the greater quantities of gold available on the European market, which led to a considerable increase in prices that was to favour the investments made by the bourgeoisie in land and subsequently in manufacturing enterprises. The formation of the mercantile bourgeoisie created the financial and technical foundation for expanding production, because this class was in possession of the necessary qualifications: the concentration of capital and the entrepreneur's vocation.

Parallel to this, the more intense development of active thought promoted scientific research to discover natural laws. And later, when these were found not to be divine laws, the road was opened for empirical rationalism from which stemmed the rapid technical evolution and the discoveries and inventions of the 18th century. Love of science and curiosity about technology on the one hand, expansion and prosperity of trade on the other – these were the most significant characteristics of 18th-century European society,

Left: A pumping system used in an old mine (from *De re metallica*, by Georgius Agricola, published in 1580). The steam engine was one of the inventions that started the Industrial Revolution. It broadened the use of coal and opened up new possibilities of transport, such as railways *(below)*.

As an economic, political, and social phenomenon, the Industrial Revolution also had its origins in geographic discoveries and the exploitation of colonies. This led to the import, through the British ports, of raw materials for industry from overseas territories. Manchester, as depicted by L. S. Lowry *(right)*, reached its full industrial ferment during the last century. It provided the classic example of a city that developed against a background of industrial mercantilism connected with the great British Empire of the 19th century. In the cities of Britain, industries were born that brought new communities into existence round the old centres. These were populated by farm workers who came from the countryside to create a new type of urban landscape, an example of which can be seen in this aerial view of York *(below)*.

Industrialization is, in developed countries today, a phenomenon that affects entire regions economically and socially. It introduces to the country-side and remote areas forms of life and technology that are the basis of vast and irreversible processes of change in old rural structures, though there may be no marked form of industrial activity in the vicinity. *Left:* The Pennsylvania Turnpike near Lehighton. The motorway introduces un-mistakable signs of industry into the countryside. In a developed country industry no longer requires the urban medium to bring about changes in ways of life. In underdeveloped countries, however, the instruments of industry appear as alien elements, and attract the attentive curiosity of people still practising ancient ways of life. *Right:* Nomads of the Moroccan desert watch oil-drilling operations.

and it was during this age that Europe reached perhaps its greatest moment of world supremacy.

The needs of mercantile activities likewise changed economic, financial, monetary, and even political institutions, and the first great doctrinal controversies concerning the organization of economy began between the mercantilists and the physiocrats. The individualistic and liberal concept of economy affirmed in Britain, and expressed in Adam Smith's work *The Wealth of Nations* (1776), enabled Britain, already favoured by its leadership of world trade, to begin the great process of transforming the structure of its production. Britain embarked on this much sooner than France and Germany, and set out from a high level of technology.

It was symptomatic that in England this process was accompanied by profound changes in agrarian structures whereby the bourgeoisie completed the system of land enclosures that had been in existence since the Middle Ages. The legislation allowing these enclosures proved a death blow to the old rural and village life and to sub-sistence forms of agriculture, and introduced the beginnings of large-scale market-based agriculture. Meanwhile the mass of the wretched peasantry, deprived of their traditional common lands and open fields, were forced to leave the countryside and live in crowded cities, where they formed the cheap labour forces for the new developing industries. Industrial development was helped fur-ther by the population increase during the second half of the 18th century, an increase due to higher standards of hygiene, improved diets, and better personal cleanliness.

Industrialization

Two aspects of the great industrial phenomenon are of basic interest in the study of geography: the technical aspect, which modifies radically the appearance of the natural landscape, and the socio-economic aspect, which, because it carries out its action on struc-tures, institutions, and orders, generates a new way of life and takes place over much larger areas and with irreversible effects.

Industrialization is, in fact, deruralization: this appears quite plainly on the historical level through the change in the concept of wealth – from land wealth to financial wealth – which is the root of the change of the economy from forms of subsistence to those based on market demands. This change leads to the intro-duction of modern techniques, with the consequent disappearance of the family-operated farm and self-consumption, and a progres-sive and large reduction of people practising agriculture.

This is a process fittingly known as urbanization. In reality, industrialization was, and is, wherever it occurs, accompanied by large-scale town-building. This appears obvious enough if we con-sider the mercantilist origin of industrialization: the bourgeoisie, which was the moving force, lived and operated in the cities, so that the rural masses were brought to the cities to become the pro-letarian class. But the cities, as well as being areas of factories and management boards for the new type of production, also became the centres of the formation and propagation of a new way of life. In times nearer our own the process of deruralization is no longer necessarily accompanied by the phenomena connected with town-dwelling, but these are still typical of the development phase in countries with a backward economy.

Source of energy

The primary sources from which power is being drawn today are all being put to a destructive use: coal, petroleum, natural gas, and fissionable minerals are extracted from deposits that will eventually

270

Oil flares in the desert of Iraq *(above)* produced by the combustion of unused methane gas. Petroleum and natural gas, today both important sources of energy, are subject to destructive use and their deposits will eventually be exhausted. Water power, however, can be used over and over again to produce electric power. It is often exploited through gigantic projects such as the Glen Canyon dam in Arizona *(left)*, but many countries have already reached the economic limit of its exploitation. The search for new sources of energy is an urgent matter today, particularly for countries poor in natural resources. In France, experiments are already being carried out to obtain energy from the heat of the Sun with the help of the huge reflector being built at Mont Louis in the Pyrenees *(below)*.

become exhausted and will be impossible to renew. Only the mechanical energy of water, which is turned into electric power, is a source not subject to exhaustion. Growing production and consumption therefore pose three major problems. The first is a general one concerning mankind as a whole, and its solution lies in the discovery of new sources of energy, preferably of an inexhaustible kind. The prospects in this field are encouraging, and several installations have been built, such as those drawing energy from the sun or harnessing the power of the tides. Plans are also afoot to obtain energy from wind power, and to make use of the temperature gradient between the upper and lower levels of the sea. The second problem concerns individual countries that have plentiful reserves of traditional sources of energy. For them, the problem is one of conserving these, and this often involves a whole series of political and economic measures. The last problem is one facing countries that have no sources of energy of their own and have reached the economic limit in the use of their potential hydro-electric power. These countries are faced with the prospect of having to import sources of energy, with a consequent threat to the independence of their economy.

Sources of energy and economic development

The most telling factor of the rapid progress of economic development over the last two centuries is the extraordinary rate of increase in the production of energy from various sources. At the

same time there has been a progressive change in the way the world has used sources of power, with a decrease in the use of coal to the advantage of oil, natural gas, and hydroelectric power.

These modifications clearly reflect the structure of consumption and this in turn depends largely on the interchangeability of the sources. The choice of a source of energy is obviously determined in each country by its availability. In Sweden and Canada the decreased use of coal as a source of energy is due to the vast hydroelectric potential available, while in the United States the large reserves of natural gas are the determining factor.

There is another factor to be taken into account. In countries where the process of industrialization is in its infancy, coal may play a dominant role in providing a source of energy, depending to a great extent on the aims of economic planning adopted – coal still plays a major part in heavy industry (for example, coke is indispensable in the production of pig-iron).

On a more general basis the use of oil provides highly competitive conditions as compared with coal. The supply of coal shows, in the first place, little elasticity regarding demand. The preparation of new mines to meet any possible increase in demand requires at least ten years of work. The high labour costs involved (about 65%) in production make it impossible to face any sudden reduction in demand. Transport costs and the expense of grading the coal (and the considerable losses through dross and slag) are particularly heavy. Petroleum production, however, is much more flexible regarding demand, and its utilization is much more simple. The organization of the market, controlled by a few large companies, permits flexible exploitation of the variety of products and zones of sale according to the needs of the moment.

The quantity and structure of energy consumption are the source of further interesting consideration. In the first place, a com-

parison of the economic development of countries over the same period of time reveals the existence of a close relationship with the consumption of energy. This is one of the factors that cause certain blocks to the process of economic development, an example of which is to be found in the southern region of Italy.

Another interesting observation is that no great oil-producing country has become the seat of large industrial complexes without having been this already by virtue of its coal production. (This is because the great coal basins became, at the beginning of the industrial revolution, areas of installation of production equipment; and the size of these installations was such that the lesser importance assumed by coal as a source of energy did not bring about a transfer or a redistribution of these installations.) At the same time, the production of hydroelectric power, natural gas, and petroleum itself is responsible only for comparatively small installations in the areas of production. There is a progressive increase in the amount of energy transported a great distance from the areas where it is produced. This partly explains the relatively small consumption of hydroelectric power and natural gas in certain countries that have a wide range of choice, as well as the enormous spread of petroleum consumption, which is the least affected by transport costs.

The coal industry

The problem in the coal-mining industry is above all one of the availability of labour. It arises first of all at the recruiting stage for new mining developments, but is subsequently complicated by the process of mechanization, which, while not resulting in a significant reduction of the numbers employed, enables miners to acquire sufficient technical ability to realize their ambitions

The confluence of the Ruhr and the Rhine at Duisburg. This aerial view shows some significant aspects of an area with one of the world's highest concentrations of industry. The industrial destiny of the region, determined about a century ago by the iron and steel works, found its original motivation in geographic factors, being situated near rich deposits and natural waterways. As a result the Duisburg port installations form the largest traffic junction of the Rhine-Ruhr navigation system. In the last few decades, the use of other sources of energy more economical than coal has not affected the productive apparatus already in existence, which continued to act as a centre of attraction for more plants and new activities of production: different sources of energy are brought to the Ruhr from distant centres of production (hydroelectric power from the upper Rhine valley, oil from countries outside Europe). The photograph gives some indication of this, with the large storage tanks seen in the port at bottom right. Other elements connected with the concentration of industrial plants, the port installations, include the dense rail network, bridges, motorways, and crossings — all expressing the volume of activity in the zone. On the left can be seen part of the great iron and steel works.

of finding work in the industries on the surface. Coal-mining is a tough occupation; not only does mining require certain physical qualities, but the miner is subjected to real physical shock every time he returns to the surface.

The first important cases for formulating laws of social security arose in the coal-mining industry. In Britain, where miners were first given considerable help in this field, there is a complete ban on the immigration of miners to avoid the situation where a cheap supply of foreign labour might cause a decrease in the rates of pay of the local miners.

The transport of coal has influenced the organization of the international trade in the product. Coal is a heavy merchandise, difficult to handle, dirty, and of little value in relation to its weight. This value also varies with the quality. It has been esti-

mated that the cost of transport practically doubles the production cost at the pit. These conditions are largely responsible for the high concentration in the vicinity of coal deposits of industries using medium-grade coal, and the recourse to the most economical forms of transport possible. Hence water transport is preferred for carrying small or medium tonnage, and coal pipelines have been installed in which powdered coal is mixed with water and pumped to power stations.

The international coal trade up to the First World War was marked by the prevalence of British coal, and in the period between the wars by the advent of Polish and German production. After 1945 the United States became the major exporting country. Now that countries who do not meet their power requirements tend to import oil rather than coal, the coal trade is gradually declining,

Section of a coal mine *(left)*, from a drawing made in the early 20th century, with vertical shafts for pit cages to ascend and descend, and horizontal tunnels leading to the coal faces and serving to ventilate the mine and provide a way for horse-drawn transport. Although technical progress has changed mining conditions, some of the labour still has to be done by hand *(below)*.

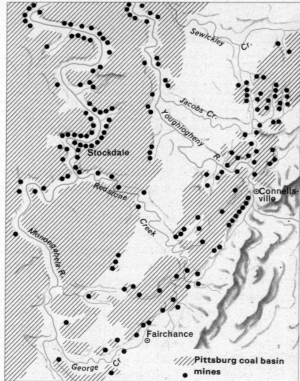

The geological conditions of deposition of the strata have a considerable effect on the cost of coal as well as the degree of mechanization used for extracting it. Relatively advantageous in this sense is the coal from the Appalachians, which is extracted from seams outcropping at the bottom of the valley slopes. The seams are mainly horizontal, as shown on the map *(right)*.

///// **Pittsburg coal basin mines**

274

The considerable labour force required by coal-mining has brought into existence large mining villages, such as the one *above*, in East Fife, Scotland.

with smaller quantities being transported over shorter distances. Only the United States remains as a long-range supplier, to Japan, the Americas, and western Europe.

Extraction, trade, and processing of petroleum

There is still no technical method of ascertaining with complete certainty that there are any oil deposits underground, even in territory where all the signs point to oil – hence the lack of interest on the part of oil companies in prospecting, which remains, at least in many countries, entrusted to small enterprises. In the United States the profession of the 'wildcatter' is fairly widespread, and 80% of annual discoveries of deposits in United States territory is the work of individual and independent operators.

The basic problem of petroleum production concerns the location of the refineries. At first, especially in the United States, refineries were built near the point where the crude oil was extracted. This was because of the lack of convenient methods of transporting a product that was only partially exploitable at a time when technology had not yet learned to obtain and use all the by-

The transport of coal, even when practised in the most convenient forms along waterways *(right)*, still adds 50% to its cost. A mechanized caravan in the Sahara *(far right)* carries equipment to be used in opening a new oil well. The track is soaked in crude oil to make travel easier. Generally, the production areas of oil are great distances from consumption centres.

products of refining. Later, with the enormous increase in demand promoting the location and utilization of large new deposits, the problem became one regarding the most convenient location of refinery processes. In the case of petroleum imported from foreign countries, the producing countries do not have control over refining. This is carried out by the consumer because of the greater profit obtained from refining and because of the greater ease in obtaining skilled labour to operate the refinery. This type of labour, which is required in larger numbers in refining than in extraction, could be found only in the consuming countries that had reached a high level of technology. It was completely lacking in countries where the oil was being extracted, as most of these were as yet underdeveloped.

The refineries were situated along sea-coasts, rivers, or navigable canals. The present tendency, however, appears to be one of situating them directly in areas of consumption, and this has been aided by the large-scale adoption of pipeline systems. These require high capital investment, but running costs are extremely low. Another reason for this tendency is the utilization of almost all the products of refining, so that the refining process has branched out into a number of activities.

The question of sea transport is complicated because of the different location of supply areas relative to areas of maximum consumption (Venezuela for the United States; the Middle East for most western European countries). As a result, decisions of a basically technical nature are often influenced by political considerations. The Middle East's position as a centre of world interest is maintained because the area has the largest reserves of crude oil and because every year it yields the greatest quantities.

The large proportion of oil transported through the Suez Canal gave that waterway tremendous importance. In order to facilitate passage through the canal (this problem also arose when the largest American oil deposits were in California and had to pass through the Panama Canal) the gross tonnage of tankers was progressively

Above: A mobile oil rig for drilling under the sea. *Top right:* An oil drilling zone in Salt Water Creek, southern Wyoming. *Left:* Oil tankers taking on their cargo at Aden, where there is a large refinery for processing crude petroleum from the Persian Gulf. *Right:* The large refinery of Sarnia, in Ontario, which exploits local petroleum and that arriving by pipeline from Alberta. It is situated in an ideal position regarding the large consumption areas of the Great Lakes, where it competes with the region's rich coal production.

A gas-processing plant *(above)* at Lacq, in the French Pyrenees, where France's largest natural-gas deposits are located. These are used as sources of power by the industries of the Garonne valley and are extended by pipeline to the Paris region.

adjusted to a maximum of about 30,000 tons. However, the present trend is to build far larger tankers; there are already several exceeding 200,000 tons, and a vessel of 300,000 tons was under construction in 1968. The determining factors were the 1956 Suez crisis and the 1967 Middle East War; shippers found the Cape route to be just as economical, provided that tankers-were large enough to carry crude petroleum in worthwhile quantities.

Utilization of natural gas

The exploitation of natural gas is more recent than that of oil, and has undergone spectacular expansion. The gas usually occurs in the same areas as petroleum deposits, and, as with petroleum, the areas of production seldom coincide with those of consumption. Economic transport of the crude product is possible only by means of gas ducts. These, however, prove to be less convenient than oil pipelines, because the heat potential of gas is less than that of petroleum, so that it takes a longer period to recoup investments. In addition, the very convenient utilization as a domestic and industrial form of fuel imparts a daily and seasonal variability in demand (this is the 'peak period' phenomenon, which also applies to electricity). On the one hand domestic distribution, which may require transport in expensive containers, increases its cost, and on the other the discontinuity of demand creates problems of sudden reorganization of supplies and stocks. To deal with these contingencies it is the practice in the United States, the world's largest consumer of natural gas, to use underground reservoirs – old petroleum deposits that have been exhausted or other suitable natural cavities.

For these reasons, natural gas does not constitute one of the goods of international exchange. As a result, deposits found in

Above: Pipelines for carrying water vapour from geysers to produce electric power at Wairakei, New Zealand. *Left:* The dam at Khashm al-Girba in the last stages of its construction on the River Atbara in Sudan (completed in 1963). The water is used for irrigation, and a hydroelectric power station will produce electricity for local domestic consumption and for planned industrial centres in Atbara.

The Grand Coulee Dam on the Columbia River in the State of Washington. It is more than 4,000 feet across, and created a lake 150 miles long. Another artificial lake functions as an equalizing reservoir. The scheme serves to irrigate cultivable land in the region and to supply power for the large centres of industry of the northwest, where hydroelectric power is the chief source of energy.

backward countries, which lack market outlets and investment capital, remain only partially utilized.

Production and transport of electric power

Electricity is not one of the primary sources of energy. The amount of electrical power produced in the world is far greater than that indicated in the general statistics, which account only for hydroelectric power; electrical energy derived from coal, oil, and other products is classified as originating from primary sources. However, electricity has the advantage that it can be applied in a wide field of activities. The chief drawback with electricity as a source of energy is that it cannot be stored, unlike the materials used in producing it, such as coal, oil, and, to a certain extent, water. In the case of water, the high costs involved in building

such installations as dams and reservoirs involve an immobilization of capital (loans and subsidies for this purpose are usually granted on a long-term basis). Also, when these installations are built, further expense is required to set up a grid system to convey the power to areas of consumption.

Hydroelectric stations of the less expensive type include those exploiting rivers or canals that can guarantee a regular supply of water. The kinetic energy of the water is converted by making the water flow down a gradient, and these installations are more or less the only type that can be used in large areas of flat land (the United States and the Soviet Union). In mountainous areas, where the gradient employed is steeper, the same water can be used several times by making it flow down a series of gradients. There are also special types of power station that use geothermal sources of energy, such as the geysers in Iceland and New Zealand.

As well as being able to produce more power than other types of installation, electric power stations have the additional advantage of being able to utilize cheap fuel and they need not be situated near mineral deposits or areas of consumption. The location of a power station is in fact determined by the cost of transporting fuel in relation to its yield and the cost of setting up a grid system, taking into account line losses.

The transport of electricity is a complex process, and problems arise because of the high costs of the materials that go into the making of cables, and the losses that occur along the grid system. The latter problem has been partly circumvented by increasing the voltage, and today most grids carry a load of up to 250,000 volts. This, however, is economical only on distances not exceeding 600 miles. In Siberia, the United States, and parts of central and western Europe, some grid systems carry a load of up to 400,000 volts, making it possible to deliver power over greater distances.

The higher elastic demand for electricity is due to seasonal factors: periodic reductions in power consumption by industries adjusting themselves to fluctuations in the market; the variations in night and day over the seasons, producing varying lighting requirements, and fluctuation in demand over the 24-hour period due to changing rates of consumption in various parts of the day. This last factor is marked by the occurrence of 'peak periods' in consumption, which in theory the power-supply sources should be in a condition to meet. To do this, however, increases the average cost of the actual power used, because of the greater volume of capacity required to meet peak requirements, a capacity that remains largely idle during off-peak periods.

The low degree of adaptability of supply to demand is partly circumnavigated in two ways: by using a system of preferential tariffs for use of power during off-peak periods and by organizing a system of production to cover the requirements of territories situated in different time zones so as to exploit the peak-period schedules. This latter system is used in the United States through a power pool, and a network of interconnections, in which a number of power stations (which may be of different types) are grouped together to feed a grid. By means of a central control, any power station can be switched in whenever more power is required.

Nuclear energy

Nuclear energy assumed a particularly important role after the Second World War. Fissionable materials, because of their strategic importance, are traded within a very closed market. Production is monopolized by the United States, the Soviet Union, Britain, France,

Los Angeles by night. Night lighting is an indication of the degree of economic development of a country, though it represents only one form of power.

and China. The western powers obtain the raw material from Canada, Congo, southern Africa, Australia, and Madagascar; the Soviet Union from East Germany and Czechoslovakia.

The production of an extremely large quantity of nuclear energy from a relatively small amount of material leads to ease of transport. One kilogram of uranium supplies energy equivalent to 2,500 tons of coal, or 1,800 tons of oil.

There are, however, a number of factors responsible for very high production costs. These include the elaborate precautions that have to be taken to provide safeguards against radiation, and the expense and complication of equipment and apparatus. As

The nuclear power station at Avoine in France (266,500 kW). Because of its high installation cost, nuclear energy cannot yet compete with energy from conventional sources, such as that derived from coal and oil and hydroelectric power.

a result, nuclear energy cannot yet compete economically with conventional sources. This is demonstrated by the policy of the United States and the Soviet Union, whose nuclear programmes are slanted towards military uses, such as atomic engines for ships and submarines. Only in Britain, where power generated from conventional sources is costly, has there been a broad programme for developing nuclear power stations.

The particular economic difficulties involved in the peaceful uses of nuclear power led to the creation, inside the European Economic Community, of the organization known as Euratom. Euratom's aims are research and dissemination of technical knowledge, the study of safety of personnel employed in nuclear plants and of the population at large, the rational use of investment by avoiding duplication in projects, the promotion of enterprises to ensure regularity and equality of conditions of supply of nuclear materials and fuels, and the creation of a common market in the supply of the necessary equipment for an atomic industry.

The exploitation of raw materials

The range of raw materials is always being increased by the discoveries and inventions of technologists, who work with economists to solve the great problem of reducing costs while increasing, diversifying, and improving the quality of production.

As has already been observed, at the time of the industrial revolution the inhabitants of Europe considered that the rest of the world was working to the advantage of their continent. Indeed, the continent mobilized the resources of the whole Earth, at least until the end of the 19th century, and colonialism was the political instrument used to carry out this mobilization.

There is a tendency for raw materials to be exploited largely

Central City, near Denver, in the Rocky Mountains, was established in 1859 during the gold-rush days. Gold, especially at the beginning of the colonial era, was one of the main causes of European migration overseas and development of overseas territories. It was later replaced by other raw materials that were just as precious and necessary to the colonial powers for their growing industries: products of tropical agriculture, stockbreeding, and minerals. Iron and coal were the most important as a basis for industrial development. Later, metals required for technological progress grew in importance. Many towns founded by gold prospectors became 'ghost towns' after the gold rush ended. Only those offering the possibility of new types of mineral exploitation survived.

Left: A section of the mines at Mount Isa in Queensland, the richest mining zone in Australia. Zinc, lead, copper, and silver are mined there. Because of the wealth of its raw materials and the special situation it found itself in during the last war, Australia was able to start a first process of industrialization. *Below:* The mines at Bisbee, in Arizona, which form one of the largest deposits of copper in the United States. This country, where the birth of industry was aided by an abundance of coal and iron, has found new conditions for industrial development in the shape of numerous other minerals on its vast territory and in supplies from other countries.

281

The case of most South American nations regarding natural resources is typical of underdeveloped countries: these countries have no industries, although they possess mineral deposits which in some cases are enormous. The raw material from their mines is supplied to the industrial countries, and in this way there is perpetuated an economic subjection that has its roots in the colonial era. This situation is to a great extent responsible for the underdevelopment of many exporting countries, including particularly Chile, Peru, and Bolivia. *Left:* The large copper mine at Chuquicamata, in Chile, the production of which goes mainly to the United States. *Above:* Miners at the entrance to a tin mine in Cerro Rico, Bolivia. *Below:* Johannesburg seen from the slag heaps of the nearby diamond mines. The city developed through the initiative of European colonists in the rich mining region of Witwatersrand, which produces gold, platinum, diamonds, silver, antimony, and chromite. South Africa is one of the world's greatest producers of these precious minerals.

in the natural sectors from which they are obtained. This tendency may be attributed to the difficulty and cost of transport, in the majority of cases it being a matter of a great volume of material with a relatively low value. Thus the transport of raw materials has always been limited.

The developed countries are those that had the greatest possible recourse to internal resources, particularly such minerals as coal and iron. Iron represents 80% of the total weight of metals being used today by the world's industry. As a result, production has become concentrated, sometimes to an extraordinary degree, on areas where the basic minerals are extracted, near coalfields or else in ports where they are unloaded, or along inland waterways.

Raw materials in economic development

Historically, the motive force of economic expansion, namely financial and technical concentration, remained the privilege of a few countries where it operated with increasing efficiency, raising living standards to higher levels. The economy of countries that function only as exporters of raw materials, already seriously beset by the lack of technically trained people, has always been at the mercy of the fluctuation of prices of these raw materials, governed by the elasticity of the market in developed countries. This has created in the exporting countries a chronic inability to accumulate capital for productive investment, the profits from their exports being mostly absorbed by the importation of consumer goods. This situation, especially in the case of the colonies, was to a certain extent encouraged by the developed countries, for whom the

Above: The iron mines at Cerro Bolivar in Venezuela. The deposits are among the largest in the world (reserves are estimated at about 500 million tons). Until recently they were exploited exclusively by North American companies. Today they provide raw materials also for a local iron and steel works working on the continuous method and built by the government at the mouth of the Orinoco River. *Below:* The huge spiral for evaporating salt water from the Texcoco lake, near Mexico City, to produce salt. The mineral is used mainly by the Mexican chemical industry.

installation of an efficient productive apparatus in economically dependent territories, with the help of cheap labour, might have brought about the creation of dangerous competition in the international market, as well as loss of markets for consumer goods, and might also have affected the price of raw materials. These economics, consisting of investments made by commercial companies aimed simply at acquiring local raw materials at low prices in exchange for manufactured goods (which increase consumption and thus absorb any profits from exports), illustrate very well the relationship between developed and underdeveloped countries.

Furthermore, many recent industrial investments in colonial or underdeveloped territories have been made on similar colonialist lines. Any enterprises set up are closely dependent for their equipment and supplies on the parent firm, situated in Europe or America, and constitute a sort of economic enclave that does little towards launching the local economy or developing social structures independently.

In mining, the prolonged and large-scale utilization of deposits

Ingots of pig-iron coming out of the blast furnaces.

in the mother country, together with the policy of preserving reserves, has recently led the larger developed countries to begin using overseas deposits or domestic ones hitherto regarded as unprofitable because they were situated too far from areas of consumption (iron in Labrador, Siberia, Mongolia, Turkestan, etc.).

The iron industry was in the past the almost exclusive monopoly of countries in possession of the raw materials needed for its development. This is the case with the United States and Canada, rich in coal and iron, which were transported along the great waterways to easily accessible production centres. *Below:* A Canadian steelworks at Hamilton, on Lake Ontario, uses iron ore from Canada and coal from Ohio.

This has enabled some African, Asian, and South American producers to step into the international market, but always with the restrictions arising from the problem of transport. As a result, deposits accessible because of their situation near coastal areas have been exploited, while rich inland deposits have been left untapped.

Heavy and light industry

A certain national self-sufficiency in raw materials, especially iron and coal, has always been one of the prime factors for economic independence. Countries with a supply of these primary products have been able to set up, without difficulty, basic industries that make it possible to produce the instruments and the means to establish all other forms of transformation processes, as well as the basic transport structure. It is evident that these basic industries, often called *heavy industry* (which includes the mining, building, iron, chemical, and heavy engineering industries), require the mobilization of vast quantities of energy and raw materials and therefore major initial capital investment, which can be recovered only in the long term. The heavy cost of transporting these raw materials is a burden that cannot be borne by

In the western regions of the United States light industries have emerged and developed in the last few decades, particularly engineering industries stimulated by the geographic and strategic situation of the western States in relation to the Pacific during the Second World War. *Left:* Assembly of an aircraft fuselage in a Los Angeles factory, where the United States aviation industry has one of its major branches. In Italy, a country poor in raw materials, light industry has developed near areas of consumption. *Below:* The Fiat Mirafiori car factory, at the foot of the Piedmont Alps where much hydroelectric power is produced.

An assembly line in a motor-car factory.

Right and far right: Two phases in the work of a textile mill at Asmara, in Eritrea, which includes spinning, weaving, and printing.

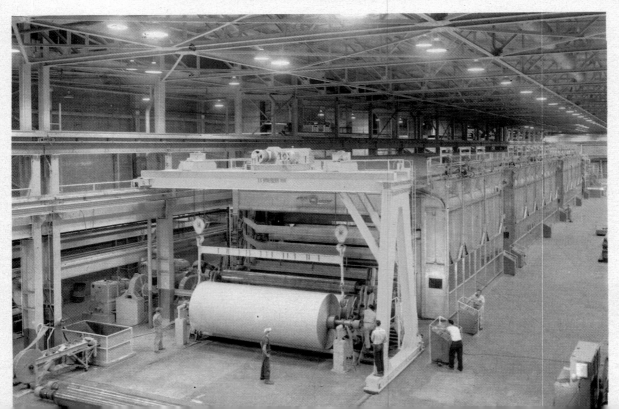

A paper mill in Providence, Rhode Island, in the United States. The paper industry has also developed in countries poor in raw materials.

Part of a large state-run establishment at Ravenna, in Italy, producing synthetic rubber, plastics, fertilizer, cement, and lamp-black. The creation of the establishment was prompted by the presence of natural gas deposits in the area and the city's favourable location near the Adriatic.

this sector alone, or by a country with an economy not possessing other sources of wealth to ensure rapid renewal of capital for productive investments. It is for this reason that some countries poor in raw materials (Japan and Italy for example) based their economies, as soon as they entered into their own industrial revolutions, on the development of consumer-goods industries, known also as *light industry*, which allow a rapid rotation of capital owing to the shorter term recovery period of the initial investments. Moreover, since these do not require large quantities of raw material or energy, they are less bound by the availability and location of sources of these primary products.

Heavy industry, because of its structure and function, represents a stake in the independence of the national economy and is particularly in the public eye. Thus it receives aid from the state more readily, and benefits from protectionist measures. Its development is affected only to a limited extent by the vicissitudes of economic cycles. It requires a large labour force, and the process of financial and technical concentration accompanying its installation does not lend itself to open competition.

By contrast, light industry is more closely connected with the consumer market and the traits and rhythms of social evolution; every fluctuation in the purchasing power of the consumer-masses has immediate and telling effects on the progress of its production. Thus a country with an industrial structure based mainly on light industries exposes its economy to dangerous fluctuations and does not normally present any great solidity in the long term.

The organization of industries

Technology plays a fundamental role in a balanced industrial structure. It obliges the entrepreneur to adopt shrewd plans of investment and to have ever greater capital resources at his disposal.

Technical evolution tends to reduce the possibility of small enterprises finding a place in a country's productive system, so

287

that the dominant process in the organization of production is that of concentration. This is carried out at the technical and financial levels. On the technical level it consists of the grouping, within the confines of the same enterprise, of similar productive apparatus, and is known as *horizontal concentration*. The grouping can also be, still within the same enterprise, of productive apparatus for a complete manufacturing cycle (from raw material to the finished product), as occurs in a textile enterprise in which production begins with spinning and ends in the manufacture of clothing. Another form is the aggregation of productive units which develop a certain range of technological processes, beginning from any level in the transformation of raw materials. A typical example of this is provided by the iron industries, which operate with enterprises mining iron and coal, producing electric power and gas and using the by-products produced by these; this is known as *vertical*, or *integrated*, *concentration*.

Technical integration does not hinder specialization of production. Even the large integrated enterprise does not produce a considerable part of its equipment – its machinery and tools. These are produced by a number of smaller, specialized companies situated in the same region as the large industrial enterprises. In this sense it can be said that industry both creates and attracts industry.

The process of concentration can take place also through financial operations aimed at expanding the interests of the enterprise to a much wider and more diverse sector of production. It is in this manner that the great technical and financial organizations are formed, which sometimes control entire sectors of the national or international economy. Characteristic examples of these, though limited to one sector of production, are the large oil companies, which directly, or through subsidiary groups, carry out prospecting, extraction, transport, refining, and distribution of petroleum, and also work in the field of petrochemicals and associated indus-

In Japan, a country forced to import practically all the raw materials required by its industries, the coastal zones near ports have become the areas of the greatest concentration of industry. This photograph shows the concentration of heavy industry in the southern part of Tokyo.

Factories in the northern industrial zone of Milan. The greater part of Italy's industrial activity is concentrated in the country's 'industrial triangle', because of its powers of attraction.

tries and manufacture the instrumental material for their activities.

Modern industrial economies are working towards the control of markets by aiming to concentrate supply and demand in the hands of the few. This aim is achieved by means of two principal forms of association: the cartel and the trust. The *cartel* is a long-term agreement between enterprises which nevertheless remain distinct as economic and legal units. The idea is to obtain a *de facto* monopoly of the market in one or more products. The *trust*, which originated in 1880, is a financial grouping which brings together, under one direction, a number of enterprises which all surrender their independence. Shareholders have the right to be paid dividends, but have no voting rights within the structure of the directorate. The trust, banned by law in the United States since 1890 (Sherman Act), is today more frequently replaced by the *holding*, a finance company which owns the majority of the shares of an association of legally independent enterprises.

The location of industries

When an entrepreneur, whether a private businessman or a state-owned organization, sets out to start up an industry, he seeks to find first of all a territory with natural and human characteristics that will enable him to achieve the aims of his enterprise. For the private individual, these aims will in every case be those of making the maximum profit, over a long period, for his investments in that particular sector of production; and for the public entrepreneur they might be to accomplish a standard level of income in the area, or to increase the economic and social level of an underdeveloped region, or to implement a particular demographic policy. Usually the public entrepreneur will have to provide first of all for the creation of certain conditions essential for a regular development of his enterprise, while the private

entrepreneur exploits as much as possible the existing favourable environmental conditions.

Once the territory is found, the next task should be to determine the optimum location for the installations. In practice, however, only a few large enterprises, and this only in recent times, possess adequate means to carry out such a survey. In most cases the choice of a location is made not on the basis of rational and rigorous economic considerations worked out by technicians and economists, but purely as a result of personal preference. Very often the list of factors that determines the choice includes reasons such as 'the wish of the Prince', 'random selection', or 'the entrepreneur's place of residence'.

Geographically, installations seem to be located in the vast majority of cases with such a high degree of density as to cover by themselves entire territorial areas known as industrial regions. The explanation for this is both technical and historical.

The technical aspect is characterized by the well-known *agglomerative tendency* of industries. This is promoted chiefly by the complexity of the types of final products and by the consequent specialization of production. In effect, the market demands goods that must satisfy technical needs that become increasingly complex and tastes that become increasingly varied. At the same time the expansion of the market reacts strongly on costs, and leads to a greater degree of specialization. This entails a more marked tendency to division of labour, and therefore stresses the complementary nature of the various branches of industry. So that this reciprocal dependence of productive processes does not result in an unsustainable increase in costs, it is necessary for the enterprises to mass together in an area that is sufficiently restricted and provided with an efficient system of infrastructures.

This concentration obviously leads to a proportional concentration of population, and thus to the formation of a market with high-absorption potential. It is clear that this area, highly organized for industry and services and also constituting a sure and solid market, acts with a considerable force of attraction for further industrial initiative. Industry can then be more easily supplied with its required productive factors; it can take advantage of a system of services the costs of which become progressively lower with their distribution among a larger number of users; and it can sell its own production at economic rates. In this way a restricted area is formed in which the principles of maximum efficiency make possible production on a large scale.

Areas of industrial expansion

It still remains to be explained why this massing together of the technical apparatus of industry occurs only in a few areas of the Earth's surface. The main ones are the Great Lakes region and the mid-Atlantic region of North America; central and western Europe, extending into northern Italy; the Donbass, the basin of the central and southern Urals; the Kuznetsk; central and southern Japan; and a few smaller, scattered areas.

An investigation into the historical process of industrialization provides some explanation. This process began at different periods for each country, but in all cases it can be linked with two stages: the installation of industry and, subsequently, its territorial expansion. The end of the first phase and the beginning of the second could perhaps be placed in the inter-war period, after the great economic crisis of the 1930s. In this respect it appears significant that it was just at that time that economic doctrines put forward the idea of greater intervention on the part of the state in the economy of a country. Typical of these doctrines was the Tennessee Valley plan promoted by President Roosevelt in the United States, and the Soviet Union's first five-year plan, which was launched at about the same period.

For a correct interpretation of the motives for location during the stage of installation, we must take into account, for each country or territory, the technological level of the time. The decisive factor appears in every case to be the presence of raw materials, particularly sources of energy, owing to the problems of transport. In fact, the areas with the greatest density of enterprises have large deposits of coal, or are situated along the courses of rivers, because these used to provide a mechanical source of energy before the invention of steam engines, and they

The counties of the central and eastern United States with more than 10,000 industrial workers. The region represents one of the world's great industrial areas.

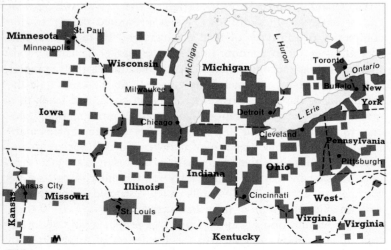

Above: Cars parked near a chemical plant in Baltimore. The number of vehicles is an even greater indication of the industrial development of a region than the extent of the industrial areas. The industrial region also imposes itself on the landscape, with roads, flyovers, large buildings, factory chimneys, railway junctions, silos, and warehouses, as seen in this view *(right)* of Cleveland on Lake Erie.

functioned as useful and economic ways of transporting raw materials. The presence of raw materials promoted the installation of base industries, which today still constitute the most developed sector of production in the chief areas of agglomeration of the world. The availability of labour, on the other hand, seems to have had a less important influence. However, it has been a more significant locational factor in those areas where the consumer-goods industries were first built such as northern Italy and southern Japan.

Technological evolution, by making possible more rational use of organization, destination, and combination of productive factors, subsequently allowed a more pronounced flexibility in the location of enterprises – the displacement of labour from the primary and secondary sectors to the tertiary one as a result of technical innovations applied to the agricultural and industrial productive processes; the substitutions in the field of primary products made possible by the chemical and petrochemical industries; the introduction of new instruments and techniques in the administrative apparatus of the enterprises which made it possible to locate the organizing and directorial offices near suppliers and customers; and the very rapid evolution of the transport sector. This was all technical progress, which gradually liberated productive apparatus from enforced location, transferring the problem of choosing locations to the level of essentially economic motives and using locations that were much nearer market areas.

When we recall the high degree of efficiency as a market area of territories with a high density of enterprises, we find that technological progress makes decentralization possible, but does not appear to promote it – in fact, it works against it. Industrial entrepreneurs seem to be strongly influenced by factors of agglomeration. Moreover, countries or territories industrially equipped to produce consumer-goods and which are enabled by the new locational flexibility to install base industries as well, also come under the influence of agglomerative factors, because new enterprises are installed in areas densely covered by previous enterprises.

This process of industrial development highlights the initial difference between countries possessing factors that promote industrial production, mostly concentrated in Europe and North America and destined to become developed countries, and the underdeveloped countries, namely those without the means to expand economically in a modern sense: a difference made more noticeable by the accelerated rate of development of the former contrasted with the practically static conditions of the latter.

Saturated areas with an excessive density of entrepreneurial activities also begin to take shape much more decisively, and some of these cease to be areas of investment and even turn into depressed areas. Others, while offering promising conditions for industrialization – obtained through the process of deruralization promoted by industry situated elsewhere – are overlooked by entrepreneurs and, lacking a specialized infrastructure, become underdeveloped.

The broadening of production and the saturation of the traditional markets make it necessary for industry to expand in other areas. The solution to the problem thus presents itself substantially as control of agglomerative factors, and this is now achieved with territorial planning.

Characteristics of an industrial region

From the point of view of the social and demographic structure, the characteristics of an industrial region can be listed as follows:

High density and mobility of the population with a tendency to centralization and urbanization.

Dense social stratification with a gradual reduction in the breaks between the traditional classes and an increasing level of technological education and specialization.

Developed awareness of political and social problems.

From the point of view of economic shape, they are:

Availability of capital goods.

Increase in resources for investment.

Tendency for profits to increase.

Tendency for wages to rise above the subsistence level.

Marked differentiation and high quantitative level of consumption.

In this way it is possible to draft a definition for an industrial region as a territory in which the majority of the population presents, both at the individual and the community levels, a marked tendency to articulate to the utmost its economic initiatives and to adopt without resistance the means and the instruments produced by technological evolution.

TRANSPORT

Traditional forms of traffic

The mobility of individuals and groups is an essential feature of
the human race; making possible this mobility is the 'road' of
communication, travelled by means made available by technology.
There is no time in the history of civilized mankind that did not
witness these movements of men and merchandise: it is the degree

of intensity of this movement that varies throughout history according to the level of expansion of the inhabited world, the knowledge of the resources available, and the extent of relationships
between human groups coming in contact with one another.

For thousands of years, exchanges and relationships made
few demands on technology. The wheel and the sail were in fact the
only innovations applied to means of transport, and it was not
until the 10th century that the yoke of draft animals was modified
in order to exploit muscular power to the utmost. The basic means of

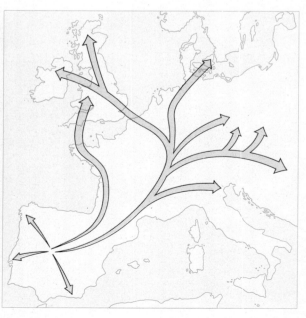

Physical obstacles are overcome
by engineering works, which are
found even in primitive societies,
such as this rope bridge in Indochina (far left). In many of the
principal communication routes
the ancient commercial and
strategic reasons that were responsible for their construction
can still be traced. The map (left)
shows the trade routes for copper
products from Spain towards
central Europe in prehistoric
times.

Rivers are natural ways of communication; they have been used since the dawn of history and have figured in the most ancient forms of human civilization. One of these arteries is the Rhine, shown (right) at its bend near Oberwesel.

land transport was the road, or rather the track or trail, because prepared roads were the expression of the strongly centralizing political orders of empires and had a pre-eminent function in strategy and politics in facilitating rapid military connections between the administrative centre of the state, the capital, and the outlying regions. Only prepared roads used technical methods to overcome natural difficulties and obstacles. Tracks and trails always carefully tried to avoid them.

A characteristic common to all these ways, which for thousands of years formed the road network of the world, is that they follow the great natural directions that make movement easier: river valleys and the lower slopes of mountains where they meet the plain. The French term *route* is significant, being derived from the Latin *via rupta*, meaning a road opened up by force through the forests of the central and western European plains.

Another characteristic common to these ways was their convergence on 'gates', great natural passages or openings through mountains. The efficiency of these early, primitive roads that served their purpose for thousands of years is underlined by the fact that today's roads basically follow their direction, if not their actual course.

The difficulty and slowness of movement by land made the sea a fundamental means of transport. It was the first to receive the attention of technology, and to be perfected to a degree of efficiency and safety. The abundance of ports remaining today, large and small, scattered along the coasts of Europe, southern Asia, and the Far East, and also, to a lesser extent, of North America, indicate the prevalence of coastal shipping over land transport, which lasted even after the advent of the Industrial Revolution. The navigation era had a fundamental influence on the transformation of economic structures, at least those of Europe, starting with the grandeur of the Italian maritime republics and the Hanseatic League, and continuing with the colonial expansion of Portugal, Spain, the Netherlands, and Britain. The history of transport up to the 18th century shows the domination of navigation and the laborious, slow movement along the ancient, difficult ways of dry land.

The Tremola road, which winds up to the St Gothard Pass in a series of hairpin bends.

The transport revolution

The Industrial Revolution cast a dramatic light on the problem of land transport. One of the first incentives to financial concentration of enterprises was the inefficiency and the inadequacy of roads which tied up the capital of entrepreneurs in accumulated stocks of raw materials. There was thus a feverish search for new methods and technology came forward with innovations in road building introduced by such men as McAdam in Britain and Trésaguet in France. But road transport still depended on the horse, and a road wagon could transport only one and a half tons of goods at just over a mile an hour.

In the first quarter of the last century the inland waterways handled the already considerable mercantile traffic. Canals, which since the Middle Ages had served many artisan activities, especially in central Europe and France, were improved and extended. Their expansion affected the choice of location for manufacturing establishments. At the same time there was technological innovation in sea transport. The clipper, developed in the 18th century, was a large sailing ship that could sail the oceans twice as fast as its predecessors. In 1819 the *Savannah* became the first steam-driven vessel to cross the Atlantic (though using its engine for four days only). In 1840 the *Archimède*, the first screw-driven ship, made the crossing. But the time was near for a change in the importance and volume of sea traffic. The steam locomotive, perfected by the 1830s, made possible the rapid development of railways, with their speed and high capacity. They made a decisive impact in the second quarter of the 19th century, after a first phase marked by the construction of disconnected trunk lines. Their subsequent linking up into systems was followed by the construction of great trans-continental lines in the last quarter of the century. These lines made possible the exploitation of the great open spaces of America and Asia, as well as convenient, rapid international connections overland. The consequences of the advent of the railway era included the collapse of prices for agricultural products in Europe because of the improved means of bringing goods from other continents in bulk.

The continued expansion and the complication of internal economic relations required further and more complete means of transport. The internal combustion engine, already functioning by 1880, and the pneumatic tyre (1885) were the new replies from technology, while there were already plans for air navigation. However, motor transport was not firmly established until the end of the First World War. It was then that roads, which had declined in the railway era to satisfy only local needs, regained their full importance.

Railways and roads in competition

The golden age of the railways was around 1910. The great crisis of 1929–1931 revealed that they no longer enjoyed a monopoly in means of intercommunication, but had already begun to surrender some traffic to competitors. Motor lorries proved to be better adapted to many modern trade flows and to pioneering the penetration of many territories; in such locations roads were cheaper to build. The function of roads is a measure of the technical improvement of the forms of transport using them. While motor vehicles for goods

A lorry on the track linking Afghanistan with Iran. Motorized transport, even in precarious conditions, is opening up the country to new ways of life.

The world traffic outline shows the degree of development of communications, which clearly distinguishes the developed countries from the emerging ones.

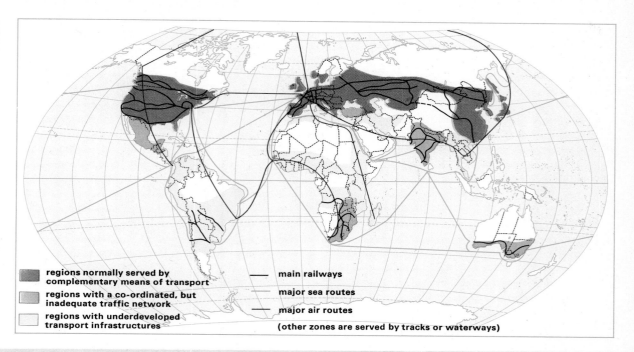

regions normally served by complementary means of transport

regions with a co-ordinated, but inadequate traffic network

regions with underdeveloped transport infrastructures

main railways

major sea routes

major air routes

(other zones are served by tracks or waterways)

A picture that expresses the possibilities and the forms of development of communications in a highly advanced country. The Mackinac bridge (shown here during its construction) crosses the Mackinac Straits between Lakes Huron and Michigan. It makes possible direct land connection between upper Michigan (United States) and Canada. It is one of the longest bridges in the world, nearly 5 miles in length.

Marshalling yards at Buffalo, where the rail network of the eastern United States converges and leads into Canada. The photograph shows the vastness and complexity of layout of large railway junctions, and may indirectly suggest explanations for the relative inadequacy of the railway as a local feeder. The supremacy of roads, asserted with the coming of the market economy, is due to the closer exchanges that now take place between town and country. At the same time, roads are able to break with the old regional structures which the railways had helped to centralize in large urban areas that were almost always large railway junctions. In some underdeveloped countries, because of the burden represented by the fixed and mobile equipment, railways today occupy a secondary place to motor transport, which can more easily penetrate territories to be developed.

transport have a power/load ratio that keeps their speed low, the distribution system uses roads for short-distance deliveries and railways for the long-distance traffic between large market centres, which are also large railway centres.

The construction of motorways was justified by the need to adapt the road network to take in the great national and international arteries and the fast-moving regional traffic routes. They first appeared in countries which lacked a co-ordinated system of road networks: Italy (1924) was the first to build them, followed by Germany and the Netherlands. The political fragmentation of Italy before 1861 and Germany before 1872 had made it impossible to build a road network with inter-regional connections. In Germany, the structure of the original motorway network shows the political and military interest of an expansionist regime. Unemployment, which followed the great crisis of 1929–1931, also prompted the construction of motorways as public works to absorb spare labour.

The United States has a transcontinental network of motorways. *Right:* Large vehicles for specialized transport on the motorway linking California and the northwestern United States.

Many other European countries have followed a more limited policy, preferring to adapt an existing and co-ordinated road system and building motorways almost solely to relieve traffic in urban areas. The United States has a programme to build 40,000 miles of toll motorway called the National System of Interstate Highways.

The system of roads in western Europe exhibits a high degree of political fragmentation, with frontiers acting as barriers to traffic. By contrast, the system in central Europe, like that in the United States, reveals an organization formed after the introduction of railways. The networks are less dense and much more co-ordinated and functional. The countries of eastern Europe show characteristics in the road system typical of those with recent economic development. Roads have a secondary economic importance (in the Soviet Union they take only 4% of the total traffic), while the railways are still very important, particularly because of the great distances to be covered.

A motorway running through the English county of Kent.

Inland waterway navigation in central Europe has its natural axis in the Rhine. Raw materials are conveyed by the river to the Ruhr and other industrial regions of Germany. *Left:* Traffic on the lower Rhine. *Below:* Barges unloading coal from the River Meuse at Antwerp, Belgium.

Inland waterways

Modern structures of production and consumption cannot entrust mass transport wholly to roads because of the limited capacity of road vehicles; the alternatives are railways and waterways. The communications policy in developed countries seeks to develop each element, but co-ordinate all three into a system.

Internal waterways, which may be rivers or artificial canals, are being reappraised after the dominance of the railways and after their first exploitation at the beginning of the industrial revolution. The particular advantage of waterways is their potential for carrying goods in far greater bulk than can be carried by other means. Their disadvantage is slowness, a drawback that may make the railways (and oil pipelines) preferred. The present operation of the waterways is therefore closely connected with the interregional co-ordination of transport; they are used to move goods that can be carried slowly without increasing costs. Such goods include chemical fertilizers, the supply of which is seasonal, constructional materials, semi-manufactured metallurgical products for stocking, and non-perishable foodstuffs, especially wines and other liquids.

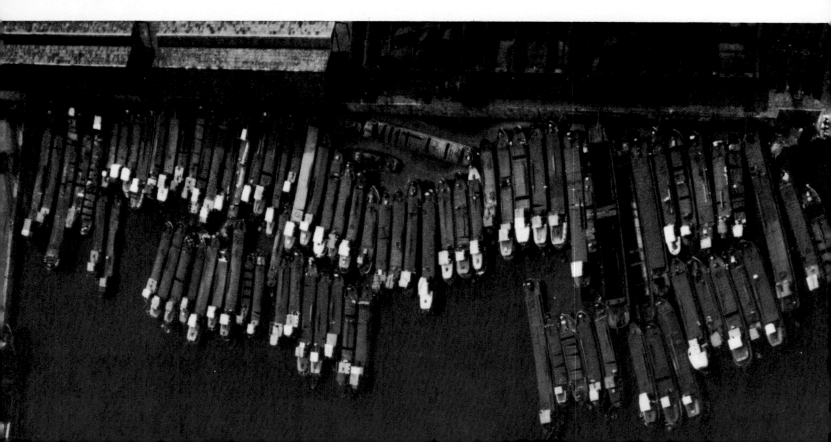

In North America canal networks supplement the basic river and lake systems, and are centred on the Great Lakes. (The construction of the great St Lawrence Seaway has introduced a maritime character to inland navigation and enabled ocean-going shipping to penetrate more than 600 miles inside the continent, as far as the ports and harbours of Lake Superior.) The more recent Soviet system has three functions: production of hydroelectric power, irrigation for agricultural development, and navigation. Soviet waterways flow mainly through broad plains, so that there is little difference in altitude between source and estuary. There are considerable increases in carrying capacity during a short period in spring, and, for the Siberian rivers flowing from south to north, an earlier thaw at the source than at the estuary. Such exceptional aspects of the river system have promoted the outstanding development of the inland navigation system (80,000 miles) joining the Black and Caspian Seas to the Baltic through the Volga and the Don.

The north-west European system, of which only the British network, with its limited capacity, has fallen into some disuse in recent times, is characterized by the comb-like system of the Rhine and the French rivers, and by the chequer-board German system based on the Rhine, Elbe, and Oder connected by parallel canals. Varied depth and breadth of some sections restrict free movement throughout the network but the E.E.C. is carrying out a programme of standardizing a 'European' canal, navigable by vessels of 1,350 tons with a draught of eight feet. The plan entails the improvement of the connections between the Meuse and the Rhine, the Rhine and the Rhône, and the Scheldt and Dunkirk, together with the canalization of the Moselle.

Above: The St Lawrence at Cornwall, above Montreal, where a gigantic system of locks has been constructed. They enable ocean-going ships to overcome the rapids of the river, which cause a total difference of nearly 250 feet in the river level. Thanks to other canal systems on the Great Lakes, shipping can now reach Duluth on the westernmost shore of Lake Superior, where other inland waterways of the continent converge. *Left:* The floodgates at Long Sault controlling the level of the St Lawrence at one of its most irregular stretches. The rise in the water level that they produce (generating conditions suitable for electric-power production) provides a path for shipping through the Snell and Eisenhower locks.

High operating and maintenance costs have considerably reduced the competitiveness of railways. The advantages of railways lie in their large carrying capacity over long distances allowing the transport of goods at relatively economic rates. It is on this principle that large American railway companies carry freight profitably. *(Left:* An American steam locomotive, in California.) In another way railways can remain competitive in passenger handling by improving their service with electrification and fast comfortable trains. The express trains that link the major cities of Italy are built to these standards. *Below:* A fast Italian electric train.

The evolution of railways

At this point railways may be considered in their most modern and, in certain aspects, most dramatic stage: their competitiveness with other forms of land transport. Their fundamental disadvantage, which derives mostly from their monopoly during the later period of the Industrial Revolution, is the great amount of equipment needed to operate them. A public service obliged to transport all that is offered, they have to maintain a permanent pool of fixed and mobile equipment to meet peak demands, daily and seasonal; this pool is extremely costly to administer and maintain. The advantages of railways remain those of possessing a much greater capacity for transporting heavy loads at reasonable rates (in the United States freight trains may carry up to 10,000 tons). These advantages apply only over long distances and with a system adapted to handle such trains. Train speeds have increased to meet growing competition from the roads and the air, largely by the widespread adoption of electric and diesel traction; the growing use of large containers which can be transferred between trains, lorries, and ships allows a co-ordinated door-to-door service.

The effort to remain competitive has been largely concentrated on rail arteries, which have been improved and modernized to allow faster travel for passengers and goods. In western Europe, the rapid Trans-Europe Express passenger service (T.E.E.) connects ninety cities, and there is a similar service for goods (T.E.E.M.). In the main, co-ordination of land transport in developed countries tends to share the carriage of heavy, bulky merchandise between waterways and railways, which compete with lighter goods carried over short distances by road.

Maritime navigation

Maritime navigation has considerably influenced the economic development of this century. An interesting phenomenon in its evolution is the reduction in the coasting trade. It remains active in serving islands with backward economies, as in Oceania and the Far East, where the sea and navigable rivers have always been almost the only system of internal or international transport.

Between developed and less developed countries there is a system

of navigation which supplies manufactured products for local consumption and capital goods for new industries, promoted either by local initiative or by foreign investors. Ships leave ports in North America or Europe with cargoes for Africa, southern Asia, or South America, from which they return with raw materials. This traffic is substantially the reason for the persistence of traditional sea routes: Europe and, later, North America have absorbed and continue to absorb such materials from other continents.

But if the large-scale import into Europe and North America of raw materials and semi-manufactured goods persists, the export of finished products from the two continents to the rest of the world is outweighing it. For the second time in the history of maritime traffic Japan has a large share in the distribution of capital goods and particularly consumer goods. This country, fourth in the world's great production areas and aided in its development by an abundance of labour, has checked the former domination of western-manufactured goods in the markets of the world.

Tramping, that is sailing from port to port in search of cargoes,

Above: The Corinth Canal. The need to cut the isthmus of Corinth and shorten the distance between the Aegean and Adriatic seas had been recognized by the peoples of the ancient world, who had to carry cargoes overland from one sea to the other. The canal, opened in 1893, is four miles long, 72 feet wide, and 26 feet deep. *Right:* A stretch of the Suez Canal near Ismailia. An attempt to cut a canal across the Suez isthmus was first made in ancient times; the modern canal was opened in 1869, and revolutionized world sea traffic by avoiding the long circumnavigation of Africa between Europe and the Far East. Broadened at various times, it has, in normal conditions, a daily capacity of 50 ships of large tonnage and a draught of up to 33 feet. *Right:* A ship on the highest reach of the Panama Canal, the Gaillard Cut. *Below:* The Miraflores lock, the first of the three on the Pacific side which raise ships 85 feet above Lake Gatún. This great link between the Atlantic and Pacific oceans has a total length of nearly 51 miles, and was officially opened in 1920.

Left: Loading sulphur at Galveston, Texas, one of the busiest ports of the United States in tonnage of goods handled. A coastal canal links Galveston Bay with Houston, a large industrial city which owes its development to this waterway.

Opposite page: Sydney harbour, one of the great ports of call for British sea traffic at the time of the great colonial expansion, remains Australia's largest port, handling the intense traffic of the southern Pacific.

Rotterdam is Europe's greatest port and the outlet for the continent's most industrialized region. The great development of its harbour, divided into specialized areas according to the type of traffic, has extended it as far as the sea at the new Europoort (see map below). *Bottom left:* Launching an oil tanker for carrying crude oil from the Middle East. Tankers of great size and capacity are now necessary to meet the demands of the world oil market. Modern cruising ships such as the Italian *Michelangelo (bottom right)* enable merchant shipping lines to compete with air travel on the North Atlantic and other routes.

has largely given way to specialized services between customer and supplier, using ships equipped to carry particular cargoes.

Air transport

Air transport is still predominantly a passenger-carrying function, and nothing can match it as a means of rapidly covering great distances. Although its greatest asset is as a fast international and intercontinental link, it is also an important means of internal transport, especially where the roads and railways are inadequate.

As a cargo-carrying service air transport is expensive, and usually only urgent, non-bulky and valuable goods are sent by air. An important development is the use of short take-off and landing (STOL) aircraft; these are particularly useful in newly-developed countries where they can provide a door-to-door service, not

EUROPOORT

- ▨ dockyards (naval and merchant)
- ▦ depots for heavy goods
- ▤ docks for oil and minerals
- ☐ urbanized areas

to The Hague

Hook of Holland

new canal

EUROPOORT

ROTTERDAM

to Utrecht

Maassluis

Vlaar-dingen Schiedam

New Meuse

to Antwerp

Old Meuse

0   5   10
km

requiring the expensive airport installation needed by larger and faster aircraft.

The increasing use of standard-size containers, which can be used in conjunction with surface transport systems, should reduce air freight costs and the amount of time lost between producer and airport, and airport and consumer.

Where land communications are poor, air travel plays an important part. When rapidly imposed on the life of underdeveloped countries, it creates contrast such as can be seen at Kandahar airport, Afghanistan (*left*). *Right:* Vienna airport, an important stop between the West and the U.S.S.R.

A section of the John F. Kennedy airport, New York. Formerly called Idlewild, it is one of the largest airports in the world.

Leonardo da Vinci airport, at Rome, is one of the chief airports in Europe for airlines serving Africa and the East.

POLITICAL DIVISIONS

States

Every geographic region, in its development over hundreds of years, tends to assume certain distinguishing characteristics that mould the people living in it. As the inhabitants gradually adapt themselves to the surroundings in which they live, their aims, work, and thoughts begin to grow alike. Once the people become aware of their common interest, they form a distinct and separate nationality. Nationality, therefore, implies the consciousness of a long history and a common destiny, and the maintenance of close relations between the inhabitants who eventually form a state.

Every nationality aims at political unity and a national state, but the concept of a nation is a modern one. In ancient times and in the Middle Ages there were no national states; dynastic group interests prevailed. The sovereign identified himself with the state, and his subjects owed him absolute obedience. The idea of national states took shape only with the French Revolution, and finally prevailed from the second half of the 19th century, leading to the collapse of the great multi-national empires such as the Austro-Hungarian monarchy and the Ottoman Empire.

The factors aiding the formation of national states are common language, religion, race, and tradition, the presence of a well-defined environment, and a natural centre of co-ordination. Nationalities are sometimes vague – they are historico-geographical entities requiring a long evolution – but the state is the most defined of human associations organized to safeguard common interests. The fundamental elements of all states are their territory, population, and organization. Once a certain territory is occupied, the inhabitants work towards dominating it, and it is the state organization that provides for this by organizing border defences, communications, economic progress, law and order, and relations between the various classes of its citizens. This task gives the state the mark of sovereignty by creating a symbiosis between the territory and the population, between soil and man. The scope of its powers and functions varies in time, and, although during time of war or under dictatorships everything is subordinate to the state organization, in peacetime, particularly in liberal regimes, its influence can be limited to essential activities. Sovereignty, which is the nucleus of state organization, represents the continuity in the life of the state, the heritage of past generations, and a safeguard of the interests of those to come. The larger the state, the more necessary it becomes for the sovereignty to be able to avoid the forces of disintegration.

The number of independent states has increased considerably since the Second World War, especially in Africa and Asia; in 1960 seventeen African states achieved their independence. The size of states is extremely varied, from the Vatican (about 110 acres) to the Soviet Union (8,649,500 square miles). Populations range from the 1,000 inhabitants of the Vatican to the 700 million of China.

The aspirations of a country looking to its future are symbolized in the statue of the pioneers *(right)* in front of Brasilia's Supreme Court building. *Far right:* the crowd at Fort-Lamy at the swearing-in of the tribal chiefs *(below right)* in January 1960, during the independence celebrations in Chad, one of the young states born from the decolonization of the former French Equatorial Africa. This moment formally marked the passage from a feudal regime to a modern and democratic republic.

A ruined fort in northern Afghanistan *(below)* is a reminder of the ancient fortifications situated in strategic positions that once provided defensive bulwarks and acted as symbols of power.

The territory of some states is often the result of long wars of unification. Gettysburg, Pennsylvania, was one of the great battlegrounds between the forces of the North and South during the American Civil War.

A view of Tripoli, with a mosque and a Catholic church in the distance. The presence of the two faiths and their contrasting styles of architecture is the consequence of a heritage of two forms of past domination: by the Ottoman Empire until 1911, and then by the Italians.

Most nations have in their territory a geographic element whose centralizing effect raises it to the status of a symbol of the state. The Ganges, besides being a life-bringing element in the geography and life of India, is the country's sacred river. *Right:* Ritual bathing in the Ganges at Varanasi (formerly Benares).

But the importance of a state, apart from its area and population, depends on many other factors, such as internal stability, administrative organization, military potential, economic resources, and participation in world trade. It is evident that only the largest states can have a sufficient range of resources on their territory to aspire to become great powers.

The expansion of states

Every state, like any vital organism, seeks to develop and grow by following determined lines; very often these are based on geographical factors. Geopolitics has tried to classify these tendential development laws of states as follows:

1) Tendency of states to expand until they occupy the entire

Below: National strength is often founded on proud awareness of the past. Heroes are honoured by monuments such as the statue of King Menelik in Addis Ababa.

Right: The Pas de la Casa between France and Andorra, the tiny and ancient republic whose survival was aided by its location in the mountainous region of the Pyrenees.

basin of a river or a large part of it, as done by Egypt (the Nile), Poland (the Vistula), Iraq (the Tigris and the Euphrates), and Venezuela (the Orinoco).

2) Tendency to open up outlets to the sea in order to maintain relations with distant countries and to take part in maritime traffic. The entire history of Russia is marked by its aspiration to open ports on the various seas washing its shores. Other countries which strove to obtain efficient ports included Austria (Trieste) and Hungary (Rijeka, now in Yugoslavia). Inland states such as Switzerland, Czechoslovakia, Hungary, and Paraguay use their rivers for this purpose.

3) Tendency to conquer an opposite shore, which has manifested itself, particularly in the Mediterranean, since the most remote times (Greek and Carthaginian colonization) and was repeated in northern Africa by Spain, France, and Italy in modern times. After Columbus's voyage and those of navigators who followed in his wake, this tendency is to be seen across the Atlantic, where Spain occupied Mexico, the islands of Central America (Cuba, Hispaniola, etc.) and various South American territories, Portugal occupied Brazil, England occupied the territory that was to become the United States, and France occupied Canada and Louisiana.

Above: The Ginza, Tokyo's busy crowded thoroughfare, is a sign of Japan's pulsating vitality. This is a country which, though limited in area, is one of the world's most heavily populated and has become one of the greatest industrial powers.

Left: 'Aqui é Portugal' (This is Portugal) announces the mosaic on Albuquerque Square in Lourenço Marques, Mozambique, in the authoritarian manner of the colonial and national Portuguese domination over African territory.

Below: Fortifications of the 16th century on the coast of Portuguese Guinea, in West Africa.

4) Tendency of a state to expand throughout a maritime basin – the *mare nostrum* tendency – as the Romans were able to do in the Mediterranean basin, and the Ottoman Empire in the Black Sea. At other times, the attempts by the Swedes in the Baltic, the Italians in the Adriatic, and the Greeks in the Aegean did not succeed; but the British made the Indian Ocean a British ocean for a time.

5) Tendency to obtain points of support to serve as stages for reaching distant possessions. The most famous example is that of Britain, which sought to consolidate its mastery of the seas by means of island possessions that acted at the same time as points of support and centres of political, military, and economic

In the last century when Victorian Britain reached the apogee of its colonial power, the Indian Ocean was an English sea in which most of the islands and of the mainland surrounding it were subject to the rule of the British crown. Ways of life, styles of architecture, customs, and mental attitudes proper to British society swept into the colonial territories, where they left their unmistakable and often formal mark. *Right:* The Queen Victoria Memorial in Calcutta, with architecture that blends both British and indigenous styles.

Below: The Rock of Gibraltar. This strategic point, which guards the western approach to the Mediterranean, has been a British possession since 1704. After the opening of the Suez Canal, it ensured Britain's domination of one of her main colonial routes for a long period and safeguarded British interests in the Mediterranean and the Indian Ocean.

influence, and by the possession of the principal straits. The United States has imitated this tendency by occupying certain islands in the Pacific and cutting the Panamanian isthmus, the Canal Zone of which it controls.

6) Tendency to adjust borders and make the state coincide with a natural region so that its territory is confined by physical barriers (mountains, deserts, rivers, seas, etc.) which act as defensive elements. Thus Italy sought to extend itself to the Alpine watersheds, Spain to the Pyrenees, France is bordered by a stretch of the Rhine and England expanded over Great Britain.

7) Tendency to improve the internal structure by distributing the density of the population according to internal resources by means of internal migrations, avoiding excessive urbanization and restraining the depopulation of the countryside and mountain areas; by eliminating or reducing contrasts between various regions; by perfecting the conditions of agriculture through reclamation and irrigation; by installing new industries; by exploiting all the resources of the subsoil; by a better distribution of property; and by building roads, railways, and navigable canals.

In Pretoria, old buildings of the colonial period (the architecture of which represents the country of origin of the Boer people) stand alongside a modern block which, with its clean lines, symbolizes a new way of life and a new kind of economy. This contrast provides evidence of the evolution of a colonial territory into a modern independent and economically developed state, even though its racial problems remain as signs of its colonial origins.

The cathedral of Managua (destroyed by a violent earthquake in 1972), capital of Nicaragua. The view, however, is typical of colonial cities in Central America.

The division of Germany into two states governed by opposing regimes is eloquently reflected in the two pictures below taken in Berlin, the most sensitive point of that division. The two different ways of life are symbolized in the two landscapes, which, though adjoining, are so much in contrast. *Left:* Motor traffic in the Tauentzienstrasse, with the Kaiser Wilhelm Gedächtniskirche in the background still unrestored after its war damage, and the modern commercial buildings of the capitalist type. *Right:* The severe Soviet-style buildings of the Karl-Marx-Alee, which has very little motor traffic.

8) Tendency to create external dependencies, spatially separated from the motherland, through the establishment of possessions and colonies. The phenomenon of modern colonial expansion (there were colonies in ancient times and also in the Middle Ages), which began in the 16th century following the geographic discoveries and the traffic across the oceans, and which reached its climax at the outbreak of the Second World War, had considerable geographic importance. It was the Europeans in particular who took to other continents their languages, laws, and civilization, which in many cases still survive, though a large number of these territories are now independent states. Between 1945 and 1965 the process of decolonization was very intense and now, save for the colonies of Portugal in Africa, colonial dependencies of European states are limited to a few territories, most of them islands of political and strategic, rather than economic, importance.

It is now much more difficult for states to expand without encountering obstacles, and they have to take into consideration the territorial integrity of the countries bordering them. But, because economic interests and political relations become interwoven in various ways, zones of friction have been formed on land and on sea where the frontiers of geographic expansion come up against each other. These zones are caused mostly by the desire on the part of nations to increase their territories, while the amount of land available, now divided up all over the Earth into states, remains the same. This can give rise to such conflicts as the Second World War, which was precipitated by Germany's attempt to increase its *lebensraum* (room to live and expand).

More faithful to the true state of affairs is the concept of the spheres of influence, according to which the world is divided up between the great powers, whose duty it is to guide the smaller states. Thus the great powers aim to satisfy their own needs within a large area, from which the aims and aspirations of other powers are excluded. In such political relationships, each one of the great powers becomes the centre of a planetary system and exerts its attraction on neighbouring satellite states. However, it is difficult to demarcate accurately one area from another, because there are states that do not fit into any large group and because of the zones of friction between the groups.

THE GREAT POWERS
AND MAJOR GROUPS

The United States

The United States of America won its independence in 1776 at a time when Spain, Portugal, and France still had vast colonial possessions on the American continent. In less than two centuries the country developed from a mere colony to a colonizing nation and a first-rank power. At first, up to 1890, the United States took little part in international disputes and followed an anti-colonialist policy. It is enough to recall the dictum of its third president, Thomas Jefferson, that 'our basic maxim must be not to take part in European disputes', and the famous declaration in 1823 of another president, James Monroe, to realize that the American continent was no longer to be regarded as a field of European colonization.

In this first period the United States aimed particularly at strengthening its internal structure by starting to develop its immense economic resources. The original 13 states, which occupied a territorial zone with a temperate climate between the Atlantic Ocean and the Allegheny Mountains, first expanded into the French possessions in Louisiana and the Spanish ones of the Mexican Gulf. Then they pushed West of the Mississippi as far as the Rocky Mountains, and beyond, as far as the Pacific, absorbing all the territory North of the Rio Grande. In 1869 the first transcontinental railway was opened, linking the Atlantic and Pacific coasts, and New York and San Francisco.

Successive waves of immigrants from Europe, mostly Anglo-Saxon Puritans with a democratic outlook, progressively populated the immense territory, developing its resources to an increasing degree and creating in the space of a few decades a civilization marked by its high standard of living, abundance of capital, love for democratic institutions, and considerable volume of gold and foreign currency reserves.

Once all the territory between Mexico and Canada was occupied, the United States began to expand its territories over the shores washed by the Pacific. Its first territorial acquisition was Alaska (with the Aleutian Islands and other lesser groups), purchased in 1867 for $7 million from Russia (which had vainly tried to expand its dominion as far as California). The territory then had little value and was used more than anything else for trapping fur animals. It later proved to be rich in minerals (including

The Capitol, where the United States Congress meets, in Washington, D.C. The city has been the federal capital since 1793. It was chosen because of favourable geographical factors at the time of the first formation of the Union.

gold), an excellent basis for the fishing industry (particularly salmon), and a support-point for aircraft flying over the polar regions. Because of its economic and strategic importance, Alaska became the 49th State of the United States in 1959. Hawaii, too, has an important commercial and strategic position in the Pacific Ocean, with its ports of Honolulu and Pearl Harbor. It was once an independent kingdom and was annexed in 1898 to the United States after the local dynasty had been toppled by a revolution. In 1959 it became the 50th State of the United States.

In 1898 Spain had to cede to the United States Puerto Rico in the Greater Antilles, the Philippines, and the island of Guam in the Marianas; Guam is now a naval base and an important junction in the underwater cable system. In 1903 Panama granted the United

Far left: A view of the Georgia landscape from Mount Kennesaw, a strategic point during the American Civil War. An old cannon is aimed at the road below leading to Atlanta, recalling the military campaigns of General Sherman's drive to the South in 1864. *Left:* Negro servants of a southern mansion. This picture recalls a social condition that is now anachronistic. The large Negro population of the United States has recently expressed with violence its aspirations, now legally recognized by the federal government, to enjoy the same rights as the Whites.

Navajo Indians in Monument Pass on the border between Arizona and Utah. The few remaining survivors of the tribes that once inhabited the vast territories of the United States today form a minority that has practically no say in the political life of the country. They live mostly in reservations, where they are the object of tourist curiosity.

An autumn view in Colorado. Vast unspoiled landscapes like this are still characteristic of many areas of the United States.

The traveller to the United States finds a dynamic, cosmopolitan world, futuristic in its planning. The enormous mass of the United Nations building *(right)* arouses this impression no less than the sight of the rocket base at Cape Kennedy *(below)*.

States permanent use and control of the 10-mile-wide Canal Zone. The canal was built by United States military engineers between 1904 and 1914, and its opening enhanced the United States' central position between the Pacific and Atlantic Oceans.

The rise of the United States continued, while Russia was making comparable advances. The thoughts of the French historian, de Tocqueville (1805–1859) proved prophetic: 'There are already on the Earth two great peoples, which having set out from different points, appear to be advancing towards the same goal: the Russians and the Anglo-Americans. Both have grown in obscurity and, while the gaze of men was directed elsewhere, they have suddenly put themselves in the first rank of the nations, and the world has learned at about the same time of their birth and their greatness. . . . Their point of departure is different, their ways are different. Nevertheless each of them seems to be summoned by a secret destiny of Providence to hold one day in their hands the destinies of half of the world.'

The principal stages by which the United States rose to promi-

nence were the victorious war against Spain (1898), which made it a world power; the opening of the Panama Canal (1914); and the two World Wars, in which its Presidents Woodrow Wilson and Franklin D. Roosevelt were responsible for drawing a new political map of the world. Its political and economic domination first made itself felt on the American continent, particularly in some states of Central America, until the Pan American conference of Montevideo (1934) laid down that no state had the right to interfere in the internal affairs of another American state. But the contributions made by United States capital to the American continent still remain considerable.

After the two World Wars the United States extended its sphere of influence to Europe and Asia. With the Soviet Union having become the major power of Europe, and with the advent of nuclear weapons, the United States took over Britain's role against the threat of domination by a power that might one day threaten the very existence of the free world. The same can be said for the intervention of the United States in Korea and Vietnam, where it

led the fight against Chinese Communism. The political and military horizon of the United States thus extended all over the world; and at the same time its economic influence has widened because of its immense internal resources. A clear illustration of the United States' expansion of influence in the military sphere was given with the foundation of NATO in 1949.

The Soviet Union

The Union of Soviet Socialist Republics (U.S.S.R.) occupies about one-seventh of the world's land area and numbers within its borders one-thirteenth of its population. It is by far the greatest continuous land-mass governed by the same sovereign power. The state, which emerged after the October Revolution of 1917, took over the exercise of power from the Tsarist system, and is based on the political and economic philosophy of communism.

The original nucleus of the Russian state was formed in an inland region near Moscow, at the centre of a zone where communications were facilitated by the system of rivers and where the forests offered a form of defence against invaders from central Asia. Once the Tatar yoke was thrown off, Russia began to expand and seek outlets to the sea in all directions. The White Sea port of Archangel was first opened in 1584. The Cossacks, having conquered Siberia, then went as far as the Pacific. In 1703 Peter the Great founded St Petersburg (now Leningrad), the famous 'window on the Baltic', which soon became the capital. Catherine the Great founded Odessa, on the Black Sea. Important stages in the subsequent growth of the country were its participation in the partitions of Poland, the occupation of Turkestan (1864–1873), which brought Russia nearer to the borders of India, and the con-

The skyscraper of Moscow's Lomonosov State University *(above)* and the citadel of the Kremlin on the River Moskva *(below)* represent the modern and ancient sides of this country, which has Moscow as its guiding centre.

A suburb of Moscow (*right*), with its severe, grey, modern buildings, and a street in Samarkand (*left*), dominated by the ruins of a mosque, illustrate the contrast between the west and the east of the Soviet Union, the old and the new.

quest of the Amur province (1860) in the Far East, which enabled it to open Vladivostok, an efficient port on the Pacific.

While there was no railway network, Siberia was an unimportant dependency where political exiles were sent. With the coming of Soviet power, the Asian territories took on a far greater importance. Siberia became a region of large industries, and Outer Mongolia also came into the Soviet orbit. For 20 years (1920–1940) the Union sought to strengthen its internal structure; it closed in on itself and strove to develop its economy by a series of five-year plans. The series of developments undertaken along the course of the Volga were particularly grand in scope; these created dams for producing electric power and extending the system of irrigation, and improved conditions of navigation. Then came the Second World War, which, ending in the defeat of Germany, enabled Russia to aspire to the domination of Europe.

In 1939 the Kremlin signed a pact with Germany and participated in the dismemberment of Poland. In the same year the Russians attacked Finland, which had to cede part of Karelia and the Petsamo corridor. In 1940 Russia invaded the Baltic countries (Lithuania, Latvia, Estonia) and incorporated them into the Soviet Union. Russia was forced temporarily onto the defensive when in 1941 it was attacked by Germany. But at the end of the Second World War it continued its expansion. In 1945 the Red Army occupied part of eastern Prussia, a large part of Poland, the Rumanian provinces

of Bessarabia and Bucovina, and sub-Carpathian Ruthenia, which were incorporated in the Soviet Union. At the same time it penetrated into the Far East at the expense of Japan by occupying the southern part of Sakhalin and the Kurile Islands.

Other countries came into the Soviet orbit as satellites, creating a double belt of buffer states which made the Soviet Union's frontiers more secure. In the years immediately following the Second World War, Moscow set up Communist governments in East Germany, Poland, Outer Mongolia, Albania, Bulgaria, Hungary, Czechoslovakia, Rumania, and North Korea. The Soviet frontier in Asia now runs from the Pacific to the Black Sea, separating contrasting forms of civilization. The territory is vast, arid, and mountainous, sparsely inhabited, and, as yet, of little economic value. In Europe the Soviet frontier runs along the satellite countries forming a chain between the Baltic and the Black Sea. This immense territory is endowed with vast quantities of raw materials, and supports a wide variety of peoples. By granting administrative and cultural autonomy to minorities in a federal system, the Union has sought to reduce breakaway tendencies, which are, however, still present. With the dissemination of the Russian language and culture, the contrast that once existed between the European and Asian territories of the country has diminished considerably.

Along with the political expansion there has been an economic domination by the Soviet Union over its satellite countries. The

Extremely evident in public life is the glorification of Marxist-Leninist ideology, which acts as the cementing force of this immense Eurasian country that has been practising socialism for over half a century. *Right:* May Day celebrations in Moscow include a parade of missiles.

Soviet Union leads and co-ordinates the economic development of these countries in its own interest, supporting it with technical and financial aid. Trade exchanges show a slight excess of exports over imports and are still of moderate proportions, two-thirds being with countries of the communist bloc.

The Commonwealth of Nations

The term describing Britain and her possessions used to be the 'British Empire', a name that implies the idea of control over subject people. But as the majority of its members were absolutely free yet wished to remain within this great political unit, the name was replaced in 1931 by that of the British Commonwealth of Nations. Subsequently, states in which the British element did not prevail came to form part of this organization, and the London conference of 1949 laid down that the name should be the Commonwealth of Nations, stressing its essential character of a voluntary association between sovereign states.

The Commonwealth includes sovereign states in five continents: Britain and Malta in Europe; Canada, Jamaica, Trinidad and Tobago, Barbados, and Guyana in the Americas; India, Pakistan, Bangladesh, Sri Lanka (Ceylon), Malaysia, Singapore, and Cyprus in Asia; Ghana, Nigeria, Sierra Leone, Tanzania, Kenya, Uganda, Zambia, Malawi, The Gambia, and Mauritius in Africa; Australia, New Zealand, and Western Samoa in Oceania.

Reciprocal relations are regulated more by mutual consent than by precise laws – the organization has no constitution. The members of the Commonwealth have associated with one another voluntarily and they all have in common the fact that they were once administered by Britain. At Commonwealth conferences, representatives of the member countries meet to discuss matters of common interest and there is large-scale collaboration between the members

The greatest cities that emerged during the expansion period of the British colonies took on typical European characteristics, and many are now the heart of independent states associated with the Commonwealth. *Right:* A modern street in Nairobi, capital of Kenya. *Left-hand page:* Sydney Harbour, Australia *(top).* Hong Kong (a Crown colony) and its bay *(bottom).*

Far right: The representative of the United Kingdom reads the Queen's message during the celebrations of the independence of Malaya (31st August, 1957).

in such areas as trade, finance, defence, education, and agriculture. Economic co-operation is based on preferential tariffs in the trade exchanges between the members.

The original nucleus of the Commonwealth was an island country, which became a great sea power. The Normans and the Hanseatics first caused the English to come out from their island and wage wars on the continent and in the Mediterranean, in the Crusades and the Hundred Years War. Once the ways across the oceans were opened up, the English began to sail the sea routes. The great expansion of England began in the reign of Queen Elizabeth I, when, having lost the last of its continental bases at Calais, the country found itself once more an island. Its security and expansion were from that moment to be based on sea power and on the acquisition of important strategic areas in the Caribbean, on the coast of Africa, in India, and elsewhere. In Europe it sought to maintain a detached position by exercising a policy of balance of power, which came to an end at the time of the Napoleonic Wars. After losing its flourishing colonies in North America in 1776, Great Britain made other conquests, which began with the occupation of Australia in 1788 and continued even during the Napoleonic Wars and later throughout the 19th century, particularly in Africa.

The two World Wars contributed to the consolidation of the Commonwealth, whose members fought to safeguard their common civilization. An important unifying element is its common heritage of political and public institutions and economic ties.

China

The Chinese People's Republic, proclaimed in Peking in 1949, is by far the most heavily populated country in the world, with more than 700 million inhabitants and an area almost equal to that of Europe. This puts it, in terms of size, in third place after the Soviet Union and Canada. China also includes Tibet, Sinkiang, Manchuria, and Inner Mongolia, all autonomous regions. Its sovereignty does not extend to Formosa (Taiwan), seat of National-

A mass demonstration in Peking. Typical of a country with a Communist regime, the symbolism and the ceremonies in China acquire a special carnival flavour.

alist China; this is the only government with whom some states have diplomatic relations, as they do not consider the Peking government the true representative of the Chinese people. The land frontiers of China bring it in contact with the Soviet Union, Mongolia, India, Pakistan, Nepal, Burma, Laos, North Vietnam, and North Korea. The Yangtze River separates northern China, which cultivates grain crops, from central and southern China, where rice is grown.

China, which until 1912 was ruled by the Manchu dynasty, has undergone profound changes in the past few decades. After the Communist take-over in 1949, the landowners' possessions and those of absentee landlords were at first transferred to the peasants, but from 1955 onwards a large number of co-operatives organized into communes were created which limited individual property to minute pieces of land. Each commune is divided into brigades, which have considerable power and stimulate competition, especially in collective labour. With the first five-year plan in 1953, followed by the second in 1958, the country reached its phase of industrialization, priority being given to heavy industry. From one million tons of steel in 1950, China progressed to 18·4 million tons in 1960. In the same year, more than 425 million tons of coal were mined. New roads and railways were opened, bridges built, navigable canals excavated, irrigation extended, and rice cultivation modernized.

China's trade with other countries also increased, although the countries of western Europe and the United States deliberately limited their trade relations with China (through the organization known as Chincom inspired by the United States), banning the export of many goods. A large proportion of Chinese trade is with Communist countries. A peak was reached in 1959, but in subsequent years trade diminished, both because of bad harvests, which prevented China from exporting its agricultural produce, and because Chinese industry was already in a position to meet demands for many of the products that had previously been imported. China also trades with non-Communist countries, particularly through Hong Kong, and sends manufactured goods (machinery, textiles, etc.) to countries with no such industries of their own. Trade with western countries include aircraft and lorries from Britain, chemical fertilizers from Belgium and Germany, and fibres and synthetic rubber from France and Italy. The continuous increase in the population has forced China in the past few years to obtain large quantities of cereal from Australia, Canada, and France; and since these countries do not need Chinese industrial goods China has had to pay for these imports in gold or silver. In the political field, China, while following similar principles to Russia, has ceased being its ally and has even started an ideological war against it, which has done great damage to the cause of world Communism.

China, with 720 million inhabitants, is the most heavily populated country in the world. The Communist regime, which came to power in 1949, brought about a radical change in the political, economic, and social structures of this large country. This was accomplished chiefly through a policy of radical agricultural reform and by intense industrial development. The human factor is still the dominant one in the country's economic activities and largely takes the place of machines, which are not yet available in sufficient quantities. *Above:* A street on the outskirts of Peking. *Top left:* An open-air theatre in Shanghai. *Far left:* Grain harvest in Manchuria. *Left:* Stevedores at work in an agricultural commune on the banks of the Yangtze. *Bottom:* A section of the harbour in Shanghai, China's most important port.

The European Economic Community

The Second World War saw the further decline in the importance of the powers that in the past had fought for the leadership of Europe (France and Germany); Italy, the Netherlands, and Belgium were seriously weakened and had to give up their overseas possessions. Faced with the powerful economic groupings of the United States, the Commonwealth of Nations, and the Soviet Union, the states of continental Europe found themselves in an uncomfortable position. Their economies had been damaged by the war and its consequences, and they were divided by frontiers that hampered trade and restricted markets. They felt the need to overcome their differences and the frictions that stemmed from past events. Therefore these states sought to establish close ties among themselves by aiming at the constitution of an efficient economic collective that would be the prelude to an eventual political union.

A first step towards achieving the economic unification of a part of Europe was taken with the creation in 1952 of the European Coal and Steel Community (ECSC) by which six states – Italy, France, West Germany, Belgium, Luxembourg, and the Netherlands – agreed to set up a common market for coal and the raw materials needed for the production of steel. The six states, with a joint population of 175 million (slightly less than the United States), are capable of an annual production of 350 million tons of coal and lignite and over 70 million tons of steel. Germany is especially rich in coal, and France in iron, and both countries were able to integrate their production. Belgium and the Netherlands both have plenty of coal, and Luxembourg is endowed with rich iron mines, so that the production of steel is constantly increasing. Italy, poor in coal and with little iron, finds herself in a less favourable position, but her abundance of labour contributes to the extraction of coal and her iron industries produce ten million tons a year.

The European Economic Community, was formed on 1 January, 1958. It envisaged the complete integration into a European common market, with a single tariff system, of the six countries forming it. The so-called Europe of the Six is the nucleus of a European unity that is intended to be transferred from the economic to the political sphere. *Above:* Brussels, the headquarters of some of the community's organizations, including Euratom. *Left:* The port of Rotterdam, the most important in western Europe.

Left: The Volkswagen works at Wolfsburg, West Germany, one of Europe's largest industrial complexes. *Above:* The entrance to the atomic centre at Ispra, Italy, part of Euratom, the European Atomic Energy Community.

On January 1st, 1958 the European Economic Community (EEC) came into being, with the same six countries as members. The organization envisaged the stage-by-stage introduction by 1970 of a common market with single tariffs for all the members, as well as the start of a series of projects aimed at reviving conditions in backward zones and achieving economic integration. They also agreed to exploit together atomic energy for peaceful purposes (Euratom). In 1972 Britain, the Republic of Ireland, and Denmark signed the Treaty of Accession to the EEC and all were to become full members in 1973.

The Common Market is the world's greatest importer (17% of the total value of goods exchanged) and is second among the exporters (16.7% of world trade), just behind the United States (17.7%), but with greater *per capita* values. Chief exports include industrial products; the main imports are raw materials for industry, transport equipment, and food. Greece, Turkey, and 18 African states are associate members of the community, the African states being former colonies of France and Belgium.

The European Free Trade Association (EFTA) pursues similar aims to the EEC. This group was formed in May, 1960, by seven European states – Austria, Britain, Denmark, Norway, Portugal, Sweden, and Switzerland. Finland became an associate member in 1961. There is also Comecon, which was set up in 1949 as the Council for Mutual Economic Aid; it is aimed at facilitating trade between the Soviet Union and the other seven European communist countries.

Inter-European communications are of fundamental importance to the development of trade between the various countries. The entrance to the Mont Blanc tunnel *(left),* which cuts straight through the massive barrier of the Alps between the Mediterranean and central Europe.